THOMAS HARDY

By the same Author

*

THE CONJURED SPIRIT: SWIFT
DONNE: A SPIRIT IN CONFLICT

*

SUMMER IN ANOTHER WORLD
(*Gollancz*)

The West Gallery of Puddletown Church, 1635

(The gallery in which Hardy's grandfather played and which bears the Latin inscription *Hither thou camest not to be looked at but to listen and to pray*)

THOMAS HARDY

A CRITICAL BIOGRAPHY

By

Evelyn Hardy

When you stand by his grave at
his funeral and think of him even the most
prosaic man's life becomes a poem.
T.H.

1954

THE HOGARTH PRESS

LONDON

PUBLISHED BY
The Hogarth Press Ltd
LONDON

✻

Clarke, Irwin & Co. Ltd
TORONTO

FIRST PUBLISHED : JANUARY 1954
SECOND IMPRESSION : FEBRUARY 1954

PRINTED IN GREAT BRITAIN
BY T. AND A. CONSTABLE LTD., EDINBURGH

To
Lord David Cecil

ACKNOWLEDGMENTS

I am greatly indebted to and wish to thank the following:

The Trustees of the Hardy Estate and Messrs Macmillan for their kindness in allowing me to quote extensively from the letters and works of Thomas and Florence Emily Hardy, and the former for allowing me to reproduce the Hardy Pedigree; the Librarian of the Brotherton Library, University of Leeds, Sir Sydney Cockerell and Dr Philip Gosse for the use of letters in the possession of the Library; the Curator of the Dorset County Museum, Lt.-Col. C. D. Drew, for his unfailing courtesy and help with all the Hardy material in the Museum.

The Syndics of the Fitzwilliam Museum and Augustus John for permission to reproduce the artist's portrait of Thomas Hardy; the Librarian of University College, Dublin, for allowing me to photograph the final page of *The Return of the Native*; H.M. Stationery Office and the Royal Commission on Historical Monuments for courteously letting me make use of a photograph before their own volumes on Dorset are published; the Salisbury Diocesan Council for information relating to the early days of the Bockhampton School; Dr E. W. Mann and Major H. O. Lock for granting permission to reproduce an unpublished letter of Hardy's and a facsimile of a page of the rough draft of *The Dynasts*.

The Times, *The Times Literary Supplement* and *The Sunday Times* for the use of passages from letters and articles; and the following Presses and Publishers for permission to make use of works published by them: The Clarendon, Oxford University, University of Columbia and Johns Hopkins University Presses, and Messrs William Heinemann, Hamish Hamilton, Jonathan Cape, Cassell and Company, George Allen and Unwin, Gerald Duckworth, the Lutterworth Press and Longmans of Dorchester.

I wish also to thank Sir Sydney Cockerell for telling me about a portion of *The Poor Man and The Lady*, and for allowing me to quote from the letters to him edited by Viola Meynell; Dr William Rutland for unstinted use of his book on Hardy's writings; Prof. W. H. Gardner for a passage from his essay on *The Mayor of Casterbridge*; and Vere Collins for generously providing me with material and information.

Florence Hardy's *Early Life* and *Later Years of Thomas Hardy*, published by Macmillan, have been designated as I and II in the footnotes after first giving the titles in full. Their Pocket Edition of Hardy's prose and poetry has been used and referred to throughout.

Contents

Illustrations

ix

A *

INTRODUCTION

THE biographer of THOMAS HARDY and critic of his work is both blessed and cursed with a mass of material concerning him: blessed because the richness provides rewarding sources of study, cursed because the abundance makes selection and emphasis more confusing. Hardy was the author of fourteen novels, four volumes of short stories, more than nine hundred poems, *The Queen of Cornwall*, and *The Dynasts* which stands alone like some hoary old monolith. There are as well the letters, essays, articles, and, most valuable of all, many of his notes jotted down without thought of publication, the seeds of inspiration for much of his work. Thus we are often in the fortunate position of being able to trace a single thought or emotion in three forms simultaneously, expressed first in a note and subsequently in its more polished forms in prose and verse. Few writers reveal these transitions so thoroughly.

Many of his manuscripts have been preserved through the foresight of others: these were sought after while Hardy was still alive. The majority of them are now in national collections and a few in private hands. An additional source of information is the remnant of Hardy's library[1]—the books which he studied long and lovingly as a growing boy and man, many of them bearing his delicate pencilled markings and a few his annotations. To handle these volumes, to remember their influence upon the formation of that powerful and original mind, is a moving experience, for books can be intensely personal, they absorb and give out, long after a man's death, something of his character: to touch them brings us close to their former owner.

The number of books written on Hardy, or his work, far exceeds those which he himself wrote. Chief amongst these must always stand the two compiled by his second wife, Florence Emily Hardy, that self-effacing woman who writ no more than she was told. Hardy is more fortunate than any of our poet-novelists, in this respect, that he married late in life a woman who measured his stature, and who persuaded him to write down, or to tell her verbally, what he remembered of his

[1] Now in the Dorset County Museum.

early life. Since Hardy had a pronounced aversion to personal reminiscences she[1] induced him to do this by arguing that they might one day be essential in order to refute false biographers, one or two of whom had already begun to misrepresent the facts of his life before he was dead. She also included many of Hardy's notes, of the utmost importance since we can hold a finished work in our hands and compare it with that which inspired the writer. The insignificant leaps to life and we come close to the mystery of creative art.

Hardy's life was not primarily one of action. He was by nature a scholar and a writer: it is what goes on in the mind that holds us, and Hardy's was rich with stored impressions. There are several reasons for this richness. First, he was an old man when he set down what he remembered, in full and vigorous mental health, yet of an age when memories crowd back into the mind filling it silently as long-parched springs revive a well. Secondly, he had an unusually retentive memory. As he himself said, he had the faculty of embalming an incident, or emotion, and of resurrecting it as many as forty or fifty years later with perfect fidelity, and he asks "Where was that sentiment hiding itself?", in the same way that he asks where have the blue-bells, which spring up when the woods are felled, been lying previously. Thirdly, he was by nature intuitive and extremely sensitive. His retentiveness of mind, coupled with his sensitivity, enabled him to recall the minutiae of existence which others would long ago have lost in the confused hurly-burly of later life, and to reanimate them emotionally.

Another important mine for the biographer remains—the Dorset countryside and its ancient monuments, miraculously preserved from spoliation, more especially Hardy's own immediate landscape and its buildings. The hamlet in which he was born has dwindled: the great heath has been clipped and shorn, but the one has not greatly altered and the other endures with stubborn tenacity. The noble manor-house and the church which dominated his childhood are essentially the same: and those other exquisite stone manors, the churches and minsters for which Dorset is famous, are all well cared for, possibly better

[1] Sir Sydney Cockerell informs me that it was he who urged Hardy to write his reminiscences for the reasons given above.

than in Hardy's youth. The sea-port and market towns still thrive, although with diminished vigour, retaining in some cases their distinctive local industries. The sullen, meandering, reed-choked rivers of north- and mid-Dorset, and the fast-flowing shining streams of the south with their plashy meadows, especially the Frome beloved by him and his ancestors, still beckon to the traveller; the rich clay valleys and the high chalk ridges decked with their fortresses and the burial places of the ancient dead still stand unmolested, with a few exceptions. The dismemberments entailed by the coming of industry are almost wholly absent.

There are also people still alive who well remember Hardy. In studying the man and his work we have to account for the fascination which he and his writings cast over others. The Poet Laureate has told us that, when he was young, he and his friends did not go south to see known historic places but to find

> where Marty South had lived, to watch the funeral gloom on Egdon, to see the Tower where two had watched the stars, and the great, lonely land of Slyre.[1]

Another man has written of Hardy himself:

> For many years I had felt as Browning felt about Byron when he said that he would "at any time have gone to see a curl of his hair, or one of his gloves."[2]

What is it that makes middle-aged men, not young impressionable girls, feel as this man felt? For Hardy himself was a gentle, unambitious man who would have denied any such power of drawing others to him. What causes people to travel three thousand miles or more, not only to see the places where he was born and his heart is buried, but the woods, fields and houses inhabited by his characters, as if these were the background for real lives, a part of chronicled history? Such is his magic that places indelibly marked on the Ordnance Map are in danger of losing their age-old, rightful names, for Hardy's inventions have replaced them. He has filled and animated the countryside with 'an imagined passion' stronger than reality.

[1] John Masefield, *The Ledbury Scene*. Jakeman's, Hereford, 1951.
[2] Vere Collins, *Talks with Hardy at Max Gate*, p. ix. Duckworth, 1928.

CHAPTER ONE

BIRTH, ANCESTRY AND INFANCY

> *As soon as she could discern the outline of the house ... it had
> all its old effect upon her imagination. Part of her body and
> life it ever seemed to be; the slope of its dormers, the finish
> of its gables, the broken courses of brick which topped the
> chimney, all had something in common with her personal
> character.*[1]

THOMAS HARDY

IT HAS sometimes been said that Thomas Hardy was not
the child of his age, that neither the events of his life nor the
literary tendencies of his period influenced his work. Nothing is
further from the truth, for Hardy echoes the swift changes
which were spreading over England, and the spiritual malaise
which infected her and the writings of her poets, more constantly
than any other novelist of the late-Victorian period. One has
only to consider the elementary problems handled in his prose
to contradict this assertion—problems such as the disastrous
effects of urban complexity on rural simplicity, the rub between
the old aristocrat and the new type of countryman—better educated than his forbears, and less content; the criss-cross matings
of people such as these, doomed to failure, since the individuals
are riddled with the destructive effects of envy and hatred: the
tension engendered by rural spontaneity tugging against the
knots of staid, urban convention. Hardy was quick to see the
pathos involved in events and scenes resulting from the countryman's uprooting, which increased alarmingly during his life-
time, and of which he himself was partly a victim. He treats
these problems indirectly, allusively if you like, but they are the
backbone of his prose-writing.

For Hardy lived in a time of physical and spiritual unrest.
In the decade 1832-42 Britain was twice perilously near revolution. He was spun round in the orbits of the great who had un-
settled thinking men by questioning traditional theology and
its accepted values. In his childhood the Established Church

[1] *Tess of the d'Urbervilles.*

had begun to lose its hold on the rustic heart, despite a revival of evangelicalism, and in his young manhood the teaching of the rationalists and scientists took deep root. Conventional belief became increasingly hard in the face of seemingly clear, demonstrable, proof of biological and chemical evolution. The spirit of the age was one of questioning and requestioning, both in secular and religious matters. Doubt, like a miasma, spread from the laboratory into the study and parlour until, as John Morley, one of Hardy's first critics, put it,

> the eternal riddles [which had at first been debated] in their crudest form in obscure societies and secularist clubs, now lay open upon the table with the popular magazines.[1]

What Hardy called the 'disease of modern life', philosophic scepticism and the ferment of unrest, touched only a few at first, generally in the towns. The vigorous country folk—the old-fashioned squires, masons and labouring men, the merchants unlading their ships, or tusselling with figures in their ware-houses—did not bother their heads about such remote problems as the meaning of existence. They were content with sport, and with work which brought its just reward. But for the artists and thinkers, those who most truly mirror the character of an age, all was different. Their very sensitivity made them more susceptible to infection.

Chief amongst the disturbing, revolutionizing changes of so-called progress was the railway, which came to Dorchester in 1847-8, seven years after Hardy's birth. When he was nine years old the railway system as we know it today had already taken on its general form. The poet Edward Fitzgerald lamented its introduction into his world of China roses and river-threaded garden. But lamenting did not stop the fire-eating monster which clove through the ancient fields, in some cases undisturbed since prehistoric man had tilled them for crops, or buried his dead.

It is surprising that Hardy never wrote a novel depicting the revolution in rural life entailed by the coming of the railway and the armies of imported navvies who invaded the countryside, corrupting it with their rough ways and speech and their

[1] *Recollections*, I, pp. 88-9.

drunken debauches. "They uprooted ancient ways of living in every place where they encamped."[1]

Hardy refers to the railway in his prose work on many occasions, and in the recollections of his youth, when describing the harvest home which he surreptitiously went to as a lad, he sums up the disastrous effects of its coming in a single sentence. The feast, he says, was

> among the last at which the old traditional ballads were sung, the railway having been extended to Dorchester just then, and the orally transmitted ditties of centuries being slain at a stroke by the London comic songs that were introduced.[2]

The quenching of ballad-making and ballad-music was a symbol of the extinction of the whole of that ancient-thing—peasant society and culture, with its age-old crafts. Even the old roads along whose miry tracks had moved a collection of characters who would themselves now die out—tinkers, tailors, packmen, drovers, reddlemen, hucksters and itinerant limners—began to grass over. The local fairs and markets diminished in size. People moved away and did not return. Hardy might have made a prose epic out of a dying country village whose interests, trades and population fluctuated and dwindled, just as William Barnes had drawn the plight of the small-holder, ejected from the common on which he depended for his livelihood before it was enclosed, in a short poem. In *The Mayor of Casterbridge* the importation by Donald Farfrae of his new-fangled agricultural machine, with its shining metal parts and garish paint, spells disaster to Michael Henchard and his old-fashioned corn-merchant's business, run on antiquated lines, but Hardy does not pause to work out the problems in detail.

In two of his published letters he showed an awareness of agricultural changes, which he deplored. When a Bishop asked what he thought of the increasing trend of migration from the land—a problem which still confronts us today—his views were that

> these modern migrations are fatal to local traditions and to cottage horticulture. Labourers formerly would plant apple trees

---

[1] Arthur Bryant, *English Saga, 1840-1940*, p. 82. Collins, 1948.
[2] Florence Emily Hardy, *The Early Life of Thomas Hardy*, pp. 25-6. Macmillan & Co., 1928, hereafter indicated by the numeral I.

and fruit bushes with zealous care, to profit from them: but now they scarce ever plant one, knowing they will be finding a home elsewhere in a year or two; or if they do happen to plant any, digging them up and selling them before leaving. Hence the lack of picturesqueness in modern labourers' dwellings.[1]

But Hardy was not merely concerned with the prettiness of the landscape. He had the welfare of the cottagers at heart, and in his article *The Dorsetshire Labourer*[2], as well as in his letter to Rider Haggard in 1902, quoted in *The Later Years*, he shows an accurate, unromantic knowledge of conditions. The ejection of Tess and her family from their cottage, and the pathetic appearance of their scanty household belongings turned out-of-doors into the unfriendly light of day, is the poet-novelist's way of showing compassion for those who were victims of insecurity of tenure.

Hardy was not a reformer. He neither attacked nor defended the order of things, nor did he feel that it became him to prophesy. But he did not sit silent. He voiced current evils as he saw them—amongst them that of instability—and he had the wisdom to record the beauty and worth of a perishing way of life, steeped in unwritten, local tradition, chronicles and folk-lore which gave it continuity. But it is against a back-cloth of doubt, upheaval and unrest that we must watch Hardy move if we are to understand his life, his philosophy and his work.

Thomas Hardy was born on June 2, 1840, in a small house of brick and thatch, surrounded by beech and apple-trees and fronted by an old-fashioned garden, in the hamlet of Upper Bockhampton (or Boc'aton, as the country people called it), in the parish of Stinsford, Dorset.

Six months later there took place in Paris the second funeral of the Emperor Napoleon. The ground was white with new-fallen snow, over which the black and glittering carriages and imperial hearse silently swept like sombre, symbolical ships of death. News of this must have reached Dorset, where, not forty years ago, the inhabitants had made preparations to repel his threatened invasion.

The Bockhampton house had been built in 1800-1 by Hardy's

[1] I, p. 270.   [2] *Longman's Magazine*, July 1883.

great-grandfather, John Hardy of Puddletown, for the latter's son, Thomas Hardy the first, to set him up in marriage. It was built on traditional lines with a large central chimney-breast and a generous hearth, annually white-washed, which caught and held the firelight, or the paler light from without on winter mornings. It also had a staircase with Venetian red walls. Both of these features, beloved by Hardy as a child, have disappeared; the chimney-throat has been closed in and the position of the staircase has been altered.

The lonely site of the old house—Hardy always disliked to hear it called a cottage—is an interesting one, for it stands at the end of a lane, formerly lined with cherry trees, with its back to a heath and its gable-ends facing a wood. Probably Hardy's grandfather chose this spot, one dear to both his son and grandson.

Hardy's father was born and died in the Bockhampton home, and Hardy himself lived for the major part of his life either in, or near, the same unpretentious house, redolent of an age that had already begun to pass when Hardy was born. For in the days of his forbears a man of energy and ability could buy for life a piece of ground and erect his own dwelling on it. He thus became a *livier*. The right to renew the copyholds of inheritance might be claimed by a satisfactory *livier* from a sympathetic landlord and thus the steading might be handed down for as long as three generations.[1] Should the *livier* become unacceptable to his landlord, or allow the lifeholds to fall out of hand, his privilege ceased, and this disastrous uncertainty of tenure is pictured by Hardy in three of his novels—*Desperate Remedies*, *The Woodlanders*, and *Tess*.

The houses, with their green shutters and brass knockers, which stood in Cherry Alley, as it was called in those days, have all disappeared, with the exception of the Hardy homestead. They were inhabited by people of independent character. Hardy himself has told us what type they were:

> two retired military officers, one old navy lieutenant, a small farmer and tranter, a relieving officer and registrar, and an old

[1] The renewal of the lease for the Bockhampton home made by William Morton Pitt to Thomas Hardy 1st, in 1835, may be seen in the Dorset County Museum.

Hardy's birthplace, Upper Bockhampton

militiaman, whose wife was the monthly nurse that assisted [him] into the world.[1]

These, then, were his immediate neighbours and we recognize amongst them the prototypes for Captain Vye, Reuben Dewy, and other characters in Hardy's novels.

When Thomas was born he was 'thrown aside as dead' and, the mother's life being in danger, medical attention was concentrated on her. Fortunately, Jemima Hardy's neighbour and nurse detected what Swift called 'the seeds of life' in the boy and drew the doctors attention to him. It is an extraordinary fact that Hardy's contemporary and friend, Sir Edmund Gosse, was also given up for dead at birth, and his life saved by the same common sense.

> I was laid, with scant care on another bed in the room . . . An old woman who happened to be there, and who was unemployed, turned her thoughts to me, and tried to awake in me a spark of vitality. She succeeded, and she was afterwards complimented by the doctor on her cleverness . . . For all the rapture of life, for all its turmoils, its anxious desires, its manifold pleasures, and even for its sorrow and suffering, I bless and praise that anonymous old lady from the bottom of my heart.[2]

Hardy nowhere gives a paean like this for his resuscitation.

His mother came of Anglo-Saxon stock and was descended from small landed proprietors of yeoman blood in the northwest corner of Dorset—the Pydel valley and (earlier) the Vale of Blackmoor. Family legends of their connection with Monmouth's rising survived. His maternal grandmother, Elizabeth Swetman (whom Hardy appears never to have seen), had a stock of thirty gowns and as many books, a library unusual both in size and kind 'for a yeoman's daughter living in a remote place'. Her grandson inherited one of her features (a nose which he liked to call Roman in shape), her love of books, her memory, and her romantic disposition. Elizabeth 'knew the writings of Addison and Steele and others of the *Spectator* group almost by heart'. Perhaps it is her copies of Fielding's Works in ten volumes which survive amongst Hardy's books, volumes in tooled leather bearing the date 1784, for Hardy tells us that she was familiar

[1] I, p. 3.
[2] *Father and Son*, p. 7. William Heinemann Ltd., 1928.

with Fielding, as well as with Milton, Richardson, Bunyan, and Culpepper's *Herbal*, with which she doctored the neighbourhood. Alas for her promise! She fell in love with, and secretly married, a man of whom her unyielding father disapproved. He disinherited her on his death, and shortly afterwards her husband also died leaving her with a young brood of children to provide for and educate.

One of these was Hardy's mother, Jemima, who could never speak of the stressful days of her childhood without pain. She was a girl of energy and resourcefulness and 'an omnivorous reader'. At one time she worked in Weymouth and London, but on her return to Dorset, met and married Thomas Hardy the second, father of the writer.

What Hardy said of Bathsheba might well have been applied to her:

> Deeds of endurance are rare in conduct . . . her philosophy was her conduct and she seldom thought practicable what she did not practise. She was of the stuff of which great men's mothers are made. She was indispensable to high generation, hated at tea-parties, feared in shops, and loved at crises.[1]

This is not merely a fanciful suggestion. Hardy once admitted that the character of Bathsheba was drawn from that of his mother's sister, and from the few remarks which he makes about his mother she seems to have been cast in the same heroic mould.

The story of his parents' first meeting has been told by Hardy in a poem.[2] The handsome fiddler of the old west-gallery of Stinsford church in his blue swallow-tailed coat with gilt embossed buttons, and flowered waistcoat, looked down at the stranger in the high pew below and 'claimed her as his own forthright'. (It is thought that Hardy made use of this incident in his first novel *The Poor Man and the Lady*, which now no longer exists. It reappears adapted in *An Indiscretion in the Life of an Heiress*,[3] a fragment of this work.)

The musician, Hardy's father, like his father and grand-

---

[1] *Far from the Madding Crowd*, p. 449.
[2] "The Church Romance," in *Time's Laughingstocks*.
[3] *New Quarterly Magazine*, October 1878.

father before him, was a master-mason and builder, who sometimes employed as many as fifteen men, among them his neighbour the tranter who carted the building materials. (Hardy
became touchy on this point as he grew older, owing to mis-
representations by would-be biographers during his lifetime:
he wished it to be understood that his father was not a mere
journeyman mason.)

In the large family Bible, dated 1817, and inscribed 'Thomas
Hardy, 1825' by the writer's father, the names and dates of
birth of the Hardy children—Thomas, Mary, Henry and
Katherine—as well as those of older members of the family, are
given. But family Bibles are apt to become repositories for
strange material. The Hardys' yields two interesting things;
an early example of printed caligraphy with adages for the
young scholar to imitate, such as:

A SLOW FIRE MAKES SWEET MALT.   BEAR AND FORBEAR

(proverbs which seem to have been distilled into the innermost
crannies of Hardy's prose work) and a sheet in the handwriting
of Thomas Hardy senior. This proves to be a rough estimate
for work at Long Burton Farm—the erection of some new cow-
houses by the master-mason. It brings his trade vividly before
us with details like this:

> Taking down old cow houses, rooting stumps of trees on site and
> drawing away same . . .

and at the close:

> Add a £10 profit, Total .   .   .   .   £179 0 0.

One instantly thinks of *Tess of the d'Urbervilles*, for Hardy must
often have been in and out of farmyards with his father as a boy,
and here was a local dairy in process of re-building.

He was, so Hardy supposed, a descendant of the Jersey
le Hardys who had traded with Dorset for centuries and had
settled along the higher reaches of the Frome, having landed at
the mouth of that river by the old town of Wareham, formerly
a port of considerable size. It was always accepted in Hardy's
family that the Admiral of the same name belonged to a
collateral branch, but, with all his immense interest in the past
and historical details concerning his own county, Hardy never

troubled to verify the relationship until he was nearly eighty. When, as an old man, he was asked wherein this lay, he merely replied that his great-uncle had known the ramifications. Hardy preferred to immortalize the Admiral in *The Dynasts*. He liked, too, to think that his namesake who had founded the Dorchester Grammar School in the 16th century belonged to his family, as well as another Thomas of the 18th century who had lived in the town and had subscribed to some anthems scored by the Organist of the Chapel Royal and Westminster Abbey.

This love of music, so pronounced in Hardy, was an inherited trait. His family provided the music for Stinsford Parish Church for more than one hundred years, and before that one of them at least had done so for the church of Puddletown. His ancestors were amongst the humble musicians who rescued the village church services from inanition by their heroic, unpaid efforts. Although smaller than the neighbouring 'bands' of Puddletown and Maiden Newton, and consisting of stringed instruments only, the Stinsford quire was superior in musicianship. This was partly because the vicar, a cousin of the Earl of Ilchester, was himself a violinist and an 'ardent musician'. Hardy's grandfather, father, and uncle (together with James Dart, the counterviol) were privileged to practise with him two or three times a week in Stinsford House.

The bass-viol was played by the old man, Thomas Hardy the first, who, before his marriage and before settling at Bockhampton, had adorned the carved oak gallery in Puddletown Church. Unlike many of its inferiors this has not been pulled down, and we can still see where this country musician performed at the close of the 18th century. On coming to Stinsford parish he found the music deplorable and straightway set about reforming it. Hardy does not say what persuasion he employed to eject the solitary old man who conducted the singing from the gallery with an oboe. He acknowledged later that the description of Thomasin's father in *The Return of the Native* is based on what he had heard of his grandfather's playing as a young man:

Whenever a club walked he'd play the clarinet in the band that marched before 'em as if he'd never touched anything but a clarinet all his life. And then, when they got to the church door he'd throw down the clarinet, mount the gallery, snatch up the bass-viol, and rozum away, as if he'd never played anything but a bass-viol . . .[1]

He seems to have been the counterpart of a Sussex choir-leader who, taking up his fiddle to play Handel, called out:

> Here, Willum, rake us over that rosin and I'll show 'em *Who's t' King of Glory*!

Hardy tells us what sort of music these untrained men played—'anthems with portentous repetitions' and 'mountainous fugues', odes, and such like long-winded things. Thomas the second, Hardy's father, began as a chorister and ended by being tenor viol, his brother playing the treble. His mother once gave Hardy an amusing description of how the three looked setting out for the services, two on Sundays and others on feast days, before her son was born.

> They were always hurrying, being rather late, their fiddles and violon-cello in green baize bags under their left arms. They wore top hats, stick-up shirt collars, dark blue coats with great collars and gilt buttons, deep cuffs and black silk 'stocks,' or neckerchiefs. Had curly hair, and carried their heads to one side as they walked. My grandfather wore drab cloth breeches and buckled shoes, but his sons wore trousers and Wellington boots.[2]

But family music was not confined to the ecclesiastical. It included jigs, reels, hornpipes, waltzes, and country-dances, and Thomas the second was much in demand at wedding, christening and other feasts. The writer treasured his father's violin long after his death: he even wrote an affectionate poem to it in which he humourously suggested that the shade of his father might need the fiddle's company to liven the monotony of the underworld. Either his own, or his father's and uncle's, violin and 'cello now stand mute with slackened strings in Hardy's re-created study in the Dorset County Museum.

The boy could tune a fiddle when he was barely breeched, and so sensitive, so responsive was he to his father's fiddling that

---

[1] p. 55.
[2] Florence Emily Hardy, *The Later Years of Thomas Hardy*, p. 10. Macmillan & Co., 1930, hereafter indicated by the numeral II.

certain tunes caused him to dance and to weep at the same time in the middle of the fire-lit room.[1] He gives the names of the tunes which he loved, among them "Miss MacLeod of Ayr" which he remembered so accurately that, more than forty years later, he could write of it:

> The tune had enticed her into [the dance]; being a tune of a busy, vaulting leaping sort—some low notes on the silver string of each fiddle, then a skipping on the small, like running up and down ladders.[2]

Old tunes and dances which Thomas became familiar with, almost from the time he was born, were to influence the writer of prose and verse. That enforced dancing, while yet he wept and danced more frantically to conceal his weeping, not only 'troubled his mind', as he says, but became a predominant theme in his work. For the self-entranced Immanent Will is the Arch-fiddler, to whose tune our over-sensitive, over-refined natures must of necessity respond, against our seemingly impotent wills.

Since he was delicate, the boy of 'ecstatic temperament' was kept at home from school until he was eight. But his physical fragility was matched by mental precocity. Amongst Hardy's surviving books is an edition of *The Cries of London* with crude red-and-yellow wood-block illustrations which his sister Kate has left on record that Tom could read before he was three. This relic of his childhood has lost its title-page, the leaves have been torn and the margins worn, but it has been carefully mended. *The Cries* in order are:

CHERRY RIPE
TURNIPS-O
POTATOES ALL HOT
THE SWEEP
FINE MULBERRIES
BUY A BROOM
ALL-A-GROWING
A LIVE LOBSTER

At the age of four his father gave him a toy concertina inscribed

[1] See "The Self Unseeing," in *Poems of the Past and Present*.
[2] *The Mayor of Casterbridge*, p. 128.

with his name and the date. (Hardy remembered this early gift shortly before he died at the age of eighty-seven-and-a-half.) A few years later he was reading *Peter Parley's Tales about the Sons of the Sea*, one of a series of small volumes eagerly awaited by children on lonely hill-farms in New England at the same date.

Hardy's sense of colour and of drama developed early. He tells us how he used to sit on the western stairs and wait for the sun to go down. In its setting it intensified the Venetian red with which his father had coloured the walls, and as it sank the child recited one of Isaac Watts' hymns, 'with great fervency'. Denied going to church on wet Sundays he used to

> wrap himself in a tablecloth and read the Morning Prayer standing in a chair, his cousin playing the clerk with loud Amens, and his grandmother representing the congregation. The sermon which followed was simply a patch-work of the sentences used by the Vicar. Everybody said that Tommy would have to be a parson, being obviously no good for any practical pursuit; which remark caused his mother many misgivings.[1]

This grandmother was his father's mother, Mary Head, of Great Fawley in Berkshire, who had been orphaned early and whose experiences as a child had been so bitter that she never wished to re-visit the place. There are several births of Hardy children recorded in the Stinsford parish registers, their father, like Thomas', being set down as a mason, but we do not know which particular cousin this was—perhaps little Theresa whose name was immortalized in *Tess*, and who died in the same year as Hardy.

Two other anecdotes relate to this early period. Both of the events were engraved so deeply on Hardy's mind that he re-counted them, together with that concerning the concertina, to his wife a few weeks before his death. He remembered being in the garden with his father on a bitterly cold winter's day and seeing a poor, half-frozen fieldfare. His father shied a stone at it, probably to see if the bird would rise. But it fell dead and on picking it up the boy discovered it to be

as light as a feather, all skin and bone . . . He had never forgotten

[1] I, p. 19.

how the body of the fieldfare felt in his hand: the memory had always haunted him.[1]

The bird evidently became for him a symbol of life so delicately poised that it might be extinguished at a stroke, by human caprice or a squall of wind. A memory of this incident came back to Hardy in his forties when he visited the grave of Shelley. In his poem, "Shelley's Skylark," he speaks of the immortal bird which

> Lived its meek life; then, one day, fell—
> A little ball of feather and bone.[2]

Secondly there is the anecdote of the boy and the sheep. 'In order to see what the sheep would do', Thomas got on his hands and knees and pretended to eat grass.

Presently he looked up and found them gathered around in a close ring, gazing at him with astonished faces.[3]

Thus, at an early age, Hardy tried to identify himself with the animal world. His later reading of Darwin only served to intensify a strain of compassionate understanding.

Few people seem to perceive fully as yet that the most far-reaching consequence of the establishment of the common origin of all species is ethical; that it logically involved a readjustment of altruistic morals by enlarging as a *necessity of rightness* the application of what has been called 'The Golden Rule' beyond the area of mere mankind to that of the whole animal kingdom. Possibly Darwin himself did not wholly perceive it, though he alluded to it . . .[4]

But life for the boy was not entirely composed of solitude or melancholy ruminations. As he grew older and learned to play the fiddle well he, too, was in demand in farm parlours and friendly sanded kitchens. As an old man he remembered the bride in white who leant down and kissed him with pleasure at his playing. He fiddled at the house of the tailor who had

[1] II, p. 263.
[2] *Poems of the Past and Present.*
[3] II, p. 263.
[4] Letter to the Secretary of the Humanitarian League written when Hardy was nearly seventy. II, pp. 141-2.

breeched him, and on another occasion he recalled that his
hostess, after three-quarters-of-an-hour of unbroken footing by
tireless couples to his fiddling of "The New Rigged Ship",
grasped his arm to stop his playing, fearing the exertion would
be too much for him. To his surprise his mother did not object
to his 'minstrelling' but his father did. (The reason for his disapproval was not given.) His mother's only stipulation was that
the boy should not accept payment for his services. But the
temptation proved too strong for Thomas on one occasion when
the hat was passed round for the fiddler. He straightway converted his earnings into a book (just as he was to do on winning
his first architectural prize) *The Boys' Own Book*, which his
mother disapproved of, since it dealt mainly with games, and
which Florence Hardy says remained with Hardy's books until
he died.[1]

But by far the most important incident recorded about
Hardy's childhood is that concerning his wish to remain in fire-
or sun-warmed domestic seclusion all his life. One day the boy
was

> . . . lying on his back in the sun, thinking how useless he was, his
> face covered with his straw hat. The sun's rays streamed through
> the interstices of the straw, the lining having disappeared.
> Reflecting on his experiences of the world so far as he had got, he
> came to the conclusion that he did not wish to grow up. Other
> boys were always talking of when they would be men; he did not
> want at all to be a man, or to possess things, but to remain as he
> was, in the same spot, and to know no more people than he already
> knew (about half a dozen). Yet this early evidence of that lack of
> social ambition which followed him through life was shown when
> he was in perfect health and happy circumstances.[2]

This feeling and this reflection occurred before Hardy was
eight years old. Yet the experience was so strong, and so per-
vasive, it remained embedded in his mind for nearly half a
century. Hardy used it in his undated poem called "Childhood
among the Ferns," and in *Jude the Obscure*, written when he
was 53-4 years of age. It then finds corroboration in *The*

---

[1] It is not among those in the Dorset County Museum now; *The Boy's
Own Book of Science* (1842) remains.
[2] I, pp. 19-20.

Early Life,[1] and thus we have a triple record of thought and emotion.

The three versions vary slightly. In the poem the boy has no hat and surveys the world through the bracken fronds: it is raining on his 'spray-roofed house' and the sun does not come out until towards the close of the poem. The account remembered in *Jude* is the fullest and most circumstantial. Hardy accurately remembered his feelings on that boyhood day: he felt (in the first account) how 'useless' he was, but in *Jude* he calls the latter's existence 'undemanded'. In keeping with the harsh, over-realistic style of that novel the boy lies down on a heap of litter near a pig-sty, and reflects:

> Growing up brought responsibilities . . . Events did not rhyme quite as he had thought. *Nature's logic was too horrid for him to care for. That mercy towards one set of creatures was cruelty towards another sickened his sense of harmony.* As you got older, and felt yourself to be at the centre of your time, and not a point on its circumference, as you had felt when you were little, you were seized with a sort of shuddering, he perceived. All around you there seemed to be something glaring, garish, rattling, and the noises and glares hit upon the little cell called your life, and shook it, and scorched it. If he could only prevent himself growing up! He did not want to be a man.[2]

Or as the poem puts it:

> *Why should I have to grow to man's estate,*
> *And this afar-noised World perambulate?*[3]

These three versions of a single thought give us the key to much of Hardy's later attitude to existence. The initial paradox which confronts us all—that life preys on other life—was incomprehensible, and overpowering in its brutality.

At eight years old Thomas was considered strong enough to be sent to the village school, which lies about a mile across the fields from his home. In those days Lower Bockhampton was

---

[1] In this case it is not an unpremeditated *note* but a recorded memory. Hardy's notes in Florence Hardy's volumes begin on p. 48, when Hardy was twenty-two. *The Church Romance* is another example, but not concerning an event in Hardy's own life.

[2] *Jude the Obscure*, p. 15. (Italics mine.)

[3] "Childhood among the Ferns," in *Winter Words*.

larger than it is today: there were ancient houses of Ham Hill stone with mullioned windows, standing by the withy-bed, and there was the Poor House 'at the corner turning down to the dairy'. There had once been a water-mill, but even this had gone when Thomas was born. And there was Robert Reason-the-Shoemaker's cottage which stood where the village Club Room now stands—a friendly house where Christmas dancing-parties were held, called Jacob's Joins, since each villager contributed his share of the cost.

This brought the boy into contact with two important influences, that of the world of books and that of the lady of the manor. "Hardy was a born book-worm, that and that alone was unchanging in him",[1] and at this early age the formation of his library was begun.

> About this time his mother gave him Dryden's *Virgil*, Johnson's *Rasselas*, and *Paul and Virginia*. He also found in a closet *A History of the Wars*—a periodical dealing with the war with Napoleon, which his grandfather had subscribed to at the time, having been himself a volunteer. The torn pages of these contemporary numbers with their melodramatic prints of serried ranks, crossed bayonets, huge knapsacks and dead bodies, were the first to set him on the train of ideas that led to *The Trumpet Major* and *The Dynasts*.[2]

Johnson's *Rasselas* has gone but the other volumes are still on their shelves; the edition of Saint-Pierre's classic and another of his boyhood books, *A Concise History of Birds*,[3] were printed in Edinburgh. In his seventh year, his godfather, a Mr King, gave to Thomas one of the publications of the Religious Tract Society —indigestible stuff for the mind of a child—*The Rites and Worship of the Jews*, and somewhat later another friend made him a gift of Thomas Dilworth's *New Guide to the English Tongue*,[4] inscribed '*Master Hardy*'.

[1] I, p. 35.   [2] I, pp. 20-21.
[3] Published by Oliver & Boyd. Undated.
[4] Published by Thos. Richardson & Son. Undated.

CHAPTER TWO

THREE LADIES OF THE MANOR

*Never were there such a gentry as the English. They will be
the distinguishing mark and glory of England in history, as
the arts were of Greece, and war of Rome. I am sure no travel
would carry me to any land so beautiful as the good sense,
justice and liberality of my good countrymen make this. And I
cling the closer to it, because I feel that we are going down the
hill, and shall perhaps live ourselves to talk of all this independence as a thing that has been.*

EDWARD FITZGERALD

THE influence of the lady of the manor was almost as
important, if not as lasting, as that of the world of books.
The manor of Kingston, in the parish of Stinsford, was once a
royal demesne which devolved upon the Maurwards. At the
close of the 14th century it passed by intermarriage to the Greys,
and after another three hundred years, again by intermarriage,
to a collateral branch of the family of William Pitt. During the
last century it has, however, changed hands no less than five
times—a comment on prevalent social conditions—and it is
now no longer a private estate.

During the 18th and 19th centuries, two ladies were connected
with it, and one with the neighbouring manor of Stinsford, who
impressed their characters on those who knew them, on posterity, even on the landscape. Hardy came under the indirect
influence of the first two and the immediate influence of the
third.

The first of these was Lora Grey, daughter and heiress of
Audeley Grey. On her mother's side she was descended from the
Stawells of Cothelstone and the Trevelyans of Nettlecombe, in
west Somerset. On her father's she came from a long line of
Dorset Greys, whose arms quartered with the Stawells are carved
over the porch of the old Kingston Maurward manor-house,
commemorating the marriage of Angel Grey. It was from this
ancestor of Lora's that Hardy took the Christian name (originally a surname) of *Angel* for Tess' neglectful husband.

Lora chose for her husband a member of a rising family in a neighbouring county, George Pitt of Stratfield Saye in Hampshire, a widower with three children. She married him in 1699, but outlived her husband, who died in 1734. In her widowhood she occupied herself with her many children, the lofty house of brick (later faced with stone), which George Pitt had built in 1717-20, with the management of her estates and with local improvements and charities. As an old obituary notice puts it, "Doing good was the business and pleasure of her life." One of her cares was the creation of a fund to help in the schooling of poor children in the parish of Stinsford.[1]

Another of Lora Pitt's concerns was the building of a bridge. Travellers to and from Dorchester complained of the flooded road and meadows lying to the east of the town. Riders in the dark were drowned, coaches were bogged and overturned, wheels were wrenched from their axles, passengers were drenched, dirtied and delayed, with a consequent rise of tempers and an outpouring of abuse on the innocent coachmen and horses. In 1747 Lora determined to do what no man had done, to apply to Parliament for permission to build a bridge to span the Frome. In the following year an Act was passed permitting its erection, and the bridge is still in use. To this day it is called *Grey's Bridge*. Either because of the conservative character of Dorset men, or because of the affection in which she and her father's people had long been held, the bridge bears her maiden name. The bridge appears repeatedly in Hardy's prose and verse and it is an important feature in *The Mayor of Casterbridge*. When he grew older and walked into Dorchester, either to school or work, he crossed it twice every day. Even before this he must have walked or driven across it with his father scores of times. The wife of a succeeding squire of Kingston Maurward, Mrs Morton Pitt, also built a bridge connected with the Hardy family—that over the Frome at Lower Bockhampton. Upon

[1] By the arrangement of the Charity Commissioners, and through the Managers of the Dorchester Grammar School, this is still paid annually to the Managers of the Church of England School in Bockhampton. The amount is distributed among all the children who attend this school "with a view to encouraging regular attendance and good conduct". Stinsford claims the right, through this charity, to have two representatives on the Board of Managers of the Dorchester Grammar School.

laying the foundation stone she presented Hardy's father, then a lad of twelve, with a *Book of Common Prayer with the Psalms in Metre, July 2, 1833.* Probably Thomas the first, as local mason, built the bridge, and the boy, as mason's son, assisted him. (As the grandson and son of country masons, and an architect's apprentice and assistant, Hardy saw more than one foundation stone laid, and it is not surprising that his earliest prose work contained a description of one of these ceremonies.)

The Lady Pitt (Lora Grey) died at Bath, where she had gone to take the waters. She is not commemorated either in Stinsford church or in that of Stratfield Saye. The imposing monument which hangs on the north wall of the former building is not raised to her memory but by her children to their grandparents', the father and mother of Lora Grey. With its beautifully cut lettering, its surmounting coats of arms, its urns, its lachrymose cherubs and pendent skull, it takes precedence over any other monument in Stinsford church.

The Hardy pew was adjacent to this aisle. Thus, as a boy, Thomas was able to read the monument's inscription until he knew it by heart, and to study its sculptured details. The skull with its curious bat-like wings, which seem to grow from the cheek-bones, hollow eye-sockets, grinning teeth, and hideous nose, from which the flesh and cartilage have been eaten away as by some cancerous agent, being the lowest part of the monument, would easily draw a child's eyes and fill him with loathing and terror. One is not surprised to hear that Hardy's sister Mary told a friend that the skull had haunted his mind as a boy. Beneath the aisle lies the Kingston Maurward vault with its cargo of still and brittle bones, a fact of which Hardy was morbidly aware, as one of his macabre illustrations to *Wessex Poems* testifies.

But a second vault and monument, in the chancel of Stinsford church, are more intimately connected with the Hardy family, one which, Thomas admits, "gained a romantic interest in his mind at an early age".

Twenty years or more after the death of Lora Pitt another aristocratic lady came to astonish the rural population. She was Lady Susanna Sarah Louisa Strangways, daughter of Stephen, first Earl of Ilchester, whose family had long held Stinsford

Manor by intermarriage with the Talboys, cousins of the Earls of Devon. Lady Susan had disgraced herself by marrying beneath her. She was born in 1743, and was one of the ten daughters of dukes and earls who acted as bridesmaids to Queen Charlotte at her marriage. Her uncle, Henry Fox, first Lord Holland, had delighted society by giving private theatricals at Holland House. At one of these Lady Susan met the young actor William O'Brien. According to Mary Frampton:

> All London was wild with admiration of his person and his inimitable manner of acting a fine gentleman in comedy. He was himself of a gentleman's family in Ireland, left by some accident for education with a Roman Catholic Priest . . . He was a very extraordinary and amiable character.[1]

Lady Susan and William O'Brien fell in love and were secretly married, in 1764, at St Paul's, Covent Garden, soon after her coming of age. Hardy, who was a great reader of Walpole's *Letters*, quotes that aristocratic gossip-monger's scorn of the match: "I cannot have believed Lady Susan could stoop so low. Even a footman were preferable . . ."[2] Such was the disrepute in which actors of the day were held. Yet O'Brien was more than a gifted ingénu. Garrick, having watched him, persuaded him to come to London, where he became junior lead at Drury Lane.

> She, when young [adds Mary Frampton], was reckoned the proudest of the proud, and the highest of the high; her elopement, therefore, was the more wondered at. They went to America for some years after the marriage, where her friends had procured him some trifling office—I believe as commissary. Mr O'Brien followed the law, and went the western circuit for a short time after his return from America, until they finally settled at Stinsford . . .[3]

When her father relented he allowed the young pair to live in Stinsford House, which stands near church and vicarage, and here they lived until they died.

> They remained always most affectionately attached to each other. Lady Susan was a woman of a very strong and highly

---

[1] *The Journal of Mary Frampton*, pp. 18-20. London, 1886.
[2] I, p. 11.   [3] *The Journal of Mary Frampton*.

improved understanding, extremely agreeable in society, a steady warm-hearted friend, and a person in whose conversation anything like gossip or abuse of your neighbour never held a place . . . No two people were more liked, or their society more courted . . . He had most amenity; she most strength of character.[1]

A few of Lady Susan's letters are included in Mrs Frampton's *Journal* and they bear out what she says of her character. She had, above all, spirit, and this was a feminine characteristic which attracted Hardy. In 1794 she was writing to a niece at Penrice Castle that she hopes, if the French invade—which she cannot believe will ever happen—that the niece will give her asylum in Wales, a detail which Hardy might well have included in *The Dynasts*.

> If they should land at Weymouth, I hope you will give me a retreat in your mountains, should I be obliged to fly, which it will be much against the grain if I do from a Frenchman. Even the prisoners at Dorchester cut off the heads of the kings and queens on the cards they played with, which is rather *outré-ing* their dislike of monarchy.[2]

In another letter she tells how she dined at Lord Malmesbury's, sitting next to Sir Walter Scott. This was in 1818, nine years before her death. In the same letter she prays that the trees at Stinsford may not have been levelled in a violent gale. (The plane in the garden of Stinsford House is still a magnificent specimen.) These two facts alone must have endeared her to Hardy, for he both admired Scott and loved every branch of his native trees.

It is interesting to see how Hardy later defended O'Brien, whose talents he enumerates—amongst them, that he was an author 'of considerable merit'. "The *stooping* might have been viewed inversely", he writes, contradicting Walpole, and for William O'Brien we may write Thomas Hardy. Hardy insists: "His marriage annihilated a promising career." For one of Lord Ilchester's stipulations on forgiving his daughter was that O'Brien should abandon the stage. Although he became a popular member of London and Dorset society, and was made Receiver General of the County, O'Brien must often have sighed

---

[1] *Ibid.*   [2] *Ibid.*, p. 80.

for the more intoxicating successes of his theatrical youth. Hardy himself took this view and wrote an undated poem [1] in which he imagines O'Brien pleading with his wife for a return to the boards, if only for one night—with dire results.

The pair were known to all by sight and Lady Susan was especially loved by the Hardy family. Thomas' father, as a boy chorister, had often seen her, old and lonely after her bereavement, in the gardens of Stinsford House, clad in a red cloak. She had pleaded with Hardy's grandfather and great-grandfather, the masons of the district, to make the vault for her and her husband "just large enough for our two selves only". [2] His grandfather had carried out her wishes, placed O'Brien and her in it, and erected a monument to both of them.

This monument, which is like a perpetual Valentine, hangs on the chancel wall and it is possible that Lady Susan designed it herself. It consists of two oval marble tablets, united by a flourish and two hearts, symbolizing her devotion. If one did not know the romantic story which lies behind this demure monument, in marked contrast to the earlier one to Lora Grey, one would imagine the device to be merely a funereal convention of the day. The only eulogy Lady Susan permits herself is that she was "the faithful wife and inseparable companion" of her husband. He who reads the short inscriptions turns away noting something else which makes him sigh for Lady Susan—she was childless.

Hardy's attraction to Lady Susan in retrospect is extraordinary. He speaks of her possessively, as if his family had a privileged right to relate themselves to her, not by birth, but by some subtle tie involving affection and the knowledge of intimate duties well-performed. He also speaks of her as if she were *alive*, at least for him. When he is in his forties he meets an old man, of incalculable age, who has known Lady Susan, and Hardy's ironic sense of humour is tickled by his account of her generosity.

She kept a splendid house—a cellar-full of strong beer that would a'most knock you down; everybody drank as much as he liked. The head gardener . . . was drunk every morning before breakfast. There are no such houses now! On wet days we used

---

[1] "The Noble Lady's Tale", *Time's Laughingstocks*.   [2] I, p. 12.

to make a point of working opposite the drawing-room window, that she might pity us. She would send out and tell us to go indoors, and not expose ourselves to the weather so reckless. . . . A kind-hearted woman, Lady Susan.[1]

When Hardy was fifty-one and on his way to dine with neighbours, he was horrified to see that Stinsford House was alight. The fire, like a cat which cruelly plays with a mouse, merely lit the rooms at first, as if for some festive occasion, and then it devoured them. Hardy described the tears streaming from men's faces, and the firelight incongruously flickering on his father's nearby grave. In the midst of a conflagration, in which he was himself actively engaged, some part of him was able to stand aside and to note details such as these. He was even aware of something more than anxiety for a neighbour's home and possessions, or for lives endangered. There was a painful revival of early emotions, a '*bruising of tender memories*', he calls it. And he recites for a second time how Lady Susan plead with his grandfather that the vault should be no larger than a lover's bed.

In 1845, the Kingston Maurward estate, with its pair of manor-houses, each remarkable examples of their periods (mid-Tudor and early Georgian), was sold out of the family by William Grey Pitt and a new lady graced the Georgian house. As far as I know, her name has never been mentioned in any work on Hardy. Perhaps this is due to a kind of over-scrupulosity on Hardy's part while she or her relations were alive, but now it is time to set her in her proper place as the woman who, next to his mother, influenced the young Thomas Hardy more than any other. In the *Early Life* she is referred to as 'the squire's wife'; and in *The Later Years*, only her Christian names are given.

She was Julia Augusta Martin, the wife of Francis Pitney Brouncker Martin, whose family may have been of the Suffolk branch of the old Martyns of Athelhampton. In one place Hardy refers to her as 'her ladyship', but this, I think, was merely a courtesy title. She and her husband remained only a few years at Kingston Maurward[2] and he was possibly that

[1] I, pp. 213-14.
[2] The Martins only held Kingston Maurward for eight years, selling it in 1853.

Kingston Maurward (South Front)
(The home of Hardy's lady of the manor)

ambitious lord of the manor who ruined himself by attempting to turn farmer of his own land, mentioned in Hardy's letter to Rider Haggard.[1]

Like Lady Susan, Julia Martin was childless,[2] and like Lora Grey she was a benefactress to Stinsford and Bockhampton. She was passionately fond of children and at her instigation a school was built and endowed on the edge of Kingston Maurward estate, alongside the lane which leads from Higher to Lower Bockhampton, not far from the old Elizabethan home of the Greys. The grant, dated January 22, 1848, states that:

> all that piece of ground situate in the said Parish of Stinsford bounded on the north by the garden now in the occupation of Robert Ricketts No. 164 on the east by the Parish road on the west by the hedge dividing the said piece of ground from the nursery ground and orchard belonging to the Mansion House of Kingston Maurward . . . and on the south side by the carriage drive now making . . . which said piece of ground . . . contains about one quarter of an acre more or less and was lately in the occupation of William Dart and the widow Oliver as part of the garden ground attached to their respective cottages.[3]

The cottages have long since disappeared, but it may be remembered that the old woman of wisdom in *The Woodlanders* was called Grammer Oliver, and Dart was the surname of the fourth musician in the Stinsford west gallery. The grant also states that the school is to "be used . . . for the education of *children of the labouring classes*".

Having seen that the school was built of good local stone, Julia Martin imported an excellent master and mistress, and spared no pains in making it one above the average for those times. Hardy's first schooling was therefore due to the generosity of two ladies of the manor, Lora (Grey) Pitt, and Julia Augusta Martin, who lavished affection on him.

[1] II, pp. 93-6. See also I. p. 24.

[2] There are no records of births of children to Francis and Julia Martin either in the Stinsford parish registers or in those of St George's, Hanover Square, the parish in which they resided after leaving Stinsford, although another family of Martins in Berkeley Square appears. Francis Martin's town house was in Bruton Street.

[3] Through the kindness of the Salisbury Diocesan Council of Education and the Right Reverend the Lord Bishop of Salisbury, Chairman of the Council.

Hardy attended the school in the year in which it was opened—1848. By some accident he arrived before master, mistress, or pupils, and stood tremulous and alone on the brink of a new and frightening world. His poem, "He revisits his first School",[1] gives a whimsical account of his sensations on returning to the Bockhampton school many years later, and he describes himself in retrospect as having been

> . . . . . . *fresh,*
> *Pink, tiny, crisp-curled,*
> *My pinions yet furled*
> *From the winds of the world.*

But long before he attended the school Julia Martin had singled him out for favour. The squire's wife was 'passionately fond of him'. She kissed him and clasped him and cradled him in her lap. She listened to songs he sang to her in his piping voice, and she treasured the childish drawings of animals which, like Bewick and William Barnes, he essayed to make. Julia Martin was, in fact, Thomas Hardy's first love. He says that 'he quite reciprocated her fondness': admits that he had 'grown more attached to her than he cared to own', and that 'his feeling for her *was almost that of a lover*'.[2] Later he speaks of her as '*the lady of his earliest passion as a child*, who had been so tender towards him—and had used to take him in her arms'.

But alas, on this idyllic scene Thomas' parents laid a ruthless hand. They had decided that he was now old and strong enough to be sent to a Dorchester day-school, and a year later, after some postponements in arranging his acceptance, the lad was transferred. His removal from the school which she had been at such pains and expense to build offended Mrs Martin, partly because the Dorchester school was nonconformist, partly because she had not been consulted as to his withdrawal, and partly because she must have considered 'Little Tommy' her especial protégé. No doubt she hoped for a prize pupil to set the seal on her scholastic venture and saw that the boy gave promise of being one.

His mother, on her part, was taken by surprise at Mrs Martin's reaction. Writing as an old man Hardy weighs the

---

[1] In *Moments of Vision*.   [2] I, pp. 23-4, 53. (Italics mine.)

claims of both women. Any thought of wounding the squire's wife, he says, was quite out of his mother's thoughts. Nor was she uncivil. The natural dignity of his family, their independent spirit and consciousness of being above the labouring classes, is plain to read. The Hardys, being life-holders of their house and land, regarded themselves as independent of the manor, and free from the necessity for an almost feudal respectfulness necessitating permission for making decisions of a private or domestic nature. Thomas became the unwilling victim of feminine dissension, and he was hurt by an abrupt termination of his friendship with the affectionate lady who had seemed so devoted. He

secretly mourned the loss of his friend the landowner's wife . . . He so much longed to see her that he jumped at the offer of a young woman of the village to take him to a harvest-supper at which he knew she would be present . . . The young woman, a small farmer's daughter, called for young Thomas on the afternoon of the festivity . . . The 'Supper' . . . was over by the time they reached the barn, and tea was going on, after which there was singing and dancing, some non-commissioned officers having been invited from the barracks [at Dorchester] by the Squire as partners for the girls. . . .

Presently the manor-lady, her husband, and a house-party arrived to lead off some dances. As soon as she saw little Thomas— who had no business whatever there—she came up to him and said reproachfully: "O Tommy! How is this? I thought you had deserted me."

Tommy assured her through his tears that he had not deserted her, and never would desert her: and then the dance went on. He being wildly fond of dancing, she gave him for a partner a little niece of hers about his own age . . . The manor-house party remained for a few figures and then left, but Tommy perforce stayed on, being afraid to go home without the strapping young woman, his companion, who was dancing with the soldiers. There he wearily waited for her till three in the morning, having eaten and drunk nothing since one o'clock on the previous day, through his fear of asking the merry-makers for food. What the estate owner's tender wife would have given him had she but known of his hunger and thirst, and how carefully have sent him home had she been aware of his dilemma! A reproof from both his parents when Tommy reached home ended the day's adventure. It was

the only harvest supper and dance that he ever saw, save one . . .
[and it] was among the last at which the old traditional ballads
were sung . . . The particular ballad which he remembered hearing
that night from the lips of the farm-women was that one variously
called "The Outlandish Knight", "May Colvine", "The Western
Tragedy", etc. He could recall to old age the scene of the young
women in their light gowns sitting on a bench against the wall in
the barn, and leaning against each other as they warbled the
Dorset version of the ballad, which differed a little from the
northern:

> Lie there, lie there, thou false-hearted man,
>   Lie there instead o' me;
> For six pretty maidens thou hast a'drown'd here,
>   But the seventh hath drown'd thee!
>
> .   .   .   .   .
>
> O tell no more, my pretty par-rót,
>   Lay not the blame on me;
> And your cage shall be made o' the glittering gold,
>   Wi' a door o' the white ivo-rie.[1]

This stolen scene made an indelible impression on the boy's
mind and in his second-hand copy of *The Ballad Minstrelsy of
Scotland* (1803), purchased some time after 1880, the Dorset
variations from the Scottish original are carefully marked in
pencil in Hardy's writing.

Mrs Martin appears in Hardy's recollections on three other
occasions. When, at the age of twenty-two, he went up to seek
his fortunes in London, he called on her. By then her husband
had sold Kingston Maurward to the Hon. Mr and Mrs Fellowes,
and the Martins were living in Bruton Street. The old butler,
whom Hardy had known as a boy and who opened the door to
him, seemed little altered. But the visit was not propitious.
The young architect was pained at the changed appearance of
his early love and, with his sensitive response to others, he felt
that she was embarrassed at the encounter. Neither could readily
adjust themselves to growth and change in the other, which
involved an entirely new relationship. Julia Augusta begged
the young man to come again, but Hardy "did not respond to
the invitation, showing that the fickleness was his alone".[2] He

[1] I, pp. 24-6. See also "The Harvest Supper", in *Human Shows*.
[2] I, pp. 53-4.

gives for excuse the fact that he got "immersed in London life",
a life of the mind, at times unconventional, even revolutionary,
with which Mrs Martin would probably not have been in sympathy

Some years later, when he was becoming established as a writer
to be seriously reckoned with, she wrote to Hardy to congratu-
late him on the reception of *Far From the Madding Crowd*:

> . . . her writing again was not merely a rekindled interest on
> account of the book's popularity, for she had written to him in his
> obscurity, before he had published a line, asking him to come and
> see her, and addressing him as her dear Tommy, as when he was a
> small boy, apologizing for doing so on the ground that she could
> not help it. She was now quite an elderly lady, but by signing her
> letter 'Julia Augusta' she revived throbs of tender feeling in him,
> and brought back to his memory the thrilling *frou-frou* of her four
> grey silk flounces when she had used to bend over him, and when
> they brushed against the font as she entered church on Sundays.
> He replied . . . but did not go to see her.[1]

At the age of 33-4 he even remembered the number of
flounces her skirts had had, their colour and texture, and
the noise which they had made. The seductive sound of
what Donne, in one of his *Elegies*, called 'whistling silks',
had early attracted the country boy of rare susceptibility, who
was responsive to feminine charm and aristocratic bearing,
and who had ears attuned to gradations in sound arising from
different substances striking on one another. His sensitivity of
ear was as pronounced as that of his other senses.

The poem, "In Her Precincts", may be Hardy's recollection
many years later of the misery of that first bewildering separation, when he felt shut out in the dark, alone. Neither the windows of the Bockhampton home, nor of Max Gate, are visible
from the park, which Hardy declared the poem's setting. It
seems likely that the verses express his remembered despair at
being separated from his childhood love.

> *Her house looked cold from the foggy lea,*
> *And the square of each window a dull black blur*
> *Where showed no stir;*
> *Yes, her gloom within at the lack of me*
> *Seemed matching mine at the lack of her.*

[1] I, p. 134.

The black squares grew to be squares of light
As the eveshade swathed the house and lawn,
And viols gave tone;
There was glee within. And I found that night
The gloom of severance mine alone.

KINGSTON MAURWARD PARK.[1]

When Mrs Hanbury came to live at Kingston Maurward Hardy prepared for her a list of the owners of the manor from 1400 downwards.[2] The name of Francis Martin is recorded as impassively as if his wife had never existed for Hardy, except as a distant, impersonal figure, no more to him than successive shadowy heiresses—Maurwards, Greys, Pitts and the like, with mere historical attributes.

Two tales with a Swiftian flavour survive from this period. The first relates to an adventure with his mother who, despite her practical 'progressive' nature, had a playful side to her character. One day she and Thomas dressed themselves up with cabbage-nets for head-gear and crossed the heath to visit Jemima's sister, who was greatly astonished at their strange appearance. Later in life Hardy told a friend that he had his mother in mind when drawing the portrait of Mrs Yeobright in *The Return of the Native*,[3] a woman of character who held herself aloof from other dwellers on the heath, feeling superior to them. If this is so, it is good to know that, as a young mother, she shared with her elder son the pranksome side of her nature.

The other tale relates an adventure with his father, from whom Thomas seems to have inherited his ironic sense of humour.

Among the queer occurrences accompanying these merry min-strellings may be described one that happened when he was coming home with his father at three in the morning from a gentle-man farmer's house where he had been second violin to his senior's first for six or seven hours ... It was bitterly cold, and the moon glistened bright upon the encrusted snow, amid which they saw motionless in the hedge what appeared to be a white human

[1] In *Moments of Vision*.
[2] A pencilled copy of this in Hardy's writing is bound into Volume II of his edition of Hutchin's *Dorset*.
[3] See Carl Weber, *Hardy of Wessex*, p. 259. Columbia University Press, 1940.

figure without a head. The boy, being very tired, with finger-tips tingling from pressing the strings, was for passing the ghastly sight quickly, but the elder went up to the object, which proved to be a very tall, thin man in a long smock-frock, leaning against the bank in a drunken stupor, his head hanging forward so low that at a distance he had seemed to have no head at all. Hardy senior, seeing the danger of leaving the man where he might be frozen to death, awoke him after much exertion, and they supported him to a cottage near, where he lived, and pushed him in through the door, their ears being greeted as they left with a stream of abuse from the man's wife, which was also vented upon her unfortunate husband, whom she promptly knocked down. Hardy's father remarked that it might have been as well to leave him where he was, to take his chance of being frozen to death.[1]

Meanwhile, at home, the recurrent question was whether Hardy the master-mason should not remove to quarters nearer town. Mrs Hardy was ambitious for him as well as for her children. The Bockhampton house lay in a remote spot, at some distance from the Dorchester-Wimborne highroad, and about three miles from the market town. The children could not easily get to school, and messengers for the builder were delayed since they could not find the spot, a lonely one "between heath and wood".

Either because of the misunderstanding with the Squire's wife, or for some other reason unknown to the boy, the building work for the Kingston Maurward estate was taken out of Hardy senior's hands. He found contracts elsewhere, one of the largest being work on that remarkable thatched building, half-fortress, half domestic-dwelling, of the time of Edward III, Woodesford Castle, which the Earl of Ilchester was then repairing. But this work would end, and what would follow? Mrs Hardy must have often pleaded with her husband to make himself better known.

But Thomas Hardy the second had not the tradesman's soul. Instead of waylaying possible needers of bricks and stone in the market-place or elsewhere, he liked going alone into the woods or on the heath, where, with a telescope inherited from some collateral ancestor who had been captain of a merchant craft, he would stay peering into the distance by the half-hour; or, in the hot weather,

[1] I, pp. 30-1.

lying on a bank of thyme, or camomile, with the grasshoppers leaping over him.[1]

Dear Thomas Hardy the second! How we love him for his lack of worldly ambition, an annoying characteristic for an ambitious wife. (Hardy has emphasized this quality of his father's in the poem "On One who Lived and Died where he was Born", in which he calls him 'wealth-wantless'.) The bank of thyme, or camomile, has a Wordsworthian flavour, a scent thrown off in hot sunshine which Jefferies would have loved, and might have described in *The Story of my Heart*.

[1] I, pp. 26-7.

CHAPTER THREE

THREE SCHOLARS AND SOME BOOKS

In childhood all books are books of divination . . . they influence the future. It is in those early years that I would look for the crisis, the moment when life took a new slant in its journey to death.

GRAHAM GREENE

WHEN he was nine years old Thomas Hardy left the village school in Lower Bockhampton and went to a Dorchester day-school run by a man of great ability—a nonconformist. Mrs Hardy had heard that he was a good scholar and teacher of Latin, and such were her ambitions for Thomas' progress, and her admiration for learning, that she disregarded her religious scruples. One might expect that he would have been sent to the Grammar School founded by Thomas Hardy of Melcombe Regis, but the teaching there at this time was said to be 'indifferent': or to William Barnes' school, but the fees there were higher.

Hardy later describes his master as 'accomplished' and 'exceptionally able'. A year or two after Thomas went to him as a pupil he opened a more ambitious Academy, one of the old British Schools, and boarders came to him from afar. This man, (who remains nameless in the *Early Life*) was Isaac Glandfield Last. All knowledge of him seems to have faded from Dorchester records and the minds of living men, and I have been unable to find to which sect of nonconformists he belonged. His son became Director of the Science Museum, South Kensington: when he died Hardy paid his old master a private tribute. Although the son, he says, had attained worldly success his intellectual ability was no higher "than that by which it had been [my] good fortune to profit".[1]

When he was fourteen years of age Hardy won his first prize, the gift from his head-master of *Scenes and Adventures at Home and Abroad, or Pleasing and Instructive Narrative Anecdotes for Young People*, inscribed 'Presented to Master Thomas Hardy by Mr

[1] II, p. 149.

Last as a reward for diligence, Dorchester, Christmas, 1854'.
When he was fifteen his master also gave him Beza's *Latin
Testament* for his "progress in that tongue—a little pocket
edition which he often carried with him in after years".[1] This
volume—a small book bound in black leather—bears the following inscription:

> 'Thomas Hardy. A reward for diligence in studies, from
> Mr Last. 1855. Mids.'[2]

Latin in Isaac Last's school was not included in the curricu-
lum. It was an extra, and Thomas began the study of this
tongue when he was twelve, using the old Eton Grammar and
Cassell's *Lessons in Latin*, by the Rev. J. R. Beard. For this
privilege Hardy's father paid the modest sum of five shillings,
as the receipt dated Christmas 1853, and signed by Mr Last,
now shows us. But a curious pair of small faded volumes, not
hitherto examined, and of the utmost importance in studying
the development of Hardy's mind, were used by him between
the ages of twelve and sixteen—by which time he had left the
Academy. They are *Thoughts from the Latin Authors*.[3] They consist
of excerpts in Latin with poetic translations, each selection being
given a suitable title, thus:

OVIDUS

THE SOUL

> *Errat, et illinc
> Huc venit, hinc illuc.*

And here and there the unbodied spirit flies
By time or force, or sickness dispossest
And lodges where it lights, in man or beast . . .

TERENTIUS

1. LIFE OF MAN LIKE A GAME AT TABLES

> *Dicunt, jus summum saepe est malitia.*
> For it is a common saying and a true
> That strictest law is oft the highest wrong.

[1] I, p. 31.

[2] Florence Hardy has given 1853-4, but the inscription now gives us the
exact date of Hardy's winning of his 2nd prize.

[3] Volume I and title-page missing.

2. THE NATURE OF MANKIND

Di vostram fidem!

Gods! that the nature of mankind is such
To see and judge the affairs of others
Much better than their own!

VIRGIL

Par varios casus, per tot discrimina rerum.

Through various hazards and events we move.

LUCRETIUS

I. EVERY MAN HAS A SKELETON CLOSET

Vitae post-scenia celant.

Men conceal the back scenes of their lives.

2. AN INFANT

Cui tantum in vita restet transire malorum.

A fit presage for all his coming ills.

These passages have been marked, at least in part, by Hardy as a boy. It will be noticed that all of them concern the uncertainty and unpredictability of life: its hazardous quality and attendant ills: the harsh and unpleasant sides of men's nature. One other ability unusual in a growing boy is implied by the markings of Terence's lines—the ability to stand aside and question generally accepted values. It is the same critical faculty which leads Hardy to underline a passage from the *Hippolytus* of Euripides—

Whosoever has chastity, not that which is taught in schools, but that which is by nature.[1]

and, when he is fifty, to write *Tess of the d'Urbervilles*.

Already Hardy is sufficiently grounded in both English and Latin literature to make a comparison in the margin between a line of Virgil's and one from *Paradise Lost*. His mother had given him Dryden's *Virgil* when he was between the ages of nine and ten: now he was able to study him in the original. He remained

---

[1] See William R. Rutland, *Thomas Hardy, A Study of his Writings and their Background*, p. 44. Basil Blackwell, Oxford, 1938.

throughout his life one of his favourite poets. But what strikes the reader of those faded volumes with their tentative markings is the cast of mind of their youthful owner. The mind appears already to have set: the pattern is already a melancholy one and the lad who carries the books in his pocket has been impressed by the harsh, the hazardous and the unjust.

The lines from Lucretius are especially interesting, indicating Hardy's early attraction to the Latin poet with whose ardent spirit he had something in common, as others have remarked.[1] Concerning Lucretius Dr Rutland has written:

> It might have been expected that in later years Hardy would read [him]. The only direct evidence that he did so appears to be the quotation from [that author] on the title page of *The Hand of Ethelberta—Vitae post scenia celant*.[2]

He goes on to mention a text printed in Paris in 1680, which was amongst the books he examined at Max Gate after Hardy's death. He does not appear to have seen these smaller volumes which were obviously in Hardy's possession long before he owned the Paris edition, and in which as a lad he marked the very passage mentioned. *The Hand of Ethelberta* was not his first novel: it was his fifth published one, and his sixth if we count his lost novel, *The Poor Man and the Lady*. Hardy was between thirty-four and thirty-five when he wrote it, and for a suggestive quotation on the title-page he returned to one which had stamped itself on his malleable mind when he was still in his teens. One of the books is inscribed with his signature in a very early hand, in which the 'd' has not yet become a Greek *delta*, a habit he adopted after taking up the study of that language.

By now Hardy's early reading had ranged over Shakespeare, Bunyan, Scott, Dumas, Harrison Ainsworth, James Grant and G. P. R. James.[3] He began to take French lessons, and to study German at home when he was fifteen in *The Popular Educator*, published first by William Kent (1855) and later taken over by John Cassell.[4] Three volumes of this periodical are still among

---

[1] Lionel Johnson and Lascelles Abercrombie.
[2] p. 26.   [3] See Weber, p. 9.
[4] Not Cassell alone, as Mrs Hardy says. His *Stepping Stones to the French Language*, received by Hardy in 1855, and *Le Voyage de Cyrus*, 1851, are reminders of this study.

Hardy's books, carefully covered in faded silk, stitched across, with an additional cover of brown paper. During his mother's childhood Ossian was held in great esteem. There are also two small volumes of this poet's work, with tentative markings by the young Hardy. It is interesting to see how the pictorial phrases took his eye:

> Arise, winds of autumn, arise, blow along the heath . . . *walk through broken clouds, oh moon* . . .[1]

and

> Arinal, my son, descended from the hill . . . *His arrows rattled by his side* . . .

and other phrases such as '*windy steep*', '*sounding rock*', 'feebly *whistling* grass'. He also liked '*Her hair flows slowly on the blast*'. and '*Fingal comes like a watery column of mist*'. But most curious of all, he has underlined 'Roll on, *ye dark brown years*, ye bring no joy on your course'.

Hardy was kept strictly at church on Sundays until he knew the Morning and Evening services by heart as well as the rubrics and large portions of the Psalms. When he was fifteen or sixteen years of age he taught in the Stinsford Sunday School, together with the Vicar's sons. Among his pupils was a pink and plump dairymaid with an astonishing verbal memory upon whom he drew for a portrait of Marian, in *Tess*, thirty-five years later.

In adolescence Hardy fell in and out of love frequently; the shy smiles and aspen forms of girls whom he passed in the lane remained in his mind until his death. Two of them are nameless. The first passed him on horseback in one of Dorchester's tree-lined Walks. She smiled at him and the mischief was done. He saw her twice again, once riding with a young man, and then she disappeared. Next he lost his heart to a girl from Windsor: then to a pretty game-keeper's daughter with 'red-bay' hair, Fancy Day in embryo. Then to a farmer's daughter who never spoke a word to him, only smiled shyly. Yet Thomas went as far afield as Weymouth, week after week, to try to find her, which at last he did, sitting in church and worshipping her from afar. The

---

[1] The words in italics only are underlined.

poems "To Lizbie Brown", and "To Louisa in the Lane", written shortly before his death, reflect these early attachments.

According to the *Early Life* Hardy was popular with his school-fellows, whose friendship he sometimes found burdensome. While not disliking people he loved solitude and he relished the long walk home, alone. He says that he was *aloof* rather than shy, making a clear distinction between the two characteristics. Clive Holland reports that his school-fellows found him 'stuck-up', even 'queer', because of his shyness.[1] Like Cézanne he had a life-long dislike of being touched. Possibly he felt, as the painter did, that others had the power of drawing strength from him by physical contact, strength which he needed to conserve. Cézanne's reiterated cry of *Moi qui suis faible* resembles Hardy's feeling that he had 'not enough staying power for life'. Such fastidiousness, a characteristic of highly reserved, sensitive people, appears in Hardy's case, to have been rooted in superstition. Another of his dislikes was that of being weighed, which he believed to be unlucky.

A pair of incidents which Hardy (with a strange disassociation from his own emotions) disavows as having 'nothing to do with his own life', and describes as being merely 'unusual' and 'dramatic', occurred, one of them shortly after, and the other before leaving, Mr Last's school.

One summer morning at Bockhampton, just before he sat down to breakfast, he remembered that a man was to be hanged at eight o'clock at Dorchester. He took up the big brass telescope that had been handed on in the family, and hastened to a hill on the heath a quarter of a mile from the house, whence he looked towards the town. The sun behind his back shone straight on the white stone façade of the gaol, the gallows upon it, and the form of the murderer in white fustian, the executioner and officials in dark clothing and the crowd below being invisible at this distance of nearly three miles. At the moment of his placing the glass to his eye the white figure dropped downwards, and the faint note of the town clock struck eight. The whole thing had been so sudden that the glass nearly fell from Hardy's hands. *He seemed alone on the heath with the hanged man*, and crept home wishing he had not been so curious. It was the second and last execution he witnessed, the

[1] *Thomas Hardy's Wessex Scene*, pp. 15-16. Longmans (Dorchester), 1948.

first having been that of a woman two or three years earlier, *when he stood close to the gallows*.[1]

Hardy gives no details, neither the woman's name, nor the crime for which she was hanged.[2] As an old man he told a friend that he had climbed on to the railings surrounding the hangman's cottage the night before the execution, and watched the executioner stolidly eating his supper. He told another that he arrived early and took his seat immediately below the staging.[3] More extraordinary still, Hardy does not mention the effect which this degrading sight must have had on a lad of his sensitivity. Yet here was a male Lachesis, apparently unfeeling and uncaring, who cut the threads of human life as easily as a child snaps the stalk of a summer flower. Human life might be extinguished as suddenly as that of the half-frozen fieldfare.

That the first execution made a deep impression on him is proven not only by his speaking to Nevinson of it, but by his reference to the event in a public speech in 1910.[4] He also wrote two poems,[5] one dealing with the 18th-century burning at the stake in Maumbury Rings of a woman who had killed her husband, and the other on the Bywaters-Thompson murder in 1923.

In one of these early executions the victim was a woman, and it was the woman who was the murderess, the figure of strength, the force in revolt. Hardy had no need to remember Clytemnaestra for an example of passion, and the fact that in his novels the women are generally the active, and the men the passive, characters may be connected with early pondering on this theme. In the second of the two poems mentioned above, Hardy's sympathy is with the murderess, as it was when he came to write *Tess*, whom of all his imagined characters he loved the most, and whom he spoke of as a living person.

[1] I, p. 37. (Italics mine.)
[2] The Governors of H.M. Prisons have not been able to give me any information concerning the execution. Carl Weber in *Hardy of Wessex*, p. 120, says that the woman was Martha Brown, wife of an innkeeper. When a former lover informed her husband of their old association she killed the lover.
[3] H. W. Nevinson and Sir Newman Flower.
[4] When he received the Freedom of the Borough of Dorchester.
[5] "The Mock Wife" and "On the Portrait of a Woman about to be Hanged".

Another tragedy told to Hardy by his father, engraved itself on his mind as mercilessly as if he himself had seen it. At the time of the rick-burnings Thomas the second had seen four men hanged, together with a stripling lad who was merely with the incendiaries by accident at the time—a poor, half-starved lad, to whose feet the Prison Master ordered weights to be tied to ensure a speedi er death. "Nothing my father ever said drove the tragedy of life so deeply into my mind".[1] This pathetic victim of man's implacability to man appears in *The Withered Arm*, written by Hardy when he was forty-eight.

At the age of sixteen the question arose as to a future profession for Hardy. He entered the offices of John Hicks, an architect and church restorer who had formerly worked in Bristol, now established in Dorchester. Thomas' regret on being transferred from Isaac Last's school to the architect's office was not for freedom and youth which were sped, but that the study of his *Æneid*, Horace, Ovid and Catullus must now be curtailed.

John Hicks had noticed Thomas when his father was carrying out the architect's plans for Woodesford Castle. He invited him to assist at a survey, and liking his work, asked to have him as a pupil. For apprenticing his son to Mr Hicks, Thomas Hardy senior paid the sum of forty pounds on July 11, 1856—"for three years instruction in architectural drawing and surveying from the date hereof".[2] His office was in that busy and narrow thoroughfare South Street, Dorchester, in ground-floor rooms which have since been part of a Temperance Hotel and are now a bicycle shop. (The rooms above were occupied by Mrs Hicks, who sent down to admonish the pupils below when they became unruly.) Their brown-painted woodwork, panelled doors, and architraves of late Georgian character, are probably much as they were in Hardy's day, when he looked out at the ancient 17th-century almshouse, Napier's Mite, with its open gallery and bracket clock.

Hicks was a jovial, easy-going master, who did not mind if the boys gave more time to books than to drawing, when so inclined. He was something of a classical scholar and had a smattering

---

[1] Sir Newman Flower, *Just as it Happened*, pp. 91-2. Cassell's, 1950.
[2] According to the extant receipt. Other details of the apprenticeship are given in the *Early Life*, I, p. 35.

of Hebrew; and there was another pupil anxious to continue his classical studies, Robert Henry Bastow, who later emigrated to Tasmania.

Hardy packed his day close. He began by reading Latin between five to eight in the mornings in the rural seclusion of his home: in summer he sometimes rose at four. On his way to and from his drawing-work he sharpened his wits by soliloquizing in Latin. Not content with Latin he began to learn Greek on his own and to read the *Iliad* and the New Testament in the original texts. Unexpected stimulus was given to his Greek studies by Bastow suddenly becoming doctrinal and deciding to be baptized. Hardy, who was easily influenced by those whom he admired, even thought of being baptized again himself. The rights and wrongs of Paedo-Baptism were furiously argued by Bastow, Hardy, and two other youths, ardent young Scotsmen, sons of the Baptist Minister. These young men were fresh from Aberdeen University (which was to be the first to honour Hardy with a degree many years later) and they could confound the youngest architectural pupil by

rattling off at a moment's notice the Greek original of any passage in the New Testament.[1]

Thomas was put on his mettle. He confesses that he felt like one with his back to the wall who has taken on three sturdy fighters. He armed himself with a new Greek Testament[2] for the fray, so that he might get his arguments for, or against, adult baptism from the original sources. This Testament bears an amusing inscription, Hardy's name in Greek lettering.

In spite of his slowness in reaching physical maturity Hardy was intellectually precocious. His critical detachment and breadth of mind helped him to see what the other students did not observe:

that Christianity did not hang on temporary details that expediency might modify, and that the practice of an isolated few in the early ages could not be binding on its multitudes in differing circumstances, when it had grown to be the religion of continents.[3]

[1] I, p. 38.
[2] In Griesbach's edition. For a description of Hardy's copy see Rutland, p. 28. He also used the Eton Greek Grammar (1852).
[3] I, p. 39.

A curious reminder of this early preoccupation of Hardy's exists in one of his note-books—that in which he jotted down material for *The Trumpet Major*.[1] This little note-book is stitched together by hand and bears a home-made paper cover on which is written in Hardy's writing:

British Museum Notes
taken for "Trumpet Major"
and other works of time of George III.
1878-1879.

But it contains material which does not relate to this novel, and incorporates notes on such varied subjects as a woman's face, the style of Jane Austen, Fournier's *Passions of the Human Soul*, poetry, and a philosophy of life. There are also several pages quoting from *The Baptism of Infants a Reasonable Service, An Argument from Apostolic Tradition*, 1765. The author, whose name is not given, draws on Justin Martyr, Tertullian, Origen, Cyprian, and Italian scholars of the 16th century to prove his point.

If Hardy copied this out in 1878 his quandary over the need for adult or infant baptism, which had troubled his mind so actively in 1859, had not yet been solved. In 1880 he was writing *A Laodicean*, which opens with Paula's refusal to be immersed in the Baptist Chapel, and in 1891, *Tess of the d'Urbervilles*, which contains the heroine's touching question to the Vicar concerning the welfare of the soul of her unbaptized babe—"Sorrow the Undesired, the bastard gift of shameless nature who respects not the social law".

To understand Hardy's preoccupation with this ecclesiastical problem one has to go back to 1847 when the West Country was shaken by the Bishop of Exeter's refusal to induct the Rev. Cornelius Gorham into a living in his diocese, because the former believed infant baptism to be a means of regeneration and the latter a symbol. The contest went on for many years. In 1850 the crisis convulsed both Church and State: the highest courts in the land were called in, and the Archbishop in accepting their final judgment was accused of 'worse than Popery'.

[1] In the Dorset County Museum. The foot of the cover bears the dates of the King's visit to Weymouth.

Seven years later, worn out by the struggle, the Vicar died. All this took place in Hardy's youth, when he was between the ages of seven and seventeen. His mother, an ardent evangelical, must have mentioned the quarrel-in-high-places at home, or Hardy himself discussed it with his Dorchester friends. The prominence of the trials and re-trial of the case, and the impression which these probably made upon him, are a partial clue to Hardy's interest in this thorny subject, which involves not merely the niceties of schoolmen but a fundamental cleavage in religion—that between mystery and reason.

While studying these problems, Hardy and the other lads used often to walk out towards Bockhampton, carrying their Greek Testaments in their pockets. Upon reaching the field-gate which opens into the Kingston Maurward ewe-leaze they climbed up and sat upon it, comparing texts and renderings. That gate and that ewe-leaze were to be the setting for a sadder scene in Hardy's life later on: but for the moment he led a charmed and varied existence. By night he slept amongst the singing nightingales, by day he lived amongst men of acute minds and was near to modern inventions, and in the evenings he relaxed with his fiddle. He led, as he puts it,

> a life twisted of three strands—the professional, the scholar's and the rustic . . . Like a conjuror at a fair [he kept] in the air the three balls of architecture, scholarship and dance-fiddling.[1]

But if Hardy lacked the advantages of a University education, which might have hardened and stereotyped his genius, causing it to run in more orthodox channels, he was fortunate in having men of unusual ability near him in Dorchester to whom he could run for scholarly assistance, and advice on life. Chief amongst these was William Barnes, the poet and philologist, who kept school at the house next door to Mr Hicks' offices in South Street.

> Knowing him to be an authority upon grammar Hardy would often run in to ask Barnes to decide some knotty point in dispute between him and his fellow pupil. Hardy used to assert in later years that upon almost every occasion the verdict was given in his favour.[2]

[1] I, pp. 41-2.   [2] I, p. 37.

When Thomas, a lad still in his teens, ran in and out for help from William Barnes, the latter was between fifty-five and sixty years of age. He had been keeping this, his second school, for more than twenty years, but upon receipt of a Civil List Pension and the presentation of a living he was soon to see an end of the poverty which had dogged him all his life. Most of his writing had been done, although it had not yet received general recognition. In 1859 the *Dorset County Chronicle* published verses of his each week. Anyone who sits in the dusty attics of that paper's offices today and suddenly comes on *Linden Lea* (with its seemingly artless grouping together of consonantal sounds in a single line) must get from it something of the pleasure which Hardy got on opening that paper's wide sheets and reading it for the first time, nearly a century ago.

William Barnes had much to offer the young Hardy: an extensive knowledge of languages; a keen interest in mathematics, music, archeology and painting; an abiding love of his own countryside, and of being actively alive in it. He was also a craftsman who delighted in making wooden toys for his children, a clock or sundial for his home or garden, a copper or wood-engraving for a friend. He was a full-orbed man with mental and physical powers stretched to their full extent, none of them atrophied by life-long residence in his beloved Dorset, or her Wiltshire borders.

Hardy's description of Barnes as an old man coming up South Street to *The Bow*, the curved street by the Dorchester cross-roads, is well-known.[1] Edmund Gosse so much admired it that he told Hardy he ought to have been a biographer instead of a novelist. Barnes' daughter, Leader Scott, has filled out the portrait with a description of her own. She says that her father kept good discipline in his school, without using the cane, and that he always wore a long, light-blue, homespun gown, like a dressing-gown, when teaching.

William Barnes was the first poet whom Hardy knew in the flesh and the only considerable one who had written in the Dorset dialect. In the year that Thomas left Dorchester for London (1862) Barnes published his sixth volume of verse, the first having

[1] Obituary Notice of Rev. William Barnes in *The Athenaeum*, October 16, 1886.

appeared as many as forty-two years earlier. Hardy must have seen Barnes' articles on versification, as well as his poems, in the local paper. His copy of *Poems of Rural Life* is marked in many places; two of his favourite poems were "Woak Hill" which appeared in the month before Hardy's migration to London, and "Melhill Feast" against which there are as many as nine separate marks. (From "Melhill" it is no great step in the imagination to the name "Mellstock.") When he was seventy-five Barnes presented the younger man with a copy of this book inscribed

> Mr T. Hardy with the author's kind regards and good wishes for his writings.

(Hardy would then have been thirty-six and well launched on his literary career with the success of *Far from the Madding Crowd*.)

Barnes was also giving public readings of his poems which we know that Hardy attended, for he has described Barnes'

> mild smile at the boisterous merriment provoked by his droll delivery

of poems such as "A Bit o' Sly Coorten".[1]

That Barnes influenced Hardy both in his prose and verse has been pointed out by others.[2] Perhaps Barnes instilled into him something he had learnt from the Welsh Bardic poets, whom he admired and strove to emulate—a philosophy applicable to life as well as to writing. According to these poets the true poet must have 'an eye to see nature, a heart to feel her, and boldness to follow her'. In other words, he must have courage to believe in his own talents (what Hardy grew to call his 'idiosyncracy'), to develop and back them against hostile critics and criticism. This was advice of which Hardy was sorely in need; if the older man, rich in spiritual serenity, could teach him this he had indeed done well.

Hardy has sometimes been criticized for not paying sufficient tribute to his old master, despite the fact that he reviewed his *Poems of Life in the Dorset Dialect* anonymously in 1879, wrote his obituary notice in 1886, and a preface to the *Selected Poems* in 1908. But when one is young it is difficult to assess those

---

[1] *Ibid.*
[2] See Rutland, pp. 8-12, and Geoffrey Grigson in *The Mint*.

invisible, intangible essences which flow from one person to another and influence him unconsciously. The eager pupil takes it for granted that his master is brilliant, his knowledge unfailing, and that his time should be given without stint. Hardy's debt was probably unconsciously incurred and he was unaware of its extent. Barnes once told Kilvert that there was not a single line uninspired by love or sympathy in all that he had written. He loved learning and the acquisition of knowledge: he loved handing on to others what it had given him joy to acquire: he loved nature, and above all mankind. Something of his tenderness and zeal for knowledge must have overflowed on to Hardy, whose misfortune it was to belong to a younger generation about to be tested in a scorching furnace.

Another of Hardy's friends at this time was Horace Moule, whose influence is generally insufficiently emphasized. Horatio Moseley Moule was the fourth of the eight sons of the Rev. Henry Moule of Fordington, whom Hardy called 'The Seven Brethren'. (One son died in infancy.) Born on May 30, 1832, he was eight years Hardy's senior. Thomas appears to have met him shortly after Horace had come down from Cambridge and had embarked on the literary career of leader-writer and reviewer for which he was so ably endowed. What seems to have attracted Hardy to him first was that 'he was a fine Greek scholar . . . always ready to act the tutor in any classical difficulty'.[1] For Horace had the divine gift, which Barnes also had, of being able to impart knowledge. He was, so his brother writes, 'rich in manifold gifts' and he had

> a hundred charming ways of interesting and teaching me, alike in scholarship and in classical history. He would walk with me through the springing corn, translating Hesiod to me. He would draw a plan of ancient Rome with lines of pebbles on the lawn . . . Wonderful was his subtle faculty for imparting, along with all due care for grammatical precision, a living interest in the subject matter, and for shedding an indefinable glamour of the ideal over all we read.[2]

Moule was of French, Welsh and English stock. His father

[1] I, p. 43.
[2] Handley C. G. Moule, D.D., *Memories of a Vicarage*, p. 35. Religious Tract Society, London, 1913.

was something of a local hero as well as a spiritual leader of the old 'methodist' evangelical school, much admired by Hardy's mother who remembered him as 'tall and noble-looking' in his youth. The Rev. Henry Moule scoured sleepy Fordington like a vitalizing fire. During the troublous time of the rick-burnings he organized and served on patrols; when cholera broke out in Fordington—when Hardy was nine and again when he has twelve—he 'stood between the living and the dead', acting with such promptitude that not a single case of infection spread to Dorchester only a stone's throw away. He visited the dying in their homes and buried the infected dead: he called the living into the fields for prayers: and he attacked the apathetic officials of the Duchy of Cornwall, which owned a large part of Fordington. When these gentlemen were too busy to attend to him he wrote to the Prince Consort and gained his ear. The conditions which had fostered the cholera outbreaks were removed and a new system of drainage, advocated by the Vicar, was adopted.

When he died Hardy wrote to one of his sons:

> Although not, topographically, a parishioner of your father's I virtually stood in that relation to him, *and his home generally*, during many years of my life, and *I always feel precisely as if I had been one.*
>
> A day or two ago Matthew Arnold talked a good deal about him to me: he was greatly struck with an imperfect description I gave him (from what I had heard my father say) of the state of Fordington 50 years ago, and its state after the Vicar had brought his energies to bear upon the village for a few years. His words 'energy is genius' express your father very happily.[1]

The parson in *A Changed Man* resembles the Reverend Henry Moule in his fearless disregard of his own life, but he deserved a finer tale, a whole volume to himself.

One of the distinguishing features of the Fordington vicarage was the warmth of its emotional and intellectual life. Mr Moule held meetings for parsons from neighbouring parishes who 'came by train, by coach, by gig or by horseback', eagerly anticipating the exchange of stimulating ideas and the hospitality which the old house on the hill afforded. And as time went on and Henry Moule's fame spread, learned men—scholars, poets

[1] I, p. 176. (Italics mine.)

and professors—brought their sons to his door, men who had known Lamb and were intimate with Disraeli, to whom Hardy later presented a petition. The vicarage contained a friendly room known as 'The Great Room',

> a delightful nondescript of a chamber . . . lighted from both ends, warmed by two fireplaces, and peopled with books in three of its corners . . . Prescott's *Mexico*. Roger's *Italy*, Cary's Dante, Milton, Scott and others.[1]

In this homely room the young Moules played their games, read out-loud, and sang or played music. Horace, who had been village-church organist at the age of twelve, taught and lead the part singers. Hardy, being a contemporary of the younger boys as well as Horace's friend, must have shared some of these pleasures, as well as their excursions into the fields, where they swam in the shining Frome waters or fished her gravelly pools for poised and darting trout.

When Hardy went up to London, it was to Horace's visits that he looked forward most ardently. Incongruously they attended service in a Roman Catholic Chapel; or dined in some old-fashioned restaurant. When Moule was ill Thomas informed his sister Mary: when Hardy tackled Newman's *Apologia* he longed to be convinced because Moule admired him. When Hardy fell in love and went down to Cornwall it was Moule who sent news of the Franco-Prussian war, together with the latest literary reviews, to the Cornish vicarage. When Moule, as Poor Law Inspector, set out for Ipswich on his rounds, Hardy sometimes accompanied him. For Moule was a born leader; he was both Hardy's friend and mentor.

Twice he tendered advice to Hardy which the younger man unhesitatingly accepted, altering the course of his life. The first occasion was when Hardy, at the age of nineteen, asked Moule whether he thought it best to go on with his study of the Greek tragedians. Moule 'reluctantly' advised him against this, on purely practical grounds, for if Hardy was to be an architect, and was to earn his own living, further study of the Greek texts would be wasted time. Hardy dutifully set aside his *Agamemnon* and *Oedipus* and applied himself to John Hicks' work,

---

[1] Moule, p. 27.

part of which was to renovate dilapidated churches, involving the destruction of ancient Gothic work, which Hardy in after years deplored. The second occasion was when Hardy was thirty-two or thirty-three years old. He was bitterly discouraged at the reception of his first novel and the rejection of his poems. He had determined to stifle his urge to write and was burying his creative energies in designing buildings for the London School Board. In crossing Trafalgar Square he ran into Horace, who had already advised him not to take the barbed arrows of unsympathetic critics too much to heart.

> Moule, a scholar and critic of perfect taste, firmly believed in Hardy's potentialities as a writer, and said he hoped he still kept a hand on the pen; but Hardy seems to have declared that he had thrown up authorship at last and for all. Moule was grieved at this, but merely advised him not to give up writing altogether, since, supposing anything were to happen to his eyes from the fine architectural drawing, literature would be a resource for him; he could dictate a book, article, or poem, but not a geometrical design. This, Hardy used to say, was essentially all that passed between them; but by a strange coincidence Moule's words were brought back to his mind one morning shortly after by his seeing, for the first time in his life, what seemed like floating specks on the white drawing-paper before him.[1]

Soon after his thirty-third birthday Hardy took the evening train to Cambridge where he stayed in college, at Queens', with Horace Moule. They walked along the Backs in the slanting light of evening; in the morning they studied the interior of King's College Chapel, and even got onto the roof, from which they could see Ely Cathedral gleaming in the eastern light. The next day Moule saw Hardy off to London. They never met again and Hardy (in retrospect) jotted down 'His last smile'.[2]

But in 1860-2 he and Horace Moule walked the Frome meadows, discussing *Essays and Reviews*, Bagehot's *Estimates*, and other books of a revolutionary nature fresh from the press. One of Horace's early gifts to Hardy was a translation of Goethe's *Faust*; but before this, when he was only seventeen, he had also given him *Elements of Experimental and Natural Philosophy* by Jabez

---

[1] I. p. 115. [2] *Ibid.*, p. 123.

Hogg, surgeon,[1] inscribed 'T. Hardy, from his friend Horace, 1857'. Furthermore, three months before he set out for London, Moule gave him a copy of the *Golden Treasury* which the nascent poet valued all his life. No doubt he knew many of its poems by heart, for he often quotes from them in his prose and has used their lines for the titles of two of his novels. More important still, Hardy confessed to his wife, shortly before his death, that if he had ever had an ambition it was that 'some poem or poems' of his should be included 'in a good anthology like the *Golden Treasury*.'[2] One might expect to find *Lycidas* heavily scored in this little volume, because of Horace's early death, but the marks appear to be youthful ones emphasizing descriptive words or passages. On the other hand Hardy's copy of *In Memoriam*, purchased after Moule's death, is marked in several places, for instance a verse from stanza V:

> *But, for the unquiet heart and brain,*
> * A use in measured language lies;*
> *The sad mechanic exercise,*
> * Like dull narcotics, numbing pain.*

and in stanza CVIII the lines:

> *And on the depths of death there swims*
> *The reflex of a human face.*

Four lines in stanza LXXVIII are compared with a stanza of *Adonais*. Hardy has also underlined ' *The winds were in the beech*' and '*The lark becomes a sightless song*'. (It was at Bockhampton that he heard of Moule's death and beeches are the predominant trees behind the old house.) All of these marks might relate to the loss of someone else in Hardy's life, but we are brought up sharp by a single word and some initials written against stanza LXXXVIII. These are the lines in which Tennyson visualizes his return to Cambridge and the haunts of the youthful 'Apostles', and the compelling appearance of Arthur Hallam, whose 'ethereal eyes' were banded by 'the bar of Michel Angelo'. Against it Hardy has written: '*Cambridge. H.M.M.*'

The fact that Hardy took Moule's advice and set aside his classical studies in 1860, marking the hiatus by writing in his

---

[1] Ingram Cooke & Co., London, 1853.   [2] II., p. 263.

Iliad, 'Left off, Bockhampton, 1860', is deceptive, for his knowledge of the Greek dramatists is too thorough, and his caste of thought too impregnated with their, for him to have abandoned them completely at this time. At some later date, when he was alone in London, or in rural solitude at Bockhampton again, he went back to them and studied them long and lovingly. Having tasted of what was, for him, 'the milk of Paradise' he could not forego it.

Dr Rutland was able to examine Hardy's classical books before the library at Max Gate was dispersed: he tells us that Hardy's knowledge of Greek was sufficient for him to compare variant readings, and to substitute the original for a poor English translation, when he was impressed by its force or beauty. He has traced the development of Hardy's thought from his first tentative Greek studies to the writing of *Tess, Jude,* and *The Dynasts,* and he points out that Hardy owed a debt to Sophocles long before he had read a word of Schopenhauer, or Nietzsche. Hardy was not yet twenty when he studied the dramatists who marked so insistently the 'vast injustice of the Gods'.

> It seems no exaggerated claim that if any purely literary influence could be held responsible for what has been called Hardy's 'twilight view of life', it would be that great and sombre art whose *leit motif* is 'call no man happy while he lives'. In Hardy's copy of the *Antigone* . . . a line is drawn against the words 'For the future, and the instant, and the past this law will suffice: nothing comes to the life of mortals far removed at least from calamity'.[1]

The words re-echo the spirit of the marked passages in Hardy's *Thoughts from the Latin Authors.* Dr Rutland rightly concludes,

> The significance for English literature of Hardy's study of Greek drama lies in the effect which that study had in confirming the cast of his thought; and this it would be hard to over-estimate.[2]

[1] Rutland, p. 20. See also pp. 26-45. [2] *Ibid.,* p. 41.

CHAPTER FOUR

THE BUOYANT TIME

O that far morning of a summer day
When, down a terraced street whose pavements lay
Glassing the sunshine into my bent eyes,
I walked and read with a quick glad surprise
New words, in classic guise—

THOMAS HARDY [1]

WHEN Bewick at the age of fourteen left his native Cherryburn to be apprenticed to a Newcastle engraver, and when William Barnes at eighteen quitted the Blackmoor Vale for Dorchester, we know that they inwardly grieved. But when Hardy, who resembles these brother craftsmen in the rural spirit of his work, left Dorset for London we do not know what he felt. That he can have left the countryside, whose lights, moods and lineaments were almost part of his being, without regret is unthinkable. There are no dated poems of this period and it is not until Hardy is sixty-eight that we catch a glimpse of his youthful feelings. Apparently, like Whittington and others, Thomas half-thought to make his fortune in London and perhaps to settle and die there. In an address which was written (but never delivered) in 1908 he draws the portrait of an imaginary young man

> just arrived in London from Dorsetshire, with a half-formed in-
> tention of making the capital the source of his life's endeavours, and
> a possibility of finding there his home and his interests, possibly his
> grave. He pauses, maybe, on Waterloo Bridge and ... experiences
> ... a vivid sense of his own significance ... isolation and
> loneliness. He feels himself among strangers and strange
> things. [2]

As an antidote to such loneliness Hardy suggests studying a map

---

[1] "A Singer Asleep" in *Satires of Circumstance.*
[2] *Presidential Address to the Society of Dorset Men in London.* See II, p. 131, and Edmund Blunden, *Thomas Hardy,* pp. 18-19. Macmillan & Co., 1942.

of London and searching for Dorset names, associations and history.

> The investigation will tend to lessen that feeling of gloomy isolation to which young men of Dorset stock are peculiarly liable in an atmosphere not altogether exhilarating after their own air—say in days of fog, when the southwest country is known to be flooded with sunshine, or in those days of piercing rawness from the eastern marches, that seem to eat into the bones, a rawness seldom or never felt in their own shire. They may gradually learn to take these inclemencies philosophically, and to decide . . . that their true locality and anchorage is where what they can do best can best be done.[1]

This has the true biographical flavour.

He had been to London once before, as a child of eight or nine, when he went on a visit to relations in Hertfordshire with his mother. He remembered two things clearly—the cries of animals about to be slaughtered in Smithfield Market, and the room at the inn in Clerkenwell where they had spent the night. Hardy's compassion for animals shines through his life and work and this early lacerating memory culminated in a special bequest in his will.[2]

The second memory is significant. Hardy was fond of identifying himself with poets and writers of the past, and (since he could not see them in the flesh), of being close to places and objects which they had seen and touched. He cherished a belief that Keats was Dorset-born and bred, and that he had walked inland to Broadmayne, which lies not far from Stinsford, when his ship was becalmed off Lulworth on that last outgoing from England to Italy. He liked to think of Fielding's having lived 'nearby' and of 'so many of his scenes having been laid down this way'.[3] Now the coaching-inn in Clerkenwell was *The Cross-Keys* where Shelley and Mary Godwin had met not more than

---

[1] *Ibid.*

[2] He left two sums of money to be spent on "the investigation of the means by which animals are conveyed from their houses to the slaughter-houses, with a view to lessening their sufferings in transit", and the prevention of caging of birds.

[3] II, p. 42. For the Keats' legend see Llewelyn Powys' "Some Memories of Thomas Hardy", *Everybody's Magazine*, April 1952. See also Hardy's footnote to his poem "At Lulworth Cove a Century Back".

forty years earlier. Hardy half-fancied that the room high up the oval staircase, which he and his mother shared, was the very one which the lovers had formerly used.

This gives us a clue to what we may expect when Hardy returns to London at the age of twenty-one, what its effect on him will be. We know what it was for Swift and for Boswell, for instance, but on Hardy the impact was different since his was a more poetic temperament. For the Dorset lad London was first and foremost the writers' town, the city where Dickens still gave his readings and Thackeray flourished, where Swinburne, Browning and Tennyson might be encountered (if one had the courage and ambition to seek them out), where Shelley, Godwin, Dr Johnson and Fanny Burney had used to live, and where Trollope worked. In other words, the shadow of dead writers is cast over it for him, and the figures of the living stand round and colour life for him.

But it was also an intoxicating place where music, painting and drama might be sampled, and in lighter moments dancing. There were oratorios at Exeter Hall, endless concerts, and a plethora of operas, either English ones like *Maritana* and *The Bohemian Girl* at the English Opera Company, or Italian ones at Covent Garden and His Majesty's, where one might hear the inimitable Italian singers. Kean and his wife were acting in Shakespeare at the Princess', and Phelps at Drury Lane. Thomas and his friends used to attend and severely test the actors by sitting in the pit close to the orchestra where, resting their copies of the plays on the barrier, they scanned the lines beneath the actors' very noses. When Thomas felt inclined to dance there were balls at Cremorne or the Argyle, or best of all Willis' Rooms, formerly Almack's, whose historic character appealed to Hardy. Here he danced the *Lancers* and *Caledonians* to their original tunes, rejoicing in the lightness of his sophisticated partner and the exquisite correctness of each quadrille step and gesture.

If he wished for solitude, or to see what was on at the Great Exhibition, he had only to run down to the reading-room of the South Kensington Museum, still housed in iron sheds known as the 'Brompton Boilers', getting on the new Underground to carry him there. When he chose to dine out there were endless restaurants, coffee-houses and supper-rooms like Bertolini's, Evans', or Newton House, which had once been the combined residence and observatory of Sir Isaac, and later the home of the Burneys visited by Sir Joshua Reynolds, Dr Johnson, and others. Hardy liked it because of its homely atmosphere and sanded floors.

But the young man with music and poetry ringing in his head had also an eye for the comic and lusty. He was amused by the phrenologist[1] in the Strand who examined his head and told him he would come to no good, and he watched the brawny pugilists of the day lounging at their ease in liquor saloons.

Having purchased a return ticket in Dorchester with prudent forethought, so that if he failed to find work he could at least return home, Hardy arrived in London with two letters of introduction, a Bible and a Book of Common Prayer, still in existence, and inscribed 'Thomas Hardy, 1861, Clarence House, Kilburn',[2] which gives us the address at which he lodged until he changed to Westbourne Park Villas where most of his early poems were written.

The first letter drew empty politeness but the second, to Mr John Norton, a West-country man, won him an anchorage and work, and a few days later, more work of an importance he could hardly have dreamt of on leaving home. On the day that he arrived to work Norton informed him that he had been asked whether he knew 'a young Gothic draughtsman who could restore churches and design rectory houses'. He had recommended Hardy, who thus began work for his new employer on May 5, eighteen days after leaving Dorchester. His offices were in St Martin's Place and were the first of an influential young architect, then thirty-three, Arthur Blomfield, son of a Bishop, and later to receive a knighthood.

It was the period of Gothic revival. Blomfield favoured the English perpendicular style in ecclesiastical architecture, although he occasionally made sallies into other fields, for instance in the Italian at St Barnabas, Oxford. Conscientious and conservative he none the less believed in individuality in

---

[1] Dr Donovan. The report is extant.
[2] Rutland, p. 110, gives 9 *Clarence Place*. Hardy was still there when he won his 1st architectural prize in March 1863.

ecclesiastical art, and felt that architects should have a right to introduce some of the benefits of modern discovery. He was to become architect to the Bank of England, to have no fewer than five cathedrals at one time under his care, to build innumerable churches, chapels, libraries and schools. In the diocese of Chichester alone, in addition to being responsible for the Cathedral, he built nine churches and restored twelve. Blomfield was that rare mixture, an athlete with artistic tastes: he was endowed with musical and dramatic gifts, and his genial disposition endeared him to friends, pupils and assistants alike. If Hardy had remained with him his success in architectural fields would have been assured and his financal worries ended.

Blomfield's second offices, into which he moved shortly after Hardy's arrival, were in Adelphi Terrace, and from the balcony a great stretch of river spanned by many bridges could be seen, including the new Charing Cross bridge, which was just going up. The embanking of the Thames (originally suggested by Wren more than a century-and-a-half earlier) was also in progress. The young architect was in time to see Nicholas Stone's Water Gate at York House—which now seems stranded like an old ship when the tide has receded—performing its proper function.

Hardy, in looking back on his life at this time, imagined links in the chain of events. Others might have read in them the hand of a thoughtful Providence: not so Hardy, who only saw in such things a curious fatality. Blomfield's first drawing-offices were shared with the Alpine Club, of which Leslie Stephen was a member, and although Stephen and Hardy were not to become intimates for another decade they must, in a kind of ironic shadow-play, have superseded each other in the rooms, the younger man passing in and out by day and the older in the evening. The Reform League, with which Swinburne was indirectly connected, met in rooms beneath Blomfield's, and Hardy in retrospect saw a link with the rebel poet whom he ardently admired.

Blomfield's offices were infected with a gaiety which one does not generally associate with the work-a-day world. When the young assistants were bored, and their master was out, they dropped paper squibs on the heads of the Reform League members passing beneath the balcony. When Blomfield found time hanging heavy he made up an office choir, and catches and glees, in which he took the bass parts, relieved the tedium. He persuaded Hardy to sing in his church choir at Richmond, and one day called out to him 'If you meet an alto anywhere in the Strand, ask him to come in and join us'.[1] (How Hardy was to recognize an alto when he saw one is not explained.) The pleasantness of atmosphere in both the Dorchester and London architectural offices in which Hardy worked is as refreshing as its leisurely quality. In the former town he had an employer who was sympathetic to his classical inclinations, and in London one who shared his musical tastes and who had, too, a sense of humour as droll as his own.

But there was also a serious side to Hardy's work. As assistant-architect one of his duties was to supervise the removal of human remains from the churchyard of Old St Pancras, through which the Midland Railway was about to make a cutting. 'Many hundreds of coffins' and 'bones in huge quantities' had to be moved. Hardy's job was to keep an eye on the clerk-of-the-works at odd hours in the evening, while Blomfield dropped in unexpectedly during the day, to see that the work was being decently done. Thus, throughout the fogbound evenings of autumn and early winter Thomas watched over the gruesome procedure. When coffins and bones fell asunder new coffins were provided, but when skeletons stubbornly held together the remains were incongruously removed on a door, or shutter. 'In one coffin that fell apart was a skeleton and two skulls', something which neither Blomfield, nor Hardy, ever forgot. It is often our fate to attract to ourselves experiences congruous to our own natures. Hardy's macabre sense of humour and his deep attraction to death and dissolution must have had their fill that year, although he may sometimes have questioned Marvell's statement that 'The grave's a fine and private place'. He had in mind lovers long dead, for under the stars, within the dark hoarding-squares lit by flickering flare-lamps, the shadows of Shelley and Mary Godwin kept Hardy company. Mary's mother, Mary Wollstonecraft, that woman of rare courage and exquisite sensibility, had been buried in this very churchyard,

[1] I, p. 59. In his office choir.

and her remains had been removed by the forethought of Shelley's descendants ten years earlier.

In 1865 Hardy went to Palmerston's funeral in Westminster Abbey, which 'greatly impressed him'. Anyone who reads his careful description of the ceremony[1] and who attended Hardy's own funeral in the same building, will be struck by the latent irony. He had been to the House to hear Palmerston speak soon after coming to London, and his sense of history had been stirred by remembering that this statesman's life overlapped those of Pitt, Fox, Sheridan and Burke, whom he recreated forty years later in *The Dynasts*.

About this time Hardy renewed his study of French, attending lectures at King's College, a fact which may account for some of the surprising Gallicisms in his early poems. But by now he had undertaken a self-regulated course of reading and writing of such an intensive nature that it precluded a serious study of languages and he neglected his French. He was also busy competing for two architectural prizes in 1862-3, both of which he won.[2] Hardy promptly converted the second prize into books— English translations of Euripides, Sophocles and Aeschylus in Bohn's series.[3] His reading ranged over the works of Latin and English lyrists and English prose writers, amongst them Horace, Spenser, Moore, Byron, Browning and Swinburne, Scott, Trollope, Thackeray and J. S. Mill. Apart from the Greek tragedians, the two writers who influenced him most in these formative years were Swinburne and Mill. But shortly he abandoned all reading but poetry, for he had come to the conclusion that if he was to write good verse he must read nothing else,

> as in verse was concentrated the essence of all imaginative and emotional literature.[4]

This he did for the space of two years, with the exception of the daily papers and weekly reviews, sometimes reading far into

---

[1] See I, pp. 67-9, in a letter to his sister Mary.

[2] The first was the R.I.B.A. Medal awarded to him for his Prize Essay, "The Application of Coloured Bricks and Terra Cotta to Modern Architecture": the sum of ten pounds was withheld since he did not develop his theme sufficiently: the second was the Sir William Tite Prize offered by the Architectural Association, a sum of three pounds.

[3] Rutland, p. 35.   [4] I, p. 64.

the night. By way of diversion he delivered lectures on English
poetry to his astonished but complacent fellow-pupils in Blomfield's offices.

Hardy varied his study of poetry with that of painting. For
many months he went to the National Gallery, 'on every day that
it was open' (and sometimes to the South Kensington Museum)
'for twenty minutes after lunch'. Here again he instituted a
self-appointed method of study,

> confining his attention to a single master on each visit and for-
> bidding his eyes to stray to any other. He went from sheer liking
> and not with any practical object.[1]

One of Hardy's most sympathetic critics, Lord David Cecil, has
implied that Hardy's love of painting was the wish of a provincial to gain culture: others have suggested that he interjects
the names of artists in his prose to exhibit his knowledge of
them, ranging from the well-known, like Giotto, Velasquez, and
Rubens, to the obscure. Or they complain that he uses their
names allusively, trusting that the reader will see as clearly as
Hardy does in his own mind the painted landscape. But Hardy's
love of painting was innate, a taste which he shared with his
sister Mary, who thought nothing of making the return
journey from Dorchester to London in a day in order to visit
the Royal Academy, when she was over seventy. (She had, too,
considerable skill as an amateur painter.) Hardy's own drawings (for the cover of *The Trumpet Major*, for *Wessex Poems* and
The Queen of Cornwall, and those printed in the *Early Life*[2]) are
thin and unconvincing, but his lack of talent did not prevent him
from responding to the work of the great masters, more than
thirty of whom are mentioned in as few as five or six novels. He
began by admiring the Dutch and Flemish schools, then the
Italian, German, Spanish and English. With the exception of
Poussin and Greuze he does not seem to have cared for French
painting. As he grew older he was especially drawn to Bellini
and Crivelli whom he considered perfect interpreters of spirit
rather than of flesh, of 'the inner meaning of things'. He also

---

[1] I, p. 69.
[2] There are a number of water-colour paintings of local scenes in the
Dorset Museum, painted by Hardy when he was nineteen, including some
of the Heath and one of the old manor-house of Kingston Maurward.

admired the work of Turner in his late phases, and thought
Zurbaran superior to Velasquez, unusual taste and opinions for
his day. He continued his study of painting well on into old
age, making journeys to see collections in private country-
houses when he no longer went to London, and when any display of his knowledge in prose was out of the question since he
had long ceased to write it.

But although Hardy was no artist with the brush or crayon
he had the painter's eye, which constantly notes, and rejoices
in, qualities of light and shade. I doubt if anyone but Hardy has
ever thought of describing light on a summer's day of thunder
and fitful sunshine as 'tin or pewter-coloured'. He was forever
being attracted by profiles, whether an imagined one, such as
Tess' against the dun side of a milch-cow, or a real, like that of
J. S. Mill against 'the blue shadow of a London church'. The
number of metaphors and similes concerned with colour and
light which appear in his descriptions—of sunsets, moonlight and
snowlight, the leafy gloom of a woodland at dusk, and (a
favourite of Hardy's) the indescribable point where shade
merges with shade (whether it is heathland meeting oncoming
night, or dusk descending on water), is astonishing. A long essay
could be written on this single aspect of Hardy's work alone.
Lastly, his notes are full of constant references to painting and
painters, the business and intention of the artist's work, so
closely allied to the writer's. It is significant that the first extant
note concerns the nature of woman; and the second an artistic
problem.

> The form on the canvas which immortalizes the painter is but
> the last of a series of tentative and abandoned sketches each of
> which contained some particular feature nearer perfection than
> any part of the finished product.[1]

It is in notes like these that we come on the very heart of
Hardy's artistic philosophy as it develops.

But the main stream of his energy, before he was thirty, had
begun to be diverted into the writing of poetry, which he had
tried his hand at as a lad in Dorchester and then discontinued.
Here we are fortunate in having a number of early poems

[1] I, p. 62.

frankly biographical in mood—documents of the greatest importance. Apart from a juvenile poem with a Wordsworthian flavour, called *Domicilium*[1] which described the Bockhampton home, the earliest extant poem dated by Hardy is one which shows that behind all the seeming gaiety of the fiddle-playing, wit-loving lad, and the joy in comradeship, ran a deeper current. It is a sonnet called *Discouragement*[2] which reveals, not some youthful failing of courage over an all-absorbing personal problem such as the failure to get a living or to succeed in love, but a terrible indictment of the shaping and shape of the very universe, and of existence as Thomas Hardy sees it between the age of twenty-three to twenty-seven. The poem was not published until 1925, sixty years later, and it was written where all these youthful verses were, in his lodgings at 16 Westbourne Park Villas, to which he removed from Kilburn, sometime in 1863.

> *To see the Mother, naturing Nature, stand*
> *All racked and wrung by her unfaithful lord,*
> *Her hopes dismayed by his defiling hand,*
> *Her passioned plans for bloom and beauty marred;*
>
> *Where she would mint a perfect mould, an ill;*
> *Where she would don divinest hues, a stain,*
> *Over her purposed genial hour a chill,*
> *Upon her charm of flawless flesh a blain:*
>
> *Her loves dependent on a feature's trim,*
> *A whole life's circumstance on hap of birth,*
> *A soul's direction on a body's whim,*
> *Eternal Heaven upon a day of Earth,*
> *Is frost to flower of heroism and worth,*
> *And fosterer of visions ghast and grim.*[3]

There are three unusual things about this poem. First, the fact that Hardy's so-called philosophy was already set in a mould from which it scarcely deviated for the rest of his life. Rough-hewn and imperfect, the poem contains in its fourteen lines the germ of that which the writer elaborated in his mature

---

[1] 1857-60, I, p. 4.   [2] 1863-7.   [3] In *Human Shows*.

c *

work, the passionate outcry against creation and an impersonal creator who permits the sacrifice of a Tess, a Jude, or the unnumbered dead of *The Dynasts*. Secondly, the line 'A whole life's circumstance on hap of birth' implies unhappiness connected with love for some aristocratic girl (which Hardy's first novel also suggests) for in his work he was advancing swiftly and had no cause for dissatisfaction with his birth as a barrier to progress. But this irritation, this discouragement, is only one cause for despair in a universe which fosters on the one hand and wantonly blights, like a killing frost, on the other. In 1903-4 William Archer talked with Hardy who expressed the view that

> incompleteness is a characteristic of all phenomena, of the universe at large. It often seems to me like a half-expressed, an ill-expressed, idea.[1]

By then he had consoled himself with the pseudo-philosophical thought that

> There may be a consciousness, infinitely far off, at the end of the chain of phenomena, always striving to express itself, and always baffled and blundering.[2]

He was then sixty-four years old and beginning *The Dynasts*, but in his twenties 'consciousness' was not merely 'baffled and blundering' it was definitely inimical. Of the 'visions ghast and grim' we shall hear more later on.

Thirdly, the poem exhibits characteristics which appear and re-appear throughout Hardy's later work. Its gloomy power embraces words and lines of poor taste side by side with others of disarming beauty. 'Naturing nature' is not a happy conjunction of words, nor is the alliteration effective. Yet Hardy continued to be fond of this use of repetitive sounds and 'dynasts discords' in 1903 shows that he did not intend to abandon it. As Dr Rutland says,

> 'genial hour' suggests a club, and 'divinest hues' and 'flower of heroism and worth' come from the cheapest magazines . . . Yet there is a certain undeniable passion about the thing.[3]

[1] William Archer, *Real Conversations*, pp. 45-6. William Heinemann, 1904.
[2] *Ibid.*   [3] pp. 266-7.

It is this passion, this overwhelming identification with a purposive mood, which gives the poem its force and carries along its imperfections.

There are in all, thirty dated poems between 1863 and 1867, the year in which Hardy first committed himself to prose, in novel form. Many poems of this early period were subsequently lost, or were destroyed by him. The four, "She to Him", come from a series originally much longer, and there are many undated poems which refer to this time in Hardy's life, written long afterwards, from which it is dangerous to draw conclusions.[1] They may be roughly divided into love poems, poems with a philosophic content, and poems on special occasions with a personal theme, such as the one called "Amabel" (1865). It is possible that this poem (in which Hardy speaks of his dismay at seeing a woman's 'ruined hues', her 'earthen brown' gown which typifies the stiffness of her mind, gait, and other depressing features) may refer to Mrs Martin. It is dated 1865 and Hardy called on his childhood love in 1862-3, with withering results for both of them. The character of Hardy's poetry remains constant: when, as an ageing man, he abandons the writing of prose for verse, it may still be divided into categories roughly the same. Furthermore the philosophy of the poems, as one might expect, is the counterpart of that displayed in the novels.

Two other curious aspects may be mentioned—the fact that Hardy, even at this early age, could penetrate a woman's mind and interpret her thoughts as well as he could his own. Many of these early poems are written from the woman's point of view, as their titles show—"*Her* Confession", "Definition", "Dilemma", "Reproach"—a habit which he later continued with "*Her* Initials", "Father", and so on. From "Her in the Country", "She at his Funeral", and the series "She to Him", are other examples. "At a Bridal" suggests that, like the Donne of the *Elegies*, Hardy was in love with someone married to another; in this poem he actually watches her being wed. This

[1] The dates appended beneath the titles of Hardy's poems are placed by him as indicative of the time at which an incident occurred, although the poem may have been written fifty years later. The dates at the foot of the poems are his own, signifying the date of composition. In the *Collected Poems* Hardy added a few additional dates.

must remain conjecture since Hardy was able to hide all traces of feeling under an intense reserve; also he could versify a scene, or dramatize a mood with such skill that we cannot tell whether the poem represents a passing, or a lasting, emotion. Yet the line in "Discouragement", the poem "At a Bridal", and what we find in Hardy's first novel, all imply something disastrous. Also, some poems written at Weymouth, where he was working in 1869, refer to 'her of a bygone vow' and his loneliness at being excluded from love and love's endearments.[1]

In 1866 Hardy sent some of these effusions to editors who promptly rejected them. They could not risk offending a public who were familiar with, and who liked, what Stephen Philips called Tennyson's 'distilled beauty'; nor did they care for Hardy's strange vocabulary, barren spirit and sombre presentation. Browning had not yet come fully into his own, nor had Tennyson developed his late, philosophic tone: Meredith had been condemned for *Modern Love* four years earlier, and the Pre-Raphaelites were advancing with difficulty. Fitzgerald's *Rubaiyat* and Thomson's *City of Dreadful Night* were not to appear or influence the public for nearly another decade, and Swinburne was about to be ostracized for *Poems and Ballads*, which appeared in this very year.

Curiously enough Thomas Hardy, if he did not anticipate, at least concurred with Swinburne's thought in another of his youthful sonnets, "Hap" (1866), which Edmund Blunden has described as having 'the neutrality of a shell before loading'. This powerful poem has a ferocious power which Hardy never exceeded. Its maturity is astonishing, and in its language it looks forward to much that is in *The Dynasts*. "Crass Casualty", "dicing Time", "purblind Doomsters" and the verb 'unblooms', carry that mixture of impersonality and submerged hatred which reminds one of the sinister iceberg in "The Convergence of the Twain", Hardy's poem commemorating the loss of the *Titanic* in 1912.

What was there abroad in the night air to cause such venomous vapours to seep into the bones of the younger poets, for it cannot have been mere coincidence which caused this *bizo*, this

[1] "Singing Lovers" in *Human Shows*.

searing north-east wind, to freeze their spiritual marrow. Just as protestantism was not produced by a single man in England, even though he were the sovereign, in the 16th century, so in the 19th neither Swinburne, Thomson, nor young Thomas Hardy were the sole originators of the new-born blasphemy of *Anactoria*, *The City of Dreadful Night*, of *Hap* and *Discouragement*. Sensitive as always to the changing temper of the age, the poets reflected that crisis in spiritual and intellectual life which came to a head in the early sixties after the publication of Darwin's *Origin of Species* (1859), *Essays and Reviews* (1860), and John Stuart Mill's *On Liberty* (1864). The emotional reaction to the scientific discoveries and philosophy of these men appeared in poetic form in Browning's *Dramatis Personae* (1864), Swinburne's *Atalanta in Calydon* (1865), and in his *Poems and Ballads* (1866). It was continued in the next decade with (in the scientific and rationalistic realm) Darwin's *Descent of Man* (1871), Huxley's *Lay Sermons* (1870), and Mill's *Three Essays on Religion* (1874): and (in the poetic) with Swinburne's *Songs before Sunrise* (1871), Thomson's *City of Dreadful Night* (1874), and Fitzgerald's *Omar Khayyám* first published in 1859 but not popular until the eighties.

But of the influence of Darwin, Huxley, Mill, Spencer and others—daring thinkers and writers whose work had something of the same shaking and shivering effect on the mid-Victorians as the discoveries of Galileo and Kepler had on the thinking world in the 16th century, and as the problems of the atom bomb have on ours—of the influence of these men on the immature Hardy we have abundant internal evidence in his work. We have corroboration elsewhere of the moulding of his thought by them when he was still in his impressionable twenties. Since he did not belong to a scholarly and scientific family Hardy had happily escaped the tragedy inherent in Edmund Gosse's childhood: he was spared the agonizing relationship between parent and child who lived through the period of conflict ante-dating the crisis of the 1860's. Readers of *Father and Son* will remember Philip Henry Gosse's inability to retract or advance in his attempts to justify science with revelation, and the son's revolt from constriction in a mental strait-jacket of acutely narrow thought. The epochal struggle was typified in the domestic, which involved two dissimilar temperaments and characters.

Apart from the statement in the *Early Life* that Hardy was reading *Essays and Reviews* with his friends Tolbort and Moule in the Dorchester meadows before he went up to London, we have further corroboration of the scientists' and rationalists' influence on him in other paragraphs of this and the succeeding volume. But it is when Hardy himself bears witness to it that we are impressed, and this he does in several places. On the centenary of Mill's death in 1906 he paid tribute to Mill's ascendancy over the young in the 1860's in ten words of a long letter wherein he described how he stood and listened to Mill's election speech outside St Paul's, Covent Garden[1], in 1865, the year in which Mill was elected to Parliament as Member for Westminster.

When I—a young man living in London—drew near to the spot, Mill was speaking. The appearance of the author of the treatise *On Liberty* (*which we students of that date knew almost by heart*) was so different from the look of persons who usually address crowds in the open air that it held the attention of people for whom such a gathering in itself had little interest. Yet it was, primarily, that of a man out of place. The religious sincerity of his speech was jarred on by his environment—a group on the hustings who, with few exceptions, did not care to understand him fully, and a crowd below who could not. He stood bareheaded, and his vast pale brow, so thin-skinned as to show the blue veins, sloped back like a stretching upland, and conveyed to the observer a curious sense of perilous exposure. The picture of him as personified earnestness surrounded for the most part by careless curiosity derived an added piquancy—if it can be called such—from the fact that the cameo clearness of his face chanced to be in relief against the blue shadow of a church, which, on its transcendental side, his doctrines antagonized. But it would not be right to say that the throng was absolutely unimpressed by his words; it felt that they were weighty, though it did not quite know why.[2]

This letter is pasted inside the cover of Hardy's copy of *On Liberty*, together with John Morley's appreciation. If we require

[1] The church in which Lady Susan Strangways and William O'Brien were secretly married.

[2] *The Times*, May 21, 1906. (Italics mine.)

evidence of the overwhelming influence of Mill on Hardy in his twenties, this volume alone will be sufficient. It is more heavily scored and underlined than any other of Hardy's extant books which it has been my privilege to examine. There are as many as fifty marked passages, a paper marker, and, in addition, several annotations. His statement that he knew the essay 'almost by heart' is visually corroborated when we see the intense study which he gave to it in young manhood.

Hardy's copy was published in 1867, three years after the original edition. It is a thin little volume in fine print with double columns on each page, and it is inscribed with his name. The second and third chapters, on *Liberty of Thought and Discussion* and on *Individuality*, are most frequently scored. An amusing pencilled comment occurs opposite Mill's paragraph on the need for impartiality in argument and opinion. Hardy has written:

> And in small domestic matters such a balancing of evidence should be adopted by women, but it never is.

Whether this comment derives from arguments with those in his home circle, or with London landladies, is not apparent. That he seems to have been easily, possibly too easily, influenced by others, is obvious from the underlining of:

> He devolves upon his own world the responsibility of being in the right against the dissentient worlds of other people.

Hardy was busy forming his own diffuse character. Two other annotations are of interest. Hardy has compared passages in Chapter III, *On Individuality*, with lines from Tennyson's *Locksley Hall* and Wordsworth's *Intimations*. Even as a lad in Dorchester he had compared the thought and expression of one writer with another, a critical faculty rare in the young.

In this same chapter, a favourite with him and one which he relied on for encouragement and stimulation, Hardy has also underlined a quotation from Sterling's *Essays*:

> 'Pagan self-assertion' is one of the elements of human worth, as well as 'Christian self-denial' . . .

and the six ensuing lines of J. S. Mill. No doubt Hardy had had enough of self-abnegation preached to him at Stinsford and

Bockhampton: his praise of 'the Pagan',[1] of (figuratively) Alcibiades and Pericles rather than Calvin or Knox at a later date, seems to have sprung from Mill as well as from his Greek studies. Eustacia's passionate abandon and Sue's revolt possibly externalize Hardy's own need to break free from a strangling evangelicalism.

The succeeding chapters, on *Society and the Individual* and on *Applications*, have less frequent markings and these cease altogether with the solemn thought:

> The fact itself of causing the existence of a human being is one of the most responsible actions in the range of human life.

Next to the influence of John Stuart Mill in liberating the thought of Hardy from evangelical trammels comes that of Swinburne, whose daring blasphemy and heady, poetic wine intoxicated the minds of young men in the sixties. The prose counterpart of Hardy's lines[2] written after visiting Swinburne's grave, in 1912, is a passage from one of his letters to this poet in 1897:

> Having rediscovered this phrase [a translation by Swinburne of a line of Sappho] it carried me back to *the buoyant time* of thirty years ago, when I used to read your early works walking along the crowded London streets to my imminent risk of being knocked down.[3]

In a second letter, after Swinburne's death, Hardy again testifies to his early reading of the older poet. In this he says that he remembers only too well how the press vilified Swinburne in 1866 on the appearance of *Poems and Ballads* . . . 'and how it made the blood of some of us young men boil'.

> I was so late in getting my poetical barge under way, and he was so early with his flotilla—besides my being between three or four years younger . . . that though I read him as he came out I did not personally know him till many years after the *Poems and Ballads* year.[4]

But further proof of the effect on Hardy of his reading of

---

[1] In *The Return of the Native* and *Jude the Obscure*.
[2] At the head of this chapter.
[3] See Rutland, p. 71. (Italics mine.)
[4] II, p. 135-6.

Swinburne in his twenties may be had from an unusual piece of small, but significant, evidence. In *Poems and Ballads*, in the poem "The Triumph of Time", there occur the lines

> *In the change of years, in the coil of things,*
> *In the clamour and rumour of life to be—*

These made a lasting impression on Hardy. The phrase 'coil of things', and especially the word 'coil', he never forgot. We find it in several unexpected and unrelated places throughout his work and letters. For example, he quotes it back to Swinburne when he sends the older writer a copy of *The Woodlanders*, in the year in which it appeared.

> Max Gate,
> nr. Dorchester.
> 9 *May* 1887

Dear Sir,

For years I have thought we might meet ('in the coil of things, in the clamour and rumour of life') : but apparently this is not likely; and I send you a copy of *The Woodlanders*, not because I think it better or worse than other novels of mine, but because it is the last I have written. If you will accept the book you will give me much pleasure.

> I am, dear Sir,
> Yours truly,
> THOMAS HARDY [1]

The word is also used in *The Return of the Native*[2] in the description of Clym Yeobright's face when Eustacia first scans it, and three times in the First Part alone of *The Dynasts*.[3]

Another line from Swinburne's *Songs before Sunrise*—'Save his own soul he hath no star'—is used as a chapter heading in *Jude the Obscure*, and is quoted by Hardy in his notes on the day of Swinburne's funeral. Florence Hardy also uses it, probably at her husband's suggestion, in describing Hardy's early years in London.

Hardy's absorptive memory drank in words which impressed him and he exuded them many years after: for instance, Shakespeare's 'bias' which he borrowed from *Hamlet* and made

---

[1] Unpublished letter. By kind permission of the Curator of the Dorset County Museum and the Trustees of the Hardy estate.
[2] p. 168.   [3] pp. 7, 15, 299.

use of in describing John Durbeyfield's drunken walk in *Tess*.
Whole lines of Browning haunted him in the same way,
especially some from his favourite poems "The Statue and the
Bust" and "Rabbi Ben Ezra", as well as from the Dedication
to "Sordello", such as 'Incidents in the development of a soul:
little else is worth study', which he jotted down on the day of
Browning's death, just as he remembered favourite lines from
Swinburne when he died.[1] Such appropriations were probably
unconscious, but even if they had been conscious, the language
is common to all and, like Handel, who was upbraided for
using the melodies of other composers, Hardy might have
replied: "Why shouldn't I? For I know how to use them."

The letter to Swinburne, quoted above, is also of interest
because it gives us a rough period during which the unrecorded
first meeting of the two poets took place. When that letter was
written, in 1887, they had not come together, although they had
corresponded. In June 1899, Florence Hardy quotes her husband on Swinburne's appearance when he visited him at
Putney. But, evidently he had been there before, since Hardy
says:

> *Again* much inclined to his engaging, fresh, frank, almost child-
> like manner . . .[2]

Hardy must therefore have met Swinburne between 1887-99,
and not in the seventies as some have thought.[3]

But it was not merely Swinburne's diction, or his passionate
power of language, which appealed to Hardy's emotions. What
he found contagious were Swinburne's 'frenzied denunciations
of Providence', especially these in "Anactoria", which, together with "Dolores", was regarded with horror by pious
Victorians.

> *Were I made as he*
> *Who hath made all things, to break them one by one,*
> *If my feet trod upon the stars and sun*
> *And souls of men as his have always trod,*
> *God knows I might be crueller than God.*

---

[1] See Weber, 'Hardy's Debt to Shakespeare and to Browning', *Hardy
of Wessex*, pp. 254 and 269-76.   [2] II, p. 83. (Italics mine.)
[3] "Offhand, I should say that Hardy met Swinburne in the later
seventies." Letter to the author, December 14, 1951, from Dr Rutland.

It is obvious that "Discouragement" was written after Hardy had grown familiar with other lines from "Anactoria". Apart from the metre which is the same, the line in roman type resembles one in Hardy's sonnet:

> . . . *Who bade exceed*
> *The fervid will, fall short the feeble deed,*
> *Bade sink the spirit and the flesh aspire,*
> *Pain animate the dust of dead desire,*
> And life yield up her flower to violent fate?

The "Hymn to Proserpine" and "Atalanta" provided further food for Hardy's tormented thoughts which he transmuted in his own manner.

Attacked from all sides by the scientists, rationalists and poets who echoed and re-echoed threnodies on the same theme— Huxley who argued that the omnipotence of an impersonal Cause was incompatible with its goodness; Mill who stated that

> If the maker of the world *can* all that he will, he wills misery, and there is no escape from that conclusion;

and Swinburne whose feverish rejection of a conventional deity in defiant, exultant verse undermined him emotionally—Hardy capitulated. Before he was thirty he had become an agnostic intellectually, and he remained one, never sloughing off disbelief. Yet, as a French critic has wisely said, Swinburne's blasphemy is only religion disguised, and the same may be said of Hardy, who was by nature essentially religious.

Swinburne's denunciation of God as 'the supreme evil' found its counterpart in the poetry and prose of a writer little-known today, although prized by William Michael Rossetti, Meredith, Swinburne and George Eliot in his own—James Thomson. When Hardy was working for Blomfield, this satirist, poet, and active propagandist of Free Thought was living in a single room in Pimlico. On glancing through a collection of the essays and reviews which he contributed to the *National Reformer* and the *Secularist* one comes on titles such as these: *The Devil in the Church of England; Great Christ is Dead;* and *The One Thing Needful,* an exhortation to honest Christians to cease begetting children, since misery on earth and hell hereafter will be their future portion.

In *Great Christ is Dead* there is a passage which would appeal to Hardy with his knowledge of *Prometheus Vinctus*; lines which suggest Sue Bridehead's outpourings:

> More than 1800 years have passed since the death of the great God Pan was proclaimed: and now it is full time to proclaim the death of the great God Christ. Eighteen hundred years make a fairly long period even for a celestial dynasty: but this one in its perishing must differ from all that have perished before it, seeing that no other can succeed it; the throne shall remain void forever, the royalty of the Heavens be abolished. Fate, in the form of Science, has decreed the extinction of the Gods. Mary and her babe must join Venus and Love, Isis and Horus; living with them only in the world of art. Jesus on his cross must dwindle to a point, even in the realms of legend under Prometheus on Caucasus.[1]

When the Swinburne controversy blazed at its fiercest, and *Punch* had lamely suggested that the poet should by right be called 'Mr Swineborn', Thomson attacked the critics for their narrow-mindedness:

> Our literature should be the clear and faithful mirror of our whole world of life, but at present there are vast realms of thought, and imagination, and passion and action, of which it is only allowed to give a reflex so obscure and distorted as to be worse than none . . .
> . . . No intelligent man in England . . . can afford to devote himself to honest treatment of any great religious or social, moral or philosophical question. If treated in a book he must himself pay the expenses of publication: if treated in an article, not even by payment could he get the portals of any popular periodical to open unto him.[2]

How true this criticism was Hardy would discover when he published his earliest work, long before the controversial *Tess* or *Jude*.

The City of Dreadful Night was dedicated to 'Dante's Younger Brother—Leopardi', and it contains passages as vehemently anti-Christian as Swinburne's own.

---

[1] *Satires and Profanities*. London, 1884.   [2] *Ibid.*

And now at last authentic word I bring,
Witnessed by every dead and every living thing;
Good tidings of great joy for you, for all;
There is no God; no Fiend with names divine
Made us and tortures us; if we must pine,
It is to satiate no Being's gall.

It was the dark delusion of a dream,
That living Person conscious and supreme,
Whom we must curse for cursing us with life;
Whom we must curse because the life He gave
Could not be buried in the quiet grave,
Could not be killed by poison or by knife.

Thomson was also the author of some serenely beautiful poems, one of which bears a resemblance to Hardy's thought in "Afternoon Service at Mellstock".

A Recusant

The church stands there beyond the orchard-blooms:
How yearningly I gaze upon its spire,
Lifted mysterious through the twilight glooms,
Dissolving in the sunset's golden fire,
Or dim as slender incense morn by morn
Ascending to the blue and open sky.
For ever when my heart feels most forlorn
It murmurs to me with a weary sigh,
How sweet to enter in, to kneel and pray
With all the others whom we love so well!
All disbelief and doubt might pass away,
All peace float to us with its Sabbath bell.
Conscience replies, There is but one good rest,
Whose head is pillowed upon Truth's pure breast.

There is a pathetic bravery here, sadder than despair. The loss of the old faith and the gaining of new knowledge brought no joy to its possessors.

When Hardy was twenty-five he bought *The Collected Poems* (1859) of Coleridge, edited by his children, Sara and Derwent.

In the preface by Coleridge, Hardy has underlined three passages. First, when Coleridge fulminates against 'the sleek favourites of fortune' who condemn all 'melancholy discontentedness', this draws appreciative response from the young architect. Secondly, in view of the fact that Hardy repeatedly alleged that no harmonious philosophy had ever been attempted by him and that his poems were merely the result of moods as shifting as cloud and cloud-shadow, it is interesting to see that he has underlined Coleridge's assertion that his poems have been written at 'different times and have been prompted by different feelings'. Thirdly, he has marked,

> . . . the mind, *full of its late sufferings* . . . *can endure no employment not in some measure connected with them.*

Here in the same year as "Amabel", and possibly of "Discouragement", is a marking which indicates a crisis in Hardy's emotional life. We know so little of him in these formative years that this clue to his suffering is important and highly suggestive.

About this time he also purchased Reed's *Introduction to English Literature* (1865) in which a paragraph on the use of prepositions is marked. This book was probably of use to him when writing, either his architectural essay, or one called *How I built Myself a House*, which appeared in Chambers' Magazine in March 1865. This was Hardy's first piece of published prose, apart from unidentified articles on Church Restoration and a lost letter in the Dorset papers.[1] He also used *A Manual of English Literature* (1867) by Thomas, younger brother of Matthew Arnold, about the time that he began his first novel, in 1868.[2] In 1865 he purchased Nuttall's *Dictionary* and Walker's *Rhyming Dictionary*.

But it is Hardy's extant copies of the English poets which appeal to us most. As a young and impecunious man he bought many of these in a cheap, uniform edition published by Moxon in the sixties. Dr Rutland mentions having seen copies in this series of Keats, Spenser, Thomson, Milton, Herbert, Young's *Night Thoughts*, Percy's *Reliques*, and Butler's *Hudibras*, at Max Gate.[3] The Keats in the County Museum[4] has a preface by

---

[1] See I, p. 43.   [2] Weber, p. 246.   [3] p. 15.
[4] Not the presentation *Lamia and Other Poems*.

Rossetti. Hardy has marked a stanza in "Isabella" and one in the first book of "Endymion":

> *And then in quiet circles did they press*
> *The hillock turf, and caught the latter end*
> *Of some strange history, potent to send*
> *A young mind from its bodily tenement.*

Hardy had been attracted earlier to the thought of the soul inhabiting first one form of life and then another which Donne in his *Progresse of the Soule* had been drawn to. In his excerpts from the Latin authors, 'the unbodied spirit' in one of Ovid's poems is 'tost from tenement to tenement'. The line suggests Hardy's fluctuations of thought when, alone in London, he was losing the faith in which he had been nurtured. But the lines from "Endymion" also remind us of the magnificent passages in *The Return of the Native*, on dancing round the bonfire, the maypole, or in grassy hollows on Egdon Heath. The green oases of the untamed waste must have come vividly to Hardy's mind if he read those lines while shut fast in his Kilburn, or Bayswater, lodgings late at night.

The copies of Swinburne's *Atalanta* in the Dorset Museum are late editions, published in 1885 and 1901. They tell us nothing of Swinburne's influence on the youthful Hardy, but a passage which he has underlined (in the preface to the second copy, edited by W. Sharp) is of interest because it gives us Swinburne's impression of his own appearance. He had lately had his portrait painted by William Bell Scott, friend of Rossetti and Ruskin, and according to the artist he

> was delighted to find it had some resemblance to what he called his portrait in the National Gallery. This was the head of Galleazzo Malatesta in the picture of the *Battle of St. Egidio* by Uccello,[1] which certainly was not merely the same type but was at this time exactly like him.

No doubt Hardy had studied the Uccello during his twenty minute periods in the National Gallery.

Meanwhile, the urgent need to get a living presented itself to Thomas. His father had guaranteed him support until 1862,[2] and would not have 'absolutely refused to advance him money in a

---

[1] Now called the *Rout of San Romano*. [2] I, pp. 43-4.

good cause'.[1] But Hardy felt bound to support himself and he considered how he might escape poverty honourably. First he thought of combining literature with architecture by becoming an art critic, a suggestion very likely made to him by Blomfield since the 'province of architectural art' was defined. Next he thought of being ordained and of filling some country living, writing his verses when not occupied with religious duties, as Herbert or Herrick had done. Next he considered being a playwright, and thus he vacillated between his gifts and leanings, towards art, poetry, drama and the church. Architecture, possibly because he was already connected with it, came fifth on the list, and music, oddly enough, nowhere. As an old man Hardy remarked that he would 'prefer to be a cathedral organist to anything in the world' and, on another occasion, that he thought the life of an architect in a small country town was the most desirable.

As for his thoughts of becoming a dramatist these were soon snuffed out, but not before he had appeared 'as a nondescript in the pantomime of *The Forty Thieves*, and in a representation of the Oxford and Cambridge Boat Race.'[2] His conversations with the stage-manager of the Haymarket Theatre and with Mark Lemon, 'an ardent amateur actor', were not encouraging. 'Almost the first sight of stage realities disinclined him to push further.' His original intentions, to write plays in blank verse and to 'try the stage as a supernumerary for six or twelve months to acquire technical skill in their construction', were not strong enough to survive contact with stage realities. Although he rejoiced in the melodramatic and fantastical and had a keen dramatic sense, Hardy was uninterested in writing for the theatre. He enjoyed going to the theatre but he once remarked that he would far rather go to a good concert: and when he was persuaded to adapt *Tess* for the stage the result was a 'theatrical impossibility'. The producer had to take a pair of 'scissors, cut up the script and rebuild the play' before it could be put on.[3]

The reasons which he put forward for abandoning architecture are interesting. Moule had already warned him about the

---

[1] *Ibid.*, p. 66. [2] I, p. 72.
[3] Blunden quoting G. E. Filmer, pp. 170-1.

possibility of straining his eyes, but Hardy says that by now he had begun to find drawing and copying 'mechanical and monotonous'. Secondly, that he lacked the

> inclination for pushing his way into influential sets which would help him to start a practice of his own:

thirdly, that his 'unfortunate aloofness served him badly'. This characteristic hampered him, too, in his literary endeavours.

> During part of his residence at Westbourne Park Villas he was living within half a mile of Swinburne, and hardly more than a stone's throw from Browning, to whom introductions would not have been difficult, through literary friends of Blomfield's. He might have obtained at least encouragement from these, and, if he had cared, possibly have floated off some of his poems in a small volume. But such a proceeding as trying to know these contemporaries seems never to have crossed his mind.[1]

This lack of ambition astonished Hardy's fellow workers.

> "Hardy", they said, "there can hardly have been anyone in the world with less ambition than you".[2]

And here Hardy is likened to the poet Donne, in his indifference' to getting into print as well 'as in some qualities of his verse'.[3] It is strange that the comparison was not carried further, for there is something of Donne's character latent in Hardy. The fire of the 16th-century poet is submerged in the 19th-century writer: it burns more clearly in his prose. His intention to enter the Church and his hesitancy to do so also resemble Donne. Both men conscientiously examined their motives and came to the conclusion that they were unfit. On looking into this 'scheme of a highly visionary character' Hardy discovered that:

> he could hardly take the step with honour while holding the views ... which he found himself to hold. And so he allowed the curious scheme to drift out of sight, though not till after he had begun to practice orthodoxy. For example:
> "To Westminster Abbey morning service. Stayed to the Sacrament. A very odd experience, amid a crowd of strangers."[4]

This was in 1865, not long after his twenty-fifth birthday

[1] I, p. 65.   [2] II, p. 185.   [3] Ibid., p. 64.   [4] I, p. 66.

upon which he had felt 'not very cheerful', and 'as if he had lived a long time and done very little'. The note of self-depreciation crops up occasionally in Hardy's notes: as a child he had thought of himself as 'useless', and as a grown man on another birthday, he calls himself 'Thomas, the Unworthy'. Perhaps, in part, its origin lies in Isaac Watts' "Evening Song", which he knew by heart as an infant.

> *But* how my childhood runs to waste!
> *My sins how great their sum!*
> *Lord, give me pardon for the past*
> *And strength for days to come.*

Within a year Hardy was writing the deeply cynical "Young Man's Epigram on Existence":

> *A senseless school, where we must give*
> *Our lives that we may learn to live!*
> *A dolt is he who memorizes*
> *Lessons that leave no time for prizes.*[1]

"Hap", "In Vision I Roamed" (the second early poem to envisage 'visions ghast and grim'), and a group of negative love-poems follow in the same year, poems which tell of a blighted love and express the view that it were better not to risk loving at all than to endure the pain of losing.

> *So may I live no junctive law fulfilling,*
> *And my heart's table bear no woman's name.*[2]

In the following year (1867) "A Young Man's Exhortation" again expresses disillusionment, over love, the evanescence of 'precious' dreams, and worldy estimation. He has gained the wry knowledge that 'aspects are within us'.

In other words, something acting like a catalyst had brought about an essential testing and change in Thomas Hardy's thoughtful soul. The early influences of his mother, and of those fine old men the Reverend Henry Moule and William Barnes, had been swept away. So far the acquisition of knowledge, whether of the age-old classics or the work of the scientists, rationalists and poets of his own day, and of life as he saw it in

---

[1] *Time's Laughingstocks.*   [2] "Revulsion" in *Wessex Poems.*

London, had both inflated and deflated him. Being of 'an ecstatic temperament' and of a highly romantic disposition he swung between ecstasy and despair. The new horizon, which attracted him as violently as any sea-adventurer, also appalled him. At one end he 'expanded with triumph' and at the other 'shrank into nothing'.[1] With all belief in a beneficent universe now destroyed Hardy depended on honesty and ardour to carry him along, but unfortunately the first had a blighting effect on the second.

Whether because of a spiritual exhaustion, engendered by the tossings and turnings of his thought and the fluctuation of his belief, or because of a physical one, induced by shutting himself away in his Bayswater rooms to study at the end of his archi-tectural day, or by the foetid atmosphere from the undrained mud-flats of the Thames below the Adelphi windows, Hardy fell ill. Blomfield, with whom Hardy always remained on the best of terms—the poem, "Heiress and Architect", is dedicated to him—urged a respite in the country but suggested that Thomas should return in October. Hardy, however, was

beginning to think that he would rather go into the country alto-gether.

No doubt Blomfield, like his assistants, was incredulous of the younger man's lack of ambition, and if the latter had explained to him that

he constitutionally shrank from the business of social advancement, caring for life as an emotion rather than for life as a science of climbing,[2]

he would have been further mystified. For this is the creed of the feeling, rather than the thinking, man, that of the poet and the seeker after 'the inner meaning of things', rather than that of the man of action.

A passage in *An Indiscretion in the Life of an Heiress* very likely portrays Hardy's sentiments at this time:

Town life had for some time been depressing to him. He began to doubt whether he could ever be happy in the course of existence that he had followed through these later years. The perpetual

<hr/>

[1] I, p. 72. [2] I, p. 70.

strain, the lack of that quiet to which he had been accustomed in early life, the absence of all personal interest in things around him, was telling upon his health of body and mind.

Then revived the wish which had for some time been smouldering in his secret heart—to leave off, for the present at least, his efforts for distinction; to retire for a few months to his old country nook, and there to meditate on his next course.

To set about this was curiously awkward to him. He had planned methods of retrogression in case of defeat through want of ability, want of means, or lack of opportunity; but to retreat because his appetite for advance had gone off was what he had never before thought of.

His reflections turned upon the old home of his mother's family. He knew exactly how Tollamore appeared at that time of year. The trees with their half-ripe apples ... the haymaking over, the harvest not begun, the people lively and always out of doors ... [1]

Once again fortune favoured him in architectural matters. Mr Hicks of Dorchester wrote asking whether he knew of an assistant who could help him in his church restoration work, since he himself was nowadays often crippled with gout. Hardy determined to be that man. He left London in July 1867, half-intending to return, leaving his books and poems behind him in his Bayswater lodgings.

[1] Edited by Carl Weber, pp. 109-110. Johns Hopkins Press, Baltimore, 1935.

CHAPTER FIVE

THREE TALES[1] AND A DIGRESSION

*The English novelist, in particular, suffers from a disability
which affects no other artist to the same extent. His work is
influenced by his birth. He is fated to know intimately, and so
to describe with understanding, only those who are of his own
social rank.*

VIRGINIA WOOLF

JOHN HICKS' architectural work was not arduous or absorb-
ing enough to employ Hardy's active, fermenting mind. His
attendance at the Dorchester drawing-offices was irregular, and
Hicks himself had set out for a remote parish in western Cornwall to inspect a ruinous church soon after Thomas had joined
him. It was natural that Hardy should turn to writing again, not
the writing of verse, which he had abandoned 'as a waste of
labour though he had resumed it awhile on arriving in the
country'. But in order to use some of his London poems he
devised the unusual plan of writing 'A Story with No Plot, containing some original verses', to be called *The Poor Man and the
Lady*. The tale was to be anonymous, acknowledged to be by the
Poor Man only; and it was to be written in the first person
singular.

The young architect had already expressed 'indifference to a
popular novelist's fame'. Yet his critical faculties had been
stirred by both Thackeray and Trollope, whose work he had
recommended to his sister Mary. Four years ago he had sent
her *Barchester Towers* and advised her to get hold of a copy of
Pelham. As for Thackeray, he had written:

> You must read something of his. He is considered to be the
> greatest novelist of the day—looking at novel writing of the
> highest kind as a perfect and truthful re-presentation of actual life
> —which is no doubt the proper view to take. Hence, because his
> novels stand so high as works of Art or Truth, they often have
> anything but an elevating tendency, and on that account are

---

[1] *The Poor Man and the Lady, An Indiscretion in the Life of an Heiress*, and
Desperate Remedies.

particularly unfitted for young people, from their very truthfulness. People say that it is beyond Mr Thackerey to paint a perfect man or woman—a great fault if novels are intended to instruct, but just the opposite if they are to be considered merely as pictures. *Vanity Fair* is considered one of his best.[1]

Hardy finished *The Poor Man and the Lady* in less than six months. He took another five to make a fair copy of the manuscript in between his intermittent work for Hicks. In spite of his resolutions not to do so he wrote more poems, outlined a narrative one on the Battle of the Nile, and tried to take down on paper the exact variations in the nightingale's song profligately spilled outside his Bockhampton window. On July 25 1868, he posted the novel to Mr Alexander Macmillan.

The Poor Man and the Lady no longer exists in entirety. The history of the manuscript, the effect of the story on those who read it, its subject matter and the spirit in which it was written, all make a fascinating study. There are three sources of information concerning it: Hardy himself, quoted by his wife, his friend Edmund Gosse, and Vere Collins[2]: a long letter from Macmillan, sent to Hardy a fortnight after he had received the manuscript: a fragment of a letter from its second reader, John Morley, and Hardy's memory of Meredith's verbal criticism, both quoted in the *Early Life*. Piecing together what they tell us we find the following:

THE SETTING:
> Dorset and London, 'the most important scenes' being laid in town and not in the country.
>
> A Dorset manor house and a town house belonging to the same aristocratic family.
>
> Scenes of gaiety at a concert and at Cremorne, or the Argyle Rooms.
>
> A meeting between the hero and the kept mistress of an architect.
>
> A melodramatic drawing-room scene. A scene in Rotten Row.
>
> A highly emotional churchyard scene, or scenes.

CHARACTERS:
> The hero, Will Strong, son of a labouring man who works on the estate of the great local squire.

[1] I, p. 53.   [2] See p. 54 of the *Talks*.

The heroine, daughter of the squire, who falls in love with Will
   Strong.
The squire, the Hon. Fay Allamont.
His wife, the lady of the manor.

THE PLOT:
   The hero shows talent at the village school and is educated as a
      draughtsman at the expense of the squire and his lady.   He
      and the heroine fall in love, in Dorset. Their attachment is
      discovered by the squire who sees to it that Will Strong is sent
      away to London, where he wins a prize which is publicly
      withdrawn. They are forbidden to write.   But the lovers
      consider themselves betrothed and break the ban. The squire
      discovers this and is wroth.
   The hero is angered and takes up radical politics, out of pique.
      He later addresses public meetings in Trafalgar Square.
   The great family come up to town and the lovers plight their
      troth anew. One day the heroine passes a street-gathering in
      her carriage : she sees that the passionate speaker is none other
      than Will and is deeply offended at his radical sentiments.
      She drives on, and breaks off all relations with him.
   They attend the same concert, Miss Allamont sitting in the last
      row of the expensive seats and Will behind her in the first of
      the inexpensive. They are deeply moved by the music and
      contrive to hold hands. Afterwards they walk away together
      and their affection is revived. The heroine asks him to call on
      her.
   Will does so and finds her out. Her mother receives him with
      anger and arrogance. . . They quarrel and she faints. Will
      tries to revive her by pouring water over her. She comes
      round and discovers that her rouge is running down her face
      which sends her off again. Enter the Hon. Fay Allamont,
      who orders the footman to throw the hero out. The squire and
      his family return to the country. The lovers do not write.
   Will hears from his relations that the heroine is to be married
      to the heir of a neighbouring landowner. He goes down to
      Dorset and haunts the churchyard on the wedding eve. The
      church is open and he sees a muffled figure steal into it.   He
      follows it and finds it to be his love. She is at first very angry
      and then confesses that she has never loved anyone but him.
   There is a scene in which a "gentleman pursues his wife and
      strikes her at midnight." (It is not certain whether this in-
      volves the heroine and her bridegroom, or her parents.

The heroine becomes critically ill and, against his principles, her father agrees to send for Will Strong at her request. She dies and her father sets up a monument to her, the estimate for which has cost him nothing.

MANNER AND STYLE:

First, according to Hardy; 'It was very crude. The only interesting thing about it was that it showed a wonderful insight into female character. I don't know how that came about'. He regarded taking an interest in the story as 'hunting very small deer'. 'But,' adds Edmund Gosse, 'the student of Hardy's mind in early development will hardly, I think, agree with him.'[1]

Secondly, according to Alexander Macmillan: the novel, which he read with 'interest and admiration', had 'fatal draw-backs to its success', and he added, with extraordinary perspicacity, that these were drawbacks to

> what I think, judging the writer from the book itself, you would feel even more strongly—its truthfulness and justice.[2]

The descriptions of rural scenes and characters were 'admirable', but the portraits of London gentlefolk were of unrelieved heart-lessness and villainy. The conversation 'in drawing-rooms and ball-rooms about the working classes' was utterly 'heedless' and 'falls harmless from very excess'.

> It seems to me that your black-wash will not be recognized as anything more than ignorant misrepresentation ... It is inconceivable to me that any considerable number of human beings—God's creatures—should be so bad without going to utter wreck within a week.[3]

The story was 'improbable', the detail was 'strained and un-natural', but the work was redeemed by the poetical handling of certain scenes and it had 'dignity and power'. He especially praised the scenes in Rotten Row and Trafalgar Square. 'Will's speech to the working men is full of wisdom'. But the whole lacked 'the modesty of nature of fact'. Here Macmillan recognized the ballad-like plot in Hardy's work, but denied that

[1] "Thomas Hardy's Lost Novel", *Sunday Times*, January 22, 1928.
[2] Charles Graves, *Life and Letters of Alexander Macmillan*. Macmillan & Co., London, 1910.   [3] *Ibid.*

'such improbabilities' could take place 'in the present day, given your characters'.

> You see I am writing to you as a writer who seems to me, at least potentially, of considerable mark, of power and purpose. If this is your first book I think you ought to go on.[1]

Macmillan enclosed his friend Morley's report, which no longer exists in full.

Thirdly, according to John Morley (who had recently published his book on Burke) the novel was:

> A very curious and original performance: the opening pictures of the Christmas Eve in the tranter's house are really of good quality: much of the writing is strong and fresh." But "the thing hangs too loosely together" and "some of the scenes were wildly extravagant", "so that they read *like some clever lad's dream* . . . If the man is young he has stuff and purpose in him'[2]

Fourthly, according to the *Early Life*, an account based on Hardy's memory of the novel's inception:

> He considered that he knew fairly well both West-country life in its less explored recesses and the life of an isolated student cast upon the billows of London with no protection but his brains— the young man of whom it may be said more truly than perhaps of any, that 'save his own soul he hath no star" The two contrasting experiences seemed to afford him abundant materials out of which to evolve a striking socialistic novel—not that he mentally defined it as such, for the word had probably never, or scarcely ever, been heard of at that date . . .[3]
>
> One instance he could remember was a chapter in which, with every circumstantial detail, he described in the first person his introduction to the kept mistress of an architect who 'took in washing' (as it was called in the profession) that is, worked at his own office for other architects, the said mistress adding to her lover's income by designing for him the pulpits, altars, reredoses, texts, holy vessels, crucifixes, and other ecclesiastical furniture which were handed on to him by the nominal architects who employed her protector—the lady herself being a dancer at a music-hall when not engaged in designing Christian emblems—all told so plausibly as to seem actual proof of the degeneracy of the age.[4]

[1] *Ibid.*   [2] I, p. 77. (Italics mine.)
[3] *Ibid.*, pp. 74-5.   [4] *Ibid.*, pp. 81-2.

D

This scene was obviously suggested to Hardy by his visit to the Covent Garden Pantomime, where he discovered that the smith who made the ironwork for *The Forty Thieves* was also the man who turned Blomfield's designs for ecclesiastical metal work; and who thus made 'crucifixes and harlequin traps with equal imperturbability'. But the sensational addition of the architect and his mistress, employed in this bizarre and seemingly sacrilegious fashion, was his own.

Macmillan had indicated that Hardy might modify *The Poor Man*, and he re-wrote some of the pages between receiving the former's letter in August and making a visit to London in December, when Macmillan made it clear that his house could not publish the tale, and introduced Hardy to Chapman and Hall. Hearing nothing from Mr Chapman, Hardy again went up to London in the New Year and talked with Macmillan, Morley, and Chapman, in whose offices he caught a glimpse of the august figure of the ageing Carlyle. Again, for inscrutable reasons, there was a delay. Although Hardy had agreed to put down the sum of £20 towards publication he heard nothing further until he was summoned to meet a third reader, this time George Meredith (Hardy's senior by twelve years), who remained anonymous throughout the interview.

Thus we have a final verdict on *The Poor Man*, Meredith's verbal one, as remembered by Hardy:

> Meredith had the manuscript in his hand and began lecturing Hardy upon it in a sonorous voice . . . He strongly advised its author 'not to nail his colours to the mast' so definitely in a first book, if he wished to do anything practical in literature: for if he printed so pronounced a thing he would be attacked on all sides by the conventional reviewers, and its future injured. The story was, in fact, a sweeping dramatic satire of the squirearchy and nobility, London society, the vulgarity of the middle class, modern Christianity, church restoration, and political and domestic morals in general, the author's views, in fact, being obviously those of a young man with a passion for reforming the world . . . the tendency of the writing being socialistic, not to say revolutionary; yet not argumentatively so, the style having the affected simplicity of Defoe's, which had long attracted Hardy.[1]

[1] I., pp. 80-1.

Meredith ended by suggesting that Hardy should re-write the story or, better still, put it on one side and write another 'with a purely artistic purpose' and a 'more complicated plot.'' Weary of the vicissitudes of *The Poor Man*, Hardy decided to do the latter. The result was *Desperate Remedies*. But he did not destroy *The Poor Man and the Lady*, whose latter history is as complicated as its earlier. He dismembered it, used portions of it in three ensuing novels, and published an emasculated form of it as *An Indiscretion in the Life of an Heiress* ten years later.[1]

But as late as 1916 'a good portion of the manuscript still survived' and Sir Sydney Cockerell, the zealous gatherer of Hardy manuscripts for the Fitzwilliam and other museums, took it away to get it handsomely bound in blue morocco at his own expense. Some years later Hardy

> came to the conclusion that it ought not to be preserved and he burnt it himself in his study fire.[2]

The student of Hardy's mind 'in its early development' aches to know what was in those burnt pages. It was in the faint hope that Sir Sydney Cockerell might remember something of their contents that I wrote to him asking if he did so. But he unfortunately replied that he had not read them, and that he had 'nothing more to tell'.[2]

The synopsis of the story of *The Poor Man*, as given above, and the comments on it by three people eminent in the literary field provoke the mind in many directions. One notices the pertinent criticism on Hardy's ability to draw rural scenes and characters with consummate skill, and his inability to do the same with those of the upper classes: and of the wild improbabilities of plot and scene. This alternation between the realistic and the artificial, the magnificent and the melodramatic, is characteristic of Hardy's work, even in maturity. One notices at once the emphasis on the marked disparity between the social backgrounds of the hero and heroine. The quarrel with social conventions, with an irrevocable unwritten man-made law which runs counter to a law governed by the rhythm of the heart, is

[1] See Rutland, pp. 111-33, for a detailed analysis of its adaptation from *The Poor Man and the Lady*.
[2] Letter from Sir Sydney Cockerell to Dr Rutland. Rutland, p. 113.
[3] Letter to the author from Sir Sydney Cockerell, January 18, 1952.

typical of the finest of Hardy's later work, but here in his first novel there is a difference, the quarrel has a strong socialistic tinge. In his subsequent work (with the exception of a single novel)[1] Hardy dropped these sentiments: either he realized, as his first readers had hinted, that it was unwise to introduce politics into fiction, or his maturing mind no longer wished to concern itself with their evanescent qualities, perceiving that those of a work of art are more enduring. But his lifelong bias against the unimaginative and stringent organization of society is obvious even in 1865 from his complaint, in *Amabel*, of the lady's 'custom-straitened views'. *The Poor Man* in 1868 develops this further, and in 1891 and 1894 with *Tess* and *Jude* it culminates in the cry against 'those creeds which futilely attempt to check what wisdom would be content to regulate.' Hardy's larger quarrel with the universe, whose latent hostility is inimical to human life, is also hinted at in *An Indiscretion*, adapted from a portion of *The Poor Man*, so we may safely assume that this characteristic of his later prose work was also present in his first, more especially as it is visible in his earliest poetry.

But perhaps the most revealing fact is Hardy's ignorance of the bitter and aggressive sides of his nature. These seem to have been so deeply repressed, or he was so completely dissociated from them, that he was wholly unaware of them. He projected them onto the impersonal creator of the universe instead, more especially in the early poems. Alexander Macmillan pointed out that the satirical parts of *The Poor Man* 'meant mischief', and Meredith stressed the 'sweeping dramatic satire'. Yet Hardy was surprised to find that

> in the opinion of such experienced critics, he had written so aggressive and even dangerous a work, *almost without knowing it*, for his mind had been given in the main to poetry and other forms of pure literature.[2]

One thing is obvious, that the quarrel between his parents and the Martins of Kingston Maurward had struck deeper into the child's mind and heart than he, or anyone else, was aware. There is no proof that the Martins behaved in either an 'arrogant' or 'angry' manner with the Bockhampton family, but Thomas was bewildered by, and then resented, the unreasonable power

[1] *The Hand of Ethelberta.*   [2] I, pp. 81 and 83. (Italics mine.)

which the aristocracy might, without warning, exert over the
lives and livelihood of others, dependent on their favour. In two
of his novels the gentry are the villains of the piece—ladies of the
manor who are selfish, capricious and pitiless. In *The Poor Man*
the hero, 'out of pique', takes up radical politics. In his own
life Hardy, seemingly out of pique, wrote a novel in which the
heroine, daughter of a butler, marries a peer of the realm and
outwits all her rivals.[1] His ignorance of the dangerous sides of
his nature was matched by unawareness of his intuitive gifts. At
eighty-one Hardy could still tell Gosse that he did not know how
it came about that he had a youthful understanding of women.

The Poor Man is indissolubly linked with *An Indiscretion in the
Life of an Heiress*, a novel-in-short which incongruously appeared
in the same year as one of Hardy's finest works, *The Return of the
Native*. There has been considerable controversy as to whether
this tale was the product of Hardy's mind at the age of twenty-
eight or thirty-eight. At first it looks as if there need be no doubt.
Hardy always took great pains to be accurate in details of the
period of his stories' settings, and to verify the superstitions and
legends which he incorporated in them.[2] He had a strong
historical sense and a love of accuracy.[3] It is this realistic framework which gives to his wildest tales a skeleton of steel, artfully
concealed. Now on the third page of *An Indiscretion* we find this
sentence:

> One day in the previous week there had been some excitement
> in the parish on account of the introduction upon the farm of a
> steam threshing-machine for the first time, the date of these events
> being some thirty years ago.[4]

This seems to date the tale conclusively and nothing remains
but to discover when this piece of agricultural machinery invaded Dorsetshire. But, when we look more closely, it appears
that Hardy inserted the detail to give realism to *An Indiscretion* in
1878, when using what remained of *The Poor Man* after cutting
it up for *Desperate Remedies* and *Under the Greenwood Tree*. In
touching it up, he changed the first person singular to the third,

---

[1] *The Hand of Ethelberta.*   [2] See Preface to *Tess*, 1911 edition.
[3] *Under the Greenwood Tree* is an exception to this, since Hardy telescopes
what he has heard from his parents and others, and what he himself had
observed.   [4] p. 23.

cut out the inflammable material and altered several salient
details. But the style remains immature and colourless, the
characterization thin, and the plot undeveloped. By 1878 Hardy
had forgotten, or did not care, that some passages in *An Indiscretion* had already appeared in *Desperate Remedies*. Three such
repetitive fragments have already been pointed out, and it has
been shown that many of the literary quotations, of which Hardy
was so fond, were used a second time in *Desperate Remedies*,
implying that they had probably first occurred in the abused
Poor Man,[1] But there is another astonishing transposal: the
opening paragraph in *An Indiscretion*, describing evening service
in Tollamore Church, is the same as one in *Desperate Remedies*,
with slight modifications.[2] That in the novel is the more detailed and forceful: Hardy probably took it over in entirety
from the *Poor Man* of 1868 for the novel in 1871, and cut it
down for *An Indiscretion* in 1878, when he wished to swell his
purse by using up old material.

An Indiscretion is still the closest we may come to the lost *Poor
Man* and some of its characteristics strike one forcibly on first
reading it. First, Hardy's youthful tenderness for old people, old
servants and poor children. Egbert's grandfather reminds us of
two other old men in Hardy's later novels,[3] while the male
factotum recalls the miller's jack-of-all-trades in *The Trumpet
Major* and Creedle in *The Woodlanders*. That kindliness, which
even in Hardy's day was dying out, is lovingly drawn, for the
old servant offers Egbert a home should London treat him
harshly. The Bockhampton house or its counterpart, appears
and, as in *Tess*, it is described as being 'almost part of himself'.
Here, too, is a description of the impressive Grey monument in
Stinsford church[4] which had haunted Hardy's childish imagination:

> Over her head rose a vast marble monument, erected to the
> memory of her ancestors, male and female . . . The design consisted
> of a winged skull and two cherubim, supporting a pair of tall

[1] Rutland, pp. 129-32.
[2] See pp. 108-9, below.
[3] Edward Springrove's father in *Desperate Remedies*, and Marty South's in
The Woodlanders.
[4] This appears in a clipped and altered form in *Desperate Remedies*, p. 288.

Corinthian columns, between which spread a broad slab, containing the roll of ancient names, lineages and deeds, and surmounted by a pediment, with the crest of the family at its apex.

As the youthful schoolmaster gazed, and all these details became dimmer, her face was modified in his fancy, till it seemed almost to resemble the carved marble skull immediately above her head.[1]

And here is the Kingston Maurward classical Temple, or summer-house, and the lime trees of the park.

The hero's name—Egbert Mayne—raises an interesting point. Hardy must have known of the west-country seminary priest and martyr of Elizabethan days, Cuthbert Mayne. (The similarity between Egbert and Cuthbert is too pronounced to be ignored.) But he was fond of taking the names of his characters from local history, ancient tombs and actual places. Thus Egbert's surname probably comes from Mayne Down on the ridge overlooking the channel, a place Hardy loved and from which he later sketched the sea in a cold spring. The village of Broadmayne, and Little Mayne Farm, lie at the foot of the down's northern slopes, the village which was endeared to Hardy because he fancied Keats' relations lived there.[2]

But it is more interesting to trace Hardy's early attitudes of mind and quirks of thought than to identify monuments and suggest possible sources for the names of his characters. For instance, the fact that the heroine questions the hero's lack of ambition, which was one of Hardy's self-acknowledged traits: that his feelings about the aristocracy are inflamed, even raw: that he has the original idea that a servant, in a certain sense, may be said to own his master, a Swiftian thought, and reminiscent of Hardy's notion that he might one day write a volume of poems depicting 'the other side of common emotions':[3] that he believes love to have three progressive stages, an idea which he elaborated in *Desperate Remedies*: the conviction that women are drawn to those who cause them pain, a thought he later transferred to his long-suffering women—Bathsheba, Tess and others,

[1] pp. 22-3.
[2] To suggest that the hero is so called because of his "main strength" is ridiculous. See Weber, *An Indiscretion*, p. 18.
[3] I, p. 76.

and that 'men survive almost anything'. The countryman's ear
for delicate sounds, so pronounced a feature of Hardy's writing,
is evident in his description of

> the dead leaves in the ditches which could be heard but not seen
> [and which] shifted their position with a troubled rustle.[1]

That adjective 'troubled' is the precursor of many sensitive
ones with which Hardy animates the minutiae of a scene.

The heroine is gentle and passive, with occasional flashes of
wilfulness which cause her to take the initiative in unwomanly
fashion: she is torn between loyalty to her father and to the man
whom she secretly loves, to the laws of the society in which she
has been bred and those of her heart: the conflict in the end
destroys her. Egbert, a young man of a 'singularly distracting
order of beauty', remains a nonentity, a stick, a peg on which
to hang the tale, with this exception, that his sense of honour is
acute. The heroine's father, the Honourable Fay, or Foy, Allamont, only comes to life when Geraldine is dying:

> It was only when he despaired that he looked upon Egbert with
> tolerance. When he hoped, the young man's presence was hateful
> to him.[2]

There is the poet's regret for the perishing beauty of woman:
there are revealing comments on the hero's change of attitude
towards the subject of painting—artists and their work cease to
be of interest 'for their own sake' and he has a new and 'breath-
less interest in them as factors in the game of sink or swim'.
There are one or two pale similes, forerunners of those remarkable ones which distinguish Hardy's finest work. When Geraldine is falling more and more deeply in love her 'passionate
likening' for Egbert's society creeps over her 'slowly and in-
sidiously like ripeness over fruit': and when Egbert sits alone in
the old house, soon to be torn down after his grandfather's
death:

> The ancient family clock had stopped for want of winding, and
> the intense silence that prevailed seemed more like the bodily
> presence of some quality than the mere absence of sound.[3]

Hardy's feelings against the gentry, vehement in *The Poor Man*
and transformed in his later work, openly appear three or four

[1] p. 80.   [2] p. 142.   [3] p. 61.

times in *An Indiscretion*. When the hero and heroine discuss going a distance of eight miles Geraldine visualizes covering it by carriage, and Egbert by foot.

> The remarks had been simple and trivial, but they brought a similar thought into the minds of both of them . . . It was that horrid thought of their differing habits and of those contrasting positions which could not be reconciled.[1]

The two other places are more significant, for they foreshadow Hardy's quarrel with the man-made laws of society which contradict, and come in conflict with, those simpler more urgent laws dictated by the heart:

> That the habits of men should be so subversive of the law of nature as to indicate that he was not worthy to marry a woman whose own instincts said that he was worthy, was a great anomaly, he thought, with some rebelliousness: but this did not upset the fact or remove the difficulty.[2]

This is Egbert's culminating reflection after his original one when he gazed at Geraldine from the church gallery:

> . . . he entered on rational considerations of what a vast gulf lay between that lady and himself, what a troublesome world it was to live in where such divisions could exist, and how painful was the evil when a man of his unequal history was possessed of a keen susceptiblity.[3]

The unfeeling capriciousness of these haughty aristocrats—distant, elusive people who have it in their power to sweep away a man's home when the fancy takes them, to enclose his land, and pull down his own roof, under which he has been born and hopes to die—is keenly felt. It was the theme-in-part of two of Hardy's greatest novels, *The Woodlanders* and *Tess of the d'Urbervilles*. Egbert calls himself a fool for loving a girl who can torment his grandfather so mercilessly and, later, in a bitter moment he professes to her that he has been helped to forget her by 'the strong prejudice I originally had against your class and family'.

During Hardy's last year in London there had been frequent working-class demonstrations in industrial towns, and riotous meetings in Hyde Park. During this same year (1867) two

[1] p. 70. [2] p. 76. [3] p. 23.

D *

memorable things occurred, the formation of the London Working Man's Association and the passage of the Reform Bill. Whether Hardy was involved to any serious extent in the ferment of this year is doubtful, but his sympathies were with the working man and the reflection of these sympathies is revealed in this immature work.

In 1868-9 Hardy paid four different visits to London, either to meet publishers and their readers, or to enquire into the fate of his manuscript. He was restless and dissatisfied, lacking not so much subsistence as

> a clear call to him which course in life to take—the course he loved, and which was his natural instinct, that of letters, or the course all practical wisdom dictated, that of architecture.[1]

Both Macmillan and Morley suggested that he should try his hand at reviewing but this did not appeal to Hardy, and although Morley kindly offered him an introduction to the editor of the *Saturday Review*, the most persistent recorder of the quarrel between science and faith in the sixties, he could have obtained this at any time through his friend Moule, and he did nothing about it.

While in London, during the winter of 1869, Hardy heard of the death of his old friend and first employer, John Hicks, whose practice was taken over by a Weymouth architect, G. R. Crickmay. Hardy agreed to stay on with the latter until Hicks' affairs were put in order, first for a fortnight in Dorchester, then for a period of three months in Weymouth, then for a further period. Crickmay was not conversant with Gothic architecture, and he was glad of the assistance of someone who had worked under so important a man as Blomfield. Having struck a compromise between architecture and literature, and gained a breathing space in life, Hardy was buoyant, and when the Weymouth town band struck up some deliciously gay music it chimed with his mood, seeming to him symbolical of new-found, careless freedom. The waltzes were new ones by Johann Strauss.

Every evening he rowed in the bay and in the mornings he bathed, diving from a boat, or wading out from the pebbly strand above Melcombe Regis. Those summer mornings when he lay on his back gently rising and falling with the tide, warmed by the hot sun, helped to dispel the melancholy which had settled on him during the previous summer, when he had felt it necessary to read Wordsworth's *Resolution and Independence* and Mill on *Individuality* to brace himself. Persuaded by a new architectural assistant he even joined a dancing-class. Hardy found the young ladies of Weymouth 'heavier on the arm' than their London cousins, and it did not take him long to realize that the class was mainly 'a gathering for dances and love-making by adepts of both sexes'. Without being a prig, Hardy dissociated himself from it since he wished to get on with the new novel he had begun (which on Meredith's advice he was striving to make more complicated than *The Poor Man and the Lady*)—*Desperate Remedies*. Hardy found that the gaiety of Weymouth interfered with his writing and, having finished the architectural drawings for Crickmay, he retired again to Bockhampton.

Hardy often regretted in after years that, on many of the journeys which he had made for these local architects, he had been forced to agree to the destruction of much of the Gothic detail of the ancient churches. He was the servant of others, a silent accomplice who, even if he had voiced his disapproval, would not have been heeded. Some of the old towers which were called unsafe proved so strong that they had to be blown up with gunpowder. Funds for so-called restoration were low, and the oak benches with their pendant poppy heads were often cast aside as being too far gone to patch and mend, and new ones of pitch-pine from America were substituted. The work was sometimes left in the hands of zealous but ignorant local men who took it upon themselves to undertake 'improvements' which had not been commissioned. Hardy remembered that one fine old rood-screen and 15th-century traceried windows were removed in entirety by the local mason-cum-carpenter, who said he would not stand on ceremony but give the congregation new ones at his own expense, thereby handsomely serving art, religion and posterity. 'A comic business—church restoration'.[1]

Desperate Remedies was refused by Macmillan and published

[1] See I, pp. 40-1 and 165, and Thomas Hardy, "Memories of Church Restoration", *Cornhill Magazine*, July 1906.

anonymously in March, 1871, by Tinsley Brothers. It is the only novel which Hardy paid to have published. It enlisted on a crowded field. The work of Scott, who had been dead for nearly forty years, of Dickens, who had died only the year before, of Charlotte Brontë, Thackeray, Mrs Gaskell and Thomas Love Peacock still attracted the minds of readers who also enjoyed that of Trollope, Kingsley, R. D. Blackmore, William Black, Wilkie Collins and Charles Reade, greatly admired by Swinburne. Towering above these in popular reputation stood the two Georges—Eliot and Meredith. In her *Scenes of Clerical Life*, which resembled excellent steel engravings, George Eliot had given promise more than a decade earlier of her power to come. As for argumentative, flamboyant Meredith—Somerset Maugham has told us that, in his youth, everyone read him. Not to have done so, whether one understood what he was saying or not, caused a stigma to be attached to one. Hardy admired Trollope for his construction, and he respected George Eliot. He considered her a 'great thinker', possibly 'one of the greatest living' writers, 'though not a born story-teller by any means'. He was not drawn to Meredith as a writer and admitted that there were times when he could not stomach his prose work in spite of its brilliance. He looked upon Meredith as being in the direct succession of Congreve and the artificial comedians of the Restoration.[1]

But what of *Desperate Remedies*, and the effect of this strange anonymous novel, imbued with a submerged poetic fire and bearing signs of the influence of that most popular of all the late Victorian novelists, Wilkie Collins, in its complicated, ingenious plot and its sense of horror? The book received friendly reviews from three well-known papers—that in the *Saturday Review* may have been by Horace Moule. It was praised for its pictures of rustic life, and the author for his

> sensitiveness to scenic and atmospheric effects, and to their influence on the mind, and the power of rousing similar sensitiveness in his readers. . . .

by the influential *Spectator*. But the reviewer of this paper also heartily disliked what it called the 'prostitution' of the writer's

[1] II, pp. 169 and 257.

powers 'to the purposes of idle prying into the ways of wickedness', and he warned readers from the book in no mild manner, suggesting that the law which allowed the publishers to issue it anonymously was 'hardly just'. The critic, had he been more perceptive and more merciful, might have detected the youth of this author who scatters his literary allusions and quotations broadside like a careless sower. The mind of this new writer is crammed with ideas, and yet it is not hungry for argument. This is the salient difference between the youthful Meredith (in *Richard Feverel*) and the young Hardy. A heavy passivity hangs over *Desperate Remedies*, cloaking its intellectual power and lyrical intensity.

Hardy had not yet learnt—and never fully learnt—to shut his ears to the 'fooleries of critics', as he was later advised to do by Moule and Macmillan's able reviewer. Ignoring the pleasant articles he characteristically pressed inwards the poisoned barbs of the *Spectator* review, which he read whilst sitting on the field-gate of the Kingston Maurward ewe-lease. When he had finished he

. . . wished he were dead. The bitterness of that moment was never forgotten.[1]

This early novel of Hardy's is generally derided as being sensational and worthless. Yet it has passages of great beauty and reveals certain distinctive traits which the writer was to develop, or which merely lie embedded like fossils in his mature work. Looking back from our vantage-point in time we can discern exciting things which the critics of eighty years ago could not possibly do, for we have the whole of Hardy's work spread out before us.

There are, for instance, many passages which verge on self-portraiture. Hardy consistently denied these in his work (with one exception) but he referred more specifically to details of his appearance and character rather than revelations of his thought, the disclosure of which no man can escape in his writings.

I should not have been so conceited as to make myself the prototype [of Stephen Smith in *A Pair of Blue Eyes*]. I describe him as a tall, handsome young fellow,

he told Vere Collins.[2]

But when Cytherea questions her brother about the new architect, Edward Springrove, who has come to the office, Owen tells her:

> though he is not a public school man he has read widely, and he has a sharp appreciation of what's good in books and art . . . His knowledge isn't nearly so exclusive as most professional men's . . . This man is of a rather melancholy turn of mind, I think . . . a thorough artist but a man of rather humble origin, it seems, who has made himself so far.[1]

And later he says:

> He's a thorough book-worm—despises the pap-and-daisy school of verse—knows Shakespeare to the very dregs of the footnotes. Indeed, he's a poet himself, in a small way.[2]

Another day some of Springrove's verses are passed round the office and there is some chatter about women and love. This is just the kind of youthful discussion which went on in Blomfield's offices, reflected in Hardy's notes of 1865, and the tinge of cynicism makes it probable that Springrove's assessment of love, and a lover's inevitable wrong choice of a mate, were Hardy's own.

Owen takes the poems home to his sister and she says:

> "If he's a satirist I don't think I care about him."

> "There you are just wrong. He is not. He is, as I believe, an impulsive fellow who has been made to pay the price of his rashness in some love affair." [3]

Later there is a revealing conversation between Cytherea and Springrove himself. He tells her that he knows that he will never advance as an architect, since he has not the necessary qualifications of character. "Those who are rich need have no skill as artists", but instead,

> A certain kind of energy which men with any fondness for art possess very seldom indeed—an earnestness in making acquaintances, and a love for using them. They give their whole attention

---

[1] *Desperate Remedies*, pp. 23-7. (Hardy's knowledge of Shakespeare was exceptional. His debt to him has been made the subject of several studies. See Weber, pp. 246-57, and Shakespeare Association Bulletin IX, April and July 1934.)   [2] *Ibid.*   [3] p. 27.

to the art of dining out, after mastering a few rudimentary facts to serve up in conversation.[1]

This exactly bears out what we are told in *The Early Life* Hardy felt. Yet, in talking to Collins many years later, the poet-architect denied 'the disgust felt for architecture by a character in *Desperate Remedies* ascribed to him by a writer'.[2] Furthermore, Edward goes on to confide his youthful predilection for verse and versifying:

> From having loved verse passionately, I went on to read it continually; then I went rhyming myself. If anything on earth ruins a man for a useful occupation, and for content with reasonable success in a profession or trade, it is the habit of writing verses on emotional subjects, which had much better be left to die from want of nourishment.[3]

There follow some melancholy lines on the effect of too much study of poetry and art on men of the middle classes in youth, a study which prevents them from getting on in the world financially, and so precludes them from exercising their powers for the enjoyment of 'conjugal love of the purest and highest kind'.[4]

Then there are the aphorisms about men and women, a curious mixture of a young man's cynicism and an old woman's wisdom wrapped up in neat packets—"To snub a petted man and to pet a snubbed man is the way to win suits in both kinds", and "Fate's nothen' beside a woman's schemen'". But it is when Hardy discusses the differences between the sexes that we become interested, for in the later novels he develops these tentative excursions and creates the once much-discussed 'Hardy woman'.

> In spite of a fashion which pervades the whole community at the present day—the habit of exclaiming that woman is not undeveloped man, but diverse, the fact remains that, after all, women are Mankind, and that in many of the sentiments of life the difference of sex is but a difference of degree.[5]

In another place he questions whether 'a difference of sex amounts to a difference of nature': and decides that there is at

---

[1] *Desperate Remedies*, pp. 49-50.   [2] Collins, p. 74.
[3] *Desperate Remedies*, pp. 49-50.   [4] p. 52.   [5] p. 210.

least one occasion when this is so. A woman reduced by sorrow to being indifferent to life itself can yet take an interest in 'those sorry trifles, her robe, her flowers, her veil, and her gloves'— when she is being married.

The unhealthy relationship between Miss Aldclyffe, the lady of the manor, and Cytherea, which remains unexplored, is also a strange theme for a first novel. Miss Aldclyffe, who is more like a boa constrictor than a woman, is attracted to the girl who becomes her companion and protégée, because she is the daughter of the man with whom Miss Aldclyffe had once been in love. One feels that this relationship was pure imaginative fancy on Hardy's part and that he had no real understanding of the psychological subtleties involved. There is also an astonishing example of feminine masochism, or self-immolation, a characteristic of Hardy's heroines even in his mature prose. Here in his first novel we have a young girl who sacrifices herself to a man, whom she does not love but who fascinates her as a snake does a bird, for the benefit of her brother. "Why should I consider my useless self?" is her cry, a cry strangely resembling Tess' own. The pressure put on her from all sides is so great that she acquiesces. The night before the wedding she is kept awake by a noise which resembles the beating of the wall below her window by a bundle of switches. She falls into a troubled sleep and

> dreamt that she was being whipped with dry bones suspended on strings, which rattled at every blow like those of a malefactor on a gibbet; that she shifted and shrank and avoided every blow, and they fell then upon the wall to which she was tied. She could not see the face of the executioner for his mask, but his form was like Manston's.[1]

This macabre dream is the sleeping counterpart of Cytherea's waking thoughts which Hardy surprisingly alleges spring from a biblical source. Women possess, he says,

> an illogical power entirely denied to men in general—the power not only of kissing, but of delighting to kiss the rod by a punctilious observance of the self-immolating doctrines in the Sermon on the Mount.[2]

[1] p. 280.   [2] p. 251.

Here also is the impersonal deity who, thirty years later, becomes The Immanent Will, after a series of transmutations.

> Reasoning worldliness, especially when allied with sensuousness, cannot repress on some extreme occasions the human instinct to pour out the soul to some Being or Personality, who in frigid moments is dismissed with the title of Chance, or at most Law.[1]

And here are the exquisite descriptions which reveal the countryman's ear and the painter's eye—Hardy's rare sensitivity to sound and colour. For here is a writer who is not only able to detect the differences in sound when rain strikes on pasture, arable, or root crops, but who also hears the 'soft hiss produced by the bursting of innumerable bubbles of foam' in the wake of a paddle-steamer: and who sees this same wake, when the moon rises, a shimmering path stretching away to the horizon

> till the flecked ripples reduced themselves to sparkles as fine as gold dust.[2]

The scene in which Hardy describes the Dorset countryside near the sea on a hot summer's afternoon is one of the most brilliant in his early writing. It palpitates with heat and colour, and it prefigures the better-known descriptions of the Heath in *The Return of The Native*.

> Nothing was visible save the strikingly brilliant, still landscape. The wide concave which lay at the back of the hill . . . was blazing with the western light, adding an orange tint to the vivid purple of the heather, now at the very climax of bloom . . . The light so intensified the colours that they seemed to stand above the surface of the earth and float in mid-air like an exhalation of red. In the minor valleys [were] . . . brakes of tall, heavy-stemmed ferns . . . in a brilliant light green dress . . . Among the ferns grew holly bushes deeper in tint than any shadow about them . . .[3]

Cytherea and her lover do not dance to the music of the harps and violins but lapse into silence, 'watching the waves from the paddles as they slid thinly and easily under each other's edges.'

Hardy's descriptive passages involve the use of similes and metaphors which, at their best, are unsurpassed. They give to his work a richness of emotional tone and a poetic justness,

[1] p. 220.   [2] pp. 33-4.   [3] pp. 28-9.

springing as they do straight from the visual imagination: they are feeling and thought embodied in a concrete perception. This 'vivid exactness' is apparent in his first published work, and there are examples, too, of those other similes which are not so felicitous, the learned ones which the 'library cormorant', as Coleridge called himself, swallows and regurgitates. When Hardy is emotionally stirred and writing at white-heat the inspired similes pour from him like sparks from a chimney on a frosty night, or they form and re-form like beaded bubbles breaking at the brim of a glass-full of heady wine, as many as five or six similes appearing in a single paragraph. It is well to seek these out in his early work and then to see how, as his talent develops and he gives his imagination rein, the similes mature in depth and range; for through his senses, Hardy, like Coleridge, explored the outer world and then re-examined it in solitude, mentally re-creating the scene which had emotionally moved him. Through the metaphors and similes alone, we can tell when he is most inspired and watch, almost over his shoulder, the half-act of artistic creation.

First, take two of the poorer sort, the learned similes, from *Desperate Remedies*. Hardy is describing a Dutch clock, with its

> entrails hanging down beneath its white face and wiry hands *like the faeces of a Harpy*.[1]

The line is a distortion of a passage from the Third Book of the *Æneid* which he had been studying three years earlier. This may be clever, but it is not pleasing writing. Then there is that extraordinary comparison of Springrove's hungry expression when Cytherea refuses to let him accompany her to her door.

> He looked at her *as a waiter looks at the change he brings back*.[2]

But a writer must be measured by his finest work, not by his oddest, and the metaphor on the following page shows Hardy's nascent power. Springrove stands below Cytherea's window in the street and watches her draw down the blind. He dwells upon her vanishing figure with

> a hopeless sense of loss akin to that which Adam is said . . . to have felt when he first saw the sun set, and thought, in his inexperience, that it would return no more.[3]

[1] p. 366. (Italics mine.)   [2] p. 34.   [3] p. 35.

The intensity of ardour and of youthful despair implied in these lines is moving and prophetic. It foreshadows the suffering and division of the lovers, and reminds one of some great painting of the expulsion, or some tragical legendary separation from the beloved—Orpheus from his Eurydice, or Lot from his wife.

The cider-making scene has often been quoted, but there is another equally delicious one—that of the 'Big House' kitchen, for Hardy excelled in painting domestic interiors, as well as rural exteriors. This one has the warmth and wholesomeness of freshly baked, home-made bread.[1]

Desperate Remedies is steeped in the landscape of Stinsford and Lower Bockhampton. In addition to the church and the towering Grey monument there is the old manor-house of the Greys (from whom Cytherea's surname is taken) with its five-pointed gables and symmetrical front—a house fallen on neglectful days ever since the Pitts came, for it has been successively a home for poor widows, evacuees, and finally squatters, and it has been stripped of all its old panelling and interior fittings. There is the great Georgian house[2] of George Pitt and Lora Grey with its Palladian front, its columns and cornices, the house which Morton Pitt was in such haste to face with freestone to please an exacting and supercilious monarch, and which, in Hardy's imagination, is presided over by the haughty Miss Aldclyffe, who cannot keep a lady's maid because of her tempers. There is the little Grecian Temple, or Fane, overlooking the great reedy lake with its burden of white swans, and there is the noise of falling waters which, even today, feed its placid beauty. From some early association Hardy retained unpleasant memories of the waterfall, the ram and the old mill-pools: in the book a sense of ominousness hangs over the marshy places with their rank foliage, which subtly suggests Manston's corruption and fills the reader's mind with foreboding. The 'stillness, flatness, and humidity' engendered by them is used to suggest Cytherea's wavering passivity under Manston's oppressive wooing.

On the other hand, the ancient river-walk with its willows

[1] See *Ibid.*, p. 282.
[2] Kingston Maurward was built between 1717-20 and completely cased in Portland stone dressings in 1794. The lake and temple are probably the work of John Pitt of Encombe. See Arthur Oswald's "Manor Houses of Dorset", *Country Life*, 1935.

and trout, its garlands of king-cups in spring and white trailing convolvulus in summer, suggests a different mood. The remarkable causeway which runs between the plaited rivulets of the Frome from Lower Bockhampton, past Stinsford into Dorchester, always charms Hardy. In *Desperate Remedies* Hardy uses it as a setting for the last meeting of the lovers, after Cytherea has been married to Aeneas Manston. The stream with its sandy bottom and shoals of minnows divides them, as in some mediaeval manuscript painting. They stretch their hands across it and are able at last to touch each other. Then Cytherea breaks away and flees back to the great house, and the

> minnows gather together again in their favourite spot as if they had never been disturbed.

One other passage must be mentioned, that in which Manston, in his confession written before he is hanged, states his belief that he is about to enter on 'his normal condition'.

> For people are almost always in their graves. When we survey the long race of men, it is strange and still more strange to find that they are mainly dead men, who have scarcely ever been otherwise.[1]

This metaphysical thought, which T. S. Eliot and François Mauriac[2] have echoed in our century, anticipates a note which Hardy made sixteen years later.

> I was thinking a night or two ago that people are somnambulists —that the material is not the real—only the visible, the real being invisible optically. That it is because we are in a somnambulistic hallucination, that we think the real to be what we see as real.[3]

These three tales—the published and unpublished novel and the novel-in-embryo—reveal marked similarities. In each there is a large amount of biographical material. The heroes of *The Poor Man* and *Desperate Remedies* are architects: the hero of *An Indiscretion* is a schoolmaster and writer, the personification of Hardy's dual inclinations. All three heroes are of (what used to be

[1] p. 457.
[2] See *The Enemy*, p. 275. "Who was it who said to him that action is but another form of sleep? The restless persons of this world are but sleepers. Real life lies elsewhere."
[3] I, p. 243.

called) 'peasant' stock. Hardy has for dramatic reasons purposely lowered their class to intensify the drama, just as he does with the hero of *A Pair of Blue Eyes*. The hero of *The Poor Man* is even called Strong, instead of Hardy: he is a brilliant student and is patronized by the gentry.

In all three tales there are passages showing class-hatred, an emotion which diminishes and is transformed in Hardy's later work. The aristocracy are perhaps not so stupid, so brusque, so pitiless and eccentric as the young Thomas Hardy would have us believe. His great people do not come to life until he learns to pity them and makes us see their weaknesses. In *Desperate Remedies* Miss Aldclyffe is almost regal in her haughtiness.

> Like a good many others in her position [she] had plainly not realized that a son of her tenant and inferior could have become an educated man, who had learnt to feel his individuality, to view society from a Bohemian standpoint, far outside the farming grade in Carriford parish, and that hence he had all a developed man's unorthodox opinion about the subordination of classes.[1]

In this he differs from Meredith who was far more successful with the gentry than he was with humble people.

But there is something more important which links the three tales together: they all contain (1) death-bed scenes, (2) church and churchyard scenes, and (3) they all reveal the fantasy life which, in spite of himself, Hardy delineated for many years to come. Let us consider the death-bed scenes first. When preparing a definitive edition of his works in 1911 Hardy wrote:

> Differing natures find their tongue in the presence of differing spectacles. Some natures become vocal at tragedy, some are made vocal by comedy, and it seems to me that to whichever the more readily responds, to that he should allow it to respond. That before a contrasting side of things he remains undemonstrative need not be assumed to mean that he remains unperceiving.[2]

That Hardy closed his first two novels and *An Indiscretion* with death-bed scenes, and that he continued to wish to do so in future novels, is not mere accident, or a longing for the sensational. Editors afterwards suggested to him that he should please the

---

[1] p. 236. Her name was probably suggested by the neighbouring Elizabethan mansion of *Clyffe*.

[2] Preface to *Tess of the d'Urbervilles*.

public by substituting what are commonly called 'happy end-
ings', but had Hardy had his own choice I believe every one of
his novels (with perhaps the exception of *Under the Greenwood
Tree*) would have closed with the death of either hero or heroine.
The contemplation of death was a fundamental reaction of
his to life. Death is significant to him, above all, because it
means an end of love: it sweeps away forever the chance of
loving with every fibre of one's being taut. The death-bed scenes
also express his conviction that life is intolerably painful, since
we are its victims both in its larger sense, and of life as man has
shaped it 'with custom-straitened views'. Geraldine describes
her life in her letter of renunciation to Egbert as

> woven and tied in with the world by blood, acquaintance, tradi-
> tion, and external habit . . . utterly at the beck of that world's
> customs . . . You have by this time learnt what life is; what partic-
> ular positions accidental though they may be ask, nay, imperatively
> exact from us. If you say "not imperatively" you cannot speak
> from knowledge of the world.[1]

Geraldine escapes through death. Her tranquil end is merely the
precursor of the more deeply tragic, more spectacular one of
Tess, but the tragedy inherent in the last tale was implicit in the
first. Both women, 'frail and sorry wrecks on the sea of life',
were punished and destroyed by going against the 'letter that
killeth'.

Secondly, the church and churchyard scenes. Those in
Hardy's first three tales are the first of many in his prose and
verse. He was once questioned about their frequency and replied
that he supposed he was fond of churchyards because he had
visited them so often as a young architect and had spent many
pleasant hours in them sketching with a friend.[2] He did not seem
to appreciate that they were congruous to his own temperament.
The long hours in Stinsford church as a child, when the
autumnal sadness of an evening service closed down over him
and he watched

> all the people as they stood and sang, waving backwards and
> forwards like a forest of pines swayed by a gentle breeze, then at

---

[1] *An Indiscretion in the Life of an Heiress*, p. 102.
[2] Letter to Sir Sydney Cockerell, March 10, 1922. *Friends of a Lifetime*
(edited by Viola Meynell), p. 291. Cape, 1940.

the village children singing too, their heads inclined to one side, their eyes listlessly tracing some crack in the old walls, or following the movement of a distant bough or bird, with features petrified almost to painfulness . . .[1]

has its counterpart in verse:

> *We watched the elms, we watched the rooks,*
> *The clouds upon the breeze,*
> *Between the whiles of glancing at our books,*
> *And swaying like the trees.*[2]

The family legends of vault-making, the gruesome scenes in old St Pancras churchyard, the frequent journeys to mouldering Gothic churches up and down the country, culminating in that to St Juliot, all combined to weave a powerful threnody in Hardy's mind, with its inherent tendency towards melancholy. Experiences such as these alone would be sufficient to make any ordinary man dwell longer on graves and grave-yards than most, but there is something else involved in their use. An analysis shows that all of the novels, and many of the stories and poems, include either church, or churchyard, scenes. In *A Pair of Blue Eyes* there are nine such, and in *Jude the Obscure* no less than eleven.

How is it that Hardy, if he ceased to be a Christian in the orthodox meaning of the word, so frequently chose these sacred places for his most dramatic and most emotional scenes? We know that Victorian life centred round the church. We know, too, that Hardy's was a mind which delighted in the morbid and the macabre—(even in the melodramatic and maudlin on occasion), in contrasts set sharply one against the other—palpitating, feverish life against a background of cold stone, charnel houses and vaults, implying an end to the fever and fret. Yet there is something which eludes us: if we look at the groups into which these scenes fall the elusive quality becomes increasingly apparent.

The first includes those in which the loved one is seen at a distance, she is worshipped, or spied on, from afar. She may know, or she may not know, that she is being observed, accord-

---

[1] *Desperate Remedies*, p. 271. See also *An Indiscretion*, p. 21.
[2] "Afternoon Service at Mellstock" in *Moments of Vision*.

ing to the novelist's purpose. These scenes involve mild flirtation, willing or unwilling wooing, evaesdropping by onlookers and commentators, and sometimes evil emotions such as covetousness—(Mrs Charmond envies Marty South's shining ropes of hair)—or even revenge. Sometimes the scenes include weeping, and the feeling of intrusion by another: at other times open spying goes on to an astonishing degree. Perhaps the most agonizing use made by Hardy of this theme is when Rhoda in *The Withered Arm* sends her illegitimate child to spy on her former lover's bride in church, bidding him bring her back word of her appearance.

In the second group of scenes the setting is the same, but the action causes a heightening of the emotional tone and great tension. The loved one is observed at some crisis in his, or her, life, and the lover, for various reasons, is powerless to intervene. One word, one act, and the whole train of tragedy might be averted, but Hardy does not put that word into the mouth of hero or heroine, and the tragedy is fulfilled. Or if by chance he, or she, plucks up courage to speak, it is too late.

The third group includes burial and grave-side scenes, involving final renunciations, remorseful considerations and chastened hearts. Troy, in the only sincere act in his life, tends Fanny's grave: the two blind lovers of Elfride (who have come perilously near farce in their journey westward on a train which also carries her body) withdraw to lick their wounds when they see her rightful husband flung across her coffin in the family vault.

Apart from its legitimate uses the church is often the setting for unchristian thoughts and activities. Hardy's sense of humour, his irony, and his realism, relished portraying this fact. Amongst other incongruous uses are a private poetry-reading: the mock-preaching of a sermon by a young girl: smuggling, (deliciously drawn in *The Distracted Preacher*): the use of the vestry for blackmail, the signing of a cheque, the playing of a fateful game of cards, and the drawing of pistols across the vestry table.

But these are incidental scenes which do not involve his own emotions to the same extent. It is in the more lurid, the more Websterian scenes that Hardy is at home. The passions of men

and women 'short sighted in good and evil', as Conrad put it,
are played out beneath the flares of funeral torches; faces
blanched and distorted remind us of the nightmare drawings of
Fuseli, or the Duchess of Malfi's tortures.

Now when a writer wishes to heighten and intensify the mood,
the importance, of a scene he does not choose for his setting a
place which is wreathed with sacred associations for his audience alone. He must share their values and their emotional
reactions, otherwise his scene will ring false, the listener and
reader be unconvinced. He must not be a mocker inside sacred
groves. For all their mawkishness these scenes of Hardy, the
unbeliever, hold the reader. We are faced with a conundrum.
The only solution seems to be that Hardy was still tethered,
emotionally, to the church which he had discarded with his
reason. The thinker had broken with the past, but the imaginative writer still hesitated to accept the thinker's loss of faith. He
felt the pull of both sides and thus, inherently, every truly tragic
tale of his is a personal drama in Hardy's own soul.

For in his best work there is always an element of doubt—a
sense of good intentions gone wrong, of noble qualities mis-
applied, of values squeezed dry of their proper meaning. It is
this trace of uncertainty, and of the holy things of former times
still binding those who are trying to escape into a freer and fuller
life, which makes Hardy's churchyard scenes moving in spite of
their melodrama.

Finally, the fantasy life revealed in *The Poor Man, An Indiscretion*, and subsequent novels—the fantasy of penetration into,
and possession of, the lives and homes of the aristocracy through
the agency of love, or romantic passion. In vain might Alexander Macmillan emphasize that

> King Cophetua and the beggar-maid made a pretty tale in an
> old ballad; but will a story in which the Duke of Edinburgh
> takes in lawful wedlock even a private gentleman's daughter?
> One sees in the papers accounts of gentlemen's daughters running
> away with their fathers' grooms, but you are not in that region.[1]

In vain might he stress Hardy's realistic gifts and attempt to
turn his powers towards the use of these, to persuade him to dis-

[1] Letter to Thomas Hardy, August 10, 1868.

card the romantic fantasy. He would have little success, for he was arguing on the rational level and Hardy's fantasy was deep in the unconscious: its depiction gratified an inner need of his own. He had been bred on tales of Lady Susan's elopement. He had been admired and petted by the lady of the manor as a child. Furthermore Julia Augusta Martin had given him her own niece for partner at the harvest-home dance, and fantasy was converted into fact. Whether Hardy met some attractive, aristocratic girl in his lonely years in London we do not know. He may have done so through Mrs Martin or Arthur Blomfield. Those early poems suggest that he did. But even if he did not the fantasy life within was sufficiently strong for him to weave a romance round some nebulous figure, seen at ballroom or concert.

This line of thought would be pure conjecture were it not for the manner in which Hardy repeatedly lives out the fantasy in his work. Take the poem " A Poor Man and A Lady "[1] 'intended to preserve an episode in the story written in 1868'. In this, the poor man places a ring on the lady's 'pale, slim hand', and the pair consider themselves betrothed. There follows a period of 'timorous secret bliss' in which they are parted.

> *I was a striver with deeds to do,*
> *And little enough to do them with,*
> *And a comely woman of noble kith,*
> *With a courtly match to make, were you.*

In time the news-sheets 'clarion' her betrothal to another—

> *. . . a man of illustrious line and old:*
> *Nor better nor worse than the manifold*
> *Of marriages made, had there not been*
> *Our faith-swearing when fervent-souled,*
> *Which, to me, seemed a breachless bar between.*

But the lady is more of a realist. When she meets the poor man, at his request in a Mayfair church, she argues that they are not married, either in the eyes of the law or of the world. She dismisses him airily, and the question which he longs to ask her

[1] In *Human Shows*.

(whether she still loves him) dies on his lips. They part for ever.

> . . . *The track of a high,*
> *Sweet, liberal lady you've doubtless trod.*
> *—All's past! No heart was burst thereby*
> *And no one knew, unless it was God.*

Here is melodrama mixed with cynicism, and here Hardy, in re-writing the poem, for artistic reasons uses the broken vow, sacred in the eyes of a God whom he no longer believes in, as an ironic climax. But if it was written before Hardy had discarded conventional religion, during, or before, the time when he had thought of entering the church, it takes on a different complexion, for then the poem may contain a filament of autobiography. His rejection of religion may have been hastened by personal disillusion.

Whether the fantasy is based on a fragment of truth or not, Hardy was not content to let it drop after writing the novel and poem of the same title. Will Strong is supplanted by Edward Springrove, Stephen Smith, Egbert Mayne, George Somerset and Swithin St Cleeve.[1] In *The Hand of Ethelberta* he undergoes a sea-change and his place is taken by the high-handed butler's daughter who weds a peer of the realm. Where the heroine is not an aristocrat she is either adopted by the lady of the manor, is descended vaguely from a titled forbear, or she inhabits the manor house or castle which the poor man covets, and eventually gains as his own. On marrying Cytherea, Edward is able to inhabit the very house which the child Thomas had entered as a favourite and from which he had been abruptly excluded. In *A Pair of Blue Eyes* Hardy has the double satisfaction of feeding the fantasy through Elfride who marries Lord Luxellian, and secondly through Stephen Smith and Knight (the architect and the literary man, representing twin aspects of Hardy's character), both of whom woo the future Baroness. The fantasy in this novel is complex and is dwelt on in more detail than in the other novels with which we are concerned.

English literature is steeped in the ups-and-downs of social

---

[1] In *Desperate Remedies, A Pair of Blue Eyes, An Indiscretion, A Laodicean,* and *Two on a Tower.*

rank. Marriage, inter-marriage, and mis-matings between members of dis-similar classes, were stock themes of the Victorian novelists. Hardy employed them in part to give tension and conflict to his work. Owing to his birth and background, his sensitivity and powers of perception, his gifts and superior education, he was able to observe the ramifications of social strata with a piercing eye.

> The defects of a class are more perceptible to the class immediately below it than to itself . . . [1]

he cynically noted down when he was twenty-six. He was perfectly aware, as Virginia Woolf puts it, that what appears to be

> the vast equality of the middle classes is, in truth, nothing of the sort. All through the social mass run curious veins and streakings separating man from man and woman from woman; mysterious prerogatives, and disabilities too ethereal to be distinguished by anything so crude as a title, impede and disorder the great business of human intercourse.[2]

But there is something more than acute perception in Hardy's attitude, something which can only be explained as an inner fantasy life, which John Morley recognized in *The Poor Man and the Lady* when he said that it read like 'a clever lad's dream'.

Hardy's employer, Crickmay, could not do without his assistant for long. Before Thomas had been in retirement at Bockhampton a week he wrote asking whether he would go down into Cornwall for him. Hardy refused, since he wished to complete his novel. A second letter came and, as he had finished all but the final chapters, he agreed to go, first despatching the novel to Macmillan, 'whom he now regarded as a friend'.

His journey was undertaken with reluctance. Owing to the distance of St Juliot from Bockhampton he had to rise at four on a cold March morning (1870).

> The candle flame had a sad and yellow look when it was brought into his bedroom . . . Few things will take away a man's confidence in an impulsive scheme more than being called up by candlelight upon a chilly morning to commence working it out.[3]

---

[1] I, p. 72.
[2] "The Niece of an Earl" in *The Common Reader*, 2nd Series, p. 215. Hogarth Press, 1935.   [3] *An Indiscretion*, p. 78.

Carrying his sketch-book, measuring-tape and rule, Hardy stepped out into the starlight and began his long cross-country journey. He reached Launceston at four in the afternoon but he had a further seventeen miles to go, by wagonette. With an almost nautical keenness of observation he noted that, although the day had been fine, the evening was cloudy, and that there was 'a dry breeze blowing'. He reached St Juliot Rectory in the dark. One of Hardy's most lyrical poems, (not one of his most characteristic), recaptures the spirit of that journey, after its felicitous outcome.

> When I set out for Lyonesse,
>   A hundred miles away,
>   The rime was on the spray.
> And starlight lit my lonesomeness
> When I set out for Lyonesse
>   A hundred miles away.[1]

[1] In *Satires of Circumstance*.

CHAPTER SIX

ST JULIOT AND THE STURMINSTER IDYLL

Love for me has always been the most—perhaps the only—
important thing in life.

STENDHAL

ST Juliot, or St Jilt as the country people used to call it, is a
small parish lying about two miles east of Boscastle with its
tortuous, rockbound harbour. With his poet's love of sound
and strange romantic names Hardy had already been drawn
to St Juliot three years ago, when first working for Hicks, and it
is likely that his love of history and ancient things would lead
him to take note of other Cornish names deriving from the
Celtic. Nor could he fail to be attracted to the wild beauty of
that rocky coast, whose winds are so savage in winter that even
the tombstones are buttressed against them, and beams and
spars of wrecked ships in barton, barn, or byre are witness to its
onslaughts.

It was formerly a place steeped in legend and superstition.
Legends of Arthur and Uther Pendragon still cling to Tintagel,[1]
Damelioc and Kelly Rounds, three places, not far distant, more
closely associated with these heroes than a thousand spurious
ones. Tales of black magic, shipwreck and piracy, of the
cruelty of the people who did not trouble to bury the dead
whom they plundered on the shore, were rife; tales, too, of the
great-hearted eccentricities of Parson Hawker of Morwenstow,
a friend of Hardy's host, who lived twenty miles off.

The ecclesiastical architect had long been awaited at the
Rectory, but it was dark when he arrived and by some mis-
chance there was no one to greet him, except a girl whom
Hardy mistook for the Rector's daughter, or sister. She was in
fact his sister-in-law. The Reverend Mr Holder was suffering
from gout and his wife had gone to attend to him. It was the
fate of Emma Lavinia Gifford to receive Thomas Hardy—a
person of great importance in her eyes because of his duties, her

---

[1] There is also a ruined chapel dedicated to St Julietta, or Julitta, in
Tintagel Castle.

devotion to the church, and the long drawn-out suspense with which the household had awaited his arrival for several years—quite alone. The isolation of the parish and Rectory, to which few strangers ever came, also made his intrusion a disturbing event. She received him with a feeling of 'curious, uneasy embarrassment'.[1] What she saw was a young man who looked older than he was because of his beard, clad in a shabby great-coat, from whose pocket there protruded a sheet of paper. A plan for the church, she thought, but it was in fact a poem.

> I was immediately arrested by his familiar appearance, as if I had seen him in a dream—his slightly different accent [and] his soft voice.

(It may be stated here that Hardy did not, as some writers have suggested, speak in the Dorset dialect. Like many others in country districts who mingled with the work-people, but held themselves aloof from pride in superior blood, craftsmanship, or intelligence, he was bi-lingual, speaking the broad, bold dialect when it pleased him to old friends and intimates but more generally the harder King's English, the use of which William Barnes deplored. Thus Hardy told Vere Collins:

> I did not speak it [the local dialect]. I knew it, but it was not spoken at home. My mother only used it when speaking to the cottagers, and my father when speaking to his workmen.[2])

What Thomas Hardy saw was a woman who appeared younger than she was, of medium height and graceful carriage, dressed in brown. Her features were irregular; she had deep-set, blue-grey eyes, a colour that came and went like 'rose-flush', and a mass of bright hair. Hardy was instantly attracted to something which he himself (from all accounts) seems to have lacked—her vitality, her 'liveness', as he called it. As for Emma Gifford's hair, Hardy never forgot its colour and texture, and after she was dead he recalled it in repeated poems. In one she is described as 'broad-browed and brown-tressed', in others he speaks of her 'brown' or 'bright hair flapping free', in another it is 'nut-coloured', in another 'squirrel-coloured', and in yet another it 'beams with live and brightest brown'. In *The Early*

---

[1] The following quotations are taken from Emma Gifford's *Recollections*, written the year before her death, part of which were printed in *The Early Life of Thomas Hardy*. See pp. 88-96.   [2] p. 74.

Life and in "This Summer and Last" it is called 'corn-brown' and 'corn-coloured': the artist who painted Miss Gifford gave her yellow hair. There is an un-noticed portrait-in-words of her in *Desperate Remedies* the novel which Hardy wrote before he met her. Its presence is explained by the fact that, in making a fair copy for the publishers, Emma Gifford helped him: by then Hardy was in love with her, and out of compliment he made the image of the imagined Cytherea tally with that of the living woman. After a long paragraph in which he describes the extraordinary gracefulness of Cytherea's carriage and movement—a characteristic which he admired in Emma Gifford—he says that her hair

> rested gaily upon her shoulders in curls, and was of a shining corn-yellow in the high lights, deepening to a definite nut-brown as each curl wound round into the shade. She had eyes of a sapphire hue, though rather darker than the gem ordinarily appears: they possessed the affectionate and liquid sparkle of loyalty and good faith, as distinguishable from that harder brightness which seems to express faithfulness only to the object confronting them.[1]

The poet says elsewhere that loyalty to him was one of her outstanding chracteristics.

Emma Lavinia's religious convictions made her feel that each step in her life had led her forward with singular intention to this provident meeting. Hardy on the other hand felt no such conviction.

> *I beheld not where all was so fleet*
> *That a Plan of the past*
> *Which had ruled us from birthtime to meet*
> *Was accomplished at last.*[2]

That evening, and on another occasion, there was music, the sisters singing duets. The next day Hardy conscientiously carried out his architectural duties. He remained most of the day drawing and measuring in the church, only returning to the house for meals, and in the evening when it was dark. He found the Cornish landscape austere and grey, dreary yet poetical. It was singular, but somehow congruous, that on his first day there

---

[1] *Desperate Remedies*, p. 8.
[2] "At the Word 'Farewell'" in *Moments of Vision*.

should be a funeral, and he was struck by the primitive manner in which the bell was tolled. Owing to the condition of the tower the bells had all been taken down and rested comically on the ground 'with their mouths opening upward'. A man made a semblance of ringing one by picking up the clapper and dropping it against the bell's sides. This incident somehow epitomized the forlorn, decayed state of the ruined church, with its dilapidated tower and nave. But Hardy noted the Saxon north door, and the ancient benches with their carved ends, and his drawings of these are preserved in St Juliot church.

On the second day he was carried off by the ladies to Boscastle, Tintagel, and the slate quarries at Penpethy from which the church roofing was to come. He never afterwards saw green slate roofs, or stacked slate in 'waggon, truck or lorry', without being carried back to that entranced time.[1] The following day he walked beside Emma Lavinia, who rode her brown mare Fanny, to Beeny Cliff, and in the afternoon the sisters accompanied him part of the way to Boscastle again, 'E. provokingly reading as she walked'.[2] At dawn the next day he had to be off. Three tantalizingly brief days, for Hardy left his heart behind him in Cornwall. He returned to Bockhampton a changed man, acknowledging that many new doors in life had been opened to him—the door of the West, the door of Romance, and the door of Love.[3]

Emma Gifford was born in the same year as Hardy,[4] in Plymouth, near the Hoe. (They were both twenty-nine when they met.) Her father was a solicitor, and her uncle a Canon of Worcester Cathedral, afterwards Archdeacon of London. From all that we can learn of her as a young woman she seems to have been impulsive, capable, courageous, and vital, possessing a certain child-like quality whereby she attracted and endeared herself to people, which never deserted her.[5] In her sister's home she cut down the household expenses, in order to contribute to the church restoration. Hardy tells us how (later) she took

---

[1] See "Green Slates" in *Human Shows*.   [2] I, p. 99.
[3] "She Opened the Door" in *Human Shows*.
[4] On November 24, 1840.
[5] Florence Hardy told Vere Collins in 1920 that she "kept to the end a strange lovableness—a gay, inconsequent, childlike charm". Privately printed note to *The Love Poetry of Thomas Hardy*.

E

command of a domestic situation long before he had roused himself: how she courageously wished to reprimand a coachman for maltreating his horses, and how fearless she was when riding; how lost he and the servants were in their home when she was unwell. She loved animals and growing things and once, when the greenhouse stove at the Rectory had been neglected and all the plants had died, her face became 'the very symbol of tragedy'.[1] She was fond of picnics, parties, and gaiety, and the small things of life which make up so much of its happiness.

She was also accustomed to solitude. In the artless reminiscences which she wrote before her death she gives us a delightful picture of her life at St Juliot—a wild, untrammelled life in which (when she was not attending to domestic, or church, duties, such as playing the organ) she scampered over the clifftops and down the steep, rough roads on her brown pony. She loved the sea in its wilder moods, especially in winter when it rolled in on that rocky coast with tumultuous waves and leaping far-flung spray. For her the Atlantic had a power, then, 'to awaken heart and soul'. In summer, Fanny might stop and browse while her mistress gathered wild-flowers, or made water-colour sketches, or clambered down over, what Hardy calls, 'the red-veined rocks'[2] of the west to the haunts of the seals. She was never happier than on these solitary rides and rambles, looking down on the little 'solemn shores' far below, 'wanting no protection', the rain sometimes going down the back of her trim brown habit, and her hair floating free on the wind. The image of her riding thus stamped itself on Hardy's mind once and for all. In the tragic sequence of poems written to her memory immediately after her death he sees the phantom rider, whom time cannot touch:

> *But she still rides gaily*
> *In his rapt thought*
> *On that shagged and shaly*
> *Atlantic spot,*
> *And as when first eyed*
> *Draws rein and sings to the swing of the tide.*[3]

[1] "The Frozen Greenhouse" in *Human Shows*.
[2] "The Going" in *Poems of 1912-13*.
[3] "The Phantom Horsewoman" in *Satires of Circumstance*.

The Cornish Coast near Boscastle

(Setting of the *Poems of 1912–13* and *A Pair of Blue Eyes*)

The nameless mounted figure whom he had idolized as a boy in the Dorchester Walks appeared in new and more tempting guise.

During the years 1867-70, when Hardy had been working for Hicks and Crickmay, St Juliot church had continued to moulder silently away. The faithful had anxiously watched the tower cracking further, the bench ends rot, and the ivy stretch its pale tendrils like long antennae into the crevices of the roof-timbers, amongst which the bats hung and the birds nested. Under Crickmay's supervision it was finally restored and the foundation stone laid by Emma Gifford. "I plastered it well, the foreman said." (This was just such a scene as Hardy had already described in *An Indiscretion* and possibly in *The Poor Man and the Lady*.) The work of restoration went on for four years, necessitating visits to Cornwall 'two or three times a year,' which Hardy was quick to seize as his prerogative. Rising once at four in the morning and priding himself on his early start he was astonished to hear a neighbour merrily whistling and whetting his scythe in the June hayfields.

Meanwhile, in March 1870, he returned to Weymouth to report to Crickmay and to work on the St Juliot plans. But he was restless and dissatisfied and in May he went up to London again in order to place *Desperate Remedies*. Using his architectural work as a stop-gap he agreed to help Blomfield out temporarily, as well as a friend of his, Raphael Brandon, a lover of English Gothic and 'a person suspect in the architectural profession' because he was 'a literary architect', who had published books on Gothic and mediaeval architecture. This remark throws light on Hardy's quandary and his low spirits during this transitional period in his life. (His copy of *Hamlet* bears a date on the margin, *Dec.* 15, 1870, and the passage, "Thou wouldst not think how ill all's here about my heart: but it is no matter", is under-scored.[1]) If he let it be known that he was a novelist, and an unsuccessful one at that, his architectural reputation would suffer, and if he failed as an architect he could not live on his earnings as a writer. Nor was he in a position to claim or support a wife.

He was clearly marking time, dining occasionally with

[1] I, p. 109.

Horace Moule, and studying painting in the galleries. When the Franco-Prussian war broke out Hardy's thoughts went back to boyhood tales in Dorset of the Napoleonic struggle. He was drawn to make the first of many memorable visits to the Chelsea Hospital where his inspection of the tattered banners, and conversations with the veterans of Waterloo and the Peninsular War, nourished thoughts for *The Dynasts*, slumbering unshapen in his mind.

Once Emma Gifford came to town to visit her brother, and once they went to Bath together where Hardy's critical eye described that city's 'rural complexion on an urban substance'.[1] But the distance of London, or Weymouth, from St Juliot, and the relative poverty of both Thomas and Emma meant that they seldom met. However, letters and 'a good deal of manuscript . . . went to and fro by post', and Emma was 'proud and happy' to help the man she had grown to love. When they came together they

> sketched and talked of books . . . We grew much interested in each other. I found him a perfectly new subject of study and delight, and he found 'a mine' in me he said. He was quite unlike any other person who came to see us, for they were slow of speech and ideas.

(That word 'mine' is strongly reminiscent of Donne's impassioned elegy.)

> The rarity of the visits made them highly delightful to both; we talked much of plots, possible scenes, tales and poetry, and of his own work.

The manuscript which went backwards and forwards was *Desperate Remedies*, and others followed suit. When Hardy, in 1871, discouraged at what he thought was Macmillan's rejection of *Under the Greenwood Tree*, determined to write no more, it was Emma Gifford who insisted that he 'adhere to authorship which she felt sure would be his true vocation'.[2] Her encouragement was all the more remarkable since it was completely selfless—

> she set herself aside altogether—architecture being obviously the quick way to an income for marrying on.[3]

[1] I, p. 123.   [2] I, p. 114.   [3] *Ibid.*

In January of the new year (1871) Hardy was at Bockhampton taking down snatches of ballads from old people. It would be interesting to know what these were—whether, for instance, those used in *The Return of the Native* were amongst them. Off and on he worked for Crickmay, lodging in Weymouth, his writing and architectural work being varied by the rare visits to Cornwall. On returning from one of these he was pained to see his novel[1] remaindered at half-a-crown for the three volumes. That the reviewer felt he had been over-harsh is obvious from the fact that he sent Hardy an unsolicited apology. His victim magnanimously forgave him and won the critic over, making him his friend. But he was still the victim of depression and underlined in his *Macbeth*:

> *Things at their worst will cease, or else climb upward*
> *To what they were before.*[2]

Yet shortly after marking this passage Hardy completed the most lyrical, most light-hearted of all his prose works—*Under the Greenwood Tree*.

He had gone once more to London where he made odd drawings for Blomfield, and assisted another London architect[3] in designing schools. Together they proved successful in the competitions arranged by the London School Board. Ironically enough Hardy always excelled at the work in which his heart did not lie. The picture of the young architect, late in establishing himself as a writer (he was now thirty-two), bending over the proofs of his rustic idyll late at night in his Bayswater lodgings is a moving one. In these same rooms he also wrote the first chapters of his next novel, for the writer had committed himself to Tinsley for a twelve months' serial shortly after the appearance of *Under the Greenwood Tree*.

This book is the most artistically balanced of all Hardy's prose work and so fresh that, as in Constable's paintings, 'the dew seems still to be on the hedgerows'. Even that canny old publisher William Tinsley, who had a sharp eye for financial rather than literary values, had to admit that it was 'as pure and sweet as new-mown hay'. Oddly enough, although it was liked it did not sell quickly, even in a two-shilling paper edition.

[1] *Desperate Remedies.*   [2] I, p. 113.   [3] Professor of Architecture at the R.I.B.A.

It is the lightweight amongst Hardy's masterpieces and in several ways it is singular.

The book depicts real, not imaginary scenes, a blending of Dorset life in Hardy's and his parents' and grandparents' day. It has that rare thing in his work, a happy ending with only a suspicion of trouble to come between hero and heroine. The theme of the uprooted, of which Hardy is so fond, obtrudes but slightly here. Although Fancy's father emphasizes her superior education and her mother's social standing she lets her heart be won, not by the Vicar who has wooed her with the promise of a lady's toys and joys (a pony carriage, a piano, flowers, tame birds and 'pleasant society') but by good solid Dick, son of a haulier or tranter, and himself a tranter-to-be.

This prose idyll is in part a paraphrase of some of Barnes' poems,[1] but there is nothing imitative about it. Each could write of young people going nutting, the taking of honey and swarming of the bees, a wise woman consulted for her advice over a love affair, Christmas scenes, and domestic warmth and gaiety, in his own way. Both rightly saw that the great chimney which thrusts its bulk up through the home's centre, which warms the new-born and the old, and to a child's mind seems to say 'I was here before you and shall be here when you are gone', is a symbol of life's core. But Barnes writes of the back-brand and the fire-light with a hungry nostalgia almost unbearable in its lyric intensity, as if he could not get domestic warmth. One remembers that he was orphaned early and excluded from his rightful inheritance of acres, which he loved so dearly that he could never bear to be far from them, and of which he bought back a few in old age. Hardy, being younger, sees with a clearer eye that the narrowing of the old hearths is a symbol of the passing of age-old domesticity, of a time when the stranger at the door was always welcome, and life began and ended round the fireside.

He may also owe the sub-title of this book—*A Rural Painting of the Dutch Schoool*—to William Barnes, for the latter had published eleven years before his essay *Thoughts on Beauty and Art*,[2] in which he praised the "beauty and truth of colour and action

---

[1] See Rutland, p. 10.
[2] *Macmillan's Magazine*, May-October 1861.

in the Dutch school". (In this, surprisingly enough, he also
admires Turner's late explosive work). Hardy's solitary study
of painting first led him to admire the Dutch and the Flemish
painters, whose sincerity and realism, warmth and liveliness,
spoke to him with direct accents, reminding him of his own
background. Thus we have those domestic interiors, minutely
noted, which glow like one of these homely paintings—Geoffrey
Day's storehouse with its bunches of dried herbs, ropes of clean
onions, red and yellow apples, potato piles, empty skeps and
barrels of new cider; or the lusty dancing on the sanded floor
of the tranter's house. From this background and from his
contact with scenes like these, Hardy was slowly estranging
himself by his work, his study of literature and art, his sojourns
in the capital, and his thoughts of marrying a Canon's niece.

Hardy's intention was to make *Under the Greenwood Tree* 'a
study of a little group of church musicians'. The drawing of the
other characters, the love story, the plot were all incidental to
this main purpose. The old Quire, which appears like an unpredictable comet here and there in Hardy's prose and verse, is
the excuse for the tale.

Many years later, when he looked back on this early work, he
regretted that he had seemed to burlesque the Quire and had
inadequately endowed its members 'with the poetry and romance that coloured their time-honoured observances'.[1] It
has sometimes been said that Hardy created types too quaintly
bucolic to be real. Yet one reviewer on the book's appearance
complained that the rustics 'were not rustic enough'.[2] But if we
compare some of the incidents and the pervading spirit of the
book with notes from another county we find that, far from
having presented a picture of men and their times purely local
in colour, Hardy has created characters and an atmosphere
general at least in the south and south-west of England for close
on one hundred years. The men of the Dorset church bands and
choirs (they were never called orchestras) were shepherds,
thatchers and farm-labourers, cobblers and tranters. Those
recorded in Sussex were, in addition, smiths, gardeners, farmers
and village schoolmasters. In this latter county as many as
twenty-four different kinds of instruments were used by them,

[1] I, p. 15.   [2] *The Athenaeum*, June 15, 1872.

ranging from bassoons and banjos to concertinas, triangles, vamp horns and serpents,[1] those hideous old instruments of leather and wood whose tonal inequalities were such that they drove even the men of the battlefield of Waterloo to distraction, according to one musical critic.

Both in Dorset and Sussex it was considered an hereditary honour to play or sing in the choir; families proudly counted up the years during which they had served church and parish through successive generations. The connection of Hardy's family with the Stinsford church music covered three generations, and more than a hundred years. To sit in the old west galleries was a coveted honour and the gallery people looked down on the congregation, in more senses than one, as Hardy has pointed out with delightful humour.[2]

Hardy is careful to emphasize that the Stinsford choir consisted entirely of strings, whereas the larger and noisier bands of neighbouring villages included brass and reed. Stinsford eschewed such vulgarity and was content with four excellent players, bass and treble viol, and tenor and second violins, with a good sprinkling of singers. This string band whose players were Hardy's grandfather, father and uncle, and a certain James Dart, prided itself on never being 'unduly emphatic, strident, or over-sonorous'.[3]

The extinction of instrumental music in our village churches entailed the death, too, of that spirit of friendly co-operation which the singing and playing engendered between choir, parishioners and Vicar, as Hardy ably pointed out in his preface.[4] The introduction of the barrel-organ, harmonium, and its 'feeble sister the American organ, was nothing short of a disaster'.[5]

That Thomas Hardy should have been born at that moment when the Stinsford quire was dying is an odd prank of fortune, for no one would have been a more fervent player than he. Yet we might have been the poorer: his ardour might have evaporated in evanescent music-making rather than in preserving for

---

[1] See K. R. Macdermott, *Sussex Church Music in the Past.* Chichester, 1923.
[2] See *Under the Greenwood Tree*, p. 48.
[3] I, p. 12.   [4] To the 1896 edition.
[5] Canon F. W. Galpin's *Old English Instruments of Music*, 1910.

us 'the old musicianers' with their boundless energy, fervent diligence, homely piety and simple sincerity. No one but Hardy, either during their lifetimes or after their official demise, recognized their signal importance and paid them tribute: he alone has re-created for us the spirit of those vanished groups so curiously neglected by novelists, diarists, and musical historians.

We are told in the *Early Life* that Hardy chose Shakespeare's words for his title because poetic titles were in fashion at the time. The book might well have been dedicated to Hardy's father, for the "Song" from *As you like It* suggests this humorous, philosophical man who loved his neighbours and music, shunned ambition, and 'loved to lie i' the sun'. If we owe to Jemima Hardy the writer's love of the old ballads which she used to sing to him, and his appreciation of that fine old carol like a Bach chorale, *Remember Adam's Fall*, which he had from her[1], we owe to his father many tales of ancient customs (recorded in the notes) and no doubt most of the anecdotes concerning the old quire. The numerous fiddlings together for weddings, christenings and other 'randies', involved long walks through woodland and pasture, and all the lore of this ancient body might be poured out in male conspiracy, away from fireside chatter and woman's 'clack'.

Under the Greenwood Tree reveals another important thing for the first time, Hardy's extreme responsiveness to music, only hinted at previously in *An Indiscretion* and in *Desperate Remedies*. The mesmeric quality of music is the theme of many of Hardy's poems, novels and stories. The supreme example is "The Fiddler of the Reels"[2] in which its malefic effects are drawn with mastery. The fiddling of Mop Olamoor, the unscrupulous musician with the foreign air which men distrust and women are drawn to, is described as having a peculiar and personal quality, 'like that in a moving preacher'. In this simile sacred and secular intermingle as in the old song books used by the Quire. Mop's playing has 'a lingual character in the supplicatory expressions which would have drawn an ache from a gate-post'. In *Far from the Madding Crowd* Susan Tall's husband admits that 'when tunes are going I seem as if hung on wires'; and the dancers on Egdon move in a delirium of exquisite

---

[1] See Rutland, p. 158.   [2] In *Life's Little Ironies*.

emotion in *The Return of the Native*. Selina wears the 'rapt expression of a somnambulist' as she dances:[1] Tess sits motionless 'like a fascinated bird' while Angel plays his harp; Margery, the impressionable milkmaid, is lured from her lover by its persuasions; and the 'regal power of music' is twice emphasized in *The Mayor of Casterbridge*. Delight is always mixed with pain: music, dancing and tears are never far apart in Hardy's responsive being: 'the aching of the heart', and 'blissful torture' are phrases expressing the slavish abandon of the dancer *against his, or her, will* to both tune and emotion, abandon to a power which smacks of witchcraft and enchantment. Even in the rustic simplicity of the tranter's house the evil goddess appears for the length of a minim, or quaver, when Dick suspects his rival, the odious Shiner, of enticing more warmth and glances from Fancy than he should. The ecstatic abandonment to both music and dance is here, too, and plain-sailing Dick succumbs to it:

> The room became to [him] like a picture in a dream; all that he could remember of it afterwards being the look of the fiddlers going to sleep, as humming-tops sleep, by increasing their motion and hum.[2]—

Hardy had made several visits to Cornwall since that first March evening when he arrived at St Juliot in the dark. The region remained for him one of

> dream and mystery. The ghostly birds, the pall-like sea, the frothy wind, the eternal soliloquy of the waters, the bloom of dark purple cast, that seems to exhale from the shoreward precipices, in themselves lend to the scene an atmosphere like the twilight of a night vision.[3]

The features of the craggy coast were for him 'wild and tragic', accustomed as he was to the less spectacular, more friendly white and golden cliffs of his native county. It is not surprising that *A Pair of Blue Eyes*, his first serial novel, is one of his most poetic, both in execution and conception, a favourite with Tennyson and Coventry Patmore. The question as to whether

---

[1] "Enter a Dragoon" in *A Changed Man and Other Tales*.
[2] *Under the Greenwood Tree*, p. 68.
[3] Preface to *A Pair of Blue Eyes*, 1896.

it contains more strictly biographical material than the other Wessex novels has already been thoroughly argued by many critics. But three details may be added. First, one concerning the question of the status and occupation of Stephen Smith's father, over which Hardy waxed hot when a writer identified the character with Hardy's own. He told Vere Collins in 1920-2:

> His father was not at all like mine. He was a Cornishman and a journeyman.[1]

It is obvious that Hardy, either in looking back over a period of fifty years or in his original conception of this character, was confused, for on page 33 of the novel he describes John Smith as a 'master mason'. On page 82 he calls him a 'cottager and journeyman mason', and on page 85 he is 'Lord Luxellian's master-mason' again, 'who lives under the park wall by the river'. John Smith's *character* is scarcely developed at all so that Hardy cannot have been contradicting an assumption that his father's and the Cornishman's differed.

Secondly, there is a scene on board a steamer which carries Elfride and her lover and family to Cornwall. Hardy had himself made this trip by water from London Bridge, on one of the Irish Mail Packets which went to the bottom shortly afterwards.

Then too, as everyone knows, Elfride's second lover, Knight, clings for his life to the face of a cliff, a scene in which Hardy, like John Donne in his poetry and sermons, introduced current scientific discoveries—in this case geological—into his prose. No one that I am aware of has remarked on the fact that Emma Gifford, in her *Recollections*, tells how as a child she had been rescued by a boatman from the Plymouth cliffs, where she had been 'clinging to a crag' in danger of her life. The adventure repeated to Hardy may have suggested his famous scene to him. The introduction of the trilobite, a creature with eyes 'dead and turned to stone' which stare back at Knight, is astonishingly successful and finds no parallel in writings of the period.

Another vivid scene in the book is that in which Knight tests

[1] p. 74.

Elfride's courage, intelligence and endurance in a chess-match, a scene which anticipates the tension of the more dramatic one in *The Return of the Native* in which Venn and Wildeve play for Thomasin's gold by the light of glow-worms. Chess may have been a favourite game of the Vicar's at St Juliot; Emma Gifford may have played it herself, for she describes her lover's first approach from a remote hamlet in Dorset, to an even more remote one in north-west Cornwall, as 'a sort of cross-jump journey like a chess-knight's move'.[1]

For the first time Hardy published a novel under his name, and the *Saturday Review* praised it for its 'singular purity of thought and intention'. The poetical quality permeates the tragedy, which is touching rather than searing, since the three protagonists submit to, rather than contend with, their fate, or with each other. For the first time, too, he openly displayed his despondent attitude to life. Elfride, Knight and Stephen Smith all frantically seek their way into life through the agency of love: all idealize the beloved to a dangerous degree, and are heart-broken when they collide with reality. (So persistent is this characteristic in Hardy's work that we are tempted to attribute it to the author himself.) Finally, all three are left, not embittered, but thwarted and baulked by life, hungry of heart and unfulfilled. Here, for the first time, Hardy dared to be himself, to state what he felt about life, death, and the inevitable fate of his characters.

The unequal quality of the writing, which we come to associate with even the best of Hardy's work, is apparent here. Through the romantic poetry and the exquisite descriptions there obtrude the stilted drawing-room conversations and episodes of society-life, like geological upthrusts. The scene in Rotten Row is perhaps a variant of the one which Macmillan had praised in *The Poor Man and the Lady*. Here, too, is a delicate description of night sounds, one of those which show us the countryman's ear. Hardy actually describes the noise which an earthworm makes when drawing a leaf down into the soil, and this humble creature may be called ancestor to the worms mentioned in *Jude* and *The Dynasts*.

From the human point of view the most interesting thing

[1] I, p. 92.

about this novel is Hardy's changing attitude to women, which he shows in a single sentence.

> It is a melancholy thought that men who at first will not allow the verdict of perfection they pronounce upon their sweethearts, or wives, to be disturbed by God's own testimony to the contrary, will, once suspecting their purity, morally hang them upon evidence they would be ashamed to admit in judging a dog.[1]

This is a highly significant sentence, for at this moment Hardy turns from his condemnatory attitude towards the aristocratic woman and, entering into the woman's point of view, condemns instead the prevalent attitude of current society towards womankind. His own compassion has been aroused and through this sympathy his women begin to live as human beings, not mere figments of intellectual imagination. Here, nearly twenty years before the writing of *Tess*, is Angel Clare's problem in embryo: here the same theme of chastity endangered; here the first championing of woman against an attitude which destroys her. Elfride succumbs because she acknowledges the rightness of current opinion; she has not the strength to vindicate herself to Knight, and she collapses, morally and physically. Her 'reluctance to tell . . . arose from simplicity in thinking herself so much more culpable than she really was': she straightway relinquished the hope of 'direct explanation' and of extenuation.

The tale is again concerned with the fantasy life discussed above. We are not surprised to hear that the basic plot had been roughed out long before Hardy had been to Cornwall, for chronologically (according to the date of conception, not perfection or publication) it belongs to the period of *The Poor Man and the Lady*. Here, once again, are the pathetic child-lovers who have plighted their troth and consider themselves irrevocably one. The introduction of Knight, Hardy's other half, is merely an added complication. This second lover wrings from Elfride an avowal of her early attachment: he assumes that she has been tarnished, in name if not in fact and, being an idealistic prig like Angel Clare, he promptly deserts her. The heroine, as in *The Poor Man*, marries the neighbouring man of property, Lord Luxellian, which she does (once again) to please her father. And

---

[1] pp. 398-9.

then, like the heroines of *The Poor Man* and *An Indiscretion*, broken by life, she dies. Since we are dealing with early fantasies we are not surprised to meet the ghost of Lady Susan O'Brien, in a Cornish instead of a Dorset vault. Even the frothy mugs of ale, which Hardy had been told lightened the thirsty building of that lady's and her husband-lover's tomb, are introduced to give a homely atmosphere, for these west-country workmen are as much at home in a vault as in their own sandstone, or granite, cottages: and although (as so frequently remarked) this scene smells of Shakespeare, it also derives from historical fact— from real life and legend.

By the time that Hardy created Tess, the fluttering bird-like Elfride and the uncertain Cytherea, turning this way and that to escape their fate, had developed into a magnificent figure of womanhood, but the element of masochistic self-sacrifice remained. The fact that Hardy never abandoned this original theme of mis-mating, desertion and belated return to the first love, implies that he was writing not merely from the conventional point of view, or for a popular market, but from his own inner conflicts, never fully resolved, which have something of an obsessional nature. Meanwhile in this early novel Hardy has only reached the stage in his artistic development where Elfride lies in her satinwood coffin with its shining scutcheon while her lovers mourn over her.

One winter's day, while Hardy was in retreat at Bockhampton writing *A Pair of Blue Eyes*, a workman came to the house bearing a mud-stained letter which the children, entrusted with its care, had dropped in the lane. It was written in a spidery hand which might have been traced with a pin-point and was from the new editor of the *Cornhill Magazine*, Leslie Stephen. He asked Hardy for a serial story since he had much admired the freshness in writing of *Under the Greenwood Tree*. Hardy explained his commitments and promised Stephen that he should have his next tale, which he had envisaged as a pastoral one whose characters were to be a woman farmer, a shepherd and a sergeant of cavalry. The editor agreed to the outline and suggested that the writer should call on him when next in town; but Hardy and Stephen did not meet for more than a year.

Hardy remained in seclusion, drenching himself in the familiar scene. In the autumn he walked to Woodbury Hill Fair which took place annually in an ancient earthwork, dyked and fossed about, near Bere Regis. This was formerly one of the largest sheep-fairs in the south of England : it lasted for three weeks, the first day being known as Gentlefolks' Day and the last as Pack-and-Penny Day. Unfortunately, like Weyhill and Pummery Fairs, it has now declined in both size and importance. Here amongst packmen, drovers, gypsies, travelling showmen, horse- and cattle-dealers jostling elbows with the pleasure seekers, Hardy found material for both *Far from the Madding Crowd* and the future *Mayor of Casterbridge*. The image of this, or other fairs, remained with him so clearly that when he came to write *The Dynasts* he could easily describe the arms of the French forces wheeling into their fighting positions on the field of Waterloo as 'glittering like a display of cutlery at a hill-side fair'.[1] He also took part in the cider-making at home for the last time, a scene dear to his heart which he had already described in *Desperate Remedies* and was to do again in *The Woodlanders*.

He wrote sometimes indoors, sometimes without, using

large dead leaves, white chips of wood left by the wood-cutters, or pieces of stone or slate, that came to hand. When he carried a pocket-book his mind was as barren as the Sahara.[2]

Here surely was a warning for him to heed, for Hardy's most poetic, most imaginative work springs from his instinctive roots. When theorizing, intellectualizing, propagating ideas culled from continental thinkers, from J. S. Mill and other English philosophers, his work becomes turgid and does not ring true.

But any joy which he may have found in the growing power visible throughout his new novel, *Far from the Madding Crowd*, must have been stifled by news of the tragic death of Horace Moule[3] at the early age of forty-one. The night before his body was brought to Fordington Hardy 'sat on the eve-lit weir' and

---

[1] Part III, Sc. I, p. 484. [2] I, p. 127.
[3] He is said to have committed suicide. See H. C. Webster, *On a Darkling Plain*. Univ. of Chicago Press, 1947.

studied 'the towered church on the rise'. He even fancied he could see the waiting grave of his friend :

> *. . . one who had stilled his walk*
> *And sought oblivion's cave.*
> *He was to come on the morrow noon*
> *And take good rest in the bed so hewn.*[1]

This was his first great loss. The man to whom he owed early intellectual stimulation, literary encouragement and honest criticism, who anticipated him in his moods of despair and tried to shield him from unnecessary pain (knowing Hardy's extreme sensitivity and his habit of fastening on the darker things in life), was gone.

Always reticent about himself Hardy, who was then thirty-three, tells us nothing of his feelings. But there are two more poems, printed forty and fifty years after Moule's death, which, like belated blooms, pay tribute to the man whom he had loved. "The Five Students", with its emphatic monosyllabic refrain and its sense of urgency, is little known, but it is one of Hardy's most austerely beautiful poems.[2]

Either because his success with two previous novels had given him more confidence, or because he was now mastering a technique alien to him by nature, *Far from the Madding Crowd* towers above its predecessors in realistic strength and imaginative brilliance. In this book Hardy abandons the fantasy which by now he has practically outworn, but the story, like all of his novels, remains a tale of love and disillusionment—this time for five people, only one of whom escapes unscathed by reason of his doggedness. The agony of disillusionment (an aspect of love which Henry James, Ibsen and Pirandello were fond of portraying) was a theme dear to Hardy. The more romantic and idealistic the lover the more severe the shock of discovering that the loved one is not the paragon of fidelity, chastity, or strength, imagined. When Knight came home from abroad and discovered that Elfride was not only (inconveniently) dead but had been previously married

---

[1] "Before My Friend Arrived" in *Human Shows.*
[2] The number of monosyllables throughout is exceptional. In the five stanzas there are only twenty words of two or more syllables. See also "Standing by the Mantelpiece" in *Winter Words.*

to another unsuspected rival, he stands over her scutcheon and wrings out "False!" The milder, kinder, Stephen repudiates 'False' and reiterates that she is merely dead. But melodrama in *A Pair of Blue Eyes* grows into something more moving in *Far from the Madding Crowd*, and the fragile, delicate Elfride is transformed into the courageous, capable Bathsheba, as Hardy's command of feminine character develops and enlarges.

We see her first through Gabriel's eyes on 'ridding' or moving day, surreptitiously regarding herself in a swing-mirror, propped up on her spring-waggon, on which she sits surrounded by her cat, canaries and bright-leaved window plants. She wears a crimson jacket which the sun lights up to a scarlet glow. Everything about Bathsheba is rosy. She is like 'a peony petal before the sun dries off the dew', or like some rose with an old-fashioned name familiar to us in floral prints or the catalogues of expensive nurserymen. Bathsheba, Eustacia and Tess, the three most passionate women in Hardy's work, all share this floral character. Tess has a 'mobile peony mouth', and Eustacia, when she laughed, unclosed her lips 'so that the sun shone into her mouth as into a tulip, and lent it a scarlet fire'.[1]

But proud Bathsheba is to love aristocratic, illegitimate, unscrupulous Serjeant Troy, an epicure in taking his pleasures and in giving pain to those who love him. He woos and wins her with his shining sabre, with the sword-exercises which are like the mating-display of some brilliantly-coloured, oriental bird, performed in the bower of bracken-fronds. Again we have a trio of male lovers, for Bathsheba is also loved by the stolid Boldwood, and by good faithful Gabriel who endures Bathsheba's capriciousness and disdain, even her elopement with, and her marriage to, Troy, biding his time (as D. H. Lawrence puts it) 'like a dog watching his bone'.

Here, for the first time in Hardy's work, his men and women show a new characteristic—that of self-dependence. Although Bathsheba is exhausted by Fate, and Gabriel wounded by it, both resist it courageously, taking command of their own lives in defiance of its maulings. Left to himself Hardy would have pre-

[1] *The Return of the Native*, p. 108.

ferred the book to end with Fanny, Troy and Boldwood dead from cruelty, revenge and mental torment, with Bathsheba widowed and Gabriel gone abroad. Yet Bathsheba's acceptance of stubborn, devoted Gabriel rings true, and here Hardy stressed something which he did not touch on again until he drew two other pairs of characters, (Marty and Giles Winterbourne, Tess and Angel Clare), the wisdom of a marriage between those bound by a knowledge of common work.

' Theirs was that substantial affection which arises . . . when the two who are thrown together begin first by knowing the rougher sides of each other's character, and not the best till further on, the romance growing up in the interstices of a mass of hard prosaic reality. This good-fellowship–*camaraderie*–usually occurring through similarity of pursuits, is unfortunately seldom superadded to love between the sexes, because men and women associate, not in their labours, but in their pleasures merely. Where, however, happy circumstance permits its development, the compounded feeling proves itself to be the only love which is as strong as death—that love which many waters can not quench, nor the floods drown, beside which the passion usually called by the name is as evanescent as steam.[1]

Neither Marty nor Tess were ever to know this 'substantial affection', this 'good-fellowship' in practice, but here the writer allows Bathsheba, tamed by sorrow, and Gabriel who has proved his worth through sheer patient watchfulness, to test it.

This is the finest of Hardy's early novels. When he is most inspired he writes with such fervour that we are carried along as on some festival platform, high above the improbabilities, the irritating coincidences, the cumbersome phrases and the erudite allusions. We care for none of these minor things if only he will continue to exalt our spirits with his imaginative power. The moving quality of his descriptions, his feeling for ancient things (whether architectural, rural or legendary), his love of colour, of music and dancing, his capacity for joy, which he experiences as intensely as he feels pain, are all so potent that one looks back on the cramped depression of *Desperate Remedies* astonished that the same sensibility has created both works. Here Hardy kindles our imaginations and emotions with his own fire.

Far from the Madding Crowd, pp. 468-9.

One of the signs of this high inspiration is his use of poetic similes and metaphors, far exceeding those in his verse in number, in poetic justness, and in imaginative brilliance. Only an artist of high visual imagination, and one accustomed to weighing hair's-breadths in shades of emphasis and meaning, knows how to use words with such imaginative skill, for the poetic simile goes straight to the heart of the descriptive matter, pointing up the passage in a few, packed words. This use of graphic similes and metaphors is one of the leading characteristics of Hardy's style at its best, and many examples may be found in *Far from the Madding Crowd* in the first period of his prose writing, and in *The Return of the Native* and *Tess of the d'Urbervilles* in his middle and last periods. Even the poorer novels contain one or two examples which act like yeast in the unleavened whole.

An analysis of these similes and metaphors shows that they fall into roughly half a dozen groups, the Biblical and religious, the classical, the humorous and rustic, the Gothic and strange, the architectural (which are unexpectedly few in number), and the highly poetic and romantic concerned with aspects of nature, or of women. A few from this novel must suffice. First the stair-case in Bathsheba's house, a Dorset manor famous for its Jacobean and Renaissance work. It is, says Hardy, made of

> hard oak, the balusters, heavy as bedposts, being turned and moulded in the quaint fashion of their century, the handrail stout as a parapet-top . . . the stairs themselves *continually twisting round like a person trying to look over his shoulder*.[1]

Boldwood suffers because he has shut off his emotion from the rest of his being *like a solitary sealed cell in a honeycomb*. A gargoyle is fashioned '*as if covered with a wrinkled hide*': a hard frost draws on '*like a stealthy tightening of bonds*': a man's oiled hair sticks to his head '*like mace round a nutmeg*': Giles hesitates to 'convey the intangibilities of his feeling in the coarse meshes of language' just as much as he would 'to carry an odour in a net'. In two of the finest scenes, the slaughter of the sheep by Gabriel's dog and the covering of the ricks before the great storm, pairs of telling metaphors and similes cluster

---

[1] p. 81. (Italics mine.)

together. The shepherd calls and calls to his lost sheep but there is no answer and

> the valleys and farthest hills resounded *as when the sailors invoked the lost Hylas on the Mysian shore.*

Suddenly he finds the over-zealous dog who has driven the sheep to their death 'standing against the sky—*dark and motionless as Napoleon at St Helena*'.[1] In the storm scene the lightning is '*like lazy tongs*' and it lights up the straw-stalks of an illumined rick until they shine with 'the brazen glare of majolica'. When the storm is at its height the continuous lightning flashes, merging into one, fill the sky with incessant light which Hardy compares to 'unbroken sound resulting from successive strokes on a gong'. Here he mingles sight and sound until their properties are confused. Lightning is transubstantiated into thunder and the two appear inextricable, which is what seems to occur when the senses are dazed and delirious.

The highly-praised scene in the malthouse, which shows Hardy at his best in delineating a rustic scene and characters, contains an amusing anecdote about Bathsheba's father and mother. Ever on the raw about marriage, and the dreadful prosaicness of couples long inured to each other's failings, Hardy inserts an original remedy for those who despair of fidelity after marriage. Leslie Stephen had warned him that he would have to treat with extreme care the harrowing passage describing Fanny's creeping to the workhouse to bear Troy's child, if he was not to offend serial readers, but it was not this scene which roused the Grundian ire but the passage referred to above from the malthouse scene. First came the complaints, but later came approbation of this very detail by *The Times*. When Hardy triumphantly remarked, "You cannot say *The Times* is not respectable", Stephen took him up sharply with a comment which is revealing as regards Hardy's ingenuousness:

> I spoke as an editor, not as a man. You have no more consciousness of these things than a child.[2]

They had at last met during the winter of 1873-4, after many delays. At first Hardy was not certain that he liked Stephen, but

---

[1] p. 40. (Italics mine.)   [2] I, p. 131.

the feeling soon changed, for Stephen had a way of winning acquaintances round to life-long friendship. Thereafter, the mantle of Horace Moule fell onto Stephen's shoulders. Both Moule and Stephen were Cambridge men, of the same age—eight years older than Hardy. But now Moule was dead, and Hardy, still in need of a mentor-friend, was thirty-three, and Stephen forty-one. Hardy's debt to the man who helped to establish him as a writer of the first rank in the pages of the 'gentlemanly' *Cornhill* is twice acknowledged in the *Early Life*:

> Leslie Stephen, the man whose philosophy was to influence his own for many years, indeed more than that of any other contemporary.

And:

> Since coming into contact with Leslie Stephen . . . Hardy had been much influenced by his philosophy, and also by his criticism.[1]

Stephen's advice to Hardy about critics agrees with Macmillan's reader's warning to ignore their 'fooleries'. Stephen, like Moule, seems to have recognized the writer's hypersensitivity on this score:

> I think as a critic, that the less authors read of criticism the better. You have a perfectly fresh and original vein and I think the less you bother yourself about critical canons the less chance there is of your becoming self-conscious and cramped . . . We are generally a poor lot, horribly afraid of not being in the fashion, and disposed to give ourselves airs on very small grounds.[2]

Although he went on writing prose for another thirty years, Hardy never completely recovered from the attack on *Desperate Remedies*; it was those early strokes which caused the later criticisms of *Tess* and *Jude* to wound more deeply than they would otherwise have done. Amongst the notes of his middle-age is the following with a distinctly Pauline ring:

> A Hint for Reviewers adapted from Carlyle: Observe what is true, not what is false; what is to be loved and held fast, and earnestly laid to heart; not what is to be contemned, and derided, and sportfully cast out-of-doors.[3]

[1] I, pp. 132 and 167.　　[2] *Ibid.*, pp. 143-4.　　[3] *Ibid.*, p. 179.

One evening in March of the following year (1875) Hardy was summoned by Leslie Stephen to his rooms. He found him,

> a tall thin figure wrapped in a heath-coloured dressing-gown . . . wandering up and down in his library slippers.[1]

He asked Hardy to witness his signature to a deed, which proved to be one renouncing Holy Orders. When it had been executed they fell into conversation, on

> theologies decayed and defunct, the origin of things, the constitution of matter, the unreality of time, and kindred matters.[2]

For all his agnosticism Stephen had about him the air of a prophet—of the new religion, rationalism. Edmund Gosse who, like Hardy, had an eye for portraits and painting, recognized this when he heard Stephen speak behind Lambeth Palace in the open air.

> It was exactly like a Holbein—the magnificent head, with its strong red hair and beard, painted against the porcelain-blue sky . . . He seemed like a prophet raised half-way to heaven, high above the people.[3]

There are certain similarities between Hardy and Stephen, as one might expect since they were drawn to each other after that first meeting. Both had been delicate and precocious as children: both were abnormally sensitive: both had retentive memories which enabled them to soak up poetry without having set themselves to learn it: both admired the poet Crabbe, for different reasons: both had been religiously inclined, sufficiently for Hardy to consider entering the church and for Stephen to be ordained, as a step to a Fellowship at Trinity Hall, and subsequently to become a fully-fledged parson; both men had a vivid sense of the importance of sincerity, and a deep distrust of the world's estimation of merit and success: both admired intellectual honesty.

A few differences will throw their characters into sharper relief. Stephen was not musical: he was also more purely a thinker, who, although he had a rich emotional life, strove not to allow it supremacy over his sense of proportion, or his acute-

---

[1] *Life and Letters of Leslie Stephen*, F. W. Maitland, Duckworth, 1906, p. 263.   [2] *Ibid.*
[3] p. 423. Compare with Hardy's description of J. S. Mill., p 68 *supra*.

ness of perception and judgment. As a biographer of Swift, and in his private letters, he stated that for him the 'sin against the Holy Ghost' was 'to blaspheme one's affections', to regret having abandoned oneself to love because loving had brought suffering. Whereas Hardy was all too prone to luxuriate in the thought of the pain after loving, although, like Stephen, he too was an ardent advocate of love. Nor could Stephen believe that to lose God and a sense of divine direction could distress any-one, least of all the loser. By the time that he and Hardy had come together both had become agnostics, following separate paths, but Stephen's loss of faith, although not without an attendant conflict, had been the easier. He has several times described this loss.

> The old husk drops off because it has long withered, and you discover that beneath it is a sound and vigorous growth of genuine conviction . . .[1]

of another kind. And thirty years later:

> I did not feel that the solid ground was giving way beneath my feet, but rather that I was being relieved of a cumbrous burden.[2]

He found the conception of man living defiantly in an indiffer-ent universe stimulating rather than depressing.

The loss of religious faith was more tragic for Hardy. The severance involved a serious mutilation. In "God's Funeral" he mourns the loss of faith which has upheld those who have lived in former ages:

> *And though struck speechless, I did not forget*
> *That what was mourned for, I, too, once had prized.*[3]

There is even something compulsive about that anguished cry which breaks from him after attendance at a Cathedral service, where, ghost-like, he stands aloof from the spirit of worship:

> *O doth a bird deprived of wings*
> *Go earth-bound wilfully?*[4]

It reminds one of Donne's lingering affection for the Catholic

---

[1] "Some Early Impressions", *National Review*, October 1903.
[2] Maitland, p. 145.   [3] In *Satires of Circumstance*.
[4] "The Impercipient", *Wessex Poems*, p. 181.

religion in which he had been nourished, which he had discarded with the intellect but not with the heart.

As late as 1920 Hardy described himself as

churchy—not in an intellectual sense, but in so far as instincts and emotions ruled.[1]

In that portion of a sentence we have the conflict clear and self-stated.

For Stephen the conflict was shorter and less intense because he was not so deeply involved with his emotions. He was what may be described as an intellectual Stoic by nature, whereas Hardy resembles a recusant from the old, not the new, faith, stubbornly refusing to yield to its emotional appeals.

Stephen remained the editor of the *Cornhill* from 1871-82. He refused *The Return of the Native* for his journal because of a suspicion that it would not please his feminine subscribers. 'Thou shalt not shock a young lady', and 'Remember the country Parson's daughter', were, he said, the dire commandments under which he lived as an editor. Hardy did not offer him *The Trumpet Major*, which Stephen regretted, and so their literary, but not their personal, association closed with the publication of *The Hand of Ethelberta* in 1875.

Hardy the poet owes something to Stephen, too, for he valued his friend's dictum on the poet's ultimate aim, which should be

to touch our hearts by showing his own, and not to exhibit his learning, or his fine taste, or his skill in mimicking the notes of his predecessors.[2]

Much of the simplicity of Hardy's later poetry springs from the pruning and paring which attention to this aim necessitates, and he would have been well advised to apply it to the more cumbrous passages of his prose.

Far from the Madding Crowd appeared in the *Cornhill* from January to December, 1874. On the strength of its success, four and a half years after he had met her, Thomas Hardy and Emma Gifford were married, in September of the same year, at St Peter's in Elgin Avenue, Paddington. None of Thomas'

[1] II, p. 176.
[2] I, p. 167.

family were present at the ceremony. The day after his marriage Hardy wrote to his brother[1]:

> Martin's Hotel,
> Queen's Road,
> Brighton.
> *Friday*

Dear Henry,

I write a line to tell you all at home that the wedding took place yesterday, and that we are got as far as this on our way to Normandy and Paris. There were only Emma and I, her uncle who married us, and her brother; my landlady's daughter signed the book as one witness.

I am going to Paris for materials for my next story. Shall return the beginning of October and shall call at once at 4 Celbridge Place to see if there is any letter.

We sent an advertisement of the marriage to the *Dorset Chronicle*. Try to see it. Thanks for your good wishes.

> Yours in haste,
> Tom.[2]

Emma Gifford's *Recollections*, as given in the *Early Life*, close with a description of her wedding day—one of 'soft, sunny luminousness'—and some reflections on life and religion—in which she states her belief in 'an Unseen Power of great benevolence', and in a life to come. If there are sorrowful, even tragic events—and in her artless way she calls them 'unhappy happenings'—these may be borne 'if Christ is our highest ideal', and she closes with the following sentence:

> A strange unearthly brilliance shines round our path, penetrating and dispersing difficulties with its warmth and glow.[3]

In these unpremeditated pages, written the year before her death, there are no traces of something of which Emma Hardy has often been accused, a feeling that she considered herself superior in birth, and equal in gifts, to her husband. Secondly, there were evidently distressing times in her life with a man of genius, but she does not dwell on these, and her faith enabled

---

[1] Amongst Hardy's books is one called *Manly Exercises*, inscribed "Thomas and Henry Hardy, Professors of Boxing".

[2] Unpublished letter on a half-sheet, in pencil, postmarked Brighton, September 18, 1874. By courtesy of the owners, the Dorset County Museum, and the Trustees of the Hardy Estate.

[3] I, p. 96.

her to see them in proportion. 'Bond servants to chance' as they both were, their antagonistic temperaments and characters eventually shut them away from each other in an isolation more terrible than mere physical separation, accentuated by their very contiguity.

But now they were young and in love. After a honeymoon spent in Paris, Rouen and other continental cities, they returned to England to lodge in Surbiton, from which they removed to Hardy's old haunt Westbourne Grove, where he was fond of thinking Mrs Siddons had held court.[1]

Here the young writer set himself rigorously to the study of prose style again. He aimed at 'crispness and movement', and quoted Herrick to paraphrase what he had in mind.

> The whole secret of a living style . . . lies in not having too much style—being, in fact, a little careless, or rather seeming to be, here and there . . . It is, of course, simply a carrying into prose the knowledge I have acquired in poetry—that inexact rhymes and rhythms now and then are far more pleasing than correct ones.[2]

Addison, Burke, Macaulay, Newman, Sterne, Defoe, Lamb, Gibbon and *The Times* leaders which he had been solemnly studying, were thrown over in a heap by this confession. After all his labours his own idiosyncracy triumphed.

This note explains why Hardy did not admire the style of one of his contemporaries, Henry James, who was concerned with problems similar to Hardy's own, treated in a wholly different manner—the grinding down or trapping of those who aspire to be free, spontaneous and natural in the mill of the conventional; people eaten away by the long bitterness of life. In exasperation he seems to throw aside one of this writer's books in order to jot down:

> After this kind of work one feels inclined to be purposely careless in detail. The great novels of the future will certainly not concern themselves with the minutiae of manners . . . James' subjects are those one could be interested in at moments when there is nothing larger to think of.[3]

Hardy's thumbnail sketches of people in his notes are always lively and incisive. Many of these were destroyed lest they give

---

[1] *The Dynasts*, Part II, p. 309.   [2] I, p. 138.   [3] *Ibid.*, p. 277.

offence to those whom he did not wish to wound, and we are the poorer. What could be better than his descriptions of Henry James, Matthew Arnold and Pater? James has 'a nebulous gaze ... and a ponderously warm manner of saying nothing in infinite sentences'.[1] Arnold seemed to have

> made up his mind upon everything years ago, so that it was a pleasing futility for his interlocutor to begin thinking new ideas, different from his own, at that time of day.[2]

Pater's manner is that of 'one carrying weighty ideas without spilling them'.[3] The acuteness of observation and unhesitating honesty in these notes were only slightly modified in Hardy's published work. For instance, after meeting Ellen Terry at a party he set down:

> Presently [she] arrived—diaphanous—a sort of balsam or sea-anemone, without shadow:

she resembled

> a machine in which, if you press a spring, all the works fly open.[4]

In *The Well-Beloved* this appears enlarged into:

> The lady on his right ... a creature in airy clothing, translucent, like a balsam or sea-anemone, without shadows, and in movement as responsive as some highly-lubricated, many-wired machine, which, if one presses a particular spring, flies open and reveals its works.[5]

But Hardy was not at his best when describing cultured drawing-room types in his novels. He stood aside from them emotionally, watching like a critical ghost, never absorbed into a vortex which at heart he despised, despite his affability.

> Even when I enter into a room to pay a simple morning call I have unconsciously the habit of regarding the scene as if I were a spectre not solid enough to influence my environment.[6]

For fame, for wealth, for social success Hardy cared but little, and in this all his finest characters resemble him, with the poss-

---

[1] *Ibid.*, pp. 217, 237.   [2] *Ibid.*, p. 175.
[3] *Ibid.*, p. 236.   [4] *Ibid.*, p. 305.
[5] p. 107.   [6] I, p. 275.

ible exception of Henchard. But if he was to support himself and a wife by literature it was essential for him to be (what he called) 'a good hand at writing a serial', if nothing more. On returning from abroad and on settling in London, 'in order to do the London scenes [of his next novel] as vigorously as possible', he was at once faced with a pair of dilemmas.

> He perceived that he was up against the position of having to carry on his life, not as an emotion, but as a scientific game; that he was committed by circumstances to novel-writing as a regular trade, as much as he had formerly been to architecture; and that, hence he would have to look for material in manners—in ordinary social and fashionable life as other novelists did. Yet he took no interest in manners, but in the substance of life only.[1]

Hardy had always loved solitude; although he was not un-social he relished that observation of the outer world, and that exploration of the inner, which can only be faithfully and fruit-fully performed when one is alone: and it is possible that, like Coleridge, he felt all his most valuable experiences to be solitary ones. He liked to think that this was an aspect of his wife's character:

> *. . . lonely I found her,*
> *The sea-birds around her,*
> *And other than nigh things uncaring to know*—[2]

but Emma Lavinia was by nature far more gregarious.

Keats, in one of his letters to Fanny Brawne, speaks of his horror of going out to 'wither at hateful tea-parties, freeze at dinners, bake at dances and simmer at routs'. He looked for 'nobler amusements'. Hardy confided a similar mistrust of his own power to enjoy 'dinners, clubs and crushes' to Thackeray's daughter Anne (sister-in-law to Leslie Stephen), but she gave him small comfort, assuring him that 'a novelist must necessarily like society'.[3]

The first dilemma involved the second, for by now the established author had to face a problem which confronts all

---

[1] *Ibid.*, p. 137.
[2] *A Dream or No*, in *Poems of 1912-1913*.
[3] I, p. 138.

writers—how to balance social demands with those of one's work. Seclusion is essential for a writer, yet he must not become a hermit. People and life must be one's study, yet they must not become one's masters. Modern writers have found this problem so suffocating that they have fled from the orbits of their world: a woman novelist takes a room in a quarter of London away from her husband and home: a poet goes abroad for long periods of time to remote fastnesses.

> Social life is all the more dangerous because it is to some extent necessary to the writer. It is one of the main doors of entrance into the life of other people: unless indeed he is one of those solitaries who gains nothing from other people. Of course, there is no great problem for those who have sound judgment and strong wills. But one may be talented without having either . . . and the writer is peculiarly dependent on his own judgment and will—made dependent by his very freedom . . . Unless he fights hard he is constantly exposed to interruptions.[1]

Hardy's success with his venture in the *Cornhill* made the editor of that paper ask him for another tale. He had thought of a plot and scene, which later developed into *The Woodlanders*, but now he put it aside, apparently out of pique. A journalist had recently hazarded that R. D. Blackmore was a market-gardener and Hardy a house-decorator. The latter, who shrank from investigation of, or assumptions on, his private life or emotions, decided to test his powers in another direction—the depiction of society life. The letter to his brother on the day following his marriage shows us that he must have made the decision as early as September, 1874. Both Rouen and Paris figure in *The Hand of Ethelberta* which began in the *Cornhill* in July 1875.

This novel had a cool reception and is now dismissed as one of Hardy's failures. Yet, as the author himself insisted in his notes, we can often learn more from a so-called failure, from tentative sketches, than from a finished masterpiece. There are some unusual, even startling, things in *The Hand of Ethelberta*. There is the quotation from Lucretius, which has been festering in his mind for more than twenty years, on the title-page. Then in his

---

[1] Stephen Spender, *World within World*, pp. 168-9. Hamish Hamilton, 1951.

preface (written some twenty years *after* the book's first appearance) we learn that his original intention had been

> to excite interest in a drama . . . wherein servants were as important as, or more important than, their masters: wherein the drawing-room was sketched in many cases from the point of view of the servants'-hall.

In one of his notes Hardy remarks that, if he were a painter, he would make a drawing of a room from a mouse-hole in the wainscot. In this novel he purposely allied himself with the servants, rather than their masters, whom he paints disparagingly throughout.

The tale is one of a butler's daughter, who, by means of her wits and beauty, marries first into the gentry and later into the nobility. Lady Petherwin, her mother-in-law, is capricious and heartless. Lord Mountclere is old and debauched and resembles 'the head-scraper at a pig-killing'. Ethelberta, who has a talent for verse and for acting, first publishes some poems and then, in order to support a large brood of brothers and sisters and her ailing mother, takes to publicly telling her own tales, after the manner of Dickens. The portraits of her brothers Dan and Sol, country builders whom she imports into her London home, are unique in the novels of the period, and through them Hardy gives vent to some of those socialistic feelings which were snuffed out with the discarding of *The Poor Man and the Lady*. Sol openly calls Mountclere's brother 'rubbish' to his face, and sternly rebukes Ethelberta for

> creeping up among the useless lumber of our nation that'll be the first to burn if there come a flare.[1]

His sister in turn rebukes him for his 'republican passions' and explains, rather weakly, that the peerage appeal to her for historical and romantic reasons, if nothing more.

The merits of town and country are balanced against each other, the country winning on all counts. Country people are more loyal, charitable and demonstrative: country poverty is endurable because it is less drab than urban: country weather is less perverse and more easily definable: country people wear brighter colours and are more healthy: the work-

[1] p. 444.

men are more honest and generous with their time, stronger, more industrious and anxious to please. Country servants are less corrupt and more devoted to their employers—in other words, human ties are altogether warmer and stronger. The heroine's uprooting from the country involves once more the problem of the déracinés. Ethelberta finds that she no longer speaks the same language, either of the tongue or heart, as her humbler sisters from whom she is estranged, whom she still loves, but whose homeliness she now finds 'wretched' and 'intolerable', Her heart aches at this 'sense of disloyalty to her class and kin . . .' from which there is now no escape. How much of this feeling Hardy himself experienced must remain conjectural.

The 'harassing social fight' is gone into in detail. Through his heroine Hardy re-lives some of his own problems on joining London society, but he is master enough of a woman's mind to interpret her difficulties with feminine understanding. Ethelberta's efforts to climb, and to remain at the top, entail a secondary war with the other sex. Although she has earned a kind of sexlessness which enables her to be free from the fettering 'conventionalities of manner prescribed by custom for household womankind', 'to move abroad unchaperoned', and 'to experience that *luxury of isolation* normally enjoyed by man alone', she finds consequent drawbacks, such as improper advances from her admirers, and an increased need to study social niceties and mystifying ramifications. She longs to be a man, since men appear to have all the advantages in life: finally she decides that, for her, the only solution is to marry an understanding man of means who will allow her to cultivate her intellectual interests. If necessary she will even contribute to a joint income.

This was advanced thought in Hardy's day and one wonders how much of it came from Emma Lavinia, whose nephew tells us that she had the interests of women at heart, and who (in 1907) walked in a woman-suffrage parade. The two struggles, the social and the feminine, involve the question of marriage, for Hardy never envisaged a woman strong enough to stand alone without the support of marriage, and in 1875 there were few careers open to women. So we find sardonic reflections on marriage, and on men. 'Proverbs', we are told, 'are all made by men, for their own advantages',[1] a sentiment which reflects Bathsheba's pronouncement that

> It is difficult for a woman to define her feelings in language which is chiefly made by men to express theirs.[2]

If the feminists were at pains to make women imitate and rival men, Hardy strove to develop women according to their own natures. The hero, Julian, remarks acidly that a 'man checks all a woman's finer sentiments towards him by marrying her'. Later, Ethelberta states that

> a proposal of marriage is only removed from being a proposal of a very different kind by an accident. . . .[3]

with which Bernard Shaw would have been in hearty agreement.

But suddenly, out of this forest of dicta, comes a strange and bitter cry. Having married her Viscount, Ethelberta finds that he is not what she has believed him to be. Even her practical forethought has not enabled her to escape the misery of disillusion, and she cries out:

> God has got me in his power at last, and is going to scourge me for my bad doings—that's what it seems like.[4]

Here the contriving woman, who feels 'over-weighted' in the race against men, reverts to the country girl who has misinterpreted her scripture teachings, and muddled her brain with fine thinking by John Stuart Mill and other writers, whose work she consults to solve her predicament. The cry anticipates Tess' cry, just as Ethelberta's concern for her family anticipates Tess' anxiety for hers. Hardy's compassion for a brood of young creatures may have sprung from his mother's, or grandmother's, tales of their own difficult childhoods. One had been 'at her wits' end to maintain herself and her family', and the other had been left an orphan at an early age. The problem of survival involves yet another—that of the value and necessity of self-sacrifice. Is it good and right that a woman should benefit others, to

---

[1] p. 161. [2] *Far from the Madding Crowd*, p. 415.
[3] *Hand of Ethelberta*, p. 331. [4] *Ibid.*, p. 453.

whom she is bound by ties of blood and affection, by sacrificing her chastity and her heart? Treatises on casuistry which Hardy had read as a young man, and which Ethelberta consults, cannot solve it.

There are also reflections of Hardy's youth. In Christopher Julian playing behind an improvised screen, twined with holly and ivy (at a Christmas dance in a country house), we detect young Tom Hardy who had once fiddled tirelessly for ardent dancers. Christopher plays until his arms ache and his fingers tap the keys 'as mechanically as fowls pecking barleycorns'.

> . . . lullabied by the faint regular beat of [the dancers'] footsteps to the tune, the players sank into the peculiar mesmeric quiet which comes over impressionable people who play for a great length of time in the midst of such scenes; and at last the only noises that Christopher took cognizance of were those of the exceptional kind, breaking above the general sea of sound—a casual smart rustle of silk, a laugh, a stumble, monosyllabic talk— . . .[1]

Ethelberta's decision to write a prose tale, when poetry will not earn her bread and butter, takes shape in a work 'written in the first person and the style of Defoe', just as *The Poor Man and the Lady* had been.[2] In the following passage Hardy puts into Ethelberta's mouth what he reiterates in his prefaces, letters and notes.

> It would be difficult to show that because I have written so-called tender and gay verse, I feel tender and gay. *It is too often assumed that a person's fancy is his real mind*. I believe that in the majority of cases one is fond of imagining the direct opposite of one's principle in sheer effort after something fresh and free; at any rate, some of the lightest of those rhymes were composed between the deepest fits of dismals I have ever known.[3]

As for drawing-room successes, which the heroine pursues in the current belief that they are essential to her literary, dramatic and social triumphs, Ethelberta secretly despises these as much as Hardy, with whom she shares a philosophic caste of mind. When, like her successor Eustacia, she stands on a tumulus on

---

[1] *Ibid.*, p. 42.
[2] *The Hand of Ethelberta*, p. 108, and I, p. 81.
[3] *The Hand of Ethelberta*, p. 87. (Italics mine.)

the heath, or examines the ruins of Corfe Castle, she fortifies herself with the following thought:

> Persons waging a harassing social fight are apt . . . to forget the smallness of the end in view; and the hints that perishing historical remnants afforded her of the attenuating effects of time, even upon great struggles, corrected the apparent scale of her own. She was reminded that in a strife for such a ludicrously small object as the entry of drawing-rooms, winning, equally with losing, is below the zero of the true philosopher's concern.[1]

Then, too, her lover Christopher is described as having:

> a countenance [which] varied with his mood, though it kept somewhat in the rear of that mood. He looked sad when he felt almost serene, and only serene when he felt quite cheerful. It is a habit people acquire who have had repressing experiences . . .[2]

This subdued emotional tone would seem to have been one of Hardy's own characteristics. Sir Newman Flower declares that he never once in all their long acquaintance heard him laugh, 'only chuckle and smile inwardly'.

The painter's eye makes Hardy note shades of colour and darkness. The doorway of a city church is lit by 'a glow of green sunlight' reflected from the churchyard grass: a cathedral fills

> with shadows, and cold breathings came round the piers, for it was November, when night very soon succeeds noon in spots where noon is sobered to the pallor of eve.[3]

This description, short as it is, shows us how Hardy ruminated on something long before he developed it fully, for it anticipates the famous description of night descending on the heath in the first three paragraphs of *The Return of the Native*.

There are also several details similar to some in *The Dynasts*. The field of Waterloo had already been mentioned in *An Indiscretion*, and Napoleon in *Far From the Madding Crowd*, and now we have the battle of Salamanca referred to by a meditative coachman who reflects:

> . . . as I wait here with the carriage sometimes, I think how many more get killed at the moment of victory than at the moment of defeat.[4]

[1] *Ibid.*, p. 272.   [2] *Ibid.*, p. 18.   [3] *Ibid.*, p. 367.   [4] p. 38.

An unusual architectural feature, a jib door, is used in both: the startlingly feminine description of Ethelberta's frock 'looped up with convolvulus flowers' heralds those careful and vivid ones of womens' clothing in *The Trumpet Major* and the great epic poem: in the novel the dancing couples 'knot themselves like house-flies', and in *The Dynasts* the British aide-de-camps dart to and fro between commanding officers 'like house-flies dancing their quadrilles'.[1] Most important of all, the discarded hero in the novel describes himself as a puppet 'moved about in the hands of a person who . . . can be nothing to me'.[2] The obsession with automatism has already begun, nearly thirty years before the completion of the epic poem.

A few beautiful similes, especially astronomical ones, of which Hardy was very fond, enliven the whole. Country people attracted by the brilliant light from a town jeweller's window 'close in upon the panes like night birds upon the lanterns of a lighthouse'. When the heroine is distressed she makes a sound 'like a note from a storm bird at night'. When she is perplexed and silent she

> wears an air of unusual stillness—the silence and stillness of a starry sky, where all is force and motion.[3]

While she dances she crosses and re-crosses Christopher's vision tantalizingly '*like a recurrent comet*', and when, on a summer's day, she gathers up her skirts clouds of quiet thistle-down rise in '*flights like a comet's tail*'. Here we have another example of something seen and expressed by Hardy in both his prose and verse. In a poem written about a day at Swanage (where he and his wife lodged with a retired sea-captain, who fed him on tales of smuggling and the tricks of the tide in Deadman's Bay) he takes six lines to describe the winged thistle-down's comet-like flight.[4]

But *The Hand of Ethelberta* is not a work of art. The satire lacks a biting edge: the story does not move us and we are left dissatisfied. There is too much shrugging of shoulders and grinning delight in ironical pronouncements; too great a stifling of the heroine's heart, a killing of her real, spontaneous self. The novel was not a success: readers complained of its 'qualities of

[1] Part III, Sc. 2.   [2] p. 41.   [3] p. 206.   [4] *Days to Recollect.*

unexpectedness' and regretted the author's departure from his old style, which they rightly felt, was his true one. Hardy himself attributed his cool reception to the fact that it was a social satire prematurely born and, later, he cited one of Shaw's successes as proof of this fact. But as another[1] has pointed out, the real cause for its failure was that Hardy was not by nature a social satirist.

It is with relief that we turn to two of the writer's notes made at this time, for these are the stuff from which poetry is distilled and are the essential Hardy. The first was made at Swanage:

> *Evening.* Just after sunset. Sitting with E. on a stone under the wall . . . The sounds are two, and only two. On the left, Durlestone Head roaring high and low, like a giant asleep. On the right, a thrush. Above the bird hangs the new moon, and a steady planet.[2]

The second is a memory of something seen on a spring day in the Somerset-Dorset borderlands, whither the pair had removed from Swanage.

> In an orchard at Closworth. Cowslips under trees. A light proceeds from them, as from Chinese lanterns, or glow-worms.[3]

The eye which could perceive, the nature which could respond to, and the memory which could retain this vision, are all those of a true poet.

Hardy never made use of this second note as it stood, but varied it when it re-appeared in two places. The faces of farm-workers on their hands and knees in a pasture are irradiated by a similar glow.

> A soft yellow gleam was reflected from the buttercups into their shaded faces, giving them an elfish, moonlit aspect, though the sun was pouring upon their backs in all the strength of noon.[4]

And in the most dramatic and tragic of all his short stories a young woman's face glows with a suffused light, 'soft and evan-escent, like the light under a heap of rose petals'.[5]

---

[1] Rutland, p. 176.   [2] I, p. 142.
[3] *Ibid.*, p. 144. The poems "Once at Swanage" and "Growth in May" refer to the same incidents.
[4] *Tess of the d'Urbervilles*, p. 180.
[5] "The Withered Arm" in *Wessex Tales*, p. 68.

After lodging in Swanage and Yeovil the young Hardys had again been abroad, this time to Holland and the Rhine. But after a time it occurred to them that to house one's goods in packing-cases and trunks is not the most comfortable way to live. The Bockhampton relations accused them of 'wandering about like two tramps': yet if they wished to rent a house they had no possessions, only books, a single bookcase, and a door-scraper bought at an auction. After looking at cottages in Shaftesbury, Blandford and Wimborne, Hardy decided to take a villa over-looking the Stour at Sturminster Newton, and here at Midsummer 1876, they settled at last, after buying £100 worth of furni-ture in two hours at Bristol.

Sturminster is an enchanting place which has not, even now, lost its rights and air of a proper market-town, something it has been without interruption since the 13th century. The two hamlets of Sturminster and Newton, with their half-timbered, thatched inns and houses, straddle the river where it turns east to flow beneath the mediaeval bridge with its six pointed arches. They share the remnant of a Saxon Castle and a Tudor manor of the Abbots of Glaston, a stone mill-house with a wide reeded pool, and higher up the hill, where Sturminster tops it, the remains of a market-cross, on which William Barnes, born at Rushay not far off, sat as a lad and frightened the cattle coming to market, Its peculiar industries were formerly the making of gloves, candles, and cloth, for the Flemish weavers came here centuries ago and their descendants made heavy cloth for the men who went out to Newfoundland with the fishing fleet. This nautical inclination, which one does not expect to find in men from an inland market-town, extended to smuggling, and Sturminster was once a disposal centre for contraband spirits brought up from the coast at Lulworth. It was also a place where legend and superstition clung tenaciously to the minds of the people. Many of them appear in Hardy's notes made while he lived here; and the folklore which plays a salient part in the book he wrote at Sturminster—*The Return of the Native*—is corroborated in a collection of such material made recently in the county of Dorset.[1]

The house which he and Emma chose stands high on a bluff

[1] *Dorset Up-Along and Down-Along.* Longman's, Dorchester, 1951.

above the river. Its gable-ends are decorated with white orna-
mental barge-boards incongruously gay, suggesting a Swiss
chalet or a New England ice-house. It faces west and the garden
is overshadowed by a Chilian Pine, the favourite Monkey
Puzzle tree of the Victorians, planted by Hardy while he lived
there. The view from the windows is over wide marsh-like
meadows, rich with alluvial soil, and pasture fat from the flood-
ings of the sullen Stour which, unlike the Frome, flows sluggishly
and is filled with reeds and rushes and, in summer, with waxen
yellow water-lilies, the 'clotes' of Barnes' poetry. Sometimes a
heron stands pensively fishing on the little willow-clad island,
on which flocks of swallows gather and roost.

Hardy's poems[1] and notes of this tranquil period bear the
impress of river and river-meads, reminding one of Constable's
declaration of passionate love for old mill-streams, rotting
planks, mossy stones and pungent river smells.

> Rowed on the Stour in the evening, the sun setting up the river.
> Just afterwards a faint exhalation visible on the surface of the
> water as we stirred it with the oars. A fishy smell from the numerous
> eels and other fish beneath. Mowers salute us. Rowed among the
> water-lilies to gather them. Their long ropy stems . . . Gathered
> meadow-sweet. Rowed with difficulty through the weeds, the
> rushes on the border standing like palisades against the bright
> sky . . . a cloud in the sky like a huge quill pen.[2]

The very mowers of the Anglian fields in the *Haywain* are
there, and one sees Emma Lavinia, with her bright coiled hair,
leaning over the boat's edges, dipping in her arms to draw out the
lilies.

Since nothing was ever lost in that seed-bed of a mind, where
actions and emotions lay dormant for as much as half a
century before germinating and flowering, we find an echo of
the Sturminster scene in the First Part of the *Dynasts*.

> . . . *they specked the water shine*
> *As will a flight of swallows towards dim eve,*
> *Descending on a smooth and loitering stream*
> *To seek some eyot's edge.*[3]

[1] "Overlooking the River Stour" and "On Sturminster Footbridge", in
Moments of Vision.
[2] I, p. 147.   [3] Act II, Sc. v, p. 55.

The Stour Meadows at Sturminster Newton

(From the bluff in front of Hardy's villa—the setting of the *Sturminster Idyll*)

In the following May, there is another note:

> A man comes every evening to the cliff in front of our house to see the sun set, timing himself to arrive a few minutes before the descent. Last night he came, but there was a cloud. His disappointment.[1]

Here was food for the novelist. In the same month Hardy was listening to

> the prime of bird-singing. The thrushes and blackbirds are the most prominent, pleading earnestly rather than singing, and with such modulation that you seem to see their little tongues curl inside their bills in emphasis. A bull-finch sings from a tree with a metallic sweetness piercing as a fife.[2]

On Coronation Day there were village games and dancing, and Hardy made a note about the pretty girls whirling on the green, a scene reminiscent of the opening one in *Tess*.

Then there is a delicious garden note headed 'Country Life at Sturminster'.

> Vegetables pass from growing to boiling, fruit from the bushes to the pudding, without a moment's halt, and the gooseberries that were ripening on the twigs at noon are in the tart an hour later.[3]

In September he went to Shroton Fair,[4] and on the way home got lost in a fog in a prehistoric earthwork, his unexpected companion being a hump-backed man. In October he took his father to drink the waters at Bath; and in November incessant rains fell and the Stour was flooded.

> Lumps of froth float down like swans in front of our house. At the arches of the large stone bridge the froth has accumulated and lies like hillocks of salt against the bridge; then the arch chokes, and after a silence coughs out the air and froth, and gurgles on.[5]

Emma and he must often have crossed either the little iron foot-bridge (erected soon after Hardy's birth) in the meadows below their villa, or the great mediaeval stone one, on their

---

[1] I, p. 149.   [2] *Ibid.*, pp. 149-50.   [3] *Ibid.*, pp. 152-3.
[4] One of the few villages in England with two names: its proper name, Iwerne Courtenay, is generally dropped for Shroton, or Sherriff's Town, which it has been since Domesday.   [5] I, p. 155.

rambles. Sometimes they dined with the local solicitor and his wife, or went to a village concert to hear a young singer whose penetratingly sweet voice roused Hardy to write a poem, and to make a note in which he stresses yet again that ecstasizing power which music exerted over him.

> She is the sweetest of singers—thrush-like in the descending scale, and lark-like in the ascending—drawing out the soul of listeners in a gradual thread of excrutiating attenuation like silk from a cocoon.[1]

But the Sturminster days were saddened by the young couples unfulfilled hopes for a child. Their servant, Jane, a girl of an old (once a county) family had run away with her lover. Thinking she might have gone home Thomas went to her cottage and found her father in the fields:

> A little girl fetched him from the haymakers. He came across to me amid the windrows of hay, and seemed to read bad news in my face. She had not been home. I remembered that she had dressed up in her best clothes, and she probably has gone to Stalbridge to her lover.[2]

A few months later there is another note:

> We hear that Jane, our late servant, is soon to have a baby. Yet never a sign of one is there for us.[3]

One might suppose Hardy's note made a month earlier to be connected with this private tragedy:

> The sudden disappointment of a hope leaves a scar which the ultimate fulfilment of that hope never entirely removes. . . .[4]

were it not for the fact that he had already expressed this thought in *Desperate Remedies*. But there was no fulfilment of that hope, and one is set dreaming on what changes in Hardy's life and philosophy might have occurred had it been otherwise.

This was a fertile time for Hardy. He was turning over many problems in his mind, was busy with his poetry and with the creation of that sombre prose poem *The Return of the Native*. His notes are full of humour and sharp observation. He ponders on the problem of artistic creation, and the nature of good and

---

[1] I, p. 156, and *The Maid of Keinton Mandeville*.
[2] *Ibid.*, pp. 152-3.   [3] *Ibid.*   [4] *Ibid.*

evil. There is an anecdote about Trollope overrunning his time for a speech; tales of the Bristol to Poole mail-coach; of an astute collector of cottage china; of poachers and keepers. There are further thoughts on Waterloo for *The Dynasts*, which he now conceives as 'an epic poem'; on types of church-goers; on laughter; on the intolerance of young writers 'who begin as judges'; and three memorable reflections on life and art. First:

> . . . all things merge into one another—good into evil, generosity into justice, religion into politics, the year into the ages, the world into the universe. With this in view the evolution of the species seems but a minute and obvious process in the same movement.[1]

Secondly:

> There is enough poetry left [in life] after all the false romance has been abstracted, to make a sweet pattern . . . So, then, if Nature's defects must be looked in the face and transcribed, whence arises the art in poetry and novel-writing? which must certainly show art, or it becomes merely mechanical reporting. I think the art lies in making these defects the basis of a hitherto unperceived beauty, by irradiating them with 'the light that never was' on their surface, but is seen to be latent in them by the spiritual eye.[2]

This is another way of saying what Hardy later condensed into 'The province of the poet is to find beauty in ugliness', or 'to show the grandeur underlying the sorriest things'.[3]

Thirdly, (a theme which Hardy was never tired of dwelling on even in the realm of painting):

> An object or mark raised or made by man on a scene is worth ten times any such formed by unconscious Nature. Hence clouds, mists and mountains are unimportant beside the wear on a threshold, or the print of a hand.[4]

By November 1878, Hardy had posted off five parts of *The Return of the Native* for serial publication. It is strange that for this book he refrained from using the scene around him which gave him so much pleasure. But the mood and characters of this tale required a sterner setting. The heath country twenty miles off near Bockhampton occupied his thoughts: even Eustacia's

[1] I, pp. 146-7. [2] *Ibid.*, pp. 150-1.
[3] *Ibid.*, pp. 279, 223. [4] I, p. 153.

F *

name was taken from a former lady of Ower Moigne manor which lies a few miles from Hardy's birthplace. Yet in writing *Far from the Madding Crowd* he had expressly said that he found it 'a great advantage to be actually among the people described at the time of describing them'.[1]

The Return of the Native is now acknowledged to be the finest work of Hardy's middle age and one of the prose masterpieces of our language. Yet when it was published it received little praise. In view of its eminence today it seems hardly credible that contemporary critics could call it 'inferior to anything of Hardy's which we have yet read', and could only grudgingly admit that there were 'elements of a good novel in it . . .' passages showing 'good workmanship' and good descriptions. It contained 'original' thought and writing', and it had a certain 'ruggedness' and 'earnestness and fantastic power'. But, having said this, nine leading journals proceeded to damn the book. It was 'artificial', the 'story did not satisfy' since it was not amusing; 'nature-worship' was all very well but this went too far; the movement, characters, action and conclusion were all lame; it repeated itself and was merely a clever parody of Hardy's earlier work: the dialect was confusing and presented readers with 'linguistic puzzles'; one was led into another world but one felt lost, and 'further than ever from the madding crowd': the author had a 'keen eye for the picturesque' but he could not draw: he had wasted his powers in painting a character like Eustacia who only wished to gratify her sensual passions, and the portrayal of what these would very likely lead to was not fit reading for the British public, who did not admire *Madame Bovary*: finally, the author missed being a really 'great man'.[2]

The *Contemporary Review* recognized Hardy's similarity to Browning, and praised his treatment of 'Nature in her lonely greatness', but the reviewer regretted that, in heightening Nature, Hardy had dwarfed the human characters, who seemed in comparison 'sordid, stunted, blundering and ignorant'.

The criticism that it was a mistake to create Eustacia, 'who only wished to gratify her sensual passions,' is still being made

---

[1] *Ibid.*, p. 131.
[2] Reviews in *The Athenaeum* and *The Saturday Review*.

today. So eminent a critic as T. S. Eliot remarks that it does not seem particularly 'wholesome' or 'edifying' to him that

> "only in their emotional paroxysms [do] most of Hardy's characters come alive. This extreme emotionalism seems to me a symptom of decadence. . . . Strong passion is only interesting and significant in strong men: those who abandon themselves without resistance. . . ."[1]

In America *The Return* was hailed as 'one of the best serial novels of the year' (1878): but Hardy had to wait ten years before a fellow-countryman and a fellow-poet, John Addington Symonds, confessed that the book had charmed him with its 'unusual freshness and vigour'. No one seems to have recognized the classical precision of design which shelters the ardently romantic conception—for here Hardy consciously observed the unities throughout; the justness of the poetic vision; the book's mastery over both the imagination and emotions of the reader, a power peculiarly Hardy's own; its essential truth, the inevitability of the tragedy inherent in it. Nor were the critics moved by the anguish of human hearts whose needs, whose hungers, are greater than their powers of perception, who perversely seek a way into life through love, very often love of the wrong person. The wringing pathos of some of the scenes also escaped them. One can hardly bear to read the description of Clym tying the strings of Eustacia's bonnet when she is leaving him and her own hands tremble too violently to do so—a scene in which the woman is washed clean of vanity by her grief, and the man steels himself against tenderness.

They did not realize in criticising the book thus that they were taking *The Return* out of its place in time—in the literature of the period and in Hardy's own life. For as McDowall has pointed out, Hardy here allies himself with the earlier Romantics

> with all the sensibility of the 19th century, in turning from orthodox beauty to the expressiveness of wild places; but instead of taking those as an escape from the fetters of life he takes them as a symbol of the facts of it. Egdon is valued for its *likeness* to what we know.[2]

[1] *After Strange Gods.* Faber & Faber, 1934.
[2] Arthur McDowall, *Thomas Hardy, A Critical Study*, p. 153. Faber & Faber, 1931.

As for Hardy's development, *The Return* was an explosion into the truth and reality of his own nature and idiosyncracy, and a revolt against asceticism and so-called Christian morality. Here for the first time he was fully himself: the mood, the setting, and the philosophy implied by that setting which it interprets, are peculiarly his. Yet he keeps himself in abeyance, his character does not over-intrude: a perfect balance is kept between the parts played by the characters and by Fate, or Chance, as well as a balance between creator and creations.

The Return of the Native is the most pagan of all Hardy's books. The pagan 'zest for life', which J. S. Mill had implied was a feature of 'early civilizations', is one of its main themes.[1] The mumming which savours of pre-Christian drama, the gipsying, the maying, the burning of the wax effigy and other superstitious practices, the lighting of the wild Beltane fires, above all the dancing, whether round the garlanded maypole or the whirling nocturnal flames, are all part of this pagan conception, expressed with a passionate vitality which exceeds allusions to it in a work concerned with a similar theme—*Jude the Obscure*.

> Indeed, the impulses of all such outlandish hamlets are pagan still: in these spots homage to nature, self-adoration, frantic gaieties, fragments of Teutonic rites to divinities whose names are forgotten, seem in some way or other to have survived mediaeval doctrine.[2] . . .

that is, the teaching of the mediaeval Church. The number of similar allusions to pre-Christian and classical races, places, heroes, heroines and goddesses, poets, philosophers, legends and monuments is remarkable; they are more numerous than in any other work of Hardy's and especially abound in the first four parts of the book. The wealth of descriptions and allusions implies something long repressed in the poet's nature, and this pagan side was never again so fully, so fitly, expressed.

As everyone knows, the Heath is the great protagonist of the

---

[1] See *Of Individuality*, passages beginning "Pagan self-assertion is one of the elements of human worth", and "Christian morality has all the characters of a reaction; it is in great part a protest against Paganism", etc. In Hardy's copy of *On Liberty* both these passages are scored.

[2] *The Return of the Native*, p. 479.

drama. But it is something more. This symbol of Nature and Necessity, this untamed, fecund, impassive force which suggests the abiding and the eternal, is (for Hardy) the equivalent of what later developed into the *Prutanis Makeron*, the 'President of the Immortals' of *Tess*, and the unweeting Will of *The Dynasts*. 'Naturing Nature and her unfaithful lord' (in the early poem "Discouragement") have merged into one—life which offers only to deny.[1] *Prutanis* and Will are here envisaged as an aspect of nature, embodied in a terrain which had dominated Hardy's childhood and boyhood, with whose moods and vapours he was saturated.

To realize what the Heath meant to Hardy we must look at some of his poems as well, since these are complementary to the famous opening description in *The Return*, and the writer's attitude to the Heath in the novel. In "Domicilium", that poem of adolescence, the Heath already dominates the dwelling and garden blossoming on its verge: the boy who wrote it devotes exactly twice as many lines to it as he does to the domestic scene: the emphasis is on the wildness of the Heath, that untamed Ishmaelitish thing. In "The Sheep Boy", a poem of maturity, another aspect of it is depicted which corresponds with two passages in *The Return* (usually neglected by critics in favour of the darker descriptions) on the Heath's summer glory. The adjective 'gorgeous' is used in both. In this poem there is a sudden transformation of 'the great valley of purple which thrills silently in the sun' (as *The Return* describes it) from—

> *A yawning, sunned concave*
> *Of purple, spread as an ocean wave . . .*

to a fog-filled landscape, folded away into 'creeping scrolls of white'. The 'gorgeous blow' and 'regal glow' are suddenly enveloped in a biblical 'moving pillar of cloud'.

In "The Moth Signal" we have a paraphrase of the scene in *The Return* in which Wildeve looses a moth to Eustacia's candle-flame, as a signal to her to come forth and secretly meet him. In "The Roman Road" a simile used in the novel is repeated, for the road (which now partially-obscured runs from Stinsford Hill

---

[1] *Yell'ham Wood.*

across the Kingston Maurward ewe-lease to Rushy Pond, and
so on up over the Heath)

> *. . . runs straight and bare*
> *As the pale parting-line in hair*
> *Across the heath.*

As the tragedy in Hardy's life deepens, the sinister qualities of
Egdon (whose name he adapted from *Eggardun*, or *don*, the
magnificent prehistoric hill-fortress on the final chalk spur of the
Dorset headlands) are increasingly emphasized, since they are
symbolic of personal misery.

> *There was another looming*
> *Whose build we did not see;*
> *There was one meekly blooming*
> *Full nigh to where walked we;*
> *There was a shade entombing*
> *All that was bright of me.*[1]

'The black, lean land of featureless contour' seems to the poet
like 'a tract in pain' in one mood. He identifies himself with the
Heath less passionately, less poetically, but more surely than in
The Return of the Native.

> *" This scene, like my own life," I said, "is one*
> *Where many glooms abide;*
> *Toned by its fortunes to a deadly dun—*
> *Lightless on every side."*[2]

In 1883 Hardy offered to take a fellow-traveller across the
Heath into his phaeton, whose lamps shone down on the man's
youthful face. But the traveller refuses: he is doomed to die
from an obscure disease and puts off death by long daily walks:
his personal tragedy is thrown into relief by the watchful intent-
ness of the Heath.[3] As age slackens the poet's own pace he
regrets that he and a loved one no longer go to watch the moon,

---

[1] "On a Heath" in *Moments of Vision.*
[2] "A Meeting with Despair" in *Wessex Poems,*
[3] "The Pedestrian" in *Moments of Vision.*

that 'wan woman of the waste up there',[1] rise over Froom Hill
Barrow.[2] Always the tumuli, the rounded barrows which bulge,

> . . . *as they bosoms were*
> *Of Multimammia stretched supinely there* . . .[3]

(a simile repeated in *Tess*) which speak to him of ancient races
and ancient things. 'A lonely mind communing with loneliness'[4]
draws inspiration and solace from the Heath whose vast care-
lessness varies in mood with the seasons. In summer, lit by
'forge-like skies', she turns from crimson to scarlet; in autumn
she wears her russet hues; and in the winter twilight sinks to a
'brown Valley of Melancholy', in which the dead are more alive
than the visible living.

The characters in *The Return of the Native*, subservient to the
Heath's moods, seem emanations from it: detached from it they
are, like Hardy himself, dominated by it. Thus the Heath par-
takes of the same nature as the Primal Cause, or the Will, for it
permits seemingly passive Eustacia, Clym and the others to seek
fulfilment or destruction yet ceaselessly coerces them, driven by
an urgency which it does not itself comprehend. Nevertheless,
a warning should be given not to read too much into the passage
in Part VI in which the First Cause is mentioned, together
with the magnanimity of humankind who 'hesitate to conceive
a dominant power of lower moral quality than their own'[5] (lines
which herald the reflections in "By the Earth's Corpse", "To
the Moon" and other late poems that it is time the Creator
ceased creating, or repents that He ever made life, earth and
man) since this was added later.[6]

This same passage has been cited as an example of Hardy's
increasing loss of hope, and his growing belief that it is less
agonizing to be a spectator, an interpreter of life, than a participant. He relinquishes life, and belief in life, and slowly renounces
desire. But resignation rather than passion has been the note

---

[1] "Seeing the Moon Rise."   [2] "At Moonrise and Onwards."
[3] "By the Barrows."   [4] McDowall, p. 154.   [5] p. 475.
[6] See Rutland, p. 185. On p. 183 he suggests that the original ending was
at the close of Part V, not VI. The MS was then in private hands and not
available for inspection. An examination of the final page of the manuscript, now in the possession of University College Library, Dublin, shows
that the close of the manuscript and published book are the same.

of even the earliest poems, and now it merely increases in *The Return of the Native*, having showed itself warily in *Desperate Remedies* and *A Pair of Blue Eyes*. But, as a Swedish writer has said, if Hardy was to be true to himself he must of necessity give artistic expression to this melancholy view of life which was 'an innate temperamental feature'.[1]

Those who, remembering the delicate descriptive passages in the earlier novels which reveal Hardy's acute sense of hearing, have been on the look-out for further examples will find many in *The Return*, notably the one of the heath awakening from its winter's trance. We listen with Eustacia, standing motionless on the barrow, to the symphony of November night sounds, a scene in which the mummied heath-bells make a noise which is likened to 'a worn whisper', 'a shrivelled and intermittent recitative', or the 'ruins of human song' from an aged throat. In another scene the listening lovers can tell from the wind half a dozen features of the hidden nocturnal landscape which a townsman would miss,

> for these differing features had their voices no less than their shapes and colours.[2]

In both these descriptions Hardy mingles the senses. The sound of the wind scouring the papery heath-bells 'brushed so distinctly across the ear' that those accustomed to it could visualize the heath bells '*as by touch*'. In the second scene Hardy expressly says that the 'compound utterances' addressed to the lovers' senses enabled them '*to view by ear*' the features of the neighbouring landscape. In the first he mingles hearing with touch, and, in the second, hearing with imagined sight. Clym's blindness accentuates his sense of hearing and Hardy makes him, when longing for Eustacia's return, imagine the fall of a leaf to be her footfall, a bird moving amongst the flower-beds to be her hand on the gate:

> at dusk, when soft, strange ventriloquisms came from holes in the ground, hollow stalks, curled dead leaves, and other crannies

[1] R. E. Zachrisson, *Thomas Hardy's Twilight View of Life, A Study of an Artistic Temperament*, p. 11. Stockholm, 1931.
[2] p. 102. 'Country places have each their own peculiar silences.' Unpublished note-book of Thomas Hardy. (By permission of the executors.)

wherein breezes, worms, and insects can work their will, he fancied that they were Eustacia, standing without and breathing wishes of reconciliation.[1]

This is reminiscent of a passage in *Desperate Remedies* and anticipates the remarkable one in *The Dynasts*. In the epic poem the flora and fauna inhabiting the battlefield are of necessity condensed into eighteen lines, whereas in a novel about the Heath they appear and re-appear in abundance—always as partners of human kind. For Darwin had taught Hardy something which his sensitive nature sorrowed and rejoiced in, that, as one of Hardy's critics puts it, 'we are all in it together'.

But it is not for these minutiae that we remember this novel, but for the beauty and passion of the descriptions, abounding in the vivid similes—the rebellious beauty of Eustacia who is '*like the tiger-beetle which . . . blazes with dazzling splendour*', or Mrs Yeobright who, '*like a planet, carries her atmosphere along with her in her orbit*'; the description of the summer heat when hollyhock leaves hang '*like half-closed umbrellas . . .* and the sap almost simmers in the stems', or of an old-fashioned hearth inside which all is Paradisial warmth and draughtlessness, where 'songs and tales are drawn out from the occupants by the comfortable heat *like fruit from melon plants in a frame*': of Eustacia and Clym in their marital felicity, 'enclosed in a sort of luminous mist, which hid from them surroundings of any inharmonious colour, and gave to all things the character of light': of Thomasin who resembles birds when in motion: of a wind-blown finch in a brake; of the dripping forests of fern; of that 'spire of blossom', the garlanded maypole; above all of the impassioned dancing. The passage describing Eustacia's dance with Wildeve by the nocturnal fires exhibits better than any other those two inter-related themes—the malefic influence of music and the disastrous results of the dance, that 'royal road' whereby quiet, respectable citizens are enflamed and destroyed like mere moths. Eustacia is drawn into the dance by her former lover *against her better judgment*: the 'equilibrium of their senses' is disturbed by the half-light, the music and their own smouldering passion until Wildeve moves in 'a dilemma of exquisite misery' and Eustacia is 'rapt, empty, quiescent', drained by an

[1] p. 428.

excess of emotion, like a woman possessed in the act of love. This 'riding on a whirlwind' of sensual abandon is the prelude to their doom.

More prosaically, we may take note of the number of times that Bonaparte is mentioned in this book. Apart from Granfer Cantel's references to his exploits as a Napoleonic volunteer there are other surprising ones to this warlike figure. He is one of Eustacia's heroes, together with Saul and William the Conqueror; she compares Wildeve with him and finds her shifty lover woefully lacking; and the reddleman, Venn, is likened to Napoleon in his hardness of heart in treating with a beautiful woman. A memory of Hardy's grandmother's (and of a London laundress) is used in describing the execution of Louis Philippe; and Nelson's *Victory*, here called *The Triumph*, appears in the next paragraph. These references show Hardy's absorption with the Napoleonic contest which was to flower in his next novel, and to take final shape in the epic *Dynasts*.

However, in 1878 Hardy had made up his mind that if he was to succeed as a writer he must live in, or near, London. He later regretted and reversed his decision but, for the time being, it seemed wise. Eight months before the publication of *The Return of the Native* in book form, and while it was still appearing serially, he said goodbye to 'the dusky house which stood apart', which had become dear to him because of his and Emma's happiness there—

> *Lifelong to be*
> *Seemed the fair colour of the time*—[1]

and because, when he returned to it after a day's outing, he was certain to find a figure

> *. . . white-muslined waiting there*
> *In the porch with high expectant heart.*[2]

On the 18th of March he wrote in his journal: "End of the Sturminster Newton Idyll"; and later, on re-reading this: "Our happiest time".[3]

---

[1] "The Musical Box" in *Moments of Vision*.
[2] *Ibid*. See also "A Two Years' Idyll" in *Late Lyrics*.
[3] I, p. 156.

CHAPTER SEVEN

THE PASSIONATE REVOLT

*I have realized that life is a point of view: to put it more
clearly—Imagination.*

ELLEN TERRY

THE days of Thomas and Emma Hardy, now that they had
decided to immerse themselves in London society, were
filled with dining out, going to theatres and concerts, studying
paintings in galleries, and entertaining, To enable them to lead
this life the writer was constantly forced to produce what he
called 'hand-to-mouth-serials'. But now he met important
people—scientists, writers, painters, publishers, legal lights and
members of the aristocracy; amongst them Huxley, whom he
had always admired; Alma Taddema, Watts and du Maurier;
Henry James, Browning, Matthew Arnold, Tennyson and young
Richard Jefferies—and measured his talent against theirs.

As a young man in Dorset he had taken down fragments of
old ballads and country lore; while watching the old people's
faces, mannerisms and tricks of speech he had squeezed them
dry of their ancient milk. In town he did much the same thing,
only less successfully. Alexander Macmillan told him a dramatic tale (which he had from Jane Carlyle) of seduction, desertion,
witchcraft and death set on Craigenputtock Moor, a life story as
tragic as any connected with Egdon. The fleeting expressions of
those whom Hardy met in streets, shops, omnibuses, clubs and
drawing-rooms were noted and reflected on. One night he went
to Irving's dressing-room and found him 'naked to the waist'
and 'champagne in tumblers'. Another time he was at Harrow
and talked with the boys in their dormitory, seeing through the
big boy's silent affectation of not being interested in what the
small boy bragged of. He joined the Savile Club and enjoyed
Leland's tales of hobnobbing with gypsies, while he silently
studied the narrator's face, 'a high flat façade, like that of a
clock tower'.

He was elected to the Rabelais Club in tribute to the virility
of his writing: Hardy was regarded as 'the most virile writer of

works of the imagination then in London"[1]. Henry James was firmly rejected. Links with essayists and poets of the past sometimes occurred. Once he was introduced to an old woman muffled in furs, renowned as the original of Byron's "Ianthe". The contrast between what Byron's charmer had been once, and now was, was not lost on Hardy's poetic, ironical nature. Mrs Barry Proctor recounted to him how she had once visited Lamb in his chambers in Edmonton and how Keats, 'a youth who nobody noticed much', had been brought to her house. He was introduced to Shelley's son, and here once again the Spirit of Irony presided, for Hardy found him an excellent man without a grain of poetry. He attended the funeral of young Louis Napoleon and was struck by the profile of Prince Napoleon, which reminded him strongly of Bonaparte's. Again he visited Chelsea Hospital to talk to the Pensioners and to listen to their grim tales of battles and military punishments in the days of Moore and Wellington.

His life in town was varied by visits to Dorset where his interest in architecture and painting took him to Ford Abbey, Kingston Lacy and other great houses. A note on a winter journey from Dorchester to Bockhampton, in driving sleet and rain, is memorable since it preserves the homely. His brother Henry had come to meet him in the family wagonette with old Bob, the pony.

> The wind on Fordington Moor cut up my sleeves and round my wrists—even up to my elbows. The light of the lamp at the bottom of the town shone on the reins in Henry's hands, and showed them glistening with ice. Bob's behind part was a mere grey arch: his foreparts invisible.[2]

He called on his old friend and master, William Barnes, at Winterbourne Came; he re-visted Weymouth, Portland and the tragic hamlet of Fleet by stony Chesil. In 1824 Fleet had been inundated by a tidal wave which had drowned people in their beds and swept away the nave of the little church, whose Mohun brasses are fortunately preserved in the extant chancel.[3] Although the spring was late and cold he sketched the Channel

---

[1] I, p. 173.   [2] I, pp. 163-4.
[3] The setting for Falkner's *Moonfleet*.

from Mayne Down, one of the most hauntingly beautiful of Dorset scenes: and in August of the same year (1879) he observed the disastrous results of a wet season for picnickers, boatmen, seaside landladies, school parties, shopkeepers and visitors.

During the recurrent visits to Dorset Hardy had been working on *The Trumpet Major* which he had agreed to write as a monthly serial throughout 1880. As might be expected, since the subject touched his heart and childhood memories, he collected 'five times as much material as he required'. The book was a new venture for him, neither an historical novel nor yet a fanciful one, but an imaginative tale compound of local tradition and historical fact, gathered from the talks in London with the Chelsea pensioners, boyhood talks in Dorset with former eye-witnesses of local scenes, from military handbooks, newspaper files, and Gifford's *History of the Napoleonic Wars* and other volumes.[1]

When in town Hardy also visited the British Museum to extract material. The notebook in which he recorded some of his information is now one of the prized exhibits of the Dorset County Museum. From it we learn that many details for the *Trumpet Major* were taken from the old *True Briton*, *The Morning Post* (which he found especially valuable), and other papers. To get the flavour of the period Hardy made minute drawings of such things as the neck of a woman's gown, a woman's cap complete with lace, ribbons and feathers, the coat of "Captain Absolute" in *The Rivals*, a Cockney sportsman's hat, the leggings, buttons and shoes of a coal-heaver of 1783, a silver cream-jug and teapot of 1792, and an iron grate, 'circa 1800'. There is also a note on a young woman's brow and nose, 'a perfect sweep'—her eye 'one sweep from corner to corner, no reverse curve'.

At home, the painted deal box carried by Hardy's grand-father 'when walking over the Ridgeway to meet Napoleon, as described in *The Dynasts*, together with other reminders of preparations for the invasion of the Dorset countryside (mentioned in the Preface to *The Trumpet Major*) were at hand for inspection. On her death in 1940, his surviving sister saw to it

[1] See Rutland, p. 189.

that this box and patterns of cloth worn by its bearer, Thomas Hardy the first, and his wife Mary,[1] should be preserved for future generations.

She also preserved some loose notes of her brother's which give the names and character of a heath-dweller and neighbour, the colloquial names of parts of the Heath (which appear in the *Poems*), and a note to the effect that the "large blue-and-white jug which hung on the middle of the [Bockhampton] dresser was called *Benjamin* and was always used [for the home-brewed ale, cider or mead provided] for the [Mellstock] singers when they came to practise in grandfather's time." This intimate note takes us back to *Under the Greenwood Tree* more swiftly than any printed page, not without meaning, for *The Trumpet Major*, Hardy's seventh novel, is closer to his second than any other of his prose works, with the exception of one or two of his short stories, both in spirit and style.

Owing to her coastline and the long sweep from St Aldhelm's Head to Portland Bill, Dorset has always been vulnerable to attack by sea: she was frequently invaded by the Danes. She is probably unique among English counties in possessing the diary of a militiaman who served for thirteen years (1796-1809), taking part in Sir John Moore's retreat to Corunna; and a home-made Napoleonic Invasion Book containing instructions for the defence of the district—Stourpaine—where it was drawn up.[2] The number of horses and wagons available for the transportation of women and children, of the cattle and sheep to be driven, of the extant tools—saws, axes and biddocks—and the names of the men to be responsible for these, are all given. People living in Dorset today, seventy years after Hardy's researches for *The Trumpet Major* and 150 years after the Napoleonic Wars, can still recall songs and legends orally handed down from these days, many of them corroborating material used by Hardy in this novel and two of his stories.[3]

---

[1] According to Kate Hardy, born and died respectively: 1777-1836 and 1772-1857. The dates on the Stinsford tombstone of Thomas Hardy 1st are 1778-1837.

[2] *Dorset Up-Along and Down-Along*, pp. 27-9. A Collection of History, Tradition, Folk Lore, etc., made by the Women's Institutes. Longmans (Dorchester), 1951.

[3] *The Melancholy Hussar* and *A Tradition of 1804*.

Hardy did not see the Invasion Book, nor the diary of Benjamin Miller, a leather-dresser from Melbury Osmund, who returned home from the bloody campaign to write of his experiences in Minorca, Eygpt, Gibraltar, Portugal and Spain, since a careful housewife rescued the first from domestic destruction after, and the Diary was discovered shortly before, Hardy's death. But that he saw another such diary is probable from a footnote about Sergeant Young in the third part of *The Dynasts*. Hardy also collected material from local tombstone inscriptions and from parish records.

The Trumpet Major is one of Hardy's most delicate, most charming works. It is full of enchanting descriptions—of an old-manor-house crusted with lichen, of the mill, mill-house, pool and gardens which smell of summer or its decline. As one reads one calls to mind the illustrations of Kate Greenaway, or Randolph Caldecott, which would interpret its moods, blending humour with pathos and light irony with romance: only a hint of the inevitable tragedy connected with war creeps in now and then. Anne Garland's attempts to give her heart to John, the Trumpet Major[1] (whom perversely she does not love), his heroic self-effacement and implied death, are never too heavily underscored.

Here is a description of pairs of lovers crossing a stream from the novel:

> They presently came to some stepping-stones across a brook. John crossed first without turning his head, and Anne, just lifting the skirt of her dress, crossed behind him. When they had reached the other side, a village girl and a young shepherd approached the brink to cross. Anne stopped and watched them. The shepherd took a hand of the young girl in each of his own, and walked backwards over the stones, facing her, and keeping her upright by his grasp, both of them laughing as they went.[2]

There are splashes of colour and music, too, for when Hardy's festive spirits are up he writes of yellow, blue and red-wheeled gigs, a girl's 'yellow gipsy hat' and lemon-coloured

[1] Hardy copied in his notebook a military warning to superior officers concerning the characters and duties of trumpeters and Trumpet Majors —that, although they were musicians, they must not be unwarlike and must be aware of the responsibilities of their calling.   [2] p. 351.

boots which make her feet look 'like a pair of yellow-hammers flitting under her dress', with exquisite lightness. The clarionets and fiddles of the church quire break forth while Bob waits outside for his intended; the fiddles, violoncellos, trombone and drum herald the descent of King George into the Weymouth waters; and the Aeolian harp which Bob makes for Anne at his brother's instigation, which twangs so distressingly during the night, is a fore-runner of Angel's harp and its disquieting effect on pliant Tess.

Perhaps because the tale's setting is a mill which grinds flour for bread the book abounds in wonderfully sensuous descriptions of food and drink. That 'man-woman', the miller's factotum David, bakes a seedy cake for the miller's prodigal sailor son so light and 'so richly compounded that it opened to the knife like a freckled buttercup'. Bob recklessly breaks eggs into the pan with an 'acquired adroitness . . . and at last made every son of a hen of them fall into two hemispheres as neatly as if it opened by a hinge'. The wedding-breakfast fare makes one's mouth water in these parsimonious days. The cider is made from old-fashioned apples with their lingering names—Tom Putts, Horners, Cleeves and Codlins: but in the description of the Casterbridge ale (and Dorchester has always been noted for its ales) Hardy excels himself:

> It was of the most beautiful colour that the eye of an artist in beer could desire; full in body, yet brisk as a volcano: piquant, yet without a twang; luminous as an autumn sunset; free from streakiness of taste; but finally, rather heady.[1]

Hardy can always charm and hold one when he swings from the humorous to the meditative, not the ponderous or deeply tragic. When describing the military manoeuvres on the downs, after giving the visual effect which the moving lines of red, white and black portions of uniforms produce on the eye, he suddenly changes his tempo and asks abruptly:

> Who thought of every point in the line as an isolated man, each dwelling all to himself *in the hermitage of his own mind*?[2]

But it is when he writes of the *Victory* and that other Thomas, Nelson's Flag-Captain, and of the Dorset men who are to die on

[1] p. 141.   [2] p. 109. (Italics mine.)

foreign battlefields that he best reveals his affectionate sympathy with his kind, and hints at the power which reaches maturity in *The Dynasts*. The description of the *Victory* as Anne watches her drop away over the horizon from Portland Bill (an event which Hardy told William Archer was 'a true story')[1] is both moving and poetically accurate. When the ship is end-on her width contracts to the proportion of a feather : next she seems to sink into, and to be absorbed by, the sea—hull, topsails, and top-gallants—until she's 'no more than a dead fly's wing on a sheet of spider's web. Yet even this fragment diminished'. The griev-ing girl watches 'with the fidelity of a balanced needle to a magnetic stone'.[2] (In this perfect simile one is reminded of Donne's comparison of the lovers' souls to the fixed feet of com-passes, one of which 'when the other far doth roam, leans and harkens after it'.)

When Hardy writes of the men clustered together on the downs, or drinking round the miller's door, unmindful of the doom which awaits them, he widens the horizon until it stretches from Dorset to the far corners of rock-ribbed Spain, and with the names of those far-off battles, and in prose which has a biblical ring, he evokes feelings of pride and pity for those who are ignorant that they will die.

> . . . but the King and his fifteen thousand armed men, the horses, the bands of music, the princesses, the cream-coloured teams—the gorgeous centrepiece, in short, to which the downs were but the mere mount or margin—how entirely have they all passed and gone!—lying scattered about the world as military and other dust, some at Talavera, Albuera, Salamanca, Vittoria, Toulouse, and Waterloo; some in home churchyards; and a few small handfuls in royal vaults.[3]

Lord David Cecil has spoken of Hardy's cinema-like method of visualizing a scene, with all its minutiae, and then of moving the camera back and giving us the long perspective. The scene is an example of that method. He also speaks of Hardy's in-stinctive modulation of sound which corresponds 'to the move-ment of the emotion it conveys'.[4] Here Hardy's innate poetic

[1] *Real Conversations*, p. 30. William Heinemann, 1904.
[2] *The Trumpet Major*, p. 318. [3] *Ibid.*, pp. 110-11.
[4] *Hardy the Novelist*, pp. 82-3. Constable, 1943.

sense makes him drop to the simple phrase—'some in home churchyards'—after the rolling, lingual foreign names, and close the sentence with a phrase in ballad metre.

Those who have analyzed Hardy's increasingly dark view of life seldom suggest that its origin was partly physical. Longevity may be enjoyed without abundant vitality. Furthermore one may be the victim of excessive nervous sensibility, and persistent melancholia, while enjoying general health. He confesses that he had 'a horror of lying down in close proximity to a monster whose body had four million heads and eight million eyes', a description which resembles a passage in *The Dynasts* describing the Monster, *Devastation*.[1] Then suddenly in *The Early Life* we come on the revealing note made in November 1878:

> Woke before it was light. Felt that I had not enough staying power to hold my own in the world.[2]

Two years later Hardy was stricken with an internal haemorrhage which nearly proved fatal. It is a curious fact that in *An Indiscretion*, published in the autumn in which the note above was made, the heroine dies from a similar weakness, and Hardy may have suffered from a mild attack previously.

Emma and he had been abroad again, this time to Normandy, thence to London, Dorset and Cambridge, where his illness was presaged by the weird shapes which he saw in the guttering candles of King's College Chapel, 'frayed shreds of scholars' shrouds'. At home, in Arundel Terrace,[3] he was forced to lie in bed with his feet higher than his head for several months. This position quickened the activities of his brain which, while Emma manfully nursed him, was especially fertile.

He fretted over financial problems and the harrowing thought that, should he die, his wife would remain unprovided for. He pondered on the relative merits of Positivism and Christianity: on the effects of multiple adversity; on that organism, Society; on general principles of Life, as he conceived it; on romanticism in literature; on realism; and on provincialism in literary style, and in feeling. From the November in which he was taken ill to

---

[1] I, p. 179, and Part III, Sc. v.   [2] p. 162.
[3] Near Wandsworth Common.

the following March he envisaged various forms for *The Dynasts* and, in the final note of this period, saw it as 'an historical drama' in which the action shall be 'mostly automatic . . . not the result of what is called *motive*, though always ostensibly so, even to the actors' own consciousness'.[1]

His worries were aggravated by the knowledge that he had agreed to provide for the new European edition of *Harper's Magazine* a tale already written in part, which was to appear in the very month of his seizure, and to be illustrated by George du Maurier.

From October to May, although often in severe pain, he dictated *A Laodicean* to his wife. The winter seemed endless. Deep snow fell and during those crucial months, Carlyle, George Eliot and Disraeli, all died. Hardy watched his keys grow rusty and his boots mouldy, while children seen through the window-panes grew alarmingly tall. His nearness to death brought him face to face with the central problem of his life—'how to reconcile a scientific view of life with the emotional and spiritual, so that they may not be inter-destructive'. After 'infinite trying', in a note written towards the close of his illness, Hardy came to the following conclusion:

Law has produced in man a child who cannot but constantly reproach its parent for doing much and yet not all, and constantly say to such parent that it would have been better never to have begun doing than to have *over*done so indecisively; that is, than to have created so far beyond all apparent first intention (on the emotional side), without mending matters by a second intent and execution, to eliminate the evils of the blunder of overdoing. The emotions have no place in a world of defect, and it is a cruel injustice that they should have developed in it. If Law itself had consciousness, how the aspect of its creatures would terrify it, fill it with remorse.[2]

This is the theme of another note, written seven years later, which closes with the oft-quoted plaint:

This planet does not supply the materials for happiness to higher existences. Other planets may, though one can hardly see how.[3]

It also forms the substance of the poems "Before Life and

[1] I, p. 191.   [2] I, p. 192.   [3] *Ibid.*, p. 286.

After", "By the Earth's Corpse", "God's Education", and others.

When he recovered, and had passed through that strangely disturbing feeling of being born anew, Hardy determined never to live in town again but only to visit it for several months of each year. He found that life in, or near, a city made him write mechanically, about ordinary things. Perhaps this, together with his illness, accounts for the paucity of imagination in *A Laodicean*, generally called his worst work. Yet it is an important one if only for this reason, that Hardy declared it to contain 'more of the facts of his own life than anything else he had ever written'[1] —one of the rare occasions on which he admits that portions of his life appear in his writing.

Thus, the hero is an architect who resembles his creator in his tastes, a fondness for—English rather than French Gothic; the 'gorgeous liveries' of sunset skies; the hymn *New Sabbath*, a favourite of his, his father's and the Stinsford quire, the tune which his father was bowing when he looked down from the gallery of that church and claimed his bride.[2] Like Thomas Hardy at twenty-two, and like the hero of *Desperate Remedies*, he is always writing poetry as a young man and admits having written little else, for two years;

> in every conceivable metre, and on every conceivable subject, from Wordsworthian sonnets . . . to epic fragments on the Fall of Empires. His discovery at the age of five-and-twenty that these inspired works were not jumped at by the publishers with all the eagerness they deserved, coincided in point of time with a severe hint from his father that unless he went on with his legitimate profession he might have to look elsewhere than at home for an allowance.[3]

This has the authentic biographical ring. 'Wordsworthian sonnets' and 'epic fragments on the Fall of Empires' corresponds with *Domicilium* and the projected *Dynasts*. Whether Thomas Hardy the second ever issued a 'severe threat' we do not know, but he may have done so. The interesting part of this description is the ensuing paragraph in which Hardy,

[1] Letter to William Lyon Phelps, Blunden, p. 49.
[2] *A Church Romance*.
[3] *A Laodicean*, pp. 6-7.

through George Somerset argues as if in opposition to parental advice:

> But light and truth may be on the side of *the dreamer*: a far wider view than the wise ones have may be his at that recalcitrant time, and his reduction to common measure be nothing less than a tragic event.[1]

As an analogy the writer then describes breaking in a colt, which he concludes, with regretful irony, can only end in one way for the animal—

> in a level trot round the lunger with the regularity of a horizontal wheel, and in the loss forever to his character of the bold contours which the fine hand of Nature gave it. Yet the process is considered to be the making of him.[2]

Here Hardy in retrospect seems actually to resent the years wasted on architectural work and to champion himself against the will of others. Not every writer is so fortunate as to be able to look back at the age of forty and to say to himself, 'I was right: I had it in me after all. The dreamer *is* as necessary to society as the practical man'.

One of the best portraits in this novel is that of the old Baptist minister, which Hardy acknowledged to be that of Mr Perkins of Dorchester, father of the lads with whom he had so earnestly argued on the subject of Infant Baptism. The heroine, Paula Power, refuses to be immersed as an adult, and the hero on her behalf takes up the cudgels with the Reverend Mr Woodwell. Hardy's extracts from a writer on the Church Fathers, incongruously bound up with notes for *The Trumpet Major*,[3] now leap into life, for on page 66 of the novel we find them condensed. This shows us something of Hardy's manner of working. *The Trumpet Major* ran from January to December, 1880, in *Good Words*: *A Laodicean* in *Harper's Magazine*[4] from December 1880—to December 1881. Thus, while still writing the former and gathering material for it in the British Museum, he was perforce already thinking of his next novel and taking down notes relevant to it.

---

[1] *A Laodicean*, pp. 6-7. (Italics mine.) [2] *Ibid.*
[3] In the County Museum Notebook. See p. 44, *Supra.*
[4] European edition.

The recurrent theme of social anomalies takes a new turn here with the portrayal of a friendship between Paula, the wealthy heroine, daughter of an engineer and builder of railways, and Charlotte de Stancy, a penniless member of a 'worn-out' family, former owners of the castle purchased from them by Miss Power's father. Paula reads Marcus Aurelius and Charlotte becomes a nun, but the improbability of these facts pales beside the actions of the villain of the piece, William Dare, illegitimate son of Captain de Stancy, Charlotte's brother. Mephistophelian characters, whose blackness is unrelieved by any strain of goodness, attracted Hardy, since his sense of the power of evil was stronger than his belief in that of goodness. The magnetic power which natures such as these have over the more impetuous, simple and sincere, a power savouring of witchcraft and necromancy, never ceases to fascinate him. Dare is the most unscrupulous and the worst of Hardy's villains. His villainy is unconvincing, even though he descends to pistols, blackmail and a game of cards with another villain in the church vestry.

Captain de Stancy is unable to control his son, who is his superior in wits, because of his own divided nature; and here Hardy comes closer to psychological subtlety than he has done heretofore in drawing a male character. When Paula refuses to marry de Stancy she wisely remarks that marriage with her will not cure his discontent, which is 'constitutional', and will persist whether she accepts him or not: and de Stancy's bifold nature is described thus:

> That mechanical admixture of black and white qualities without coalescence, on which the theory of men's characters was based by moral analysis before the rise of modern ethical schools, fictitious as it was in general application, would have almost hit off the truth as regards Captain de Stancy ... It was this tendency to moral chequer work which accounted for his varied bearings towards Dare.[1]

Yet despite the mention of 'new ethical schools' and their ameliorating precepts, Hardy remains fascinated by the black-and-white characters of ballad and folklore. One expects William Dare to disappear in a clap of thunder, or in a ghostly

[1] *Ibid.*, p. 240.

chariot drawn by black phantom horses, like the mysterious Baron in *The Romantic Adventures of a Milkmaid*, hastily written two years later.

Being a man before his time, in some aspects of his thought, Hardy had an uncanny knack of foretelling events in his work. In *The Poor Man and the Lady* the hero had made inflammable speeches to working-men in Trafalgar Square, but Hardy pointed out to Sir Edmund Gosse in relating the plot of this novel to him that

> this was rather a remarkable prophecy, because at that time no such meetings had ever been held in Trafalgar Square, and John Morley actually pointed out this scene to him as absurd and impossible.[1]

In *A Laodicean* the heroine, new owner of the ancient castle, says: "People hold these places in trust for the nation, in a sense." As the National Trust was not founded until 1895 this is a remarkable forecast of their attitude. Hardy also foretells the fate of the upper classes in a socialistic society; de Stancy's ne'er-do-well son declares:

> The truth is we must not take too high a tone. Our days as an independent division of society, which holds aloof from other sections, is past.[2]

But his introduction of the railway into this novel is disappointing. In *The Return of the Native* the travelling reddleman is used as one of the symbols of a vanished, poetic past which the coming of the railways has jeopardized. In *A Laodicean* the railway is used merely to emphasize Paula's ancestry, or as an excuse for throwing the lovers together in the face of imminent danger, a device which Hardy had earlier used in *An Indiscretion*.

Hardy was fond of imagining a 'new type' and a 'new face', which the close of the century was producing. In *The Return of the Native* Clym Yeobright exemplified this 'future human type', harassed by thought which, like a disease, infects the old rural and religious simplicity of mind. To over-develop one's intellect is to destroy one's happiness, a belief which (as Hardy must have

---

[1] *Sunday Times*, January 22, 1928.
[2] p. 359.

known) he shared with the Catholic Church. But, as D. H. Lawrence has said, in a little-known essay on Hardy's novels,

> One does not catch thought like a fever; one produces it. If it be in any way a disease of flesh, it is rather the rash that indicates the disease, than the disease itself.[1]

In *A Laodicean* both Paula and Somerset show signs of this 'disease', not only in their expressions but in their actual features; and on the last page of the book the 'modern spirit' makes its appearance. Paula senteniously asks her husband whether he thinks she may become a perfect example of it,

> . . . representing neither the senses and understanding, nor the heart and imagination, but what a finished writer calls 'the imaginative reason'.[2]

It is this sort of writing which irritates unsympathetic readers of Hardy's work. We may more readily understand him if we look at his notes. The 'finished writer' was Matthew Arnold whom he had been reading, and the undigested thought is here set down to be pondered on, rather than to be used in a stilted conversation, at an improbable moment, in an unlikely place, as in the novel.

> Style: consider the Wordsworthian dictum—the more perfectly the natural object is reproduced, the more truly poetic the picture. This reproduction is achieved by seeing into *the heart of a thing* (as wind, rain, for instance), and is realism, in fact, though through being pursued by means of the imagination it is confounded with invention, which is pursued by the same means. It is, in short, what M. Arnold calls 'the imaginative reason'.[3]

This somewhat muddled record of a train of thought came to Hardy while lying on his back in Arundel Terrace in January 1881. The final chapters of *A Laodicean* were despatched to the publishers in May, before he ventured out of doors for the first time after his illness.

In the year before his illness (1879) Hardy had published his

---

[1] "Six Novels of Thomas Hardy and the Real Tragedy", *Book Collectors' Quarterly*, January-March 1932. Cassell & Co.

[2] p. 499.

[3] I, p. 190. (Italics mine.)

second, and one of his most spirited, short-stories.[1] This was *The Distracted Preacher*, a tale full of vigorous action, and of characters who delight in smuggling contraband spirits, concealing them in the Church tower and in empty tombs with the Vicar's knowledge. The heroine, Lizzie Newberry, one of Hardy's most resourceful feminine characters, is an active participant in the sport, although she is weakly converted to proselytising in the end. Perhaps the tale was suggested to him while he and Emma were lodging with the old sea-captain in Swanage, but smuggling in Dorset was not confined to seaports or coastal spots, and Ower Moigne, setting of the tale, lies some distance away from the downs. Even an inland market-town like Sturminster Newton thrived on its proceeds, and an unpublished notebook of Hardy's tells us that the Bockhampton home had been one of the smuggler's outposts in his grandfather's life-time, until, other houses being built nearby, the secrecy necessary for good trade became endangered.

From 1879 until 1900 Hardy published one or two short stories annually, the greatest number in any single year being four in 1891, a year of exceptional literary activity for him.[2] These short-stories bear little resemblance to those of the great masters of this art as we now know it, whether French, Russian, English or American. Hardy's *adagio tempo* does not readily lend itself to this kind of prose, which requires a style more incisive and a form more highly compressed. Although he is able to point home the exact shade of meaning by means of a simile, or metaphor, in one of the long descriptions of his novels, and to portray an event or series of events, sometimes covering a long period of time, in a poem, when he submits himself to the discipline of short-story writing Hardy fails to be concise. Like a foreigner speaking an alien language, or a man uncertain of his bearings, he is often wordy, or moves over a larger area than that required to reach his destination.

The explanation seems to lie in this—that Hardy regarded his short-stories as novels in miniature. We know that he did not care for the word 'novel' for his longer works, preferring merely

---

[1] The first was *Destiny and a Blue Cloak*, published in the *New York Times* in 1874.
[2] In 1886, 1892, 1894 and 1898 none appeared.

G

to call them stories, or even tales, and when he had written *The Romantic Adventures of a Milkmaid* (now generally called a short-story) he himself described it as ' a short, hastily-written *novel* '.[1] He evidently did not regard them as independent literary forms. Hence he finds obvious difficulty in compressing an entire family history, such as that of the father and his three children in *The Tragedy of Two Ambitions*, into a few pages. Not satisfied with mere incidents, with a solitary action, or its effects, Hardy prefers to paint his canvas large. He finds it hard to dispense with the passages of mounting poetic fervour, which occur in the novels when he is moved by nature and uses her moods to symbolize those of humankind. Nor can he find space for those problems of life which fret and chafe his spirits—the plight of those who are spiritually disinherited; of those perversely matched, or divided by impassable barriers; the compassionate heart in conflict with the law, whether the law of the courts, the church, or society. Subjects such as these can not be treated easily in short tales.

Many of the stories are what D. H. Lawrence tellingly called 'little tales of widows and widowers'. Yet how delicious Hardy's best stories are, and how beautifully does he weave into them the stuff of vanishing legend and superstition, humour and irony deepening into bitter satire in some; and how exquisite are the vignettes of country life and the rural scene.

For instance, when the mowers in *A Superstitious Man's Story* sit down to refresh themselves under a tree, and fall asleep in the heat of the day, one of them on waking sees a great white miller-moth —a 'miller's soul' in Dorset—fly from the other's mouth while he sleeps. This belief in the visibility of the soul of a sleeper who is about to die is as old in English literature as the 14th-century tale of *Havelock the Dane*, in which the soul appears as a fluttering flame. But Hardy in using it was not copying ancient literature, he was relishing the poetic beauty of the superstition, and, furthermore, recording what was still believed in Dorset.

All that about the Miller's soul is, or was until lately, an actual belief down here. It was told me years ago by an old woman. I may say, once and for all, that every superstition, custom, etc., described in my *novels* may be depended on as true records of the

[1] I, p. 205. (Italics mine.)

same, whatever merit they may have in folklorists' eyes, and are not inventions of mine.[1]

This story is one of those linked together by the Chaucerian device of making the tellers fellow-travellers in a carrier's van. *A Few Crusted Characters*[2] is a collection of some of Hardy's most spontaneous and refreshing tales, including an inimitable one about the old Quire, which once again has its counterpart in Sussex lore. The humour of these tales is rich and natural; it springs from the life that Hardy knew and loved as a boy.

In *The Romantic Adventures of a Milkmaid*, a fairy-tale of the Dorset countryside, whose theme resembles that of *The Fiddler of the Reels*, we catch for an instant some of the vanished colour of the English landscape. From his garden terrace the mysterious Baron watches the haymakers at their work:

> The white shirt-sleeves of the mowers glistened in the sun, the scythes flashed, voices echoed, snatches of song floated about, there were glimpses of red waggon-wheels, purple gowns, and many coloured handkerchiefs.[3]

But for psychological subtlety and dramatic power the two finest stories are *The Withered Arm* and *The Fiddler of the Reels*. *The Withered Arm* is a novel in embryo, and in the hands of Gogol, or Dostoevsky, would have been developed with an analytical subtlety which would have made it one of the great masterpieces of European literature. It is the most complex of all Hardy's tales, emotionally, for we have the criss-cross relationships of a prosperous farmer with his bride, Gertrude, his former mistress, Rhoda, and his illegitimate son; of Rhoda and her boy; and finally, of Rhoda and Gertrude, who are drawn to each other despite mistrust and hatred. The lad, whose character is never developed, is the human pawn of his elders, themselves the victims of powerful emotions which they do not understand. The interplay of hatred and attraction, of the unsuspected forces agitating the actors, and of those ironic ones controlling their circumscribed world, are all the stuff of a tragic drama of the highest order.

[1] Letter to Edward Clodd in the Ashley Library. See Rutland, footnote, p. 220. (Italics mine.)   [2] In *Life's Little Ironies*.
[3] *A Changed Man and Other Tales*, pp. 357-8.

The Fiddler of the Reels is the supreme example in Hardy's work of the malefic power of music, and the only one in which the fiddler, knowing his powers, consciously uses them to destroy his victim. The 'ecstasizing air' of the Duchess of Richmond's Ball on the eve of Waterloo, the enticing tune which prevails over sober Elizabeth Jane's resolves, the 'exaltation' which lifts pliant Tess and causes her to listen to Angel's playing 'like a fascinated bird' until 'her heart is nearly dragged out of her bosom',[1] in this tale draws the soul of a weak-willed girl 'out of her body like a spider's web'. There are recollections of that emotion which had troubled Hardy when, as a susceptible child, he had danced and wept simultaneously.

The subjection of a person's will, through music, dancing or some other agency, a power allied to witchcraft and necromancy, fascinates Hardy. His preoccupation deepens into a conception of mankind as puppets, *fantoccini*, manikins in the power of the Immanent Will. The two themes finally emerge into one in *The Dynasts*, when the Spirit of the Years speaks of puppets manipulated by strings in one line and continues:

> *You'll mark the twitchings of this lonely Bonaparte*
> *As he with other figures foots his reel.*[2]

The Withered Arm was published in 1888, in the year following the appearance of *The Woodlanders*, and *The Fiddler of the Reels* in 1893, two years after *Tess of the d'Urbervilles*.

At midsummer 1881, after his severe illness, Hardy rented a small house in Wimborne, a pleasant market-town in east Dorset with memories of Roman and West Saxon occupations, and a fine old minster wherein are buried an elder brother of Alfred's, and Defoe's two daughters—facts which pleased Hardy with his sense of history and love of English writers.[3] The curious 14th-century clock whose Napoleonic wooden Quarter Jack, wearing the dress of a British Grenadier, strikes the hours with queer contortions took his fancy as being yet another symbol of human life animated by unseen forces. It appears in the opening

---

[1] In *The Dynasts*, *The Mayor of Casterbridge*, and *Tess of the d'Urbervilles.*
[2] Part I, Fore-scene. (Italics mine.)
[3] See "Copying Architecture in an Old Minster."

pages of *The Dynasts*, wherein the Spirit of the Pities urges the other Spirits forward with:

> *So may ye judge Earth's jack-a-clocks to be*
> *Not fugled by one Will, but function-free.*

The garden of their little house was full of summer fruit and old-fashioned flowers which made Hardy feel at home, and on their first night he and Emma saw through the glass of the greenhouse a long-tailed comet. After a visit to Scotland where they talked to an old man who had known Scott, they settled down in Wimborne. Hardy corrected proofs sitting under a vine whose tendrils twisted about seeking to attach themselves in almost human fashion, and whose giant leaves canopied his pages, giving them a strange subaqueous light. His notes at this time are concerned with the art of writing fiction—how to create illusion and yet preserve the balance between common and uncommon, how to relate this proportion to characters and events. A humorous poem "The Levelled Churchyard", written at Wimborne, would have given pleasure to Swift or Tom Hood.

Far from being dull as they had expected, Emma and he found themselves swept up into a whirl of provincial gaiety. There were afternoon calls, dinners with music, and Shakespearian evenings during which Hardy marked the characters and reactions of the performers as they read their parts, making a play-scene within a play, to the confusion of the readers had they known what he observed. And there was a Christmas ball. Lord Wimborne deplored the dampness of Canford Manor, caused by the penning of water for the mill below, and Hardy was glad that he refused to pull the mill down, or to drain the pool, since the mill 'ground food for the body' just as an old church 'ground food for the soul'. He noted with a wry, inward smile that his Lordship's reasons were more prosaic than his own, for the loss of the mill would have reduced his income by fifty pounds a year.

The comet which had heralded Hardy's return to Dorset, and an 18th-century tower (re-built the year before his birth) in Charborough Park, south-west of Wimborne Minster, set his mind running on his new book, *Two on a Tower*, the first of his novels to appear in an American paper before an English.[1] As he explains in a preface written some thirteen years later, his intention was 'to set the emotional history of two infinitesimal lives against the stupendous background of the stellar universe', and to suggest that 'of these contrasting magnitudes the smaller might be the greater to them as men'. This theme, the *credo* of Hardy's work, which appears in his notes as

> Clouds, mists and mountains are unimportant beside the wear on a threshold, or the print of a hand,[2]

implies that the novel may include passages which, to use Dr Rutland's phrase, are a kind of 'spiritual autobiography'. But this preface was absent when the tale first appeared, and readers were not discerning enough to spy out Hardy's intention behind the plot.

In order to give a semblance of actuality to this visionary story, the writer read some technical works on astronomy, and applied to the Astronomer Royal for permission to go over Greenwich Observatory, a request which he was granted by means of a clever ruse on Hardy's part.[3] Here, for the last time, he plays out his childhood fantasy of the man of humble origin wedding the great lady. The hero, Swithin St Cleeve, is a clever lad with 'two stations of blood in his veins' that is, he is the son of a curate and a farmer's daughter. He is loved by Lady Constantine, who is older than he, believes herself to be a widow, marries St Cleeve, discovers her husband to be alive, and also that she is with child. She realizes that she is a burden to St Cleeve, an impediment to his rising in his profession. She heroically sets her love on one side, and half out of true self-sacrifice, half out of conventional necessity, marries a suitor for her hand—a Bishop, who conveniently dies.

Hardy had himself known something of what he calls that 'divine tenderness' which an older woman may show for a child, or, in the novel, for 'a lover several years her junior'. It may be nothing more than coincidence but Swithin's mother's maiden name, and that of his old grandmother with whom he lives, is *Martin*, and it is possible that, in this final resurrection of

---

[1] In the *Atlantic Monthly*.   [2] I, p. 153.

[3] The Astronomer Royal is unable to trace Hardy's letter to the Observatory.

the early fantasy, the memory of Julia Augusta shadowed Hardy's pages. Be that as it may, the hero in this tale wins the highborn lady herself, not her daughter, or descendant. With this triumphant end to the lingering fantasy it drops out of sight and does not re-appear, for it has at last played itself out.

The book was not at all to the taste of the Victorian public: the critics, who always demanded that a story should be plausible even if life is not, found it 'extravagant, impossible, unpleasant' and even 'objectionable'. The marital complications, and what they conceived as a slur on the Church, stuck in their throats, and the wistful beauty of the tale was lost to them. Since it impinged too closely on their own times they failed to recognize the blighting effect of 19th-century scientific thought on the mind of a sensitive writer, and, with the exception of Havelock Ellis, an early admirer of Hardy's work, there were few who praised it.[1]

But Hardy had always loved the stars. Long before he had thought of *Two on a Tower* he had been fascinated by their brilliance and beauty. A young girl and an old woman, the cook's attendants in the Big House kitchen, and dancers in a shepherd's hut have all been compared to stellar bodies previously.[2] In one tale the stars 'flutter like bright birds': in another they seem 'indecisive and palpitating': in *Tess of the d'Urbervilles* they are described as 'steely', and Jupiter hangs like a 'bright, full-blown jonquil' in the western sky—similes repeated with slight variations in *The Dynasts*. The wheel of the constellations in *Far from the Madding Crowd* gives to the opening chapters a poetic grandeur unequalled by any other writer of the period, and we watch with Gabriel the stars 'timed by a common pulse'.

In Hardy's notes Orion reflected upside down in a roadside pool, imprisoned in a network of crossed branches, catches his eye and imagination. Strangely enough, the stars do not appear so frequently or shine with such brilliance in his poems as they do in his prose. There is the 'leaping star' of "The Sign Seeker,"

[1] In the *Westminster Review*, April 1883.
[2] See *The Hand of Ethelberta*, *The Return of the Native*, *Desperate Remedies*, and *The Three Strangers*.

and the "Comet at Yell'ham"—'a strange fiery lantern' with a 'strange swift shine'—appears in two poems. The immense glittering form of Orion strides through another: and in a remarkable phrase, in a fourth, the 'tired stars' of a sky breaking from night-into-dawn 'thin together'.

But, after the first youthful exhilaration which he derives from them, the stars, like the earth, bring Hardy little happiness. There is in his work none of that divine content, that sense of mystery, which a metaphysical poet like Vaughan felt when contemplating the miracle of light, or 'the planet's ordered flight'— nothing to alleviate his spiritual loneliness. The pastoral world of enchantment, like that beloved by the painter Samuel Palmer, is for Hardy a mockery and a delusion. Astronomy is a 'tragic' study, the results of which are to dwarf human significance into nightmare insignificance ; a study of stellar bodies and chasms brings not only unendurable loneliness but overpowering 'pulsations of horror'.[1]

But, as we have seen, disillusion with the universe was no new thing for Hardy. His depiction of the decaying stellar universe in which stars 'burn out like candles', or are become 'black invisible cinders', in *Two on a Tower* is merely an echo of what he had written as a young man in *A Lunar Eclipse*, and *In Vision I Roamed*. The basic thought of these two poems of the year 1866 is the same as that expressed in the novel of 1882, a letter written to a friend in 1902, and a passage in *The Dynasts*, 1903-8. It is significant that a single expressive adjective occurs in *all* these writings—the word *ghastly*, or *ghast*. In *In Vision I Roamed* the young poet speaks of the loneliness engendered by contemplating 'ghast heights of sky': in *Two on a Tower* St Cleeve describes the gradations of quality in the starry wilderness, ranging from 'dignity, solemnity and awfulness' to 'a size at which *ghastliness* begins'. In the letter to a friend[2] Hardy explicitly says that the more we pry into nature's secrets the more we gain only sadness, and 'the more *ghastly* a business one perceives it all to be', with further adumbrations. Finally, in *The Dynasts* the 'solar craters spew and spit' as balefully as when, in *Two on a Tower*, St Cleeve studies them at the South

---

[1] See *Two on a Tower*, pp. 33 and 318.
[2] Edward Clodd, February 27, 1902. See Rutland, pp. 64 and 192-7.

Pole, gaining only a terrifying sense of loneliness and a new horror.

> *. . . the roars and plashings of the flames*
> *Of earth-invisible suns swell noisily,*
> *And onwards into* ghastly *gulfs of sky,*
> *Where hideous presences churn through the dark—*
> *Monsters of magnitude without a shape,*
> *Hanging amid deep wells of nothingness.*[1]

Thus, for more than forty years, Hardy's reactions did not change. His youthful dismay and discouragement only deepened and set hard.

Darwin, for whose integrity of thought he had always had great admiration, died in April 1882, and Hardy went to his funeral in Westminster Abbey, a month before the publication of the first instalment of *Two on a Tower*. His thoughts may have ranged back to the days when he first read *The Origin of Species* (and other scientific works) and to the disturbing emotions which they roused in him at that time.

His notes of this period indicate that 'melancholy marked him for her own', despite the consolations of Wimborne and Dorchester society. He sees people as caged birds, 'the only difference being in the size of the cage;' and the world around him 'weeping and mourning', and he considers this 'the widened view of nowadays'. While he studies a skeleton hung against the window-panes in a First Aid room he sees the children dancing on the green (past the skeleton dangling in front), just as in Paris with his brother eight years later he stares at the silent, moonlit graves over the heads of the dancing, grimacing, *can-can* girls of the *Moulin Rouge*.[2]

A solitary note, made on a trip to Paris and Versailles with his wife in the autumn of 1882, indicates the writer's gradual relinquishment of hope.

> Since I discovered, several years ago, that I was living in a world where nothing bears out in practice what it promises incipiently, I have troubled myself very little about theories . . . I am content with tentativeness from day to day.[3]

[2] I, pp. 264 and 300.   [3] *Ibid.*, p. 201.
[1] Part III, *After-scene*. (Italics mine.)

Disillusion, like an insidious sea-fog, has stealthily crept in. But if, as Mazzini once said, 'disillusion is disenchanted egotism', what self-disenchantment is involved? There has evidently been a blight on ardour, affection, hope, on the springs of life itself. It is possible that the lack of a child, added to the early loss of faith which one of religious inclinations needs for support, saddened Hardy. Living with 'tentativeness from day to day' hardens into Tess' fatalistic acceptance of her, and her family's, lot, played out beneath the 'cold pulses of the stars beating . . . in serene disassociation from . . . wisps of human life'.

Yet hand-in-hand with melancholy and discouragement went a healthy pleasure in the quirks and oddities of human nature, which always delighted Hardy. When Emma's brother-in-law, the Rector of St Juliot, died Hardy recalled the humorous anecdotes with which he had formerly regaled him; and there are other tales of country and town behaviour which set him inwardly laughing at this time in the *Early Life*.

In June 1883, Hardy made up his mind to remove to the county town of Dorchester. He had begun to feel that he would like a home of his own designing and, in October, the foundations of Max Gate, where he lived for the rest of his life, were laid. Meanwhile he rented a cramped old house in Shirehall Lane, of which Blunden records a townsman as saying, "He have but one window and she do look into Gaol Lane."[1] In order to build his own home Hardy had first to purchase some ground from the Duchy of Cornwall, (their first sale to a private individual for many generations), choosing a piece of land in that field of mediaeval tenure and proportions, Fordington Field, which covers some 3,000 acres.[2] The spot was a bare one on the outskirts of the town, on the road to Wareham, near Conquer Barrow, a fine prehistoric earthwork crowned with Scotch firs, and close to an old tollgate-house inhabited by one commonly called Mack—hence Mack's Gate. The house took some time to build and Emma and he were unable to move in until the end of June 1885. Hardy wished to avoid pretentiousness and

---

[1] p. 51.
[2] Bishop Moule says that until 1870 it was unbroken by a fence and was tilled by farmers on a pre-Christian system of annual exchange.—Max Gate was built by Hardy's brother, Henry.

unnecessary expense. The house he designed was solid and comfortable but singularly lacking in charm. Granted that villas were the fashion of the day, and that Emma Hardy may have been responsible for its general style rather than the poet-architect, it still remains incongruous. How could a man who loved beauty in painting and architecture, who wrote with affection of Dorset's exquisite stone manors (one of which in the 1880's could have been bought for a reasonable sum) build such a house? For Max Gate remains uncompromisingly unattractive, almost suburban in character, and the belt of trees which was planted round it, with the double intention of forming a wind-brake and of gaining privacy, now gives it a gloomy, shut-in appearance. One can only imagine that Hardy, like many artists, was oblivious to beauty in his immediate domestic surroundings, that he dwelt in a world of the imagination so intense that it excluded any need for the former. Decency, a modicum of comfort, but above all privacy, were what he required.

Living at Max Gate enabled him to keep in touch with the surviving Moules in Dorchester, his family at Bockhampton, and William Barnes at Winterborne Came. With an ironic appreciation of Barnes' single-minded purpose to minister to his flock, rather than to preach fine sermons for literary men, Hardy recalls how he and Edmund Gosse went to hear Barnes preach in the church outside which he now lies buried. The older poet 'almost pointedly excluded' them from his sermon, but he made atonement to them after the service by taking them to the Rectory, where he showed them his collection of paintings and engravings made over a period of many years. This display was of especial interest to both Gosse and Hardy, whose love of painting and poetry drew them together. Amongst Barnes' paintings was one which he had had the wisdom to purchase before the artist was valued in his own country, *The Three Marys* by Richard Wilson, which Hardy purchased at Barnes' death and which is now in the possession of one of Hardy's friends.

Walking in the Bockhampton plantation (part of Thorncombe wood) on this forty-fourth birthday, Hardy saw in the twilight 'strange faces and figures', leaves which shone 'like human eyes', and 'sky glimpses . . . like white phantoms and cloven tongues'.[1]

But before he might inhabit his new home he was obliged to live in Dorchester, which afforded him glimpses of street-musicians, circuses, and strolling players to whom he was always attracted. He gives a dramatic sketch of *Othello* played in a canvas booth in Dorchester market-field. Although he stands critically aloof from the rural audience, who mock the tawdry players, Hardy is half in love with the vermilion scene lit by the sinking sun, a primitive setting suited to the 'immortal words which spread . . . into the silence around, and to the trees, and to the stars'.[2]

His residence in Dorchester,[3] broken by visits to London, the Channel Islands, and Lord and Lady Portsmouth's home in Devonshire, revived his boyhood memories of the ancient borough and gave him a setting for the novel which he had been working on, with many interruptions, for some time past—*The Mayor of Casterbridge*. Anyone reading this book for the first time will be struck by the wealth of simile and metaphor, signifying a work of the highest visual and imaginative power.

As one might expect, knowing Hardy's love of the ancient, the aspect of Dorchester which he emphasizes is her Roman past. But he was not alone in a consciousness of historic and archeological wonders at this time. Antiquities, Roman or otherwise, were much in the minds of Englishmen, including the poets. As early as 1839 William Barnes had sent a letter on *The Roman Amphitheatre at Dorchester* to the *Gentleman's Magazine*, and Wordsworth had written some beautiful lines on an archeological discovery in the north in which he spoke of

> , . . *mere fibulae without a clasp,*
> *Obsolete lamps, whose light no time recalls;*
> *Urns without ashes, tearless lachrymals.*[4]

There had been spasmodic local 'digs' and discoveries during Hardy's childhood in the neighbourhood of Dorchester. In 1842 the Roman villa with its tessellated pavement (a common find in these parts) had been unearthed at Preston: many years

---

[1] I, p. 216.   [2] I, pp. 218-19.   [3] From June 1883-5.
[4] *Athenaeum*, Sept. 21, 1884.

later, in a barrow not far from the town, there was discovered something which must have strongly appealed to Hardy's sense of pity—an oblong grave containing a woman's skeleton clasping a black vessel, together with her three children, each carrying his small viaticum. Even at Max Gate what looked like hard, modern, umpromising soil had yielded three elliptical graves, each with its skeleton neatly fitted in, 'like a chicken in its shell', as Hardy described it. On the head of one there rested a fibula, or clasp of iron and bronze, of which the front had once been gilded. And there were other ancient signs of tenure and burial, which Hardy liked to discourse on to his friends, and on which he published articles.[1]

He liked to think that the fibula which had fastened the fillet across the brow of a living person, 1500 years before, had belonged to a woman. "I took it from her skull with my own hands and it lies in the corner cupboard yonder."[2] He also told William Archer that the workmen had 'decapitated five Roman soldiers, or colonists, in moving earth to make the drive' at Max Gate; and a large, possibly a sacrificial, stone which he named the Druid Stone and which it took 'seven men with levers and appliances' to lift it into position, became a familiar ornament of the garden.

The Dorset Field Club had been formed in 1875, and in 1884, the year in which The Mayor was written, the new building for the County Museum was opened by its enterprising organizer, Henry Moule, brother of Horace, who delighted in giving talks to working-men on the ancient history of their countryside and in collecting antiquities, amongst them the head-gear of a Roman lady dug up at Fordington, and some vicious man-traps with jaws like crocodiles, whose dramatic implications Hardy was quick to seize on, and to use in The Woodlanders.

These discoveries and collections merely added zest to memories stored in Hardy's mind—memories of Dorchester as he had heard it spoken of by the old people at home, by William Barnes and others, and as he had known it from childhood

---

[1] See Some Romano-British Relics found at Max Gate, Dorchester, Dorset Field Club Proceedings, Vol. XI, 1890, and Chapter XI of The Mayor of Casterbridge for almost identical descriptions of the Max Gate discoveries.
[2] Archer, p. 38. It is now in the County Museum.

upwards. At the age of six he must have heard fragments of the controversy which agitated Dorchester as to whether Poundbury and Maumbury, her prehistoric fortress and amphitheatre (then believed to be Roman), were to be cut in half by the makers of the new railway. They were barely saved from truncation and, as the workmen dug near them, numerous evidences of ancient settlements—stone coffins and other impressive objects —were unearthed. Maumbury was excavated in 1879 when Hardy was thirty-nine. He reflects his interest in it and in *Mai-dun*, or Maiden Castle—the gigantic fortress with its complex entrenchments which looms large, like a silent, straight-backed, sleeping animal, in the plain on the road to the south-west—in poem, short story and letter.[1]

But Hardy was not merely interested in ancient monuments as an archaeologist; he could penetrate the past imaginatively and clothe these hoary hulks of antiquity with vanished magnificence. He invested them with 'the power, the pride, the reach of perished Rome', and used them as a backcloth, not for a highly-coloured historical romance, but for the dramatic rise and fall of a violent man, obsessed with ambitions for power. Just as he had drawn the untamed savagery of the Heath as the counterpart of Eustacia's lawlessness and unconcern for those around her, so now Hardy draws an implied parallel between the genius of Rome which was energy, and the sole talent of that blundering Titan of a self-made man, Michael Henchard. But here the parallel ceases. The Roman genius for law and order, and for submission to them, was lacking in Henchard and for this reason he falls. He is a primitive type, defeated by his own defects, as well as by his rival's ability to adapt himself to changing conditions. The imperturbability, the enduring qualities of the background against which the tragedy of his life and death is enacted, are heightened by his very instability.

The Mayor of Casterbridge is unique in Hardy's work for more than one reason. For the first time he draws a protagonist who towers above the other leading characters in height and strength. Heretofore he has drawn a constellation of interrelated characters and no single one has dominated the others, as

---

[1] *A Tryst at an Ancient Earthwork*, in *The Old Theatre, Fiesole*, and *Maumbury Rings*, letter to *The Times*, October 9, 1908.

Henchard does, by sheer force of personality. It is the beginning of the epic conception and treatment, fulfilled in *Tess* and *Jude*, in which the interest centres on a single life. Henchard is drawn on the heroic scale: he stands six foot and more, he has eyes that 'dig into men's souls', and he moves 'like a great tree in a wind'.

Secondly, he is the most complex and subtly drawn Hardy's male character, a man at war with himself, who, ignorant of his motives, works against and destroys himself—a smouldering, volcanic fellow whose pattern is to cheat himself of success, companionship, happiness, love, to castigate and brand himself until he dies an outcast, self-excommunicate. Henchard is cruel, jealous, possessive; suspicious, vain, proud; dishonest, prejudiced and rigid; yet for all his villainy there is something lovable about him. He is a confusing mixture of good and evil. With his negative qualities there are blended courage, generosity, forthrightness; patches of honesty, a sense of justice, a massive fortitude which disdains suffering and, like Atlas, bears all. Impulsive acts of kindness are accompanied by a need to wound himself, and a pathetic inability to plead his own cause, since he does not value himself enough to 'lessen his sufferings by strenuous appeal or elaborate argument'. His pitiable need to love and to be loved is matched by a fiery disdain of both. In the end he stands 'like a dark ruin' on the threshold of life and love, from which he is excluded by acts of blundering egotism. As others[1] have pointed out, Henchard is Lear-like in his tragic grandeur; but Hardy has consummately proved that such a tragic figure need not be a regal one: he evokes in us both terror and pity through his portrayal of a homespun trusser of hay.

Thirdly, Henchard is the most virile of all Hardy's men. Giles and Gabriel are male enough and they touch us by their staunchness, fidelity, sincerity and simplicity—the great Wessex virtues—but Henchard, like a wild bull roaming the hillside, triumphant in his prime, subdued and driven from the herd by a younger, more agile rival, attracts us through his animal

---

[1] W. H. Gardner, *Some Thoughts on The Mayor of Casterbridge*, Eng. Association Pamphlet 77, November 1930 (Oxford University Press), and Arthur McDowall, *Thomas Hardy—A Critical Study*, p. 74. Faber & Faber, 1931.

strength. There is not another character like him in Hardy's work. Perhaps the writer saw some such red-and-grey volcanic man in one of the Dorchester inns or streets, who set him pondering on his life, character and fortunes.[1]

The majority of Hardy's men stand aloof from, and are spectators of, even spies on, life which revolves round them, rather than active participants who intervene to shape life and the lives of others to their own ends. They are victims of the Victorian ethical convention which required that men, at least in fiction, must be virtually sexless. The self-effacing quality in his men makes Hardy's women all the more vital: the contrast is so marked that it has caused one writer to question whether this lack of virility in his masculine characters may not be unconsciously autobiographical.[2] He speaks of the 'pallid reticence' of the male characters, who drift like sleep-walkers through the scenes, envying the women who love and hate with passionate abandon. The future biographer of Hardy, he suggests, must determine whence 'this almost pathological unaggressiveness springs' and decide whether it is significant material.

We are not likely now to uncover anything which will throw light on this delicate subject. The most that one can say is that the dominant character of Hardy's mother, and of his first wife, together with his own suppressed aggressiveness (which only reveals itself in his writings and in his masochistic tendencies), made him tend to regard women as the more energetic and forceful of the sexes, around whom men revolve like obedient satellites. His intuitive gifts, imaginative powers, and feminine nature enabled him to understand them better than men, and thus to portray them far more subtly.

If we turn to Hardy's poems and notes we may find something to explain the phenomenon of Henchard's character. The dated poems of this period in his life are scanty. Between 1872-82 there are only six dated ones.[3] We know that some others of a descrip-

---

[1] Weber, p. 102, suggests that Hardy drew Henchard on the lines of Trollope's father, whose *Autobiography* appeared in 1883.

[2] Albert Guerard, *Thomas Hardy, The Novels and Stories*, pp. 43, 114 and 117. Oxford University Press, 1949.

[3] When he came to edit his *Collected Poems* Hardy placed further dates relevant to the action of the poems, beneath the titles. I refer again to the dates at the *foot* of the poems.

tive nature were written, *vide* those from the Sturminster
Newton and Swanage days. Then suddenly in 1883 we find a
beautiful poem, compact with certitude and decision, "He
abjures Love"[1] in which the writer shakes off love's enchantment and speaks

> . . . *as one who plumbs*
> *Life's dim profound,*
> *One who at length can sound*
> *Clear views and certain.*

Hardy was now forty-three and his disenchantment with love
coincides with an increasing disillusion with life. Deeply
romantic, he has hitherto made love the lodestar of his being:
when this fails there is nothing left. Even though the poem may
be merely the record of a passing mood (which Hardy later
declared it to be: he also called it a love poem, adding 'and
lovers are chartered irresponsibles')[2] it contains a poignant
admission. A deeply reticent man lays bare his heart to tell us
that he was once

> . . . *as children may be*
> *Who have no care;*
> *I did not think or sigh,*
> *I did not sicken;*
> *But lo, Love beckoned me,*
> *And I was bare,*
> *And poor, and starved, and dry*
> *And fever-stricken.*

Lacking the consolations of religion, with a soul 'laid bare by
faith's receding wave'; lacking, too, a detached philosophical
attitude to the inherently tragic and insoluble problems of life,
which seemed to him so vast they defied more than mere
conjecture; blessed, and at the same time cursed, with excessive
sensitivity and compassion for human and animal life, Hardy's
only escape was to live as an avowed stoic. By this means he
thought to ward off pain; by scaling down his hopes and desires
he might be content to realize that 'happiness [is] but the

[1] In *Time's Laughingstocks*.
[2] Letter to Alfred Noyes, II, p. 218.

occasional episode in a general drama of pain'.[1] This is a summary of that doctrine of resignation and renunciation which has been forming in his mind, a negative attitude to life which totally contradicts Hardy's naturally responsive heart. The fastidious mind rejects what the eager heart cries out for, and the endless conflict engendered is doomed to continue.

No greater proof of the darkening of Hardy's mood is needed than the record (in his notes) of his reflections on two New Year's Eves, those of 1884 and 1885, during and after the days when he had written those final remorseless pages of *The Mayor of Casterbridge*. On the first he visited the ringers in the belfry of old St Peter's Church, Dorchester, whose tenor bell had been the admiration of his father and which appears in two of his novels. Hardy helped the ringers by climbing over the bells to fix the mufflers, he looked into the mouth of the worn tenor, and examined the 15th-century masonry of the tower. His description of the men taking up their positions and beginning to ring is an example of his acute powers of observation fused with emotion, which always appears in his finest work. He closes with one of his vivid similes:

> The red, white and green sallies bolt up through the holes like rats between the huge beams overhead.[2]

But by New Year's Eve 1885, something has happened to sadden Hardy. He does not join the ringers nor celebrate in any way. A few days before Christmas he had written, almost viciously:

> The Hypocrisy of things! Nature is an arch-dissembler. A child is deceived completely; the older members of society more or less, according to their penetration, though even they seldom get to realize that *nothing* is as it appears.[3]

Seven months after he had finished writing *The Mayor of Casterbridge*, in April 1885, Hardy states in his notes:

> . . . a tragedy exhibits a state of things in the life of an individual which unavoidably causes some natural aim, or desire, of his to end in a catastrophe when carried out.[4]

The date of this note, so long after the novel's completion, im-

---

[1] *The Mayor of Casterbridge*, p. 406.   [2] I, p. 221.
[3] *Ibid.*, p. 231.   [4] *Ibid.*, p. 230.

plies that the latter was written in the white heat of inspiration and reflected on later; but the importance of developing character, rather than stressing incident, had occupied Hardy's mind for some time past. On the day of the tale's first appearance he had admitted his fears that *The Mayor* might not be as good as he had intended it to be:

> . . . but after all, it is not improbabilities of incident but improbabilities of character that matter.[1]

Hardy's fear that this novel had been 'recklessly damaged' refers to the alterations which once again he had been forced to make to placate magazine editors and the squeamish public. He had had to tone down the portrait of Henchard and to introduce incidents, as he thought, far too freely. The passionate revolt against destiny which Henchard typifies, and which was rising in Hardy's breast as he drew this character, consorts but poorly with the unrealities of life as Victorian ladies conceived it. Both the man and the writer were increasingly galled. For one who loves truth there is nothing more shameful than to be forced to hedge and hide, to *cease to be oneself*, something the artist *must* be if his work is to ring true, and if he is to reap the satisfaction from it which a good craftsman covets. A modern poet has described his predicament thus:

> There is something about the literary life which, although it offers the writer freedom and honour enjoyed by a very few, at the same time brings him a cup of bitterness with every meal. There is too much betrayal, there is a general atmosphere of intellectual disgrace, writers have to make too many concessions in order to support themselves and their families . . . I think that almost every writer secretly feels that the literary career is not worthy of the writer's vocation. For this vocation resembles that of the religious . . .[2]

Hardy found it difficult to get *The Mayor* published in volume form. The excuse which was given was that 'the lack of gentry among the characters made it uninteresting.' So much for Victorian taste. A more likely reason was that the publishers feared the reception that a novel seared with so much bitterness

[1] I, p. 231.
[2] Stephen Spender, *World within World*. Hamish Hamilton, 1951.

might win, for in book form Hardy 'made not the slightest concession' to public taste: *The Mayor* 'moves remorselessly to its remorseless close', and it 'exemplifies what had become Hardy's personal philosophy of life with a starkness to be found in none of his previous books'.[1] It may even be a final, defiant challenge to manhood and virility, the bitter cry of one who saw himself cheated and childless, trapped by Fate into an unfertile, life-long union.

When it was finally published the *Saturday Review* declared that *The Mayor of Casterbridge*

> failed to contain a single character worth arousing a passing interest[2]

On the other hand Stevenson, who had been amongst the first visitors to Max Gate, praised it to Hardy, and the *Athenaeum* divined that the author had a gift for

> so telling a story that it sticks by the reader for days afterwards, mixing itself with his impressions and recollections of real people, *just as a very vivid dream will sometimes do*, till he is not quite sure whether it also does not belong to them.[3]

Once again that power of Hardy's to write from the unconscious, which John Morley had recognized, impressed perceptive critics. Hardy now strove to mould this native ability with conscious skill, and to heed the advice of Coleridge:

> to aim at *illusion* in audience or readers . . . i.e. the mental state when dreaming, intermediate between complete *delusion* . . . and a clear perception of falsity.[4]

In Germany, where Hardy's work has never been as popular as in France and America, *The Mayor* was translated under the title of *Der Burgermeister*. The fact that it was a study of a power type no doubt appealed to the Germanic mind, but Hardy's love of music, revealed in two telling passages, must also have pleased it. The first is the passage in which Henchard forces the members of the Quire to play and to sing an anathema on his rival, who is himself described as having the 'crispness, stringency and charm of a well-braced musical instrument'. Henchard's superstitious, revengeful nature is pacified, but the fact that it was *he* who chose the tune (which made 'his blood ebb and

---

[1] Rutland, pp. 198-9.   [2] *Ibid.*   [3] *Ibid.*   [4] I, p. 197.

flow like the sea') makes the imprecation all the more ironic. The second is the description of the symphony which the weir-waters play to Henchard's moody soul when he thinks of taking his life:

> If he could have summoned music to his aid, his existence might even now have been borne; for with Henchard music was of regal power. The merest trumpet or organ tone was enough to move him, and high harmonies transubstantiated him. But fate had ordained that he should be unable to call up this Divine spirit in his need . . . To the east of Casterbridge lay moors and meadows, through which much water flowed. The wanderer in this direction . . . might hear singular symphonies from these waters, as *from a lampless orchestra*, all playing in their sundry tones, from near and far parts of the moor. At a hole in a rotten weir they executed a recitative: where a tributary brook fell over a stone breastwork they trilled cheerily; under an arch they performed a metallic cymballing; and at Durnover Hole they hissed. The spot at which their instrumentation rose loudest was a place called Ten Hatches whence during high springs there proceeded a very fugue of sounds.[1]

These are the Frome waters, and the stone bridge on which such emphasis is laid is none other than Grey's Bridge, which Hardy had crossed and re-crossed countless times.

A passage in the book shows us once again how the novelist expands an original note, startlingly fresh in the *Early Life*. Here then is the note, followed by the prose passage:

> A gusty wind makes the raindrops hit the window in stars, and the sunshine flaps open and shuts like a fan, flinging into the room a tin-coloured light . . .[2]

> . . . There was a gusty, high, warm wind; isolated raindrops starred the window-panes at remote distances; the sunlight would flap out like a quickly opened fan, throw the pattern of the window upon the floor of the room in a milky, colourless shine, and withdraw as suddenly as it had appeared.[3]

Either because Dorchester (Casterbridge) is an agricultural market-town, formerly dependent for her prosperity on the crops produced by the surrounding fields, or because the summers

---

[1] *The Mayor of Casterbridge*, pp. 358-9. (Italics mine.)
[2] I, p. 220.   [3] *The Mayor of Casterbridge*, p. 228.

which Hardy spent inside her walls were tempestuous ones, the
weather plays a dominant part in this book. The sun is lord of
all, elating the hearts of the corn-merchants, who 'watch the
weather-cocks as men waiting in antechambers watch the
lackey'. Its tawny locks and furious heat, its unpredictable
qualities, seem the counterpart of the moods and uncertain temper of Henchard, the firebrand Titan, brother to the sun-god,
with his red-brown fiery eyes. Lucetta lies in her room and
watches its reflected brightness pouring into her rooms, and
added to the steady light she sees 'a fantastic series of circling
irradiations upon the ceiling'. A laden hay-wain passes up the
street and 'a yellow flood of sunlight fills the room for an
instant': or the 'tin-coloured light' changes to 'topaz'. The
declining sun 'takes the street endways, enfilading the long
thoroughfare from top to bottom': or the cottage which
Henchard rents for his wife is irradiated by sun which

> seemed to shine more yellowly there than anywhere else . . .
> stretching its rays, as the hours grew later, under the lowest syca-
> more boughs, and steeping the ground-floor of the dwelling, with
> its green shutters, in a substratum of radiance.[1]

While Hardy was writing *The Mayor of Casterbridge* he made
several significant notes on two inter-related themes, one of
which appears to have troubled him ever since his youthful reading of the Greek tragedians—the illusory nature of the world,
and, secondly, the resemblance of humankind to enchanted
beings, or automata. This is a subject which properly belongs
to a chapter on *The Dynasts*, were it not for the fact that Hardy's
interest in it at this time increased to an inexplicable degree.
Taking the allusions to it in his notes and prose chronologically
we find the following. There is nothing in *An Indiscretion* which
savours of it, and there may or may not have been in *The Poor
Man and the Lady*. But, as we have already seen, Manston's dying
speech in *Desperate Remedies* (1871) contains a sentence which is
the forerunner of much else.[2] *The Return of the Native* (1878) gives
an important variant of this, somewhat disguised.

> The truth seems to be that a long line of disillusive centuries has
> permanently displaced the Hellenic idea of life, or whatever it may

---

[1] p. 97.   [2] See p. 106, *supra*.

be called. What the Greeks only suspected, we know well; what their Aeschylus imagined, our nursery children feel.[1]

Hardy here refers to a corrupt passage from the *Agamemnon* which has baffled translators for centuries, and is variously rendered. When good tidings speed through the city of Argos, heralding Agamemnon's return, the elders ask:

'Who knows if it be true, or some delusion of the Gods?'[2] Can the tidings be believed, or are the Gods making sport with human beings? As the years went by this single line gathered round it in Hardy's mind a clot of meaning which it is doubtful if Aeschylus ever intended—put briefly, that the world is an illusion. His quandary became a general one—whether the visible world which at first enchants us utterly, whether happiness, is not entirely delusive. What is real? What can we trust, and believe? He transposes the question of the old men, written five centuries before the birth of Christ, and applies it to the 19th century. The thought re-appears in *Jude the Obscure*, and it crowns one of the most powerful passages in *The Dynasts*. In 1880 Hardy, who was accompanying Emma to a fashionable shop, remarks (in a note) that the trained saleswoman 'acts as by clockwork . . . like an automaton'.[3] In 1882 he sets down an important note, forerunner of the dicta of students of the Unconscious.

> Write a history of human automatism, or impulsion—viz., an account of human action in spite of human knowledge, showing how very far human conduct lags behind the knowledge that should really guide it.[4]

This harks back to a note made when Hardy was only twenty-six wherein he sagely comments that, had we reaped what we should from experience, we should now equal God in omniscience.

Next in 1884, he questions whether

> . . . the present quasi-scientific system of writing history [is not] mere charlatanism? Events and tendencies are traced as if they

[1] pp. 205-6.
[2] Hardy's translation written against Paley's reading in his own copy of *The Agamemnon*. See Rutland, p. 37.
[3] I, p. 184.
[4] *Ibid.*, pp. 197-8.

were rivers of voluntary activity, and courses reasoned out from the circumstances in which natures, religions, or what-not, have found themselves. But are they not in the main the outcome of *passivity*—acted upon by unconscious propensity? [1]

Then comes the writing of *The Mayor of Casterbridge* (1884-5) with the powerful portrait of a man driven by inner destructive forces beyond his comprehension and control, followed by a note which outlines the supernatural framework of *The Dynasts*, nearly twenty years before it was finally used. In 1886 Hardy had begun to substitute the chilly consolations of philosophy for those of religion. He considers Hegel's dictum that 'the real is the rational, and the rational the real'. Five months later he develops the thought that people in the street, or in drawing-rooms are like

> beings in a somnambulistic state, making their motions automatically—not realizing what they mean :[2]

and again, four months later:

> I was thinking a night or two ago that people are somnambulists—that the material is not the real—only the visible, the real being invisible optically. That it is because we are in a somnambulistic halucination that we think the real to be what we see as real.[3]

In 1888 Hardy sees women praying in a church

> as if under enchantment. Their real life is spinning on beneath this apparent one of calm, like the District Railway trains underground just by.[4]

In 1890 the fashionable crowd at the Royal Academy move for him 'like people under enchantment, or as somnambulists'. A single poem written in 1893 sums up the preoccupation which eight years later finds its final expression in *The Dynasts*:

> *No use hoping, or feeling vext,*
> *Tugged by a force above or under*
> *Like some fantocine, much I wonder*
> *What I shall find me doing next!*

.   .   .   .   .   .

---

[1] I, pp. 219-20.   [2] *Ibid.*, p. 241.
[3] *Ibid.*, p. 243.   [4] *Ibid.*, p. 276.

Part is mine of the general Will,
Cannot my share in the sum of sources
Bend a digit the poise of forces,
And a fair desire fulfil?[1]

These questionings differ from those of the metaphysical poets of the 16th and 17th centuries, which at heart they resemble, in this respect—that, for the older men, that which lay behind the seen and unreal, glowing like a yellow diamond to light them in the dark, was of infinite value, whereas for Hardy there was ultimately only

> *. . . a dreaming dark, dumb Thing*
> *That turns the handle of this idle show*
>
> .   .   .   .
>
> *. . . some hocus-pocus to fulfil.*

[1] "He Wonders about Himself" in *Moments of Vision*.

CHAPTER EIGHT

THE CLIMAX AND END
OF PROSE WRITING

Nay, know ye not, this burden hath always lain
On the devious being of woman? Yea, burdens twain,
The burden of wild will and the burden of pain?

EURIPIDES

IN 1886, while Hardy was at work on his twelfth novel, *The Woodlanders*, one English poet wrote to another that in his judgment 'the amount of genius and gift which goes into novels in the literature of this generation is perhaps not inferior to what made the Elizabethan drama'. So wrote Gerard Manley Hopkins to Robert Bridges. Hopkins illustrated his statement with examples from Hardy's work, choosing the bonfire scene from *The Return of the Native*, the sword display in *Far from the Madding Crowd*, and the sale of Susan Henchard in *The Mayor of Casterbridge*, passages which he described as 'breathing epic'.[1]

Although the germ for *The Woodlanders* had lain dormant in Hardy's mind for ten years or more it did not grow to maturity easily. He wrestled with the details from mid-morning till midnight, altered the plot and worked in 'a fit of depression, as if enveloped in a leaden cloud'.[2] This note was written in November 1885; the book was not finished until February 1887, nearly two years after its inception. In looking back on it he declared it to be his favourite,

> *as a story*—perhaps . . . owing to the locality and scenery of the action, a part I am very fond of . . .[3]

that is, the villages nestling under High Stoy, where the country drops away into the Vale of Blackmoor.

In this novel, more than in any other, Hardy exhibits that sympathy with growing things, so instant and so perfect that it

---

[1] Letter dated October 28th. See Blunden, pp. 55-6 and 89. Havelock Ellis made the same comparison.

[2] I, p. 230.   [3] II, pp. 151-2.

is like a lover's intuition. If in *Domicilium* he attributed human
wishes to the aspiring honeysuckle so now he draws the analogy
of trees which sigh and appear to feel pain, planted by a man
and a girl whose sufferings will far exceed those of the inanimate
soughing firs, and who will die long before the trees are felled.
The small creatures of the woods—a robin, a squirrel, a
pheasant 'a-croupied' down close to the bough, insects dancing
in the sunbeams, or the winged seeds of a lime tree—are drawn
with that faithfulness to detail which reminds one of Dürer's
meticulous work.

The note which Hardy had made in the Bockhampton wood
is enlarged until it reads:

> The plantations were always weird at this hour of eve—more
> spectral far than in the leafless season, when there were fewer
> masses and more minute lineality. The smooth surfaces of glossy
> plants came out like weak, lidless eyes: there were strange faces
> and figures from expiring lights that had somehow wandered into
> the canopied obscurity; while now and then low peeps of the sky
> between the trunks were like sheeted shapes, and on the tips of
> boughs sat faint cloven tongues.[1]

The interest of this passage is fourfold: we see, first, how Hardy
has altered the time of year to suit his plot, from June to late
autumn or winter—altered, too, its construction: we see how a
note made in 1884 can be made use of nearly three years later;
and lastly, that the powerfulness of the writer's imagination
enabled him to draw the small plantation adjoining his birthplace as a large wood, just as he expanded Egdon, a relatively
small heath in comparison with the great moors of the West or
the North, magnifying it to epic proportions.

But now there is a new aspect to the familiar trees and wood,
for these, as well as Mother Nature, are hostile in behaviour and
intent. The tree which John Smith has watched since it was a
sapling 'threatens his life' and seems to possess the intention of
'dashing him into his grave'.

> Here, as everywhere, the Unfulfilled Intention, which makes life
> what it is, was as obvious as it could be among the depraved crowds
> of a city slum. The leaf was deformed, the curve was crippled,

---

[1] *The Woodlanders*, p. 375. See pp. 193-4, *supra*.

the taper was interrupted. The lichen ate the vigour of the stalk, and the ivy strangled to death the promising sapling.[1]

A new and ominous note has crept into the attitude to nature in English literature. In the poem[2] which corresponds to the note and prose passage, Hardy turns from the trees to human faces and human-kind for solace, for these at least smile, discourse joyfully, and show 'life-loyalties'; but the mood is the same in all three examples.

The Woodlanders is a transitional novel, which looks both forward and backward in Hardy's work. It harks back to *An Indiscretion*, in treating the plight of the *liviers*, the cottagers who may be ejected from their homes when the leases fall into hand. The injustice of this old-fashioned legal right torments Hardy and he cannot let it go, making it a part-theme of *Tess of the d'Urbervilles*. When Giles, in order to prolong John South's life, starts to cut off the lower branches of the inimical elm he hesitates for a moment, conscious of the fact that he is mutilating the landlord's property in order to increase a *livier's* life, to the detriment of the landlord's pocket. Then, Hardy's compassionate, rebellious spirit triumphs over such man-made laws through Giles, who risks maiming the tree in order to prolong the threadbare life of a labouring man.

The landowner in this novel is a woman—one of the two capricious ladies of the manor in Hardy's prose work. Like all his 'foreign' characters, who enter the paradisial Wessex land to disturb and destroy its serenity, Felice Charmond has come from, and is going, abroad; furthermore, she has an Italianate nature. Hardy has often been criticized for making these highborn, foreign characters mere lay figures. Yet a curious parallel to his description of Mrs Charmond has recently appeared in current literature. Hardy has foretold the behaviour of a living person in drawing an imagined character.

When the dissatisfied beauty attempts to rouse herself from melancholy he describes the scene thus:

> The morning had been windy, and little showers had scattered themselves like grain against the walls and window-panes . . .

[1] *The Woodlanders*, p. 62.
[2] "In a Wood." See also "The Ivy Wife" and "The Pine Planters."

[Felice] was in a little boudoir, or writing-room, on the first floor and Fitzpiers was surprised to find that the window-curtains were closed and a red-shaded lamp and candles burning, though out of doors it was broad daylight. Moreover a large fire was burning in the grate, though it was not cold.

"What does it all mean?" he asked. . .

"O," she murmured, "it is because the world is so dreary outside! Sorrow and bitterness in the sky, and floods of agonized tears beating against the panes. . . . O! why were we given hungry hearts and wild desires if we have to live in a world like this?" [1]

Now in describing her mother's reaction to the weather of Dartmoor, the reactions of an Italian woman 'accustomed to the delicate lights of the Tuscan Hills,' Freya Stark says:

After three days of the unbroken southwest wind, when she had ridden or walked morning and afternoon, and had been soaked every time . . . my father came home in the middle of the fourth day to find the whole house shuttered up, the lamps and candles lit, and my mother savagely reading, trying to forget the existence of the climate. [2]

The Woodlanders also harks back to *The Poor Man*'s defiance of the gentry in a magnificent piece of descriptive writing. Hardy's horses and dogs are always drawn with the same compassionate understanding that he gives to humankind (the portraits of Gabriel's sheep-dogs are unforgettable) and behind this description there lies a hint of tragedy, for in defying Mrs Charmond Giles risks losing his home. His challenge bears the marks of that rectitude, that strength of rural character, which Hardy knew was not to be outmatched in any of the great houses to which he now had the entrée. The scene described is the carting of a heavy load of timber early one morning through the narrow Hintock lanes.

The horses wore their bells that day. There were sixteen to the team, carried on a frame above each animal's shoulders, and tuned to scale, so as to form two octaves, running from the highest note on the right or off-side of the leader to the lowest on the left or

[1] pp. 248-9.
[2] *Traveller's Prelude*, p. 21. John Murray, 1950. Felice's outcries against the rigours of society resemble those of Mrs Stark in the same chapter of her daughter's book.

near-side of the shaft-horse . . . The tones of all the teams in the district being known to the carters of each, they could tell a long way off on a dark night whether they were about to encounter friends or strangers.[1]

The team with its chiming-bells and five-ton load of timber rises out of the fog-laden valley only to encounter what the bells had guarded against—the lamps of an oncoming carriage, followed by a second light vehicle. The coachman imperiously demands Giles' carter to turn back the load. Giles refuses. Annoyed at the delay Mrs Charmond leans out of her window to enquire the cause and, in her turn, she orders the woodmen to turn back. Giles sends his apologies but explains that they cannot.

> In fine, nothing could move him, and the carriages were compelled to back till they reached one of the sidings or turn-outs constructed in the banks for the purpose. Then the team came on ponderously, and the clanging of its sixteen bells as it passed the discomfited carriages tilted up against the bank, lent a particularly triumphant note to the team's progress . . .[2]

The great capricious lady goes on her way to Italy with Giles' refusal embedded like a barb in her sensitive skin. Our admiration is for Giles and his team, and our sympathy for him is deepened when Mrs Charmond punishes him with the loss of his home.

The novel harks forward in its recognition of disorders of the mind, bordering on pathology, and its treatment of the marriage question, both of them themes of *Jude the Obscure*. Hardy increasingly felt it to be an injustice that the nervous system had developed to an alarmingly high degree in creatures never intended to bear the consciousness of pain; he voices this sentiment again and again in his notes and poems. Here this conviction is personified by Grace Melbury, tormented by her husband's infidelities and the equivocal position in which she is placed by his disappearance. Hardy calls her an

> impressionable creature, who combined modern nerves with primitive feelings, and was doomed by such co-existence to be numbered among the distressed, and to take her scourgings to their exquisite extremity.[3]

---

[1] *The Woodlanders*, pp. 118-9.   [2] *Ibid.*, p. 120.   [3] p. 373.

Here is Sue Bridehead foreshadowed. We have had the 'modern face', and 'modern spirit', and now we have 'modern nerves'. There are, in addition, two other examples of people suffering from nervous disorders in *The Woodlanders*—the 'tree possessed' John South and Grammer Oliver with her pathetic delusions. The dilettante Fitzpiers, unstable, unfaithful, attracted to half-a-dozen studies and excelling in none, is never very convincing, but he reflects for us Hardy's interest in current 'abstract philosophy', culled from his reading of German literature and metaphysics at this time. Fitzpiers' dislike of being married in a church clearly antedates passages in *Jude*, and strikes a new note in Hardy's fiction—his quarrel with society for its unrelenting attitude to sexual relationships. But the ethical discussions which obtrude unpleasantly in his final novel are here merely unlikely interruptions, and the contemplative beauty of *The Woodlanders*, tinctured with a pensiveness in keeping with the moods of the sighing plantations, remains predominant. Homeliness and humour have not yet vanished from Hardy's prose, and passages of a broader, more Shakespearian kind, and of delicate irony, still delight us.

The paragraph in the opening chapter of *The Woodlanders* wherein Hardy defines his belief that actions as tragic, as significant as any in Attic drama may be enacted in the Dorset woods and fields, (a belief he also expressed in the 1911 Preface to *Tess*), has been quoted times out of number, but generally without the sentences leading up to it which, with their homely domesticity, give the contrast Hardy intended.

> At length could be discerned in the dusk . . . gardens and orchards sunk in a concave, and, as it were, snipped out of the woodland. From this self-contained place rose in stealthy silence tall stems of smoke, which the eye of imagination could trace downward to their root on quiet hearthstones, festooned overhead with hams and flitches. It was one of those sequestered spots outside the gates of the world . . . where, from time to time, dramas of a grandeur and a unity truly Sophoclean are enacted in the real, by virtue of the concentrated passions and closely-knit interdependence of the lives therein.[1]

The force of Hardy's antitheses lies in this essential contrast of

[1] *The Woodlanders*, pp. 4-5.

the homely with the grand, the minute with the vast, the temporal with the eternal: in this way he tethers our emotions while projecting our imaginations through space onto distant battle-fields, to the Pole, or into stellar crevasses. A few pages further on, the pin-pricks of light from Giles' and Marty's lantern cast giant rings on the 'tent-shaped sky', and these two isolated lives are described as

> part of the pattern in the great web of human doings then weaving in both hemispheres from the White Sea to Cape Horn.[1]

The descriptions of the autumn countryside, and of Giles when he is cider-making, have about them a warmth and a fullness which is pastoral in the classical sense—they are reminiscent of Theocritus and Virgil's *Georgics*—yet they are essentially English. Firm and beautifully modelled he suggests a figure from Paestum or Samothrace; while the landscapes glow like Samuel Palmer's paintings, in which the fruit-trees heavy with blossom and the thatch encrusted with emerald moss preserve for us a rural beauty typically English.

> He looked and smelt like Autumn's very brother, his face being sunburnt to wheat colour, his eyes blue as corn-flowers, his sleeves and leggings dyed with fruit-stains, his hands clammy with the sweet juice of apples, his hat sprinkled with pips, and everywhere about him that atmosphere of cider which at its first return each season has such an indescribable fascination for those who have been born and bred among the orchards. Her heart rose from its late sadness *like a released bough*—[2]

That last line includes another of Hardy's poetic similes, exquisite in its fitness, both to the mood of Grace and to a book devoted to woodland subjects. To give only two more—the ancient waggons formerly used for carrying sheep-cribs, hurdles, poles and spars, are likened aptly yet incongruously to

> shapes bulging and curving at the base and ends *like Trafalgar line-of-battle ships*, with which venerable hulks these vehicles evidenced a constructive spirit curiously in harmony:[3]

Marty's shorn tresses which she has sacrificed for Mrs

---

[1] *Ibid.*, p. 23.
[2] p. 260. (Italics mine.)
[3] p. 17. (Italics mine.)

Charmond's benefit, lying on the pale, scrubbed deal of the coffin-stool, stretch '*like waving and ropy weeds over the washed white bed of a stream*'.[1] Hardy's predilection for thorn (or other dark) patterns moving across a lighter background, a face or a wall, reappears here, and is to do so again in *The Dynasts*.

A pair of passages bears a striking resemblance, hitherto unremarked, to two poems of Donne's. The first is that in which the heads of lovers bent towards each other (and seen from behind by the self-effacing Marty South) are described as being 'drawn together, no doubt by their souls; as the heads of a pair of horses are drawn in by the rein'. Secondly, that in which the drowsy Fitzpiers fancies he sees the girl of whom he has been thinking enter the room. The sentence—

> that he saw her coming instead of going made him ask himself if his first impression of her were not a dream indeed . . .

reminds one sharply of Donne's "The Dream" with its age-old conceit; and the former of some famous stanzas in "A Valediction: Forbidding Mourning".

Meanwhile, there were friendly visits to William Barnes, whose life was drawing to its close; and to London, where Hardy attended the debate in the House on Gladstone's Bill for Irish Government. Alternately impressed and depressed by the earnestness and rigidity of the Irish members—'the phalanx', as he called them, 'sitting tight'—he could not forbear making his inimitable thumb-nail sketches of the speakers—

> Sir R. Cross sturdy, like the Dorchester butcher when he used to stand at the chopping-block on market-days.[2]

Yet he saw more clearly than the politicians involved the true dilemma—that national policy and humanity did not coincide, and both parties, instead of recognizing antithetical moralities,

> speciously insisted that humanity and policy were both on one side —of course their own.[3]

He also attended the Law Courts where his sympathy went out to the witness, who was at once 'king and victim . . . the fool of the court'. (Hardy showed the same responsiveness to the

---

[1] p. 21. (Italics mine.)   [2] I, p. 233.   [3] *Ibid.*, p. 234.

H

plight of a lad charged with setting fire to a common at the
Dorchester Assizes,[1] remembering perhaps the terrible tale
told him by his father of the lad hanged for arson.) He went
often to the British Museum where he was infected with the
feelings of dissolution which the reading-room of this august
building communicates to some:

> Souls are gliding about here in a sort of dream—screened some-
> what by their bodies, but imaginable behind them . . . Time is
> looking into Space . . . Coughs are floating in the same great vault,
> mixing with the rustle of bookleaves risen from the dead, and the
> touches of footsteps on the floor.[2]

There were the inevitable dinners in London houses where he
met and made new friends, or re-encountered old—Browning,
Wilde, Gissing, Whistler, Bret Harte, Stevenson and Oliver
Wendell Holmes: or visits to his club where he talked again
with Meredith and Henry James. Now and then flashes of
humour light up for us this list of impressive names, as when he
found himself sitting next to a genial old lady at dinner, Lady
Camperdowne, and 'could not get rid of the feeling that [he]
was close to a great naval engagement'.[3]

But it is when Hardy the artist speaks that we listen atten-
tively, for the artist is apt to become submerged during these
London interludes. He was quick to realize the ironically symbolic nature of the architecture of the Law Courts:

> . . . everywhere religious art-forces masquerading as law symbols!
> The leaf, flower, fret, suggested by spiritual emotion, are pressed
> into the service of social strife.[4]

He sets down the principle of the Impressionistic painters, as
he sees it—that the painter should retain and interpret those
details which appeal to his particular eye and heart, a reflection
akin to one he had already stated in his journal more than
four years earlier:

> . . . in life the seer should watch that pattern among general things
> which his idiosyncracy moves him to observe, and describe that

---

[1] I, p. 218.
[2] *Ibid.*, pp. 270-1.
[3] *Ibid.*, p. 237.
[4] I, p. 240. See also II, p. 117.

alone. This is . . . a going to Nature; yet the result is no mere photograph, but purely the product of the writer's own mind.[1]

Sitting in his drawing-room at home he studies a landscape attributed to Bonington, and grows dissatisfied with it since it seems to him to depict Nature 'as a Beauty, but not as a Mystery'. He increasingly seeks to dig beneath mere 'optical effects' to deeper realities, to

> the expression of what are sometimes called abstract imaginings. The 'simply natural' is interesting no longer. The much decried, mad, late-Turner rendering is now necessary to create my interest. The exact truth as to material fact ceases to be of importance in art—it is a student's style—the style of a period when the mind is serene and unawakened to the tragical mysteries of life.[2]

This admission of his preference for late Turners is extremely interesting, not only because here Hardy follows in the footsteps of Ruskin and of his old master, William Barnes,[3] but because his descriptive passages, especially those of evening skies, become increasingly like a Turner painting:

> . . . the whole west sky was revealed. Between the broken clouds they could see far into the recesses of heaven, the eye journeying on under a species of golden arcades, and past fiery obstructions, fancied cairns, logan-stones, stalactites and stalagmites of topaz. Deeper than this their gaze passed thin flakes of incandescence, till it plunged into a bottomless medium of soft green fire.[4]

That description of a sunset is from the novel which Hardy was writing when he made the note (quoted above) referring to Turner in January 1887.

As early as 1873, when writing his fourth novel, Hardy had mentioned Turner, not merely to display his knowledge, but to give the exact shade of colour to an old sheep-dog's coat

> marked in random splotches approximating in colour to white and slaty grey: but the grey, after years of sun and rain, had been scorched and washed out . . . leaving them reddish brown, as if the

[1] I., p. 198.
[2] Ibid., pp. 242-3.
[3] See Thoughts on Beauty and Art, 1861. Hardy was reading Modern Painters when he worked in Blomfield's offices in 1862.
[4] The Woodlanders, p. 261. See also Desperate Remedies, p. 266; Far from the Madding Crowd, p. 243; The Hand of Ethelberta, p. 401.

blue component of the grey had faded, like the indigo from the same kind of colour in Turner's pictures.[1]

A year after making his first note referring to Turner, Hardy viewed the old masters at the Royal Academy and devoted the most intense study to this artist's water-colours:

> ... each is a landscape *plus* a man's soul. What he paints chiefly is *light as modified by objects*. He first realizes the impossibility of reproducing on canvas all that is in a landscape; then gives for that which cannot be reproduced a something else which shall have upon the spectator an approximative effect to that of the real. He said, in his maddest and greatest days: 'What pictorial drug can I dose man with, which shall affect his eyes somewhat in the manner of this reality which I cannot carry to him?'—and set to make such strange mixtures as he was tending towards in "Rain, Steam and Speed", "Approach to Venice", and other paintings.[2]

Painter and poet had much in common—their early interest in architecture, in classical subjects, and in ships-of-the-line which had fought at Trafalgar. But there was a closer emotional kinship between them, appearing in their more sensational work. In Turner this reveals itself in paintings of violent wind and weather, of whirlwinds, avalanches, crags and tempests, in the fatalistic fires-in-flood which resemble Donne's terrible Epigram *A Burnt Ship*, and in volcanic eruptions. Nature in her rebellious, cataclysmic moods attracted Turner, for in interpreting these he expressed the luridly romantic side of his own nature and, like Hardy, emphasized the impotence and insignificance of man. What Sir Kenneth Clark has called the 'sunset cloud-architecture of his mind's eye' is Hardy's as well.

Constable once wrote that Turner was 'stark mad with ability'. There is something of this divine frenzy in Hardy's descriptions of the storm in *Far from the Madding Crowd*, of the nocturnal heath fires in *The Return*, and the arctic winter in *Tess*. In his last period (about five years before Hardy was born), Turner painted a small picture called *An Iceberg*, in which the whiteness of the towering ice stands out from the whiteness of the mist and icy water without apparent visible means. It is the very essence of light, cold and whiteness in varying shades. In

---

[1] *Far from the Madding Crowd*, p. 38.   [2] I, pp. 283-4.

his last prose period Hardy paints, in words, an Arctic scene in which he pictures

> the crash of icebergs and the slide of snowhills by the shooting light of the Aurora . . . the whirl of colossal storms and terraqueous distortions.[1]

The white face of Tess emerging from the meadow-mists is drawn with the same consummate ability. The light in which the scene is set is 'spectral, half-compounded, aqueous', a 'mixed, singular luminous gloom' of 'neutral shade'. Tess' face

> . . . rising above the mist stratum, seemed to have a sort of phosphorescence upon it. She looked ghostly, as if she were merely a soul at large . . . her face had caught the cold gleam of day from the north east.[2]

Turner accompanied many of his drawings with lines from some poems of his own called *The Fallacies of Hope*. What seems at first merely exhilaration with storm and stress, or over-dramatization for its own sake in his painting, proves to be a wild inner despair, a need to depict the violence in his own soul which few suspected on looking at the mild old man. Thus even in their pessimism, *and the subdued fires of their nature which flared only in their work*, painter and writer are alike.

Hardy sent a copy of *The Woodlanders* to Swinburne. Stevenson engaged the help of Edmund Gosse in scouring London to find copies for him before he went abroad at the age of thirty-seven: and Coventry Patmore, while refusing to admire it as much as some of Hardy's earlier novels, wrote appreciative criticism of his work in general in the *St James Gazette*.[3] *The Athenaeum* declared it to be 'distinctly not for the Young Person' but admitted that it was 'masterly'.[4] Hardy's own comment at the end of the year shows that, master though he now was of the art of fiction in a new form, he found novel writing exigent. The book, he wrote in his journal, had enabled him 'to hold his own in fiction—whatever that may be worth'. His heart was still set on poetry.

---

[1] *Tess of the d'Urbervilles*, p. 369.
[2] *Ibid*, p. 169. See also the complex description of snow-light and moon-light in *Far from the Madding Crowd*, pp. 114-15.
[3] Weber, p. 111, and Blunden, p. 56.   [4] Rutland, p. 212.

While *The Woodlanders* was appearing in serial form, in October 1886, William Barnes died. Hardy attended the funeral, and it was like him to see and to translate the flash of light which, blazing briefly from the coffin-plate, lit for an instant the eastern sky dark with cloud.

> *Thus a farewell to me he signalled on his grave-way,*
> *As with a wave of his hand.*[1]

The younger poet had always had an eye for light striking from polished surfaces, whether from a bell-metal crock or andirons on the hearth, the bits and spurs of riders in the Row, a lady's parasol-handle or bracelet, the accoutrements of soldiers on the march 'shining like a school of mackerel', or oar-blades 'tossing twinkles to the moon'—'anything that shined', as the old Chelsea Pensioner, with his arm round Emma Hardy's waist, had said to them when recounting what he remembered of that fateful day at Waterloo sixty years before. But here was something more than a mere artistic detail: the gleam seemed to Hardy a deeply significant, deeply personal one, a final salute from one whom he had loved and revered since a boy. The novelist paid tribute to Barnes in the *Athenaeum* and in the selection of Barnes' poetry which he made and edited.

In the following year the Hardys, like Felice Charmond, set out for Italy in the month of March. The writer's response to Rome and other Italian cities was characteristic; he found them both stimulating and deeply depressing. He was moved to tread in the footsteps of those English poets who have interpreted Italy for us in their own imperishable manner, but the weight of past centuries, heavy with history, troubled and exhausted him. In Rome the shadow of the dying Keats accompanied him: he studied the front of the house in which he had died and derived a melancholy pleasure from the façade and steps of Santa Trinità dei Monti immersed in an orange sunset. In Pisa he watched the sun go down from one of the bridges over the Arno and, like any ardent poetic schoolboy, wondered how may times Shelley had mused on the same scene. In Venice, as he stood on the Riva degli Schiavoni, or regarded the sea-girt palaces from the black-bowed gondolas, the ghost

[1] "The Last Signal" in *Moments of Vision.*

which haunted him was that of Byron, the poet whom Hardy
declared was

> for the English, the most fascinating personality in the world . . . a
> romantically wicked, noble lord.[1]

Both in Rome and Florence, Browning was also much in his
mind. The title of a group of poems written about experiences
on this Italian tour clearly shows that Hardy regarded it as a
kind of sacred pilgrimage, not to The Holy City or St Peter's,
but to the burial places (and the places where they had lived
before their deaths) of the English poets. Hardy has called them
Poems of Pilgrimage and the most original and forceful of them is
one called "At the Pyramid of Cestius, near the Graves of
Shelley and Keats", in which the poet characteristically
throws the name and fame of Cestius to the winds, declaring
him to mean nothing to him except that his monument acts as a
signpost to more meaningful graves.

> *Who, then, was Cestius,*
> *And what is he to me?—*
> *Amid thick thoughts and memories multitudinous*
> *One thought alone brings he.*
>
> .   .   .   .   .
>
> *Cestius in life, may be,*
> *Slew, breathed out threatening;*
> *I know not. This I know: in death all silently*
> *He does a kindlier thing,*
>
> *In beckoning pilgrim feet*
> *With marble finger high*
> *To where, by shadowy wall and history-haunted street,*
> *Those matchless singers lie . . .*[2]

The effect of the Holy City was to intensify Hardy's pagan,
rather than his Christian, sympathies, and to stimulate his
artistic senses. A column from an ancient temple buried in
church, or basilica, elated him. The richness of colour in ala-
baster pillar or amber sculptured drapery, the sharpness of
shadows thrown from buildings 'steeped in afternoon stagna-

---

[1] I, p. 272.   [2] In *Poems of the Past and Present.*

tion,' the reflected, 'secondary light' from the statue of a pagan god, all were garnered by this writer with a painter's avid eye.

A Dorset man, with 'the tin-tray timbre' of the Dorset village church-bells still in his ears, he went and stood before the portraits of the Doges and felt himself an alien in their presence. Sensitive to the 'watching eyes' of portraits, whether the crude and primitive ones of the Woolbridge Manor heiresses, or those of the Royal Academy dining-hall, Hardy describes the faces of the Doges as 'floating out into the air of the room' before him.

> "We know nothing of you," say these spectres. "Who may you be, pray?" The draught brushing past seems like inquiring touches by their cold hands, feeling, feeling like blind people what you are. Yes: here to this visionary place I solidly bring in my person Dorchester and Wessex life . . .[1]

The oppressive number of ancient buildings burdened his senses until he was glad to return to Florence, 'soothing after the gauntness of Rome', and then to go north to Venice and Milan, where his mind reverted to thoughts of Napoleon while he studied the city between the flying buttresses on the Cathedral roof. The haunting refrain of one of his father's fiddle-tunes, *The Bridge of Lodi*, set him searching for signs of the vanished battle in the small 'saffron-walled' town of that name, without success.

The overlapping of the strata of history increasingly impressed Hardy. If, in Rome, he had felt 'its measureless layers of history to lie upon him like a physical weight,'[2] in Paris he found a melancholy pleasure in standing close to the keys of the Bastille, letters from the dead Kings of France, the edicts and shady documents; while in the British Museum the young girls 'traipsing gaily round the mummies',[3] or laughing and flirting beneath the shadow of Rameses the Great, caused him to contrast their flippancy, and the transitoriness of human life and endeavour, with the statue's seeming imperishability. He liked to hear that an old man who talked to Emma at dinner 'had danced in the same quadrille with a gentleman who had danced with Marie Antoinette',[4] and was pleased to think that

---

[1] I, p. 253.   [2] I, p. 247.   [3] *Ibid.*, p. 309.   [4] *Ibid.*, p. 263.

Wordsworth might have seen him in his own cradle and that Gray might have looked on Wordsworth.[1] But the world's progression brought him no happiness.

> It is the on-going—i.e. the 'becoming'—of the world that produces its sadness. If the world stood still at a felicitous moment there would be no sadness in it.[2]

To hold oneself aloof from unfelicitous evolution and the pain which it involved, to resign oneself philosophically, was the only solution. But resignation implies suffering, and passivity in suffering, which Hardy attributed to animals and people around him. He was struck by the pathetic eyes of some horses in the street, and the thought of their suffering haunted him as he lay awake at night—'The absoluteness of their resignation was terrible':[3] he thought, too, that he divined 'sad, impotent resignation' in the attitude of the leading actress of the *Taming of the Shrew*, after her conquest by Petruchio; and on the faces of some dancing girls at the *Alhambra*. In June 1888, he sums up his state of mind thus:

> For my part, if there is any way of getting a melancholy satisfaction out of life it lies in dying, so to speak, before one is out of the flesh: by which I mean putting on the manners of ghosts, wandering in their haunts, and taking their views of surrounding things. To think of life as passing away is a sadness; to think of it as past is at least tolerable. Hence even when I enter a room to pay a simple morning call I have unconsciously the habit of regarding the scene as if I were a spectre not solid enough to influence my environment; only fit to behold and say, as another spectre said, "Peace be unto you!"[4]

Thus when Hardy conversed with a young Italian Contessa, a descendant of the Doges, although he noted with feminine precision her garments, their colour and style, he committed himself in part only to her beauty, charm and conversation, for his mind was abstracted, perpending on 'those behind the centuries'. And when Leonard Woolf talked with him at Max Gate (when Hardy was eighty-seven) he described him as standing:

> firmly and realistically on this solid ball, as an oak or ancient stone in a meadow; yet coexistent with this, through his talk of

[1] II, p. 187.   [2] I, p. 265.   [3] I, p. 278.   [4] *Ibid.*, p. 275.

H *

plain local and diurnal business, there came the feeling that he was also attending to some quite different, distant, unspoken, incommunicable world of consciousness . . . his time and place were suspiciously distant.[1]

This seems to have been one of Hardy's earliest characteristics. Clive Holland quotes a school-friend as saying that he remembered Hardy as a boy 'of a meditative disposition, *as though in search of something outside his work at school*'.[2] His ability to hold himself aloof from the world mentally and emotionally made Hardy see people at a concert, a picture-gallery, or in the Museum Reading Room as 'Souls outside Bodies', or 'Souls . . . screened by their bodies'.

In 1889 he published (separately) some stories which later appeared under the title of *A Group of Noble Dames*. The tales (which may be classed with the short stories rather than the novels) failed to please his publishers, the directors objecting to their character, and Hardy was forced to 'smooth them down somehow'. The theme of two of the stories is the effect of hallucination. They dabble in the occult and macabre, and spring in part-measure from an interest in genealogical trees which contributed to the birth of *Tess*. Anyone who turns the pages of Hardy's copy of the three great volumes of Hutchin's *History of Dorset* will see how genealogy held him in thrall. His annotations are numerous and specific. Hardy would have us believe that the tales in *A Group of Noble Dames* are founded on fact and that they are related to events in the lives of the ancestors of Wessex people of quality.[3] He had recently been reading Chaucer: thus he uses Boccaccio's device of stringing together a series of tales, and compares a lady to one of Chaucer's heroines who has 'all the craft of fine loving at her fingers' ends'. But the tone of these tales is unpleasant, and their chief value for most of us lies in a realization of Hardy's increasing interest in 'subtle instructive studies' with a psychological bent, which he declared were 'so much in demand'.[4]

Meanwhile, like advancing waves whose frilled edges slide imperceptibly beneath each other, thoughts of *The Dynasts, Jude*

---

[1] Blunden, pp. 172-3. [2] I, p. 18.
[3] Preface, and letter to Edward Clodd, Rutland, p. 219.
[4] *A Group of Noble Dames*, p. 185.

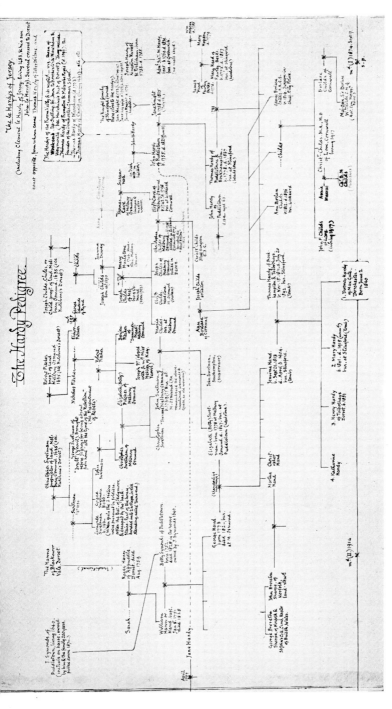

The Hardy Family Pedigree in Hardy's handwriting
(Showing the disputed relationship with Admiral Sir Thomas Masterman Hardy)

and *Tess* intermingled in Hardy's creative mind. Although *The Dynasts* was the last to take shape it obtruded most persistently, and the theme of *Jude* came to him earlier and more clearly than that of *Tess* although it was not written until three years after. *Tess of the d'Urbervilles* appeared in the same year as *A Group of Noble Dames* (1891), and the fact that Hardy was at work on his best-known novel and these tales simultaneously accounts for the relative poverty of the minor work, in which neither the fire of the greater, nor any of the poetic quality which pervades it, is apparent.

Between the appearance of *The Woodlanders* (1886-7) and *Tess of the d'Urbervilles* (1891) there is a gap in Hardy's writing-life, which is partly explained by the refusal of *Tess* by the editors of two magazines. During this time he also wrote *The Withered Arm* and was collecting the *Wessex Tales* together for publication (1888) as well as *A Group of Noble Dames*. He contributed some letters and articles to periodicals.[1] The most significant of these is "Candour in English Fiction" in which the following passage occurs:

> If the true artist ever weeps it is when he discovers the fearful price he has to pay for the privilege of writing in the English language, no less a price than *the complete extinction in the mind of every mature and penetrating reader of sympathetic belief in his personages*.[2]

In his notes he also stressed the fact that insincerity is 'the besetting sin of modern literature'.[3] This was a subject close to Hardy's heart. But he was not alone in appreciating the strangulating demands of the late-Victorian public. After announcing his determination to devote his life to literature, Gissing had already written to Hardy in 1886:

> The misery of it is that, writing for English people, one may not be thorough: reticences and superficialities have so often to fill places where one is willing to put in honest work.[4]

[1] "The Profitable Reading of Fiction", *New Review*, January 1890; "Some Romano-British Relics found at Max Gate", *Dorset Field Club Papers*, 1890; "On the Treatment of a Certain Author", *The Athenaeum*, November 1890; and "The Science of Fiction", *New Review*, April 1891. "Why I don't Write Plays" followed in 1892, in the *Pall Mall Gazette*, August 31.

[2] In the *New Review*, January 1890. (Italics mine.)

[3] I, p. 281.

[4] *Ibid.*, p. 239.

Thackeray had been forced to envy frankness permitted to Fielding in the 18th century, and the constricting bonds had continued to tighten since his day. Dostoevsky might publish *The Brothers Karamazov* on the continent (it appeared a year after Gissing's letter) but no such novel about spiritual and sexual problems might yet be published in England.

Hardy's distress at this constriction was acute. His major preoccupation during these four years, apart from the fluctuations of his mind between the conflicting claims of *The Dynasts*, *Jude* and *Tess*, and the exactions of minor literary work, was with the creation of his best-known novel *Tess of the d'Urbervilles*, which required greater freedom in treatment than his previous stories.

In his notes Hardy had stated his urgent desire to penetrate to the heart of things after the manner of Bellini and Crivelli. So we are not surprised that when he wishes to draw Angel returning from far-off Brazil, worn and cadaverous, he likens him to the *Dead Christ* of the latter artist ... a comparison somewhat laboured, but showing us Hardy's emphasis throughout *Tess* on *suffering*, made with such persistence that it implies personal suffering during these years.

Despite its lyrical qualities, and the imaginative fire which makes it glow like an inspired canvas, *Tess* is didactic: it seeks to teach a great moral lesson. The urgency and the passion which drive Hardy forward spring from two convictions. First, if writing is to be valid it must be true to life, the author must be allowed to tell his tale in his own way, to represent aspects of life as he sees them. An aspect which had always deeply troubled Hardy's compassionate heart was the betrayal of innocence. Every one knew that seductions occurred, both in rural and town life, the only difference being that if a man's daughter had an illegitimate child in town lodgings the family were not necessarily ejected from their home, whereas in the country, tenants being more sparsely scattered and their lives more readily observed, they were apt to be victimized by the squire.[1] Yet no one dared to write of such things, or, if they did, the girl remained a shadowy figure alluded to indirectly, or relegated to an inferior position in the drama. Hardy's sin in the eyes of professional

[1] II, p. 95.

critics was threefold—he handled this theme at length, he made
Tess the heroine of his tale, and he dared to call her 'a pure
woman'.

Now a great and daring work raises up detractors and cham-
pions simultaneously, especially when the chief character of that
work is a woman. Convention must first be outraged before it
may be altered. After the publication of *Tess* Hardy found himself publicly shunned, ridiculed by some and ardently defended
by others. One society hostess divided her guests into sheep and
goats—those who championed *Tess* and those who derided it.
As for the professional critics they called the novel 'disagreeable,
ridiculous and affected', or showed their own paucity of imagination by declaring, in a phrase which now seems ludicrous, that

> Few people would deny the terrible dreariness of this tale, which,
> except during a few hours spent with cows, has not a gleam of sun-
> shine anywhere.[1]

There were more of this nature. On the other hand the critic of
The Times described it as Hardy's greatest work,

> daring in its treatment of conventional ideas, pathetic in its sad-
> ness, and profoundly stirring in its tragic power.[2]

H. W. Massingham called it 'as pitiless and tragic in its intensity as the old Greek dramas',[3] and William Watson, the
poet, declared that to have read it was

> to have permanently enlarged the boundaries of one's intellectual
> and emotional experience.[4]

The reviewer of the *Westminster* wrote:

> From beginning to end it bears the hall-mark of truth upon every
> page . . . It is the greatest work of fiction produced in England
> since George Eliot died.[5]

Yet another critic 'found . . . a union of the ideal and the realistic
which struck him as masterly' and it must have pleased Hardy
to read:

> Your work has much of the Greek spirit in it, and is, therefore,
> unique in the present day.[6]

---

[1] *New Review*. See Rutland, pp. 228-9.   [2] *Ibid.*
[3] See Blunden, pp. 72-3.   [4] *The Academy*, see Rutland, pp.228-9.
[5] *Ibid.*   [6] John Steuart, see Blunden, p. 80.

A feminine critic perceived that the book's value lay in under-standing that

> a woman's moral worth is measurable, not by any one deed, but by the whole aim and tendency of her life and nature.[1]

Hardy's insistence that Tess, although an adulteress and a murderess, remained *A Pure Woman*, was based on his second conviction. To a reviewer who questioned him on this point he replied:

> I still maintain that her innate purity remained intact to the very last; though I frankly own that a certain outward purity left her on her last fall. I regarded her then as being in the hands of circumstances, not normally responsible, a mere corpse drifting with a current to her end.[2]

It was this contention which outraged Victorian sentiments. How could one bring up one's daughter to revere chastity if a well-known writer perverted the moral law? In these days, when *Tess* is given to sixth form girls to study, it is difficult to re-create the prevalent emotional values, and to understand the controversy which raged round this book.

Yet Hardy's conviction was based on the words of no less a teacher than Christ himself. 'Judge not that ye be not judged', or 'Go and sin no more', might have been placed on the title-page instead of the lines from *Two Gentlemen of Verona*. When the reviewer of the *Quarterly* spoke of Hardy's 'affectation of ex-pounding a great moral law', and *The Times* reviewer contra-dicted him (by perceiving that Hardy was an idealist and main-taining that it is well for us that he 'should remind us how terribly defective are our means of judging others') they were criticizing aspects of the same theme.

In this novel more than in any other (with the exception of *Jude*) Hardy goes back to the reading of adolescence and young manhood for the roots of his mature convictions—both to the Greek tragedians, whom he had studied with youthful avidity, and to his later reading of Darwin, Huxley and Mill. To take the tragedians first: quite apart from the controversial Aes-chylean phrase at the close ('The President of the Immortals

---

[1] Clementine Black, *Ibid.*, p. 73.   [2] *Ibid.*, p. 79.

had ended his sport with Tess') which was not in the original manuscript and was an afterthought,[1] the spirit of Tess' persecution by a relentless fate or force, of the condemnation of that persecutor, and the plea for a new understanding of moral laws through the great emancipator, the human intellect, all recall the early Greek dramatist who dared to question without fear of disfavour. Aristotle said of the *Prometheus Vinctus* that 'out of little myths and ridiculous language' Aeschylus had created high tragedy. Out of local gossip and sometimes in dialect speech (which the novelist had to defend in an article)[2] Hardy made a masterpiece.

The need for sincerity which obsessed Hardy at this time was likewise rooted in the reading of young manhood. Florence Hardy has told us how her husband was forced to mutilate and emasculate *Tess* for serial publication. An examination of the manuscript reveals that the final chapter began with a telling paragraph, later deleted.

> The humble delineator of human character and human contingencies, whether his narrative deal with the actual or with the typical only, must primarily and above all things be sincere, however terrible sincerity may be. Gladly sometimes would he lie, for dear civility's sake, if he dared, but for the haunting afterthought that 'this thing was not done honestly and may do harm'. In typical history, with all its liberty, there are as in real history, features which can never be varied with impunity and issues which should never be falsified. And perhaps in glancing at the misfortunes of such people as have, or could have, lived, we may acquire some art in shielding from like misfortunes, those who have yet to be born. If truth required justification, surely this is an ample one.[3]

This measured dictum may be traced to John Stuart Mill who, in his *Liberty*, makes the following declaration:

> Were an opinion a personal possession of no value except to the owner; if to be obstructed in the enjoyment of it were simply a private injury, it would make some difference whether the injury was inflicted only on a few persons or on many. *But the peculiar evil of silencing the expression of an opinion is that it is robbing the human race;*

---

[1] See Rutland, pp. 226-7.
[2] "Dialect in Novels", a letter in *The Athenaeum*, November 30, 1878.
[3] See Rutland, pp. 221-38.

posterity as well as the existing generation; those who dissent from the opinion, still more than those who hold it. If the opinion is right, they are deprived of the opportunity of exchanging error for truth : if wrong, they lose *what is almost as great a benefit, the clearer perception and livelier impression of truth, produced by its collision with error.*[1]

Hardy is clearly thinking of another passage in *Liberty* when writing *Tess*, that in which Mill questions the confusion by mankind of what he calls First and Second Nature. Mill is discussing the restraints which must be laid on the individual either by law, or opinion, to protect society—restrictions about which no two ages or countries agree.

> Yet the people of any given age and country no more suspect any difficulty in it than if it were a subject on which mankind had always been agreed. The rules which obtain among themselves appear to them self-evident and self-justifying. This all but universal illusion is one of the examples of the magical influence of custom which is not only, *as the proverb says, a second nature, but is continually mistaken for the first.*[2]

Side by side with this read Hardy's note made in the month in which he began *Tess* :

> The literary productions of men of rigidly good family, and rigidly correct education, mostly treat social conventions and contrivances —the artificial forms of living—as if they were cardinal facts of life.[3]

The words given in italics in the two passages above are among those underlined by Hardy in his youth in his copy of Mill's revolutionary work.

But the most fervent are not always the most lucid. Hardy writes with passionate conviction but his arguments lack consistency. Sometime he arraigns the social law, sometimes the cosmic. The force which comes from single conviction and a single purpose is not his. Nevertheless we are conquered. In spite of the unreality of many of the characters (chief amongst them Angel with his unfeeling arguments and cold, sterile behaviour, and Alec, the 'twopence-coloured' villain with his cigars and moustaches) in spite of the staginess of the final

[1] *Of Thought and Discussion.*
[2] "Introductory", *On Liberty.*   [3] I, p. 279.

setting, and the over-persistent dwelling on unkind Fate and Chance, we are carried away by reason of the book's poetic truth and Hardy's creative fervour. *Tess of the d'Urbervilles* remains a masterpiece which the French, Germans, Italians, Dutch, Russians and Japanese were quick to appreciate.

All of the critics of this novel have, with one accord, taken it for granted that Tess is the victim, and not the instigator of, her misfortunes, as Henchard was of his. They point to these two characters as opposites and stress the fact that Hardy pursued Tess and visited on her head, as Jove on Io, or the mediaeval romance-makers on their heroines, a superfluity of evils to weight the balance against her. The cry which Hardy was fond of uttering with regard to other heroines—Elfride, Grace, and Napoleon's Josephine—that it is the woman, the innocent one, who always pays, and which he here strove so passionately to express, has blinded readers to something which may be otherwise. Tess, for all her simplicity, is a subtly-drawn character with contradictory traits. Her simplicity and purity are adulterated with a strain likely to bring about her downfall, no matter what circumstances attend her—the tendency towards martyrdom and self-sacrifice which Hardy has touched on in his feminine characters in previous novels. Thus when Tess, driven almost to madness by her physical sufferings and Alec's undermining of her high resolves, finally strikes him 'flat on the mouth' with a heavy gauntlet, she is not merely protecting the honour of her husband, whom Alec has insulted, she is giving expression to a fury which precedes her collapse before her insidious torturer:

> "Now punish me!" she said, turning up her eyes to him with the hopeless defiance of the sparrow's gaze before its captor twists its neck. "Whip me, crush me; you need not mind those people under the rick! I shall not cry out. Once victim, always victim—that's the law."[1]

A solitary critic seems to me to have interpreted this cry rightly when he says that

> this is a very remarkable speech . . . it recalls to my mind T. E. Lawrence's account of his terrifying abasement before the

---

[1] *Tess of the d'Urbervilles*, p. 427.

Arab who flogged him. One feels that it is quite unpremeditated, as if it proceeded from some deeper level of the mind than Hardy fully understood . . . It is the cry of a passionate woman . . . to her demon lover . . . but I do not believe Hardy thought of it as anything but proof that the docility of the rabbit demonstrates the wickedness of the weazel.[1]

The self-reproach which Tess heaps upon herself for her negligence in falling asleep on the cart and so causing the old horse, Prince's, death, makes her regard herself as 'a murderess'. She continues to 'sink in her own esteem'.[2] The neighbours hardly expect

> welfare possible to such a family, harmless as the Durbeyfields were to all except themselves.

When Tess attempts to prefer the other dairymaids before herself to Angel, Hardy openly calls it 'self-immolation'. When, to avoid unwelcome attentions from men, she snips off her eyebrows and makes herself unattractive in other ways she exclaims:

> I'll always be ugly now, because Angel is not here, and I have nobody to take care of me.[3]

When Angel tells her that he is going abroad and that she must not follow him Tess' pride forbids her to cry out.

> Her mood of long-suffering made his way easy for him, and she herself was his best advocate.[4]

Like Eustacia, Tess prides herself that she is not 'a crying sort of animal'.

Hardy attempts to explain this tendency in human nature by contrasting it with its opposite, the urge towards happiness. Only the word 'circumstantial' betrays his incomprehension of the psychological phenomenon involved.

> So the two forces were at work here as everywhere, the inherent will to enjoy, and the circumstantial will against enjoyment.[5]

---

[1] Desmond Hawkins, *Thomas Hardy*, p. 82. Arthur Barker, 1951.
[2] *Tess of the d'Urbervilles*, pp. 39 and 54.
[3] *Ibid.*, p. 359.   [4] *Ibid.*, p. 326.   [5] p. 367.

He has already been astonished by the spirit's ability to renew its strength. In 1886, in *The Woodlanders*, he comments on the miracle:

> Even among the moodiest the tendency to be cheered is stronger than the tendency to be cast down; and a soul's specific gravity constantly re-asserts itself as less than that of the sea of troubles into which it is thrown.[1]

And in July 1888 he jots down:

> Thought of the *determination to enjoy* . . . It is achieved of a sort under superhuman difficulties. Like pent-up water it will find a chink of possibility somewhere. Even the most oppressed of men and animals find it, so that out of a thousand there is not one who has not *a sun of some sort for his soul*.[2]

But he does not appear to have studied the *determination to suffer*. Suffering is endured by Hardy's characters passively, with resignation. Those who contend with it, like Michael Henchard, only destroy themselves. Yet passivity and inaction can sometimes be as destructive as action, and Hardy hints at this when he says that had Tess pled with Angel 'in that lonely lane . . . he would probably not have withstood her'. Her 'passive responsiveness' to all that Angel suggests, her mute obedience to his wishes which prevents her repeated attempts to be honest with him, imply the longing of a passionate woman to be possessed and dominated by a more powerful mate. But there is also something abject, something unconsciously self-destructive in this passivity, and thus, when Angel carries her in his arms, in the sleep-walking scene, she finds herself wishing that they could fall together 'and both be dashed to pieces—how fit, how desirable'.[3] When Alec woos her beside the ancestral tombs she melodramatically wonders why she is not on the other side of the vault.

All these feelings—of guilt because she inhabits 'the fleshly tabernacle with which nature had endowed her'[4]: of having

---

[1] pp. 31-2.
[2] I, p. 279. (Italics mine.) "Hope, and the invisible instinct towards self delight" closes the second part of *Tess*.
[3] p. 213.   [4] P. 395.

caused her family's misfortunes by the accident of falling asleep, (first in the cart and secondly when 'she is in the hands of the spoiler'),[1] cause Tess to sink so low in her own esteem that she commits herself to Alec's care, while secretly despising him. She then loads herself with further guilt, until she 'spiritually ceases to recognize [her own] body as hers—allowing it to drift, like a corpse upon the current, in a direction dissociated from its living will'.[2]

This is the true tragedy of Tess Durbeyfield—not a girl's loss of virginity, or even a woman's murder of a man when goaded past endurance. Only a despairing soul allows itself to be destroyed by someone else, to be subtly lead away from its true self, not only by the threats or persuasions of another, but by an inner, unconscious consent more treacherous than the act of any hired lackey. Hardy understands this in the affairs of nations, for in *The Dynasts* he makes an English statesman say:

> *Wrongly has Bonaparte's late course been called*
> *A rude incursion on the soil of France.—*
> *Who ever knew a sole and single man*
> *Invade a nation thirty million strong,*
> *And gain in some few days full sovereignty*
> *Against that nation's will!—The truth is this:*
> The nation longed for him, and has obtained him . . .[3]

Tess was not only the victim of Fate, Circumstance, a malign progenitor, of shiftless, cowardly or bestial people, she was also the victim of her own strong sensuality, and of an insidious need to immolate herself under the deceptive guise of benefiting others. Hardy called his portrait of Henchard that of a 'self-alienated man'. Tess is even more alienated from her true self, and the portrait of her may be called that of a human sacrifice. In choosing Stonehenge as the setting for her last hours with Angel, Hardy stressed the sacrificial elements involved, but he looked upon Tess as having been destroyed by 'the letter of a law that killeth'. I do not think he was fully aware of the significance of his symbolism, of that which he had

[1] Unprinted phrase from Hardy's original manuscript. See Rutland, p. 227. [2] *Tess of the d'Urbervilles*, p. 491.
[3] Part III, Act V, Sc. 5. (Italics mine.)

rightly apprehended with his intuition. As Virginia Woolf says:

> It is as if Hardy himself were not quite aware of what he did, as if his consciousness held more than he could produce, and he left it for his readers to make out his full meaning . . .[1]

But there is so much beauty in this book, both in the descriptions of the heroine and in those of nature, we are led away from the contemplation of suffering, over and over again. When Hardy is moved by his creation Tess assumes divine proportions; she is enlarged symbolically until she towers above us like one of the great Byzantine Saints or Empresses. When setting out to meet Alec she has 'an amplitude which belies her age' and gives her a womanly carriage. When she baptizes her child, in the cottage bedroom, she appears to the sleep-dazed children . . .

> singularly tall and imposing . . . a being large, towering and awful—a divine personage with whom they had nothing in common . . .[2]

and when she walks with Angel in the 'singular, luminous gloom' of the mist-laden valley, before the dawn, she looks 'like a soul at large'; her features are 'those of a divinity who can confer bliss'.[3]

This novel is filled with astonishing descriptions of darkness and light and has about it, for all its stern (or melodramatic) tragedy, an ethereal quality not equalled in any of Hardy's other works. In the dread morning at Stonehenge, before the officers come to take Tess away, the dawn is described as having (like the heath in *The Return of the Native*) a human, sentient quality.

> The band of silver paleness along the east horizon made even the distant parts of the Great Plain appear dark and near; and the whole enormous landscape bore that impress of reserve, taciturnity, and hesitation which is usual just before day.[4]

[1] "Thomas Hardy" in *The Common Reader*, p. 248.
[2] *Tess of the d'Urbervilles*, p. 121.
[3] *Ibid.*, pp. 169-70.
[4] p. 513.

When Tess fears to face her neighbours, and chooses the twilight for walking alone in the woods, she knows

> . . . how to hit to a hair's-breadth that moment of evening when the light and the darkness are so evenly balanced that the constraint of day and the suspense of night neutralize each other, leaving absolute mental liberty.[1]

'Stealthy' and 'flexuous', Tess merges with the shadows and the unreal world, which is after all only 'a psychological phenomenon'.[2]

And in the Frome meadows dawn light and twilight are contrasted:

> The grey half-tones of daybreak are not the grey half-tones of the day's close, though the degree of their shade may be the same. In the twilight of the morning light seems active, darkness passive; in the twilight of evening it is the darkness which is active and crescent, and the light which is the drowsy reverse.[3]

"*Tess*," says Florence Hardy, "was the beginning of the end of Hardy's career as a novelist." The poet in him increasingly longed for utterance, and the attacks made on *Tess* and *Jude the Obscure* left him disinclined to 'deliberately stand up to be shot at'.[4] But it was the beginning of the end in another way. Never again, either in prose or verse, did Hardy attain to the same fullness, the same rich lyricism. The similes and metaphors in *Tess* rise like bubbling springs from the Frome meadows: sometimes there are as many as five or six on a page, or two in a single sentence. In one description alone, that of Angel carrying the dairymaids over the flooded footpath (a passage which had to be altered for the *Graphic* so that Angel pushed them across in a wheel-barrow) there are five, intensely poetic examples. In his first novel Hardy had described pigeons with especial delicacy.[5] Here, in *Tess*, the dairymaids in their summer frocks cling to the hedgerow-bank '*like pigeons on a roof-slope*'. Their gauzy skirts have brushed-up flies and butterflies 'caged in the transparent tissue *as in an aviary*'. When Angel declares that he will carry them all over the water the 'four flush *as if one heart*

---

[1] pp. 109-10.   [2] p. 110.   [3] pp. 168-9.
[4] I, p. 315, and II, p. 7.
[5] *Desperate Remedies*, p. 10.

beat through them', and when he bears Marian, the heaviest of the girls,

> his slim figure, as viewed from behind looked *like the mere stem to the great nosegay suggested by hers.*[1]

To take three more examples: the herons in the mist-filled, summer meadows come out of the boughs of a nearby plantation 'with a great bold noise *as of opening doors and shutters*', or, standing in the water, watch Tess and Angel pass,

> moving their heads round in a slow, horizontal, passionless wheel, *like the turn of puppets by clockwork.*[2]

Anyone who has lived near a heronry will recognize the skilful and poetical way in which Hardy blends minute observation with intuitive appreciation in those two short phrases. The last example occurs when Tess mournfully gazes at the tombs of her ancestors . . .

> their carvings, defaced and broken; their brasses torn from the matrices, the rivet-holes remaining *like martin-holes in a sand cliff.*[3]

Here Hardy engagingly mixes the rural and archeological. Yet the comparison is not one which would readily be made by either the countryman or the antiquarian. It is instead a brief and brilliant recapitulation of what a country *child* would think. Hardy stands and looks at the sepulchral brasses with his own childhood eyes, which he lends to Tess. For this woman of sorrows, who courts suffering so fatalistically, is still only a young girl at heart, and with a delicate brush stroke such as this Hardy makes us remember it.

It is strange that Tess, familiar as such to millions the world over, should have begun life in Hardy's mind as Sue (the name of the heroine of his last great novel), and then became Rose Mary. Not until the thirty-fifth chapter did she change to Tess,[4] a name which her creator seems to have borrowed from his own cousin, who continued the family association with the Stinsford church music by playing the new-fangled organ. Tess became so real to Hardy that he always spoke of her as if she were, or had been, a living person. Emma complained that her husband

---

[1] *Tess of the d'Urbervilles*, pp. 185-7   [2] *Ibid.*, p. 170.
[3] *Ibid.*, p. 469.   [4] Rutland, p. 225.

thought of every servant as a Tess, and this belief in the living quality of his heroine was transferred to others in Dorset. Upon meeting a pretty country-girl Hardy paid her a compliment to which she retorted with

> "Ah, but you don't think me as nice as Tess."—Hardy replied, "But she isn't real; you are . . ." She was much relieved, Hardy gathered, to know that Tess was no practical rival.[1]

There are many threads from the past woven into the making of *Tess* which we can identify. First, the tales of Hardy's mother and grandmother of the former yeoman status of Swetmans, Childses and Hardys. Tess' father-in-embryo actually appeared in the flesh and was pointed out to Thomas as he walked with his mother.

> This particular couple had an enormous lot of children. I remember when young seeing the man—tall and thin—walking beside a horse and common spring-trap, and my mother pointing him out to me and saying he represented what was once the leading branch of the family. So we go down, down, down.[2]

As a boy Hardy had been employed by the village girls to write their love-letters for them in Richardsonian fashion. Thus, as William Archer put it, the 18th-century writer had 'trained for Clarissa, Hardy for Tess'.[3]

Stinsford church gave him Angel's name and Stinsford Sunday School the dairymaid with the amazing verbal memory. The servant-girl at Sturminster Newton who belonged to 'an old county family': the whirling maids on the village-green: the field-women of his childhood (the 'bevy now underground' whom he described in a poem)[4]: a girl whom he met driving a cart and belabouring her horse 'with unnecessary vehemence of language':[5] a woman with an unforgettable 'stopt diapason note to her voice', and the study of dry, diagrammatic county pedigrees behind which Hardy discerned 'palpitating dramas'[6]—all these and more went into the making of *Tess*, the 'revelation of a soul unreconciled to life'.

---

[1] Blunden, p. 79.   [2] I, p. 281.   [3] Archer, p. 32.
[4] "At Middle-Field Gate in February."
[5] Blunden, p. 47.   [6] Preface to *A Group of Noble Dames.*

Hardy once told a reporter that old Parson Clare was

> a Dorsetshire parson whose name still lives enshrined in the
> hearts of thousands.[1]

One immediately thinks of Horace Moule's father, and this
thought is strengthened when we read that Hardy told Sir
Sydney Cockerell he had modelled Angel on Charles Moule,
Horace's brother. But in Angel's reading of a book described as
a 'system of philosophy' than which there is 'no more moral,
or even religious work published' (possibly a reference to *On
Liberty*), in his refusal to subscribe to the Fourth of the thirty-nine
Articles ('leave alone the rest'), and his decision 'to do without
Cambridge' since he could not contemplate taking Orders, all
these are strongly reminiscent of Hardy's own early manhood.
To carry the comparison further, Angel tells his father:

> I love the Church as one loves a parent. I shall always have the
> warmest affection for her. There is no institution for whose
> history I have a deeper admiration; but I cannot honestly be
> ordained her minister . . . while she refuses to liberate her mind
> from an untenable redemptive theolatry.[2]

He goes on to say that his 'whole instinct in matters of religion is
towards reconstruction' and later, we are told that he could
never sacrifice 'what he valued even more than a competency—
intellectual liberty'[3]—something which Hardy deeply prized.
Angel's experiences in Brazil bring him a kind of conversion
and his heart softens towards Tess, whom he has deserted because of her former misfortune. Here we are told that Angel
had 'persistently elevated Hellenic Paganism at the expense of
Christianity'—another reflection of Mill, and in a fine passage
the voice of Thomas Hardy is clearly heard:

> What arrested him now as of value in life was less its beauty
> than its pathos. Having long discredited the old systems of mysti-
> cism, he now began to discredit the old appraisements of morality.
> He thought they wanted readjusting. Who was the moral man?
> Still more pertinently, who was the moral woman? The beauty
> or ugliness of a character lay not only in its achievements, but in
> its aims and impulses; its true history lay, not among things done,
> but among things willed.[4]

[1] Blunden, p. 68.   [2] p. 151.   [3] pp. 151-3.   [4] p. 438

The final sentence is the equivalent of two of the writer's private notes emphasizing wherein beauty or significance lies—in the province of painting, writing, or of life.

While Hardy was writing *Tess* he made other notes which indirectly bear upon it, but more especially on the problem of suffering which predominated in his mind.

Evil, he decides, has its place in art as well as good, only the 'choice of evil must be limited by the sense of worthiness'.[1]

> Altruism . . . will ultimately be brought about by the pain we see in others reacting on ourselves, as if we and they were a part of one body. Mankind, in fact, may be, and possibly will be, viewed as members of one corporeal frame.[2]

This note harks back to one made in the previous year when he pondered on whether:

> In time one might get to regard every object, and every action, as composed, not of this or that material . . . or movement, but of the qualities *pleasure and pain* in varying proportions.[3]

Thirty years earlier he had written in the margin of his copy of *On Liberty* 'Do unto others as you would they should do unto you', when Mill condemns the disconnection of 'each man's feelings of duty from the interests of his fellow-creatures'.

In the Sturminster Newton days (1876) Hardy had written in his notebook

> "All is vanity," saith the Preacher. But if all were only vanity, who would mind? Alas, it is too often worse than vanity; agony, darkness, death also.[4]

In 1891 the words, with slight alteration, are made a reflection of Tess' own. And earlier, before he was twenty, Hardy had marked Terence's lines which, in his excerpts from Latin authors, was translated,

> *For it's a common saying and a true*
> *That strictest law is oft the highest wrong.*

That he was re-reading the Greek tragedians, and reflecting on them with a mind seasoned by maturity, while writing *Tess*

---

[1] I, pp. 229, 294.
[2] *Ibid.*, p. 294. This idea was enlarged in *The Dynasts*.
[3] I, p. 285.   [4] *Ibid.*, p. 148.

is implied by his note, clearly related to the action of the story:

> When a married woman who has a lover kills her husband, she does not really wish to kill the husband; she wishes to kill the situation . . .[1]

and he added thoughts on Clytaemnestra and Iphigenia.

Six months before he began the writing of *Tess*, in March 1888, Hardy contributed an article called "The Profitable Reading of English Fiction" to the *Forum*, in which he stresses the 'constructive art' of the Greek tragedians, and it is interesting to find that he praises Richardson for similar skill, for with Pamela, Tess shares many misfortunes. At some time, too, we cannot say exactly when, Hardy underlined a passage in the *Hippolytus*:

> Whoever has chastity, not that which is taught in schools, but that which is by nature.[2]

(This reminds one of Schweitzer's remark that 'there is a chastity of the mind as well as of the body'.) In *The Early Life* there are notes on Plato and Sophocles in February and July of the same year.

At this time the writer was often in the company of society women, many of them famous beauties, at county-balls, town dinners and 'crushes'. But his heart remained faithful to rustic types. 'These women!', he exclaims in his private journal. 'If put into rough wrappers in a turnip-field, where would their beauty be?'[3] Although Hardy claimed friendship with many women of rank who valued his gifts he confessed that there were 'few, very few for whom he would make a sacrifice'.[4] He looked at a fragile woman of wealth being bowled along in a landau and pair, weighted with metal trappings, complete with coachman and footman heavy with livery, and saw the ridiculous contrast between her passive, slim form and the

> mass of matter moved along with brute force and clatter through a street congested and obstructed [when she might], if held up by her hair and slipped out of her clothes . . . be not much larger than a skinned rabbit, and of less use.[5]

---

[1] *Ibid.*, p. 289.   [2] Rutland, p. 44.
[3] I, p. 293.   [4] *Ibid.*, p. 276.   [5] *Ibid.*, p. 311.

(The tone of derogation is easily perceptible and reminds one of Delacroix's burning condemnations of French society.) Hardy was writing in a time of agricultural depression and he was vividly aware that the society which he moved in, for the supposed good of his writer's soul, was unmoved by this distressing, fundamental situation. The welfare of the people 'was never once thought of' at these gatherings. There is an echo of this thought in one of Hardy's works:

> The pity is that politics are looked on as being a game for politicians, just as cricket is a game for cricketers; not as the serious duties of political trustees.[1]

His sympathy was also with the suffering in a lunatic asylum, and with young and ignorant girls in Women's Training Colleges, which he visited at this time.

In the latter his protective tenderness was aroused. He felt the contrast between the 'noble aspirations' of the girls and the disillusionment which he felt certain they would encounter outside the walls. Their belief in the superficial structure of life—'the rightness of things, circumstances, convention' (so easily confused with First Nature) which he now knew to be 'damnably wrong', touched him profoundly. His sisters had attended a Training College in Salisbury and their experiences, together with what he himself now observed, were used when delineating Sue's life at Christminster in his next novel.

In 1892 Hardy made a journey to Great Fawley in Berkshire, the village from which his paternal grandmother, Mary Head,[2] had come. So intent was he on remembering her presence by the Bockhampton hearth in his own childhood, and what she had told him of her painful experiences as an orphan, that he scarcely remarked the living children here at play. He was impressed by the silence in a ploughed vale which he entered, calling it 'The Valley of Brown Melancholy', a phrase reminiscent of a marked passage in his *Ossian*.

The visits to Great Fawley and to Oxford, which he made in 1892-3, were for the purpose of gathering body and colour for

---

[1] *The Well Beloved*, p. 97.
[2] The poem "One We Knew" in *Time's Laughingstocks*, was written to her memory, in 1902.

his next novel *Jude the Obscure*, the name being taken from a Berkshire surname. (It will be remembered that Jude was an orphan like Mary Head.) Hardy had once met a lad driving a baker's cart who asked if he might borrow a Latin Grammar from him and this incident is vividly made use of in the book. He had lately[1] been reading Milton on *Divorce* and Weismann on *Heredity*, as well as many of the satirists—Latin, French, English, German and Spanish. He attended the new plays of Ibsen in London:[2] and discussed the question of marriage with society women, discussions, he is careful to tell us, initiated by them. One of them told him how nervously exhausting it was to be tied to a man who could 'throw you over at any moment'.

But as early as 1887 he had been making notes for *Jude* and in April 1888 had written in his notebook:

> A short story of a young man—'who could not go to Oxford'. His struggles and ultimate failure. Suicide. There is something in this the world ought to be shown and I am the one to show it to them—though I was not altogether hindered going, at least to Cambridge, and could have gone up easily at five-and-twenty.[3]

The seed for *Jude the Obscure* lay germinating for seven years. Before its appearance in serial form (December 1894—November 1895) Hardy published a letter called "On the Tree of Knowledge" in the *New Reveiw*, in company with other contributors who had been asked whether a young girl should be informed of sexual matters before marriage. He alone amongst the contributors makes the suggestion that boys as well as girls should be initiated,

> for it has never struck me that the spider is invariably male and the fly invariably female.

Jude's sexual ignorance is one of the causes of his lamentable marriage and his ultimate downfall.

Hardy's aims in writing *Jude* are clearly given in his preface to the novel, and in letters written to a 'close friend', in 1895,

---

[1] 1887 and 1890.

[2] Hardy was a foundation member of the Independent Theatre Association sponsoring Ibsen's plays. See Rutland, p. 252 *et seq.*

[3] I, pp. 272-3.

after its publication. In the former he tells us that he had attempted to

> deal unaffectedly with the fret and fever, derision and disaster, that may press in the wake of the strongest passion known to humanity; to tell, without a mincing of words, of a deadly war waged . . . between flesh and spirit; and to point the tragedy of unfulfilled aims.'[1]

In the letters he says:

> The 'grimy' features of the story go to show the contrast between the ideal life a man wished to lead, and the squalid real life he was fated to lead. The throwing of the pizzle at the supreme moment of his young, dream is to sharply initiate the contrast . . . The idea was meant to run all through the novel. It is, in fact, to be discovered in everybody's life, though it lies less on the surface perhaps than it does in my poor puppets.[2]
>
> Of course the book is all contrasts—or was meant to be in its original conception . . . Sue and her heathen gods set against Jude's reading the Greek Testament; Christminster academical, Christminster in the slums; Jude the saint, Jude the sinner; Sue the Pagan, Sue the saint; marriage, no marriage; etc. etc.[3]

In a third he stresses the point that the book

> makes for morality: and that delicacy or indelicacy in a writer is according to his object. If I say to a lady "I met a naked woman," it is indelicate. But if I go on to say "I found she was mad with sorrow", it ceases to be indelicate. And in writing *Jude* my mind was fixed on the ending.[4]

In 1890 Hardy also wrote a poem called "Thoughts of Phena"[5] to a cousin who died in this year. We learn nothing of the cousin's character from the verses which merely hint at her 'gifts', 'compassion' and 'sweet ways', but that she contributed to the poet's drawing of Sue Bridehead we gather from the preface to *Jude* which states that 'some of the circumstances were suggested by the death of a woman in the former year'. One would like to know more of this mysterious

---

[1] Dated 1895-1902.   [2] II, pp. 41-3.
[3] *Ibid.*   [4] II, pp. 43.   [5] In *Wessex Poems.*

cousin, since Hardy writes in the second letter quoted from above:

> Sue is a type of woman which has always had an attraction for me, but the difficulty of drawing the type has kept me from attempting it till now.

But, determined to keep his private life secret and close, Hardy tells us no more. That at some time she was his companion in her youth is obvious from the lines:

> . . . *whom I knew when her dreams*
> *were upbrimming with light,*
> *And with laughter her eyes.*

Three months before her death Browning had also died. Although baffled by Browning's optimism and zest for life, Hardy had always admired, and even striven to imitate, his poetry, and now he set down in his notebook that line from *Sordello* which summed up for him the poet's gift;

"Incidents in the development of a soul! little else is worth study.[1]

Jude was to be such a study, Hardy's closest approach to the psychologically subtle after Michael Henchard.

Few are now concerned with the meaningless and emasculated form of the novel as it appeared in serial instalments. But some memory, some scent, as from a sacrificial holocaust, of the execrations heaped on it when it appeared in volume form still cling to this much abused book, which an irate Bishop in England, and a man in Australia, burnt. The former denounced it in a letter to the *Yorkshire Post*, calling it 'garbage', and the latter informed Hardy that the packet of ashes enclosed were those of the pages of *Jude*. The antagonistic reviewers called it 'titanically bad', 'an exposition of the unclean', and 'a deplorable falling-off'. On the other hand, admirers gave it extravagant praise. It was 'the most splendid of all the works which he had given to the world': 'one of the most touching records in all our literature': Aeschylean in its 'profound and unfathomable depths of gloom and greatness'. Swinburne comforted Hardy by assuring him that 'the tragedy was equally beautiful and terrible in its pathos'.[2]

[1] I, p. 292.   [2] II, p. 39.

If *Tess* had aroused curiosity as to Hardy's religious faith, *Jude* brought a more distressing series of letters and articles questioning, and making assumptions on, the author's private life. The book was said to be 'a treatise on the marriage question' as well as autobiographical; Christminster was pointed at as being Oxford. All of these things Hardy (and, in later years, his second wife) stoutly denied. For by now he was nettled and stung into defiance, bewildered by the virulence and number of the attacks, and determined to escape the legend of himself. Once again he seems to have been unaware of the vehemence of the bitter and aggressive sides of his nature. He thought of himself as a mild, inoffensive countryman; a 'harmless agnostic' rather than a 'clamorous atheist'; a teller of tales, a recorder of 'seemings' or 'impressions', a chronicler of moods and deeds rather than a philosopher, or reformer. He liked to be called 'the man with the watching eye'.[1] Humility made him say to a reporter that he was only a 'learner' in the art of novel-writing and that, as regards *Tess*, it was too much to hope that he had been able to bring about any changes in the treatment, or attitude to, those intricate problems which hedge about the sexes.[2]

What is it which angered and disgusted the readers of *Jude*? Granted that the Victorian world was hardly ready for the psychological intricacies of Sue, or the unconventional illicit relationship between her and her cousin, Jude, there is more to their objections than cavilling at convention: their response is that of the healthy to the morbid. The book is steeped in bitterness, and redemptive forces seldom spring from this emotion, generally a sign of defeat and spiritual immaturity. *Jude* verges on the pathological; it is a theorem clothed in language rather than the study of warm-blooded human beings; above all, it stands as Hardy's final testament to disillusion, the theme which had attracted him from the beginning. The romantic goes under, 'bloody, but unbowed' it is true, but with an aching, empty and broken heart, disenchanted with marriage, an unmarried relationship, the consolations of religion, the possibilities of a poor and gifted man scaling the ladder of learning without in-

---

[1] II, p. 246. [2] See Blunden, p. 80.

fluence; disillusioned over the charitable hearts of scholars and theologians, the fidelity of women, their ability to think and grow dispassionately; disillusioned finally by the quenching of the light from his own soul which, like Jupiter 'the golden jonquil', had steadfastly guided him as a youth. The darkness and bitterness of his mood, the reverse of that ardent buoyancy which had elated him as a young man, is so intense that one cannot help identifying it as the unacknowledged story of the development of Hardy's own soul.

Looking back on those early days the poet wrote one of his loveliest lyrics, *In the Seventies*. If we compare this with the three poems called *In Tenebris*, two of which were written in 1895-6 after the reception of *Jude*, we get the full contrast. Here are three stanzas of the lyric:

> *In the seventies I was bearing in my breast,*
> > *Penned tight,*
> *Certain starry thoughts that threw a magic light*
> *On the worktimes and the soundless hours of rest*
> *In the seventies; aye, I bore them in my breast*
> > *Penned tight.*

. . . .
. . . .

> *In the seventies those who met me did not know*
> > *Of the vision*
> *That immuned me from the chillings of misprision*
> *And the damps that choked my goings to and fro*
> *In the seventies; yea, those nodders did not know*
> > *Of the vision.*

> *In the seventies nought could darken or destroy it,*
> > *Locked in me,*
> *Though as delicate as lamp-worm's lucency;*
> *Neither mist nor murk could weaken or alloy it*
> *In the seventies!—could not darken or destroy it,*
> > *Locked in me.*[1]

And here are stanzas from the first of the triology called

[1] Undated poem in *Moments of Vision*.

I

In Tenebris, beneath the title of which Hardy appends a line from the 51st Psalm—in the Latin of St Jerome:

> *Wintertime nighs;*
> *But my bereavement-pain*
> *It cannot bring again;*
> *Twice no one dies.*

> .   .   .   .

> *Leaves freeze to dun;*
> *But friends can not turn cold*
> *This season as of old*
> *For him with none.*

> *Tempests may scath;*
> *But love can not make smart*
> *Again this year his heart*
> *Who no heart hath.*

> *Black is night's cope;*
> *But death will not appal*
> *One who, past doubtings all,*
> *Waits in unhope.*[1]

This poem reminds one of lines from the Book of Jude in which the false teachers are described as "*wandering stars, to whom is reserved the blackness of darkness forever*". For without hope, faith, strength, friends, and feeling, one is indeed (in the words of the Bible) 'twice dead, plucked up by the roots'. It is evidence that Hardy, like Coleridge, had an 'encumbered heart'.

For poetry in *Jude the Obscure* we must turn to the passages on Christminster, wherein Hardy creates the exquisite consolations which the thought of reaching this academic city holds for a poor lad, first a rook-scarer and then driver of a baker's cart. We need not identify these occupations with Thomas Hardy's as a boy. As far as we know, that *intense* longing to get a University education or to enter the Church were not even his, but he had been close enough to these ambitions, and had been sufficiently hard-pressed to attain classical knowledge without regular

---

[1] *Poems of the Past and Present.*

tutelage, to enable him to write with particular pathos of Jude's hunger for learning and his primitive attempts to obtain it. Jude Fawley may be regarded as a heart-breaking caricature of what Hardy, but for his talents, his mother's ambitions, and the good fortune of having Isaac Last, William Barnes and Horace Moule to guide his intellectual growth, might have been.

In visualizing Jude's struggles to learn Latin and Greek Hardy very naturally went back to his own first classical studies, and we find this character mastering and admiring passages of the *Iliad*, the lyrics of Horace, and the Greek Testament in Griesbach's text, just as Thomas had done more than forty years before. On the other hand Sue, the rationalistic counterpart of her poetic cousin Jude, is a devotee of Mill, like Ethelberta. In a scene which verges on the ludicrous, she quotes a sentence from *On Liberty* to her long-suffering husband who finally breaks out with:

"What do I care about J. S. Mill! I only want to lead a quiet life!"[1]

Sue also admires Swinburne, and quotes from the very poems which had stirred Hardy so profoundly in the 1860's—the "Hymn to Prosperine" and "Songs before Sunrise." Furthermore Jude delights in deciphering 'the Latin inscriptions on 15th-century brasses and tombs', a favourite pastime of Hardy's, who had a predilection for mediaeval Latin.

It is against the ethereal vision of Christminster-desired that we must set the action of *Jude*, for in this novel there is no substantial background such as the Heath, woodland, downs, meadows, or Romano-Victorian town. Jude's obsession with Christminster, and what it may lead him to, is a 'fixed vision', and the vision (and the emotion it arouses in him) resembles the New Jerusalem with which Bernard of Murles or the tortured Elizabethan recusants consoled themselves, a city 'expected by eager hearts'.

Some way within the limits of the stretch of landscape, points of light like the topaz gleamed. The air increased in transparency with the lapse of minutes, till the topaz points showed themselves to be the vanes, windows, wet roof-slopes, and other shining

[1] *Jude the Obscure*, p. 280.

spots upon the spires, domes, freestone-work . . . Christminster
unquestionably; either directly seen, or miraged in the peculiar
atmosphere.

The spectator gazed on and on till the windows and vanes lost
their shine, going out almost suddenly like extinguished candles.
The vague city became veiled in mist.[1]

He meets a carter, like Giles, with a heavy load and a string of
belled horses, who tells the boy that 'as for music, there's
beautiful music everywhere in Christminster'; and when he
walks on alone he reflects to himself:

It had been the yearning of his heart to find something to
anchor on, to cling to—for some place which he could call
admirable . . . .
'It is a city of light,' he said to himself.
'The tree of knowledge grows there,' he added a few steps
further on.
'It is a place that teachers of men spring from and go to.'
'It is what you may call a castle, manned by scholarship and
religion.'
After this figure he was silent for a long while, till he added:
'It would just suit me.' [2]

The boy's mystical ardour dims as he grows older, yet even
in young manhood he can describe it with poetic imagery,
using an astronomical simile.

. . . there is more going on than meets the eye of a man walking
through the streets. It is a unique centre of thought and religion—
the intellectual and spiritual granary of this country. All that
silence and absence of goings-on is the stillness of infinite motion
. . .[3]

Contrasted with this vision of the academic city are those other
aspects of it which the varied sides of Hardy's nature depict;
Christminster which raises parsons 'like radishes in a bed', or the
town with a life

infinitely more palpitating, varied, and compendious than the
gown life—the *reality* of Christminster.

To reveal this second city Hardy uses the cynical voice of country
workers, or the flippant one of Sue with her 'modern' sight

[1] *Ibid.*, pp. 19-20.   [2] pp. 24-5.   [3] p. 137.

and restless, speculative mind. It is she who declares that the academic city is 'full of fetichists and ghost-seers', who has the courage to declare that

> The mediaevalism of Christminster must go, be sloughed off, or Christminster itself will have to go. . . .

and who caps her denunciation with a line from Swinburne's "Hymn to Proserpine"[1]—a reflection once again of the theological-scientific battle of the '60's. 'The freezing negative which the scholared walls had echoed to his desire' make Jude cry out at last that the city hates all men like him. . . .

> scorns our laboured acquisitions, when it should be the first to respect them . . . sneers at our false quantities and mispronunciations when it should say "I see you want help, my poor friend". Nevertheless it is the centre of the universe to me, because of my early dream: and nothing can alter it. Perhaps it will soon wake up, and be generous . . .[2]

As others have pointed out the pattern of *Jude* is that of *Tess* reversed. The sensuous Arabella, with her temporary religious conversion, is a female Alec; the fastidious Sue, with her moral questioning and her admiration for Pagan gods and philosophy, a female Angel; and Jude himself, while not necessarily resembling Tess in character, is destroyed by two women of opposite natures, as *Tess* was between two men. Phillitson, despite his open-mindedness and generosity, is too much of a lay figure to count as anything more than a useful fourth to complicate the plot with its dual mismatings. He has no counterpart in *Tess*.

With the character of Tess regnant and dominant Hardy had come a long way from his early portrayal of women as capricious, wilful, indecisive creatures who flutter like robins, but in Sue he returns to this type, in part, although Sue's 'liquid-eyed, lightfooted, aerial' qualities make one think more of a faun. Hardy dowers this fragile, mercurial creature with maddening intellectual quandaries, and distractingly weak emotions that cause her to test and tantalize herself and torture the men who are her victims. She is in fact the elfin *Belle Dame sans Merci*, more masochistic than all of his heroines put together, and the

---

[1] p. 185.   [2] p. 402.

scene where she forces herself to return to the bed of the man whom she respects, but abhors, is one of the most loathsome in the whole of English literature. We turn from it to the homely recitals of the old-fashioned country woman, Widow Edlin, with infinite relief.

> Nobody thought o' being afeared o' matrimony in my time, nor of much else but a cannon-ball or empty cupboard! Why, when I and my poor man were married we thought no more o't than of a game o' dibs . . . In my time we took it more careless: and I don't know that we was any the worse for it! When I and my poor man were jined in it we kept up the junketting all the week, and drunk the parish dry, and had to borrow half-a-crown to begin housekeeping.[1]

If Hardy wrote *The Woodlanders* in a mood which made him feel 'encased in lead', his state of mind while writing *Jude* gives the impression of having been that of man who wore a shirt of Nessus and cried out with irritant pain. 'We are horribly sensitive, that's what's wrong with us,' says Jude to Sue, and it is useless for Hardy to deny self-portraiture in passages such as these, which he would have considered of small account. In addition to the remarkable similarity between the 'unwanted' Jude (staring through the interstices of his straw hat, and hoping he may never grow up) and the 'useless' Tom Hardy[2], there are others. Jude feels a kinship with the hungry rooks, defenceless earthworms, trapped rabbits and growing things around him. 'A magic thread of fellow-feeling united his own life with theirs.'[3]

> . . . he was a boy who could not himself bear to hurt anything. He had never brought home a nest of young birds without lying awake in misery half the night after, and often reinstating them and the nest in their original place the next morning. He could scarcely bear to see trees cut down or lopped, from a fancy that it hurt them; and late pruning, when the sap was up and the tree bled profusely, had been a positive grief to him in his infancy. This weakness of character, as it may be called. suggested that he was the sort of man who was born to ache a good deal before the

---

[1] *Jude the Obscure*, pp. 361 and 464.
[2] See p. 17, *supra*.
[3] *Jude the Obscure*, pp. 11 and 13.

fall of the curtain upon his unneccessary life should signify that all was well with him again.[1]

This has the ring of self-revelation: and

that flaw in the terrestrial scheme by which what was good for God's birds was bad for God's gardener—[2]

is this not the paradox presented to us at birth which Hardy could never accept? Again, later: "I am only a feeler, not a reasoner," Phillotson declares, which might have been Hardy's own epitaph.

Jude stands as a denial of life as we know it, the crux of the problem being that we are self-contradictions from the start, animal beings endowed with intellectual and spiritual aspirations which seldom harmonize with our primitive sexual urges, and a sensitivity in excess of our courage, or physical strength. Added to this there is the further complication which man has consciously evolved, a society so artificial that it seems to turn

the normal sex-impulses into devilish, domestic gins and springes to noose and hold back those who want to progress.[3]

All this Hardy has pointed out less forcibly in other prose works, but in none of them has the will *to die out of life*, which reaches its apex in the unappetising figure of Jude's son, been so strong. This negative urge is generally set down to Hardy's reading of Schopenhauer, but we have seen other examples; the masochistic cry of Tess to Alec is matched by that of Jude, who bids Sue 'crucify' him if she wishes, for he is hers and hers alone. There is so little alleviation from tragedy, so small a respite from the major theme of wormwood marriages which corrode and corrupt, that we turn away feeling the book is inartistic, false to life and to art.

In an unfinished essay on Hardy's novels [4] D. H. Lawrence makes the trenchant comment that *Jude the Obscure* is not a true, an essential tragedy:

Necessarily painful it was, but they were not at war with God, only with society. Yet they were all cowed by the mere judgment of man upon them, and all the while by their own souls they were

[1] *Ibid.*, pp. 11 and 13.   [2] *Ibid.*
[3] *Ibid.*, p. 272.   [4] See p. 182, *supra*, footnote 1.

right. The judgment of man killed them, not the judgment of
their own souls, or the judgment of eternal God.

And he stresses that this is the weakness of *Jude*, and of modern
tragedy in which

transgression against the social code is made to bring destruction,
as though the social code worked our irrevocable fate.

The real tragedy of the lives of Eustacia, Tess, Sue and Jude is,
he suggests, that

they are unfaithful to the greater unwritten morality, which
would have bidden Eustacia fight Clym for his own soul, and
Tess take and claim her Angel, since she had the greater light;
would have bidden Jude and Sue endure for very honour's
sake, since one must bide by the best that one has known, and not
succumb to lesser good.

In other words, Sue's recantation and return to the husband
whom she does not love, and Jude's return to Arabella, who had
merely entrapped him sexually with her skin 'like a Cochin
hen's egg' and her vulgar wiles, were essentially false, and Hardy
weakened the tragedy by not daring to write from his own inner
belief that Sue and Jude should have remained faithful to one
another and defied society. What Lawrence rightly calls

the little human morality play, with its queer frame . . . and
mechanized movement [which goes on] seriously, portentously till
some of the protagonists . . . weary of the stage and look into
the wilderness raging round. . . .

is (in this novel) the centre of the embittered action: the 'beauty
and the wonder' of Hardy's other novels, which set the morality
play against the unexplored, eternally incomprehensible outer
immorality of Nature, is nowhere visible here.

Since Hardy himself never broke away from the moral code
which many of his protagonists transgressed it is worth con-
sidering whether he himself was not taken in by that which, in
his novels, he affected to despise. Lawrence closes his essay by
saying that to most of us, as to Clym, the map of the social code
appears more real than the land.

Shortsighted almost to blindness, we pore over the chart, map
out journeys and confirm them: and we cannot see life itself giving
us the lie the whole time.

It is possible that life was giving *Hardy* the lie all the time: that at heart he was a rebel, who dared not trust those anarchic instincts which he only lived out in his tales of soldiers, smugglers, murderers, and—for him most dangerous, most sinful of all—adulterers.

One wonders that Hardy had the heart to dance on a village green, and visit music-halls while writing, or altering, *Jude*. In the spring of 1893 he and Emma went to Ireland where they stayed at the Vice-regal Lodge, and although he solemnly went the rounds of sight-seeing, the races, the Queen's birthday review procession, and semi-official dinners, Hardy remained objective and aloof, writing in the privacy of his own note-book: "Very funny altogether, this little court."[1] During their social season in London they saw Duse act, and Hardy went to a lecture on Tolstoi. In August they visited Hereford, Shrewsbury, and Ludlow where the roofless state of the castle, so closely connected with *Comus* and *Hudibras*, distressed him; and there were other visits to friends in manor houses whose architecture and gardens delighted him. It was during one of these visits that Hardy proposed dancing on the green by the light of the full moon: at a masked ball in town he and Henry James were brave enough to go unmasked and without costumes; nor was he too self-conscious to take a society beauty by the hand and tread a measure with her to the strains of the Blue Danube Waltz, amongst promenaders who had come to hear one of the famous bands of Europe, at the Imperial Institute. He also supped with Mrs Patrick Campbell and Forbes Robertson at Willis' Rooms, where he had danced more than thirty years before.

In 1892 his father had died and Florence Hardy records 'almost his last remark', which epitomizes the man's integrity and simplicity. He

> had asked for water fresh drawn from the well—which was brought and given him: he tasted it and said, "Yes—that's our well-water. Now I know I am at home."[2]

He died in the house in which he and his son had been born, and Hardy (who grieved that, in spite of his intention to be with him at the end, he was not) wrote a poem entitled "On One who Lived and Died where he was Born."

[1] II, p. 19.   [2] *Ibid.*, p. 10.

I *

The Pursuit of the Well-Beloved, Hardy's last novel, is something of a literary curiosity. Two-thirds of it were written and published serially before *Jude the Obscure* was ever heard of, and the final part later. It was published in book form two years after *Jude*. Its sub-title is *A Sketch of a Temperament* and elsewhere Hardy calls it 'a fantasy'. It is concerned with

> a subjective idea—the theory of the transmigration of the ideal beloved one, who only exists in the lover, from material woman to material woman.[1]

As a young man Hardy had been drawn to the Platonic Idea and, as he grew older, his belief that 'all men are pursuing a shadow, the Unattainable', strengthened. In 1888 he had written in his notebook:

> The story of a face which goes through three generations or more, would make a fine novel or poem of the passage of Time. The differences in personality to be ignored.[2]

And now, with lines of Swinburne's ringing in his head, he carried out his nebulous notion. Hardy does not specifically acknowledge his debt to Shelley yet his frequent quoting from *Epipsychidion*, in his earliest to his last great prose work, and the fact that lines from it are quoted in consecutive novels from 1887-96 (except for *Tess*), show us Hardy's increasing interest in the idea expressed in Shelley's poem:

> *In many mortal forms I rashly sought*
> *The shadow of that idol of my thought.*

Hardy was probably attracted to Plato through his knowledge of Shelley; the epigraph of *The Well-Beloved* is from his *Prometheus Unbound*. The reviewers 'affected to find unmentionable moral atrocities' in this slight work and Hardy, sickened by their prejudices, did not trouble to defend himself, since silence was the more dignified answer. Yet, to his astonishment the book sold well.

Ever since boyhood Hardy had been able to look across the bay to the Isle of Slingers—Portland—which lies 'like a great snail upon the sea'. As the son of a mason, and himself an architect, he had always been attracted to it, for he knew Wren's praise and

---

[1] *Ibid.*, p. 59.   [2] I, p. 284.

discovery of Portland stone, had seen the fine buildings taken from the island's loins, and was never weary of watching truckloads of the stuff wending their way to London, and other great cities. Even in Rome the 'quarried ruins' had set him thinking on 'the quarries of maiden rock at home', and the juxtaposition of Pagan and Christian in the Eternal City which had impressed him had once been found in Portland where customs, legends, dialect, even names, were ancient and peculiar to the stony island.

He delights in stressing the ancient, pre-Christian custom of the island girls giving themselves blithely before marriage to their betrothed : and that idealistic concern with the Pagan, which had fascinated Hardy since his youthful reading of *On Liberty* (which appears in *The Return of the Native*, *Jude*, and a poem called "The Young Glass-Stainer" written at this time— 1893), comes out strongly here. A landslip gives him the excuse for a display of his sense of the relative newness of the Christian faith :

> The church had slipped down with the rest of the cliff, and had long been a ruin. It seemed to say that in this last local stronghold of the Pagan divinities, where Pagan customs lingered yet, Christianity had established itself precariously at best.[1]

The sculptor Pierston fancies in a moment of remorse that some 'Christian emanation' from this church

> might be wrathfully torturing him through the very false gods to whom he had devoted himself both in his craft, like Demetrius of Ephesus, and in his heart. Perhaps Divine punishment for his idolatries had come.[2]

The island setting is also a convenient background for Hardy's historical interests, and his recent taste for studies in heredity which play such an important part in *Jude the Obscure*. He liked to think that Roman faces and features might be discerned in those of the island race and he gave his heroines Roman and Italianate names to make them seem more foreign—Avice Caro, and Marcia, a name to be found on a Stinsford mural tablet close to the towering one of the Greys. There is another reminder of Hardy's youth in this, his final, novel—a re-creation

---

[1] *The Well-Beloved*, p. 19. [2] *Ibid.*, p. 178.

at some length of his mad schoolboy love for the nameless girl
on horseback who had smiled at him as she passed him in the
Dorchester Walks. Even the boys from whom he sought her
name and sympathy are included here.[1] But the tone of the
book is light, not to say unintentionally farcical at times. The
tragi-comedy, as Hardy called it, has little of real tragedy. The
visionary Pierston, a confirmed ego-centric, doomed to live on
in an ageing frame with a youthful heart perpetually torn by
adolescent love, becomes ludicrous. There is no passion and no
real love. We are never moved to pity for this ageing Don Juan
who cynically perceives that "to wed a woman may be by no
means the same thing as to be united to her", but who is in-
capable of abandoning the idea of wedding. Marriage is
suggested as a remedy for escaping from maiden aunts or smoky
chimneys, to assuage a prickly conscience, to satisfy some theory
of beauty and justness, or for mere convention, or custom's,
sake.

Hardy has said these things better in his short story *For
Conscience's Sake*, and in a poem in which he bewails his undying
sensitivity, not only to feminine beauty, but to pain.

> *I look into my glass,*
> *And view my wasting skin,*
> *And say, "Would God it came to pass*
> *My heart had shrunk as thin!"*
>
> *For then, I, undistrest*
> *By hearts grown cold to me,*
> *Could lonely wait my endless rest*
> *With equanimity.*
>
> *But Time, to make me grieve,*
> *Part steals, lets part abide;*
> *And shakes this fragile frame at eve*
> *With throbbings of noontide.*[2]

To which one might answer in Hardy's own words:

Yet he would not have stood where he did stand in the ranks of
an imaginative profession if he had not been at the mercy of every

---

[1] Compare I, p. 32, and *The Well-Beloved*, pp. 52-3.
[2] "I Look into My Glass" in *Wessex Poems*.

haunting of the fancy that can beset man. It was in his weaknesses as a citizen and a national-unit that his strength lay as an artist, and he felt it childish to complain of susceptibilities not only innate but cultivated.[1]

But the significant thing to be noted in reading *The Well-Beloved*, more especially the third and final part, is Hardy's increasing use of words suitable for poetry rather than prose, and of words in poetic order. 'Fantast', 'darkling'[2]—'as he sat darkling here', 'Now she me for your son', and 'the raw rain flies level' are similar to words and phrases to be found and matched in Hardy's lyrical poetry with its terse, compressed, and often monosyllabic style. The prose writer had come to the end of his wish to interpret life further through this medium. He wearied of a trade that earned him a living, fame, wealth; pleasant companionship with the intelligent, titled and famous; even encounters with royalty; but which brought in its train misinterpretation of his motives and harsh, unsparing criticism. Furthermore, for thirty years he had been forced to stifle his deepest longing, and with infinite relief for the buried lyric and epic poet in Thomas Hardy we read this note:

> *Christmas Day* (1890). While thinking of resuming 'the viewless wings of poesy' before dawn this morning, new horizons seemed to open, and worrying pettinesses to disappear.[3]

In February of the year following the appearance of *The Well-Beloved* (1897) Hardy envisaged:

> Wessex Poems: with Sketches of their Scenes by the Author . . .[4]

and in 1898 he published this collection of verses which he had been writing since 1865, pondering on them in his heart and keeping them close since the chilling rejection of some of them in his youth. At the age of fifty-eight, when most authors have turned from the making of verse to prose writing, Hardy reversed the process. The novel-writer risked abandoning himself

---

[1] *The Well-Beloved*, pp. 156-7.
[2] "The Darkling Thrush" (formerly called "By the Century's Deathbed"), was written at the close of this decade. See Carl Weber, *The Colby Mercury*, November 1940.
[3] I, p. 302.
[4] II, p. 58. The original MS, with 32 illustrations by Hardy, is now in the Birmingham City Museum and Art Gallery.

publicly to that form of art which had always been more instinctive with him. In his own words:

> A sense of the truth of poetry, of its supreme place in literature, had awakened itself in me. At the risk of ruining all my worldly prospects I dabbled in it . . . was forced out of it . . . It came back upon me . . . All was of the nature of being led by a mood, without foresight, or regard to whither it led.[1]

[1] II, p. 185.

CHAPTER NINE

'THE DIVISION' AND 'THE DYNASTS'

*I have heard that there grow oaks out of the walls of Silchester
which seem to strike root in the very stones.*

JOHN EVELYN

WHY, during this period of his life, was Hardy embittered about marriage and the possibility of a solution to the intricate problems relating to the sexes? Why was he increasingly obsessed with the thought of 'man entangled against his will', reduced to mere automatism like the Wimborne Jack-a-clock? Why was he preoccupied with suffering and its revelation? Why, above all, with the subject of heredity and the effects of madness in *Jude the Obscure*? A man does not become obsessed with these things altruistically, for the benefit of others, unless he feels himself involved in the common predicament, is himself one "into whose soul the iron has entered, and entered deeply at some time".[1]

It has become the fashion to imagine that great men are unhappy in their marriages, to pity them for having inadequate mates. Yet the personal tragedy implied in Hardy's life by the writing of *Tess*, *Jude*, *In Tenebris* and other lyrical poems, is substantiated by those who knew and watched him with anxiety during these years. Edmund Gosse noticed that the

> wells of human hope had been poisoned for him by some condition of which we know nothing:

and there were others equally observant, although Hardy himself revealed nothing by pen or word of mouth. His doctrine was to suffer in dignified silence:

> *Ache deep; but make no moans:*
> *Smile out; but stilly suffer:*
> *The paths of love are rougher*
> *Than thoroughfares of stones.*[2]

[1] Letter to Swinburne, II, p. 40.
[2] "The End of the Episode," in *Time's Laughingstocks*.

He seems to have felt excluded from love and understanding, from the traffic and intercourse of the mind which binds a pair together more closely than physical rapture. The finality of death can be accepted by some with greater composure than the shock of disillusion, or the slow chilling effects of living with a companion with a closed heart and a shuttered mind.

A few passages from Hardy's prose writing imply his state of mind, of which there is corroboration in the poems. The first is in *Tess*. When she and Angel come to bid farewell to Dairyman Crick and his wife, after their marriage and after Angel's stony decision to part, Hardy says of them:

> . . . as she and Clare stood side by side at leaving, as if united body and soul, there would have been something peculiarly sorry in their aspect to one who should have seen it truly; *two limbs of one life as they outwardly were*, his arm touching hers, her skirts touching him, facing one way, as against all the dairy facing the other, speaking in their adieux as 'we', *and yet sundered like the poles*.[1]

In *Jude* there occur the acid comments on marriage, which has always been a dangerous venture for Hardy's heroines, and the validity of which he had begun to openly question through the characters of Grace and Fitzpiers in *The Woodlanders*. In *Jude* it is described by Sue as 'a hopelessly vulgar institution', and by Jude as something which 'squashes up and digests' people 'in its vast maw as an atom which has no further individuality'. Hardy could disown these passages by retorting that these were not *his* ideas, only those in keeping with imagined characters. But a trenchant statement in the *New Review*, a public and personal testament under his signature, also appeared at this time, so that we have a right to assume that the passages in the novels bear some relation to Hardy's own thoughts. His contribution to *On the Tree of Knowledge* (in the *Journal* mentioned above), closes with the following melancholy query:

> whether marriage, as we at present understand it, is such a desirable goal for all woman as it is assumed to be, or whether civilization can escape the humiliating indictment that, while it has been able to cover itself with glory in the arts, in literatures, in religions and in the sciences, it has never succeeded in creating that homely thing *a satisfactory scheme for the conjunction of the sexes*.

[1] p. 324. (Italics mine.)

Another passage in *Jude* has a personal bearing. In discussing Sue's recantation from her belief in pagan joy, and her former freedom from conventional ideas, Jude asserts to Widow Edlin that

time and circumstance, which enlarge the views of most men, narrow the views of women almost invariably.[1]

As we shall see, this is more than a stray comment on the difference in the sexes.

That Hardy identified himself with suffering seems probable when we learn that his copy of *Prometheus Bound* is marked at the close, in the tremendous, defiant, passage in which Prometheus arraigns the Gods and their malignity. Hardy has underscored *Thou seest the wrongs I endure*,[2] and added his signature. Furthermore, at this time he selected and commented on a passage from the *Œdipus Tyrannus* ... "and if there be a woe surpassing woes, it hath become the portion of Œdipus". Here Hardy was following an old habit of his, that of comparing the mood and words of similar passages in dissimilar works, in this case Jebb's translation with a line from Tennyson.[3] But *why* was he drawn to these two passages, from two different tragedians, expressing the nadir of grief *at this time*? The creation of a *Tess* or even a *Jude* is not sufficient answer.

One of the themes of *Jude the Obscure* is the destruction, the disintegration of a strong, courageous man by two women through the agency of love, physical and intellectual. Hardy had been reading von Hartmann's *Metaphysics of the Unconscious* in which the 'illusory nature of successful love after union', the pain which it brings him who experiences it—pain outweighing pleasure and presaging doom—is stressed. Man cannot help himself or escape since 'he is entangled against his will in passion'.[4] This theory so exactly corresponds with what Hardy had tried to portray again and again in his novels that when he read it he must have started, not with joy, but with a fearful foreboding that he had indeed been right in his old surmises. And when Emma Hardy's character began to harden and set along unpremeditated lines (which it would have been easier for one outside the charmed entanglement to see and foretell), is

---

[1] p. 505.   [2] Rutland, p. 39.
[3] I, p. 289.   [4] See Rutland, p. 255.

it not possible that Hardy felt this to be true about his own love and union, which had begun so auspiciously, and about *himself*— that he was but one more example of the fly ensnared by the spider through the lure of sex?

We have lost sight of Emma Lavinia in the profusion and complexity of her husband's work, in his increasing fame, in the number of social engagements which they fulfilled, and which she especially enjoyed. We have watched her at a distance, moving gay and competent through the throng of celebrities into which she has been thrust by his talent and her charm and exertions. Florence Hardy speaks of her riding up the passes of Zermatt, through the Gap of Dunloe, or onto the Malvern Beacon; of her managing a frightened mare who rears but does not throw her. Thereafter Emma becomes a keen cyclist and we hear of her accompanying her husband and his friends on rides in Dorset, or of her cycling abroad, to the confusion of French railway porters. Sometimes she is unwell and is unable to accompany Hardy on one of his excursions, or again it is he who is ill and she who nurses him competently. Always, outwardly, she is his constant and energetic companion.

We know, too, that she shares the vexatious ardours of her husband's work—the making of reference notes, the copying of manuscripts, the writing of perpetual letters, the welcoming and entertaining of visitors, the rejection of tiresome and impertinent intruders on their domestic privacy. We see that Hardy was struck now and then by a chance phrase of hers which he noted down. The massive drifts of snow, Emma says, are 'architectural': the crowd at the Lord Mayor's Show, as seen from above, resembles 'a boiling cauldron of porridge'. (Hardy's description of this crowd remained in his notebook to be made use of in *The Dynasts* twenty years later.)[1] She even suggests details for his novels which the writer accepts, for it was Emma who overheard and called her husband's attention to the labourer who boasted of the numerous 'skelingtons' of his ancient family, made use of in *Tess*: furthermore, it was she, so Hardy told a reporter, who had thought of making Tess wear the jewels on her ill-fated wedding night at Woolbridge Manor.[2]

[1] See I, p. 171, and *The Dynasts*, Act VI, Scene vi.
[2] See Blunden, p. 69.

Then, suddenly, there is some violent disagreement and Emma is excluded from discussions and counsel over her husband's work. The outward sign of an inner disharmony, the excuse for a rupture, is the subject and handling of *Jude the Obscure*. We are told by one writer that, just before its publication, Emma made a journey to London to see Dr Garnett in an attempt to persuade him to influence Hardy to suppress the book—in which she was unsuccessful;[1] and her own nephew has told us that she 'strongly objected to this book'.[2] What was it that Emma Hardy disliked and feared in *Jude the Obscure*—the handling of the marriage question, the comments on religion and the church, or the theme of hereditary eccentricity? Did she suspect that others would read into *Jude* more than they should of her, and her husband's, private life? Was it herself she wished to protect, or her husband's reputation? The letter mentioned above states that she 'strongly objected to the book', and to 'some of the characters depicted therein' because she

> was a very ardent churchwoman and a believer in the virtues of women in general.

A great deal has been made of some verses of Hardy's called "The Division", written in the 1890's, an uninspired, doleful poem in which he regrets that, although 'he' sits in the same room as 'her', they are separated by 'a hundred miles', which in no wise sum up their 'severance'. There is no conclusive proof that this poem was written to his wife, but certainly 'the thwart thing' which lies between them, and 'which nothing cleaves or clears', is strongly suggestive of the incubus which checked expressions of tenderness between Thomas and Emma during these years, but fortunately did not stifle Hardy's greater genius. The word 'division' is also used in "After a Journey".

In 1906 Hardy sat for his portrait to the painter Jacques Émile Blanche, nicknamed 'the French Sargent' on account of his popularity with Edwardian society people. In his book *Portraits of a Lifetime* Blanche tells how Hardy came to sit for him in a summer of intense heat which gave him a greenish pallor and made his head droop further and further to one side 'like a

[1] Weber, p. 167.
[2] Letter to *The Times Literary Supplement* from Gordon Gifford, January 1, 1944.

plucked bird's'.[1] Blanche is not always accurate in his factual statements but there is no reason why his reactions should be mistrusted. He felt drawn to Hardy and his work, and although his portrait is not an astonishing success (nor did Hardy like it) he seems to have had sympathetic conversations with him during the sitting, concerning agricultural conditions and customs in France and England, and other matters. He reports Hardy as saying:

> "You know the corn sprouts in November? Listen well to the secret movement of the earth under its crust of frost and snow." This was possibly an allusion to himself for he was entering on a period which, for others, was the beginning of decay . . .

and he adds that "the term 'gentle drover', which Barrès applies to his countryman from Lorraine, I should use for Hardy."[2] Blanche also makes a revealing comment on the attitude of English society people to Hardy's writing.

> They asserted that a foreigner could not possibly appreciate the lack of taste in his English. Were it written in French you would consider it 'coco'.

Blanche evidently did not agree with them, for he set himself to read several of Hardy's novels and relished them.

Two other things which he tells us are revealing. Blanche says that when he met Emma Hardy she begged him not to make her husband 'look miserable' in his portrait, adding 'A real gentleman never does'. The Blanches and the Hardys attended the Royal Garden Party at Windsor in 1907. Hardy had been unwell and when it was suggested that he should ride up the hill in one of the carriages provided, but Emma asserted that the walk would do him good. 'A real gentleman never does' is the key to one of the causes of increasing friction at Max Gate and even in public, elsewhere. Emma Hardy had unfortunately come to the conclusion that she had married beneath her: the numerous meetings with aristocratic hosts and hostesses, and now with Royalty, had gone to her head. She seemed unaware that these introductions and invitations were the result of her husband's

---

[1] One of his portraits of Hardy is now in the Manchester City Art Gallery.
[2] Jacques Émile Blanche, *Portraits of a Lifetime*, trans. by Walter Clement. J. M. Dent, 1937.

gifts, and not her own. She openly resented what she called his 'peasant' traits, his meanness, and other boorish qualities.[1] It is also said that she was jealous of the society beauties and other women who sometimes surrounded her husband, treating him with affectionate adulation.

A second cause of dissention was their religious differences. When she had first met Thomas his connection with the church, through the important avenue of ecclesiastical architecture, had impressed her. He had been attracted to her, as Synge was to his first love, because her ardent evangelicalism resembled his mother's. His intimate knowledge and love of the Bible, of church music, of village churches in the southwest, all impressed her in her turn. In their youthful days, loverlike, they could not see the sadly divergent paths along which their natures would lead them. Now the effects of that sterilization of the religious emotions, experienced by Hardy and others from an early acquaintance with Darwin's works, had become appallingly apparent. Hardy, in spite of himself, was drawn further and further away from conventional belief, whereas Emma was more and more entrenched in hers. She had, in fact, begun to suffer from a mild form of religious mania.

Her convictions that she was superior to her husband in breeding and in spirituality, and his equal in intellectual achievements, slowly increased. Hardy's humility, gentleness and courtesy, his habit of consulting her about details of his work, inflated her ideas of her own literary powers and judgment; and his lack of self-assertion seems to have goaded her into persecuting him, in some horrible animal way, by belittling him in public. She assured callers at Max Gate that she too had ability, had written works which lay upstairs, and even read out her poems to those who were polite enough to listen.

A collection of the harsh and limited sayings of Emma Hardy during these embittered years has already been made.[2] They are painful to read. Some people maliciously repeated and

[1] See Desmond MacCarthy's *Memoirs*, MacGibbon & Kee, 1953; Carl J. Weber, *Hardy and the Lady from Madison Square*. Colby College Press. Waterville, Maine, 1952, and others.
[2] See Weber, pp. 161 *et seq.*

recorded them; others, anxious for Hardy's welfare, pitied a man whom they saw powerless to defend himself. His tendency to suffer (which he had transferred to the feminine characters in his novels, and to Jude), his romantic and chivalrous nature which made him idealize women, and his disinclination to cause strife, all prevented him from standing out against a dominant partner.

Emma Hardy was thrown back on her own resources. While her husband retreated into creative work she surrounded herself, like many childless, dissatisfied women, with numerous cats, of whom Hardy charmingly remarked to an American visitor:

> . . . Some are cats who come regularly to have tea, and some are still other cats, not invited by us, who seem to find out about this time of day that tea will be going.[1]

Unfortunately she also tried to compete with her husband in literary fields. This implies, either a desperate effort to raise her own self-esteem, or a lamentable lack of judgment, for she had no poetic gifts whatsoever. One or two London journals accepted verses on the strength of her husband's reputation, with embarrassed comments, and the *Dorset Country Chronicle* followed suit. In 1911 and 1912 she persuaded a Dorset publishing house to print privately her collected verse and some religious lucubrations under the strange, possibly symbolic, titles of *Alleys*, and *Spaces*.[2] The subjects of the poems are the planting of a rose-bush, walnut trees, the end of a wet summer, flowers, birdsong, churchyards, youth, age, and advancing time. A few show signs of marked eccentricity. The innocuousness of "Ripe Summer"—

> *The meadows lie beneath*
> *The summer sun's hot rays,*
> *O happy, happy summer,*
> *O golden, golden days . . .*

merges into seeming derangement in others, such as:

---

[1] Blunden, p. 109.
[2] The following excerpts are made from these volumes lent to me by the courtesy of Mr H. G. Longman.

TEN MOONS

In misery swirled
  Is this one-moon whirled,
But there's no sorrow or darkness there
  In that mighty planet where
There is no night.
  Ten moons ever revolving
All matter its long years resolving
  To sweetness and light.

and:

ELECTRIC CURRENTS

By electric currents working
  Sweetest influences abound
And fearful powers our lives surround
For not known to us they're lurking
By electric currents working.

Spaces is entirely concerned with religious themes and is divided into four parts called "High Delights of Heaven", "Acceptors or Non-Acceptors", New Element of Fire", and "Retrospect", the last being in the form of a dialogue between Satan, God, and the Archangel Michael. To read them gives one the feeling experienced on studying the more curious and extravagant incongruities of the surrealists: things prophetic and hieratical are indiscriminately mingled with objects of modern scientific invention. Here is her description of the Last Trump:

The ominous rumbling of thunder sounds unaccompanied by lightning or rain will precede the gradual rising of a sound, terrible, penetrating, continuous, and arresting attention, producing fear, paralyzing effort, after awhile stopping all energy whatever and causing a general distress of nations, which calling to each other to know if this thunder is everywhere to be heard receive terrifying confirmation. And then will occur the general darkening of the sun, moon, and stars by blackest clouds, as at the Crucifixion, and the power of that awful trumpet accelerated till the final blast, when suddenly a spot of light will appear in the East at 4 a.m. according to western time—and dark night of eastern time or about that hour, varying at distances, the hot sunshine there gone completely, leaving, however, the weariness and dreariness of afternoon heat of hot latitudes. And while bodies will be seen rising and floating in the phosphorescent great oceans, in seas, lakes, rivers, the graveyards will be crowded with strange moving figures seen dimly in the darkness and that much watched spot of Eastern light will brighten and be enlarged . . .

From these effusions one gathers the impression that Emma Hardy found consolation of an ecstatic kind in religious beliefs.

But it will readily be seen that a mind which could create and live in harmony with these fantastic exaltations must be at loggerheads with another type of mind—that of her husband—which feels constrained to translate the emotional overtones of Biblical language into plainer, more scientific ones before it can trust them. Crashaw and John Stuart Mill, St Theresa and Charles Darwin would make poor bedfellows and would jostle each other uncomfortably. That in 1899—on his fifty-ninth birthday—Emma Hardy still had hopes of leading her husband back to a more conventional faith is evidenced by her gift to him of the Holy Bible inscribed "T. Hardy from E. L. H., June 2, 1899, Wynstay Gardens, Kensington". It is in this copy of the Bible (there are three amongst the Hardy books in the County Museum) that Hardy has written:

Jer. vi. *v.* 4. *Salisbury Cathedral*, 1897. For the day goeth away, the shadows of the evening are stretched out. . . . .

and made notes (at the back) of numbers of verses from six books of the Old Testament and one of the New. He and Emma had been to the Cathedral together in that year, and Hardy had been moved late at night by the spectacle of the moonlight striking through both the north and south clerestory windows onto the turf of the Close where he stood. He watched it

creep round upon the statuary of the façade—stroking tentatively and then more and more firmly the prophets, the martyrs, the bishops, the kings, and the queens . . .[1]

But another note shows that Hardy was probably going through a mental crisis at this time, for he has also marked:

I Kings: xviii. *v.* 21. How long halt ye between two opinions?

[1] II, p. 71. See also "A Cathedral Façade at Midnight" in *Human Shows*.

and:

Lamentations i. *v.* 12: Is it nothing to you, all ye that pass by?—

passages which are doubly marked with strips of paper.

During these distressing years, although the Hardys continued to live side by side, to travel abroad together, to visit in manor houses, to examine cathedrals, castles and churches in each other's company, and to appear in public as one, bitter things were said, wounds were given, and unhealed scars remained. The poems[1] tell of 'soul-sick blight', 'our unforeboded troublous case', 'a thing . . . that loomed with an immortal mien':

> *Some heart-bane moved our souls to sever*
>
> .   .   .   .
>
> *And misconceits raised horrid shows,*
> *And agonies came thereof . . .*[2]

of a wound that pierced the poet through; of a 'cowled apparition' which comes between the loved ones in sinister guise, of

> *. . . divisions dire and wry*
> *And long drawn days of blight.*[3]

At some time, we do not know exactly when (possibly as long ago as 1896 when two of the *In Tenebris* poems were written), Emma's eccentricities and the bitterness in her heart took a more serious form. Here we have a possible answer to that final question—why was Hardy interested in the problems of heredity while writing *Jude the Obscure*. In the novel, Jude and Sue are cousins: their family suffers from a pathological fear of marriage and marriage-ties which 'snuffs out spontaneity and cordiality', and finally love, until they break the ties and flee. (This theme had already appeared in *Far from the Madding Crowd* and in the inimitable malthouse scene we have a recital of an original solution to these miseries. The poem "The Christening" is concerned with the same problem). But in *Jude* it is suggested that a tainted family may turn 'a tragic sadness into a tragic horror'. Hardy perceived, or thought that

---

[1] "Lost Love", "The Place on the Map", "Self-Unconscious", "The Wound", "At the Piano". Examples could be multiplied.
[2] "The Spell of the Rose" in *Satires of Circumstance*.   [3] *Ibid.*

he perceived, that his wife sometimes suffered from delusions. We have confirmation of this belief in three separate places. First, in a letter written by Hardy three weeks after her death in 1912, wherein he says:

> In spite of the differences between us, which it would be affectation to deny, and certain painful delusions she suffered from at times, my life is intensely sad to me now without her.[1]

In 1920 Vere Collins discussed with Hardy at Max Gate certain passages in his poems which the former found obscure. He had been perplexed by several in which

> there intrudes every now and then . . . a disquieting shadow, which seems to conceal some tragic mystery. The allusions are obscure . . . The obscurity is often connected with some sinister but vague and indefinite spirit, or figure, in the scene.[2]

Mr Collins was disturbed by the fact that, not only is there expressed the idea of a calamity which could not have been foreseen, but that "the two persons concerned are represented as helpless and guiltless". In his beautifully balanced and deeply sympathetic essay he quotes from Hardy's poem "The Man with a Past"

> *Innocent was she,*
> *Innocent was I,*
> *Too simple we!*
> *Before us we did not see,*
> *Nearing, aught wry—*
> *Aught wry!*
>
> *I can tell it now,*
> *It was long ago;*
> *And such things cow;*
> *But that is why and how*
> *Two lives were so—*
> *Were so.*[3]

---

[1] Letter to Mrs Henniker, Dec. 17, 1912. *Thomas Hardy*, W. R. Rutland, Blackie and Son, 1938, p. 108.

[2] *The Love Poetry of Thomas Hardy*. Essays and Studies, English Assoc., Vol. XXVIII, 1942. Oxford University Press, 1943, p. 81.

[3] In *Moments of Vision*.

A poem which especially troubled Mr Collins was "The Interloper":

> *Nay: it's not the pale Form your imagings raise*
> *That waits on us all at a destined Time . . .*
>
> . . . .
>
> *It is that under which best lives corrode;*
> *Would, would it could not be there!* [1]

He asked Hardy whether he could not append, as he had so often done, some word, or line, beneath the title to elucidate the poem. Hardy re-read the poem and suggested the word "Madness"; then, "Insanity, that is a better word than Madness. I wonder how I could make it clear."[2] He had been careful to point out previously that a Biblical quotation would be useless since 'madness' was not used in the same sense then as that in which we use it now.

> When Hardy uttered that word . . . there burst on me a revelation. This was the clue. *The Blow, The Blot, The Wound*; the spectre haunting that beautiful girl while she sang and played; the shadow darkening and chilling that passionate union; the lovers struck by an unexpected, unprovoked, undeserved foe; now at last I grasped what . . . had put an end to happiness in Hardy's marriage and life—that had tended to concentrate his attention on the tragedies and ironies in love—that had accentuated the 'grim message' from his reading of life.[3]

(This was in 1920). In the 1923 edition of his *Collected Poems* Hardy substituted the line "And I saw the figure and visage of madness seeking for a home" beneath the poem's title, where it still stands.

Meeting Mr Collins alone on the next day Florence Hardy corroborated what we now know—from his letter above— Hardy thought. She said of Emma Hardy:

> She was subject at times to delusions. She would then make the wildest accusations against anyone, including her husband . . . At such times life with her was almost unbearable.

How gently and with what compassionate care would Hardy have treated his wife had he fully realized her predicament.

---

[1] In *Moments of Vision.*
[2] Unpublished note to the above.   [3] *Ibid.*

Some poems imply that this was not always the case. But the tragedy of close relationship is that it often obscures rather than illumes: life is not only 'corroded' but eroded, chiselled and eaten away by the distempered minds of those near to us, whose illnesses we are powerless to hinder, or heal. In a grave, perpending poem, called "His Heart—A Woman's Dream", Hardy describes a woman bending over her dead husband's body, examining his heart to discover:

> *What hereto had been known to him alone,*
> *Despite our long sit-out of years foreflown,*
> *"And if," I said, "I do this for his memory's sake,*
> *It would not wound him, even if he could wake."*
>
> .   .   .   .   .   .
>
> *It was inscribed like a terrestrial sphere*
> *With quaint vermiculations close and clear—*
> *His graving. Had I known, would I have risked the stroke*
> *Its reading brought, and my own heart nigh broke!*
>
> *Yes, there at last, eyes opened, did I see*
> *His whole sincere symmetric history;*
> *There were his truth, his simple singlemindedness,*
> *Strained, maybe, by time's storms, but there no less.*[1]

She counts the daily deeds performed, often blindly, but always in good faith: the times when he has reproached himself for not cherishing her: the record of blissful hours spent together, the painful ones when they were parted: the chronicle of 'dulled hours' which separated them until they were rejoined: the times when he has verbally defended her. Here Hardy touchingly pleads his own cause, which he could not put into words for his defence in daily life. If we invert the poem, and imagine a man examining the graven lines and 'quaint vermiculations' of his wife's heart when she is dead, we get a reflection of what the poet felt when his wife died.

But in the years before the end there were still the gaieties which Emma loved. In 1905 she rose to the occasion and entertained two hundred journalists who descended like locusts

[1] In *Moments of Vision.*

on Max Gate: in July 1912 she gave what turned out to be her last garden-party. For some time past she had been suffering from giddiness and fainting fits, and complaining of digestive disorders. [According to a friend[1] a major disagreement occurred between them sometime during the summer, or autumn, of this year. Hardy had an outside staircase built so that he might ascend to his study without going through the house. There he might work and have his meals alone. Here, one day in November, Emma sought him out: in exasperation the writer turned on her to vent his long repressed irritation and misery.] The uneasy truce of years was broken. A dramatized version of *The Trumpet Major* was being performed in Dorchester and Hardy was forced to attend the final rehearsal. He came in late and went directly to his own room. The next morning, when Hardy went to her, Emma was unconscious, and she died shortly after. Hardy never ceased to reproach himself for that fatal outbreak.

Now she was gone he poured out poems to her memory with all the pent-up force of a retentive, remorseful nature—poems in which he castigated himself for not speaking of the days of their first love, for not striving to renew the joy of that time, for not being more affectionate, for not taking her to revisit St Juliot and that enchanted coast, or on lesser journeys, for not singing the old songs with her or listening while she played. He passionately regrets that it is not *he* who is dead, or that they are not lying together

> . . . *folded away there*
> *Exposed to one weather.*[2]

The note of a division between them before the end is plain to read. In "The Voice" she calls persistently to him, assuring him that now she is not as she was in her embittered days

> *But as at first, when our day was fair.*

In "After a Journey" he puts into Emma's ghostly mind the questions:

> *Summer gave us sweets, but autumn wrought* division?
> *Things were not lastly as firstly well*
> *With us twain, you tell?*

[1] Sir Newman Flower, *Just as it Happened*, pp. 96 *et seq*. Cassells, 1950.
[2] "Rain on a Grave."

The sequence of poems written to her memory immediately after her death[1] is one of the most poignant in our literature, the more so since it unashamedly reveals the love and grief of a reticent nature, taken unawares by the phantom reaper who cuts us down 'like sedge beneath the scythe'. The anguish of Hardy's undoing in the first poem—"The Going"—is almost unbearable: there is nothing false in the emotion which makes him cry out:

> *I seem but a dead man held on end*
> *To sink down soon . . .*

The sub-title to the poems is *Veteris vestigia flammae* and although the flame had been quenched for a long time, and Hardy was seventy-four, it renewed itself miraculously with a young man's intense ardour, burning with amazing vitality. For the poems in this sequence (and many others throughout succeeding volumes) written about Emma Hardy, about places in the west they had loved and known, or their experiences together, are not merely remorseful or sorrowful. In an astonishing way they recapture the vision of his loved one, as first seen, and the emotions attendant on that vision. The rocky coast, the deep-cleft combes with the sound of the sea breaking over them 'like distant cannonades', the 'flounce flinging mist', the water 'prinked' with purple, the hidden, unexpected house embowered in flowers and candlelight, all come back to him as if it were only yesterday that he 'burst on her my heart could not but follow'. One vision never forsook him, that of a young woman on horseback 'with bright hair flapping free'. Now that she lies amongst the 'mute and manifold souls of old' he finds release and consolation in dwelling on the memory of

The woman whom I loved so, and who loyally loved me.[2]

Amongst Emma's papers, after her death Hardy found two relics of her ill and embittered days called *The Pleasures of Heaven and Pains of Hell*, and *What I thought of my Husband*, both of which Hardy rightly destroyed.[3] But he also found those fresh and charming *Recollections*, written the year before she died, in

---

[1] "Poems of 1912-13" in *Satires of Circumstance*.
[2] "Beeny Cliff."   [3] Sir Newman Flower, p. 96.

which Emma's mind had likewise gone back to those Cornish days; in her own simple manner she had recaptured their magic, a discovery which must have brought him comfort.

Eight years after Hardy's birth, Thackeray, in looking back on his own domestic tragedy, wrote to a friend:

> I would do it all over again; for behold love is the crown and completion of all earthly goods.[1]

Had anyone asked Hardy whether he, like Thackeray, would take with the ecstasy all the anguish, the 'soul-blight' and 'dire division', I believe he would have nodded assent. Love for him was the quintessence, the elixir of life: he tells us in another poem that he counts it his greatest blessing that he gained and kept in life the love of two 'bright-souled women'.[2]

Hardy's mother, from whom he had inherited his love of books and learning, the ancient ballads and memories, who had been the driving force behind his childhood life, had died in 1904. Her gaiety of spirit had remained almost to the end. When nearly eighty she had walked in slippery winter weather from the Bockhampton home to Max Gate, and upon her son remonstrating with her had coolly replied that she had done so "To enjoy the beauties of nature, of course, and why shouldn't I?"[3]

Hardy laid his wife beside her under the yew-trees in Stinsford churchyard. Both Swinburne and Meredith had also died, in 1909, and the poet commemorated them in verses; those to Swinburne contain the stanza recalling how Hardy, as a young man, 'with quick glad surprise' had read

The passionate pages of his earlier years.[4]———

They were indeed 'thinning out ahead'.

In 1913, and again in 1916, he revisited Plymouth, St Juliot and other places in the west connected with Emma's memory, regretting that he had not taken her there once more with him when she was alive, and he also went to Sturminster Newton, the setting of their 'Idyll'. He saw that a tablet was placed to

[1] *Private Letters and Papers of W. M. Thackeray.*
[2] "A Poet."
[3] Letter from Hardy to Sir Sydney Cockerell, p. 286.
[4] "A Singer Asleep" in *Satires of Circumstance.*

her in the walls of St Juliot church where, in their betrothal days, she had played the organ and he had read the lessons, her brother-in-law taking the services. In 1920, eight years after her death, when his publishers sent him copies of his new-published works the only pages which he troubled to cut were those of *A Pair of Blue Eyes* and the *Poems of* 1912-13, enshrining her memory.[1] He was then eighty years old. In 1924, four years before his own death, Hardy wrote in his notebook: "E. first met fifty-four years ago".[2] The memory of the unhappy years had been absorbed into the golden.

For Hardy, the artist, there had been a clear and conscious division between his public appearance as a writer of prose and of verse; in his private life·there had been that tormenting, bewildering division between him and her whom he had loved. But for a third person there was also an acknowledged cleavage between past and present. Ten years after Emma's death Hardy's second wife wrote to a friend:

> Looking back, I seem to see a clear *division* in my life, for on that day I seemed suddenly to leap from youth into dreary middle-age . . . I suppose because I had had no responsibility before.[3]

But, fortunately for us, neither personal sorrow nor international calamities could stem the tide of Hardy's poetic genius. If anything, they intensified it, forcing him to draw on the depths of his inmost vision. We have seen how various aspects of *The Dynasts* attracted him from youth upwards. In 1897, at the age of fifty-seven (fourteen years before the death of his wife), he began close work on it, which continued for ten years. A second visit to the battlefield of Waterloo where, solitary and preoccupied, he noted "the *nearness* of the French and English lines to each other", helped him to envisage the carnage which had taken place little more than eighty years before.[4]

In studying the life and work of a creative artist one seldom

---

[1] Carl Weber, *Centenary of E. L. Gifford.*
[2] II, p. 237. It is said that he died with words concerning her on his lips.
[3] Letter to S. C. Cockerell, November 26, 1922, p. 308. (Italics mine.)
[4] Byron visited Waterloo in 1816, bringing away souvenirs of the battlefield. He was a great admirer of Napoleon.

finds a single work which represents a life-long absorption, and it is rarely that one can trace, almost without interruption, the stimuli which impelled him to create. Yet both of these things are true of *The Dynasts*, which stands like a huge oak in the middlefield of Hardy's life and achievements. With its tap-root striking strong and deep into ancestral loam and its laterals ranging wide, in its twisted and gnarled language, and the toughness of its fibre, the great poem resembles this essentially English tree. A philosophic history and an epic drama of the Napoleonic Wars the poem emphasizes England's greatness throughout. Now and then Hardy takes a poet's licence to deviate from historical particulars to drive home his major theme—that England alone amongst the European powers defied Napoleon, never once deviating from her uncompromising policy—and he draws Bonaparte as a heartless tyrant whose overmastering obsession was to vanquish Albion, bearing in mind the medal which Napoleon had prepared to be struck in London when he should have made her a mere outpost capital of his far-flung realm.

Despite its original reception in England and America as 'a fearful sort of wildfowl',[1] and 'so ridiculous that the second Part would never be heard of',[2] *The Dynasts* now stands in public estimation, at least in this country, as Hardy's greatest and most enduring work. But at first a great many people felt as Wilfrid Scawen Blunt, the poet-traveller, did:

> On your recommendation I sent for *The Dynasts* and read it conscientiously through, without finding anything at all in it which has any business to be called poetry, except a little piece on the battle of Trafalgar imitated from Kipling. The subject is of course interesting as a resumé of a great epoch. But it is nothing more than that . . . all ditchwater from start to finish.[3]

Bewilderment and ridicule have been succeeded by acceptance and praise: our minds have become accustomed to the intention and scale of the whole which at first confused, and then ended by enlarging, the vision of those who studied and listened. It

---

[1] *Times Literary Supplement*, see Rutland, p. 280.
[2] *New York Tribune*, see II, p. 114.
[3] Sir Sydney Cockerell, pp. 183-4.

has been ranked unashamedly with the work of Milton and Shakespeare.

> The very size of his achievement in this one work gave an added prestige to English letters, whose present tends always to be dwarfed by their gigantic past; it is no little thing that the literature which bore *Hamlet* and *Paradise Lost* should still have so much life that it can bear *The Dynasts* . . .[1]

When more than one hundred young poets paid tribute to Hardy on his eighty-first birthday they thanked him profoundly for 'all that [he] had written . . . but most of all, perhaps, for *The Dynasts*.'[2] Recently it has shown itself, rather unexpectedly, to be pre-eminently fit for broadcasting, a medium which Hardy only knew in its infancy. The kaleidoscopic scenes might also be filmed by a producer of exceptional imagination. But *The Dynasts* must always remain one of the great dramas for the exercise and delight of the mind, which can range over vaster fields and more transcendant heights than those on wireless, or screen.

Its inception goes back to the days of childhood, to the tales of his father's mother and father. The first remembered till the day she died the pattern of a muslin frock she was ironing when she heard that the Queen of France had been beheaded; hot and thundery summer weather always recalled to her that season which had been bathed in blood.[3] Later, Hardy was to hear of a dumb woman who broke her long silence with a prophecy as terrible as that of an ancient sibyl:

> A cold winter, a forward spring,
> A bloody summer, a dead King.

She then dropped dead. The French Revolution followed immediately after.[4]

The second—his father's father—had been a volunteer in a local regiment and had subscribed to the *History of the Napoleonic Wars* which survived until Hardy's boyhood in a Bockhampton cupboard.

The slow growth of Hardy's interest in things Napoleonic

[1] Rutland, pp. 283.   [2] II, p. 222.
[3] I, p. 282.   [4] *Ibid.*, p. 165.

continued with the study of familiar relics of the wars between England and France, which occurred about thirty-years after the French Revolution and only forty before Hardy was born—

> ... an outhouse door riddled with bullet-holes ... a heap of bricks and clods on a beacon-hill, which had formed the chimney and walls of the hut occupied by the beacon-keeper, worm-eaten shafts and iron heads of pikes for the use of those who had no better weapons, ridges on the down thrown up during the encampment, fragments of volunteer uniform ... [and a] hieroglyphic portrait of Napoleon, [which] existed as a print in an old woman's cottage ...[1]

Another childhood influence is evident in *The Dynasts*, that of

> the old Christmas mummers, the curiously hypnotizing impressiveness of whose automatic style—that of persons who spoke by no will of their own—may be remembered by all who ever experienced it.[2]

The manor of Kingston Maurward had long been and was still, in Hardy's childhood, in the hands of a collateral branch of the family of the great William Pitt. In the churchyard of neighbouring Bincombe there are the graves and headstones of two German legionaries who grew homesick for their fatherland, whom Hardy immortalized in "The Melancholy Hussar". Weymouth contains a few battered relics and reminders of George III, whose likeness in chalky whiteness prances over the shorn downs; Lulworth and other places have their legends of a supposed invasion by Bonaparte himself.

The first reflection of Hardy's preoccupation with the Napoleonic Wars occurs in *An Indiscretion* (1868); next in some early poems (1878), possibly those which Hardy first thought of shaping into a larger whole to consist of many ballads strung together necklace-wise.[3] *The Trumpet Major* follows in 1880, but before its appearance, Hardy had seen Palmerston in the flesh and watched his state funeral, talked with the Chelsea

---

[1] Preface to *The Trumpet Major*, 1895.
[2] Preface to *The Dynasts*, 1903.
[3] The ballads are "San Sebastian", "Leipzig", "The Peasant's Confession" and "Valenciennes" in *Wessex Poems*. Only one is dated 1878. See Rutland, pp. 125 and 274.

Hospital pensioners, visited the battlefield of Waterloo and searched for the vanished site of the Duchess of Richmond's Ballroom in Brussels, attended the funeral of Louis Napoleon, been struck with the similarity between the profile of 'Plon-Plon' and Napoleon, and made two notes on a projected Napoleonic "Iliad of Europe from 1789-1815". Thereafter, during his severe illness and in succeeding years, the conception of the future *Dynasts* developed, remaining unnamed, or bearing other names—"A Grand Drama", "A Great Modern Drama", "A Drama of Kings", "A Homeric Ballad in which Napoleon is a sort of Achilles", an "Historical Drama in which the action is mostly automatic".[1] It is interesting to read that as early as 1877 Hardy has a clear determination *not* to fashion it like Shakespeare's dramas.[2] And so the notes continue as the philosophic framework grows at a slower, more mature pace than the youthful zest for military matters, and the details of the whole slip across the writer's mind to lodge in some dark cranny until their perfect formation and ultimate birth. Always the conception of the whole is on the grand scale.

Hand-in-hand with those notes which bear a definite relation to the epic poem, made between the years 1880-1902, must be taken those which at first do not seem concerned with it, the nebulous ones on automatism, somnambulism, volition, the power of will, and others which recur intermittently and indicate Hardy's preoccupation with these themes, whether studied from the personal, or the broader philosophic, angle. It is not until we read the material which Hardy gave (late in life) to his second wife[3] that we fully comprehend his dual conception of a titanic figure driving forward compulsively—a rôle which Napoleon is to play out for the diversion of the Spirit Ironic—together with Hardy's conception of him as a figure worthy of compassion, which culminates in the pleading of the Spirit of the Pities.

In *The Dynasts* we feel the full force of Hardy's matured character and thought: by comparison his stories, poems and novels, even the finest of them, seem puny and somehow lacking in masculine virility. To a large extent this is because, for the

---

[1] I, pp. 140, 150, 188.
[2] For the difference between Shakespeare's and Hardy's treatment see Rutland, pp. 346-51.   [3] II, p. 226-7.

first time, the writer allows himself to conceive, and to express, robust thoughts and matter which hitherto he has been forced to conceal, or suppress, to placate an over-pudentious public. It had been his plaint more times than one that if what he wrote had been set in verse no one would carp or criticize. Now he took the full liberties which blank verse proffered. Now, as in some invigorating sea-scape or some vast panoramic painting of a battlefield with all its encumbrances of gear and animal and human life, we find the realistic detail of a van de Velde, the virility and lustfulness of a fleshly Rubens canvas, or the tossed and whirled atmospheric confusion of a late Turner. During the Battle of Trafalgar a woman dives naked into the sea:

> . . . Our men in charge,
> Seeing her great breasts bulging on the brine,
> Sang out, "A mermaid, 'tis, by God!"—then rowed
> and hauled her in.[1]

Women bear babies behind the lines of Waterloo, others faint while tending the wounded, while children watch men dying. Here at last the common soldier can speak out his mind, regretting that he has not left foreign doxies and wine alone, and "stuck to the true doxology":[2] or sardonically reflecting on the veracity of the wives of two officers come to seek their husbands behind the lines.

> "'Wives!' Oh, not today! I have heard such titles of courtesy afore; but they never shake me. 'W' begins other female words than 'wives'."[3]

Furthermore, because it is history and not fictitious matter, Godoy may openly trifle with his favourites in Spain, Nelson acknowledge his Emma and Horatia, and Napoleon cast off Josephine.

This frankness gives a solidity, a realism, to *The Dynasts* which Hardy was forced to sacrifice in prose, and which ill-consorted with the technical requirements of his lyrical verse. It bears that refreshing quality which enlivens the broad humour of Chaucer and Skakespeare. Hardy expands his lungs and breathes deeply at last. He employs all his senses to stir us to

---

[1] Part I, p. 95.   [2] Part II, p. 211.   [3] Part III, p. 332.

imagine this colossal scene, which must embrace parliamentary debates and military strategy; the carnage of the battlefield and ships-of-the-line; ball-rooms, continental cafés, palaces and clubs; cornfields, chalk downs and mountain-passes, great cities, villages and isolated farms in half-a-dozen different countries, without losing touch with humanity. Hardy achieves this by skilfully lifting us above the scene until, like God himself, we see the whole of Europe spread out beneath us at a glance, the grey-green seas embracing her. He then invokes our senses. We smell the fumes of nitre and the stench of warm entrails and un-dressed wounds; hear the agonized screaming of wounded horses and of men beng trampled on: the cry of a heart-broken woman who repeats the terrible entreaty of Tess, and of Jude, with:

> *I give up all—ay, kill me if you will,*
> *I won't cry out!* [1]

We taste the desperate meal of grilled horse-flesh, salted down with gun-powder, of the survivors from Moscow, or the unholy grog in which Nelson's body has been pickled on its long journey home. We feel the texture of clothing sodden with flood-water, rain or blood, and of bodies not yet cold when the dark plun-derers stoop over the battlefields at nightfall to rifle the uncaring dead.

In contrast to this realistic, this factual treatment of the immediate and earthly scene, there is the shadowy and remote. Hardy retains his detached, rarified vision through the various voices of the Spirits Ironic, Satiric and Pitying, and the various Choruses, which he adapted to his needs from the Greek tragedians, Shelley's *Prometheus Unbound*, the *Numantia* of Cer-vantes[2] and (possibly) Doughty's dramas on the invasion of England—voices which range over the philosophical thought of his day. Moreover the Spirits are the thinking characters of *The Dynasts*, who comment and reflect on the passage of events, who interpret the hidden elusive meaning behind multifarious action. In addition they give voice to various aspects of Hardy's

---

[1] Part II, p. 262.

[2] Hardy had been reading Cervantes in December 1887 and again in 1890.

own nature. Thus, when the Spirit of the Years describes Napoleon's rites in Milan cathedral as pertaining to 'a local cult, called Christianity', which endures for a brief, parenthetical period of time, and the Spirit of the Pities replies:

> *I did not recognize it here, forsooth;*
> *Though in its early, lovingkindly days*
> *Of gracious purpose it was much to me . . .*[1]

we recognize the poet's early attachment to the faith of his fathers', a reflection of his scientific and philosophical studies, and his final relegation of that faith to a position of subsidiary importance in the aeons of time which have whirled away to the Pleiades. The Spirit of the Years may be said to embody (in so far as a Spirit may) Hardy's abiding sense of history: the Spirits Sinister and Ironic that deeply ironic sense of his which had always rejoiced in, and sorrowed over, the ill-timed or perverse in life: and the Spirit of the Pities his intense compassion, which embraced, not only, the 'feverish fleshings of humanity', but the flora and fauna of the battlefield, so tenderly that we grieve with the poet for the standing corn which will never be cut, its sap mingling with human gore at nightfall; we pity the swallows, larks and butterflies so soon to be silenced by satanic fumes, and tremble for the hare crouched in her form, the snail and humble earthworm. This famous Chorus struck Hardy in after years as 'the most original page' in *The Dynasts* and he humorously remarked in a letter to a friend that he believed that

> in the many treatments of Waterloo in literature, those particular personages who were present have never been alluded to before.[2]

The Spirits, in fact, are the means whereby Hardy achieves what had been one of his most steadfast ambitions—to penetrate behind the surface of life and seeming reality to the 'substance of things not seen'. It is this metaphysical aim and quality of *The Dynasts* which makes it tower above a purely representational work lacking in philosophy.

The Dynasts is unique in the literature of Western Europe, for there is no other comparable epic of the Napoleonic Wars.[3] It is

---

[1] Part I, pp. 32-3.   [2] II, p. 275.   [3] See Rutland, p. 271.

also something entirely fresh in Hardy's field of work, the poetic flowering of a lifelong preoccupation with a subject, an inspired collection of literary material kneaded together with oral records of the experienced. In other words it stands as a great work of imaginative art, and is not a mere prose chronicle, or history of the wars. For the first time in his life Hardy drew on a vast amount of written material of an historical nature. The work done on *The Trumpet Major* had been a prelude for this study, but in comparison with the symphonic grandeur of *The Dynasts* the novel must be regarded as a mere overture. The hundred odd books which Hardy collected and used as a basis for his work stand in their cases still, with a few exceptions.[1] He also worked in the British Museum, and in a private library specializing in Napoleonic material, formed by a Dorset man.[2] Compounded into this written material are oral traditions, family and local legends, and eye-witness descriptions of the battles from the Chelsea Hospital veterans with whom Hardy had talked so often and so lovingly. This is further alloyed with the study and reading—classical, religious, philosophical and scientific—of half a century, tinctured with that caste of thought which is peculiarly Hardy's own.

Thus we find echoes from (to name only a few) Sophocles, Milton, Shakespeare, Wordsworth, Shelley, Byron, Swinburne, Stuart Mill and Schopenhauer; legitimate borrowings from French and English historians, journalists and biographers, even from state archives and recorded public speeches, handled with the most scholarly and meticulous attention to detail in the study of his sources. Then there is the introduction of grotesque, dramatic detail, such as the hauling up of the French 'mermaid', and the broaching of the cask in which Nelson's body was preserved on its long journey home, details which do not appear in Hardy's sources. These are either imaginative inventions of Hardy's own fertile mind, or recorded fragments of Dorset tradition. Occasionally we find that juxtaposition of unexpected things and places, together with their associations and values for Hardy, which has been evident in his prose: to take a single example, the site of the vanished ballroom is compared first

---

[1] Some were sold after his death, at his direction.
[2] See Rutland, p. 295.

with something from the world of mediaeval romance ('towered Camelot'), then with something classical ('The Palace of Priam'), and finally with something from Christian religion ('the hill of Calvary').

An Aeschylean conception of the world as an illusion (as Hardy interpreted a line of this tragedian's), runs through and binds the whole, while a reflection of those early tormenting scientific studies of his occurs in the After Scene. His later reading of philosophy and psychology is woven into his conception of the Immanent Will; and when Hardy sets aside the brightly-coloured uniforms of the troopers, cuirassiers, lancers and chasseurs which he had always loved as

> *A mere lingering on, till late in Christendom*
> *Of the barbaric trick to terrorize*
> *The foe by aspect*. . . . . [1]

we suspect him of having read anthropology as well. (In 1905 'Golden-Bough Frazer', as Hardy called him in a letter to Clement Shorter, tried unsuccessfully to visit Hardy in London while he was still engaged on the epic poem.)

The Dynasts can not be regarded as a poetic curiosity springing up spasmodically in the life of a prose writer: it is part and parcel of his thought over a long period of time. One appreciates this more fully as one becomes aware of those familiar details which attracted and drew Hardy's visual eye and imagination in his earlier work. There is, for instance, his predilection for sunsets, whose flaming clouds have architectural mouldings; for profiles, for patterned bough-shadows. His love of painting is abundantly clear, and his love of music appears in the similes referring to organs and organ music, and in the picturesque names of the old tunes played at assemblies, balls and pleasure-gardens. Occasionally Hardy cannot resist putting in a line of the music as well, so anxious is he that the right air shall be resuscitated. The regimental tunes of fifers and drummers are lovingly recorded, and, with the economy necessary in a work of this magnitude, a single adjective sums up for us his old belief in the emotional effects of music-and-dancing combined—the air at the Duchess of Richmond's ball, played on the eve of the battle,

[1] Part III, p. 496.

K *

is called 'ecstasizing', an adjective he substituted for 'electric' in the rough draft. The planets and stars accompany the men on their forced, tragic marches, frozen to death beneath Sirius, and the stars of belted Orion. There is also a significant reminder of Tess. Her most deeply touching, most tragic, question is her final one to Angel, when she asks him if he thinks that they will meet beyond the grave. In *The Dynasts*, when Nelson lies dying in the cockpit of the *Victory*, he thinks of Emma Hamilton and asks his Flag-Captain:

> *Does love die with our frame's decease, I wonder,*
> *Or does it live on ever?*[1]

Neither Angel nor Captain Hardy vouchsafe an answer. The negation of silence in the face of death to the two passionately eager questioners is more terrible than empty reassurance. Hardy's integrity would not let him proffer what, for him, would be false consolation.

In a work of this gigantic stature, which reminds one of Michelangelo's heroic painting of the Sistine Chapel in its single-handed conception and execution, there is small place for the poetic similes which came so readily to Hardy's mind, and which he used so frequently in the novels. Action, and comment on the action, predominate of necessity throughout, and description must be curtailed. Yet even in *The Dynasts* a few similes and metaphors reveal his ability to pierce to the heart of the matter by means of this device. Napoleon's staff-meeting before the battle of Leipzig is likened by the Spirit of Irony to the Last Supper, which swiftly brings home to us Bonaparte's intention to rival Christ in significance, emphasized again in his speech at the close. When Hardy likens the seas encircling Spain to 'a disturbed bed on which the figure lies' we are reminded of his youthful description in *A Pair of Blue Eyes* in which the

> sea bears a fringe of white . . . moving and heaving like a counter-pane upon a restless sleeper.

The comparison of Napoleon's increasing predicament to 'a narrowing room' recalls Grace's 'sense of contracting time' in

[1] Part I, p. 97.

The Woodlanders, likened to 'a shortening chamber'. The comparison of the cries from a distant battlefield to the rising and falling noises of 'a vast rookery far away' gives that rural and domestic touch characteristic of Hardy's work which juxtaposes the strange and the homely, and startles us with the rightness of his poetic touch. Flashes of light on metal attract him:[1] a little further on the 'coils of starch-blue smoke' again remind us of *The Woodlanders*, and who but Hardy would have thought of *starch-blue* for a colour? The comparison of rows of waiting cannon to 'black bulls at gaze', is as masterly as that of the distracted aides-de-camps to 'house-flies dancing their quadrilles' is deft. The laughter of the doomed men under fire is 'hollow, as from people in hell'; and departing souls, in the passionless sight of an opening Chorus, are called 'pale cysts', in lines which depend on their sibilant alliteration for their effect.

In his analysis of the sources and significance of *The Dynasts*, which has never been surpassed, Dr Rutland regretted that

> ... no material bearing upon the history of the text of *The Dynasts* has been forthcoming ... It is surely a pity that no early drafts or notes of so important a work have been made available to scholars whose interest in them is not a financial one. For some such manuscripts certainly exist ... Would it not be a service to English scholarship to deposit these beginnings of one of our masterpieces in some public library or museum?[2]

This was written in 1938. Since that time both Hardy's second wife and his sister Katherine have died, and through their foresight, and the courtesy of executors and beneficiaries, we are now able to examine that rare thing, a portion of the rough draft of *The Dynasts*, most of it in Hardy's handwriting. The manuscript of the final form, which varies slightly from the published, is safe in the British Museum. But if we want to 'come close to the mystery of creative genius' we must go, not to this final, august reading, but to the rough draft in its tangled form. As if looking over his shoulder we may watch the poet at work.

> Here is the bringing of order out of chaos; the making of something out of nothing. And this alone among men the artist can

---

[1] See p. 220, *supra*.   [2] p. 283.

accomplish. All others are bound by the principle of the conservation of matter—they can but work with that with which they began; but the artist, taking that which is without form and void, makes thereof a living world. In more general language, out of the insignificant, the trivial, the occasional, the artist fashions that whose significance is universal and perdurable. Out of a chapter in the Book of Judges, Milton made *Samson Agonistes*; out of a chronicle of Saxo Grammaticus, Shakespeare made *Hamlet*. Out of history that is being forgotten and memoirs that are no longer read, Hardy made *The Dynasts*.[1]

An examination of the rough draft reveals several salient things about Hardy's method of working. First, some of the most brilliant minor features of *The Dynasts*, with which we are now familiar in its published form, do not appear. They were inspired after-thoughts, inserted either when the manuscript was going through the transitional stage from rough draft to perfected, or perfected draft to proof. For example: the startling indirect comparison of the vanished Duchess-of-Richmond's-Ballroom to "Camelot, the Palace of Priam, or the hill of Calvary"[2] is squeezed into a last-minute footnote and it is absent from the original manuscript. The brilliant description of Sirius and the stars of Orion 'flashing like stilettos'[3]—a simile which immediately suggests the steel-like, Arctic cold—is nowhere to be found in the rough draft. The hare in the memorable Chorus of the Years before the Battle of Waterloo—

And the hare's hid litter the sapper unseals—[4]

was originally a hedgehog, the line running thus:

And the hedgehog's {hollow the sapper unsealed.
{home

This was an animal for which Hardy felt especial tenderness. He once told a friend that he thought of it as

a piece of Divine creation which God for some reason or other had put under spikes.[5]

[1] Rutland, p. 313.
[2] Part III, Act VI, Sc. II, 1st edition, 1908.
[3] Part III, Act I, Sc. XI.
[4] Part III, Act VI, Sc. VIII.
[5] Sir Newman Flower, p. 93.

Lines from the rough draft of *The Dynasts* in Hardy's handwriting
(The Empress Josephine's dying speech. Part III, Act IV, Scene VII)

Hardy's fondness for the hedgehog was so strong that, despite the fact that the line containing the hare is more poetical, he reverted to the hedgehog in the revised editions later, so that the line ultimately published reads

And the hedgehog's household *the sapper unseals.*[1]

Secondly (and this is another facet of the first discovery) his method of creating in *The Dynasts*—it may have been otherwise with him when writing the shorter lyrics—differs from that of most writers who depend on inspiration rather than solid craftsmanship to carry them through. He does not write with full, flamboyant vision, and then rub out the inessential, the elaborate and redundant, leaving the essential to stand out like a brilliant imago from the protective chrysalis which it has shed, *he inserts the imago afterwards, in his final attempt.* Take some examples on consecutive pages in Part III[2] from the scene outside the city of Moscow. Here, towards the close of the scene, the Spirit of Rumour's speech describing the appearance of the deserted city closes with a couplet published thus:

Enchantment seems to sway from quay to keep
And lock commotion in a century's sleep.

What Hardy first wrote was far less poetic:

It is as if the city were enchanted
And the inhabitants in a century's sleep.

In a second attempt he altered this to:

Enchantment seems to {*rule* the city through*
            {*hold*
And lock its dwellers in a century's sleep.

'Enchantment' and 'a century's sleep' have remained throughout, but Hardy had first to get rid of the unpoetic 'inhabitants' who became 'dwellers', before pointing the lines up with the fresh word and image —'commotion'. That he had visualized the bustle of life in a great city had nowhere first appeared, and it now does so in the final version.

[1] Pocket Edition, 1924. (Italics mine.) The hedgehog also appears in the poem "Afterwards".   [2] Act I, Scene VII.

Another example follows a few lines further on. Here the Chorus of the Rumours is describing the distant figure of Napoleon gazing from the Ivan Tower before darkness falls:

> *Mark you thereon a small lone figure gazing*
> *Upon his hard-gained goal? It is he!*
> *The startled crows, their broad black pinions raising,*
> *Forsake their haunts, and wheel disquietedly.*

This is the published version, of which the last two lines alone need concern us. Hardy first wrote:

Thousands of crows disturbed by him from their perches in and about the lone tower, speckle the air around.

In a second and third attempt he altered this to:

> | *Thousands of startled crows, their vans upraising*
> | *Now crowds of crows, their broad black wings*
> *Swing from their haunts and wheel* | *uneasily*
> | *disquietedly*
> | *amazedly.*

In this pair of lines a single word remains from his first attempt in the final form, the word *crows*. From the second and third attempts he retained "*startled*", "*broad black*" and "*raising*". From the third attempt he also retained the whole of the last line as it now stands, inserting an entirely new word in the next to the last line, *pinions*, instead of the original "vans", or "wings", between which he had hesitated.

The description of Moscow on fire follows, in which there are three significant changes. The 'lurid, malignant star', to which the strange light in the black sky is likened, was originally only a 'ruddy' one. In the two closing sentences—concise, vigorous and vivid, the product of the poet's own observation and imagination—Hardy hesitated between "aflame", "ablaze", and (by far the most telling) "aflare", as an adjective to describe the large pieces of canvas sailing away in the gale. Finally, to the joyful 'Cocks crow, thinking it sunrise' he added the horrible 'ere they are burnt to death', which does not exist in the rough draft.

Thirdly, we see that, time and time again, Hardy set down his thoughts in plain prose, altering it to blank verse later. This discovery shows us that the writing of blank verse was an alien medium in which he was not instinctively at ease. In the press of tremendous thought which a work of such gigantic structure and intention entailed, the poet first set down the facts which came into his mind to 'peg' them, so to speak, and went back over them to polish them, afterwards, like rough-hewn gems. This observation does not hold true when we come to the common soldier's speeches, those of a man who is generally (in Hardy's mind) a countryman, often from Wessex. For instance, the sentinel who challenges Mrs Dalbiac, seeking her husband outside the walls of Salamanca, straightway declares:

> "Where there's war there's women, and where's there's women there's trouble!" (Aloud) "Who goes there?"[1]

Hardy never altered this pithy proverb. The same is true of his satirical conversation between the English soldier and the captive Spanish lady (whom Hardy originally thought of as French) at Vittoria.

Hardy's belief that the life of common man, or woman, is an ample theme for the artist (a belief shared by Aeschylus) is herein justified.

> *Wise, wise was he to whom the thought first came*
> *. . . that Love should aim*
> *Not at the stars but at his own lowly kind:*
> *Not amid delicate damsels bright with gold,*
> *Not in the pride of them with lineage old,*
> *The toil-worn hand shall dream his bliss to find.*[2]

For not only the princes and powerful ones of the earth—Kings, Queens, Dictators and self-styled Emperors, their progeny, and satellites—suffer and bleed, or are tossed about by the 'high gales' of the Primal Force like 'thistle-globes', but the whole of human and animal-kind, since we are parts of one body: are all, like the French 'mermaid' fished up from the deep by the English sailors, 'desperate for life', and at our wits' end to unravel its urgent meaning.

It is no small tribute to Hardy's powers of imagination and

---

[1] Act I, Scene II.
[2] *Prometheus Bound*, p. 62. Translation of Gilbert Murray. Geo. Allen & Unwin, 1931.

tenderness of heart that, on laying down *The Dynasts*, we feel his compassion mothering humanity, 'even as a hen doth gather her chicks under her wings'. He both portrays and pities mankind whom Aeschylus viewed as 'entranced', or moving 'as if in a dream', whose strength is 'hazardous', whose senses confused, and who does all that he does 'without knowledge'. Hardy's despair at the stupidity of man in the face of cumulative experience, and his rebelliousness against the unheeding Will, cause him, Prometheus-like, to take upon himself those protective qualities, properly divine, lacking in either a Zeus or a Thoughtless Cause.

CHAPTER TEN

LYRIC POETRY AND AFTER-SCENE

Time so complained of,
Who to no one man shows partiality,
Brings round to all men
Some undimn'd hours.

MATTHEW ARNOLD

ONE of the most bitterly ironic passages in *The Dynasts* is the dialogue between the Spirit of the Pities and the Spirit Ironic during the battle of Waterloo, when the former asks:

> *Is this the Esdraelon of a moil*
> *For mortal man's effacement?*

and the latter replies:

> *. . . Warfare mere,*
> *Plied by the Managed for the Managers;*
> *To wit: by frenzied-folks who profit nought*
> *For those who profit all!*[1]

Hardy had dared to believe that war was 'doomed' at last because of its 'absurdity'. In 1904, during the time that he was writing *The Dynasts*, he told William Archer:

> It is doomed by the gradual growth of the introspective faculty in mankind—of their power of putting themselves in another's place, and taking a point of view that is not their own. In another aspect, this may be called the growth of a sense of humour. Not today, nor tomorrow, but in the fulness of time, war will come to an end, not for moral reasons, but because of its absurdity.[2]

The third part of *The Dynasts* which appeared in 1908 ended on a note of hope. "It was just as well," wrote Hardy, "that the Pities should have the last word since, like *Paradise Lost*, *The Dynasts* proves nothing."[3]

---

[1] Part III, Act VII, Scene VIII.
[2] *Real Conversations*, p. 47. The poems "His Country" and "The Sick Battle God" play on the same theme.
[3] Letter to Edward Clodd, II, p. 275.

The convulsion of nations which occurred in August 1914 therefore came as a profound shock to Hardy's convictions and susceptibilities. Relieved at having completed *The Dynasts* he confessed to Edward Clodd that he had been living in spirit so much in the campaigns of Wellington that he felt he had almost taken part in them and had written of them from memory. Now imagined carnage was to be exceeded by the real. The percipient commented on what they called Hardy's prophetic vision in having depicted the horrors of war on such a scale, and the coincidence that he had written a lyric called "Channel Firing" only a few months before war broke out. Now the last shadow of a hope that a 'fundamental, ultimate Wisdom' might lie behind creation was swept away. The writer deplored the advance of material and scientific knowledge to the detriment of simple, old-fashioned kindness. He foresaw that the wars of the future would be even more fiendish, and began to doubt if the world was 'worth the saving'. His old view of the gradual ennoblement of human nature was destroyed: he 'despaired of the world's history' and saw with horror its retrogression. He had

> visions ahead of ignorance over-ruling intelligence and reducing us to another Dark Age.[1]

To the same friend he had written earlier:

> What a set back this revival of superstition is. It makes one despair of the human mind. Where's Willy Shakespeare's 'So noble in reason' now! In another quarter of a century we shall be burying food and money with our deceased, as was done with the Romano-British skeletons I used to find in my garden.[2]

And to another friend he wrote:

> . . . the recognition that we are living in a more brutal age than that, say, of Elizabeth, or of the chivalry which could cry: "Gentlemen of the Guard, fire first!" (far more brutal indeed: no chivalry now!), does not inspire one to write hopeful poetry, or even conjectural prose, but simply makes one sit back in an apathy and watch the clock spinning backwards . . .[3]

[1] Letter to Edward Clodd, dated June 6, 1919, from the Brotherton Collection.
[2] *Ibid.*, February 1918.
[3] Letter dated August 28, 1914. Sir Sydney Cockerell, p. 279.

But, during the war years with their agonized fluctuations, Hardy did not sit miserable and silent at home. At the age of seventy-four he offered his services wherever he thought they might be acceptable to his country. In Dorset he adjudicated on food-profiteering cases at the Police Courts, or visited the English and German wounded in hospital or Prisoner of War Camps. In one of these a Prussian soldier died whilst Hardy was with him, 'to my great relief and his own'. When writing *The Dynasts* he had been struck by the terrible ironies of war and had portrayed soldiers of opposing armies drinking from the same stream at nightfall, only to rise in the morning and do as they were bid—kill each other outright. Now here in Dorchester itself he found the same senseless horrors—English and Germans helpless from wounds, dying only a few hundred yards apart, "each scene of suffering caused by the other". Of what use was compassion? In a mood of sheer desperation Hardy later wrote to a friend:

Why does not Christianity throw up the sponge and say. 'I am beaten', and let another religion take its place?[1]

Together with others eminent in the field of letters he was summoned to London at the instance of the Cabinet. These men met together to see how best to put forward Britain's case to neutral countries. As he looked at their grave, perpending faces Hardy's old sense of form and colour re-asserted itself. He remarked the yellow sun shining in on the large blue table, the upcast shadow giving the earnest faces a tragic caste.

His new-found domestic happiness somewhat consoled him for the savagery of nations at war. In February 1914 he married Florence Emily Dugdale, the daughter of an Enfield headmaster who came of Dorset stock. When they were introduced the fact that they might be distantly related was half-humorously pointed out to Hardy; in his thorough manner he later recorded in his Hutchins' *Dorset* that a certain William Dugdale of Wareham, the great-great-uncle of his second wife, had married a Hardy.

From various letters we learn that Hardy began by calling her 'my little cousin F.' By 1910 she had become 'Miss D.—my

[1] II, pp. 173 and 192.

handyman with her typewriter . . .", for she had undertaken informal secretarial work for the author, whose eyes by now were often afflicted with rheum. In 1911 Hardy took her and her sister on a brief tour of some favourite cathedrals, and she accompanied him once or twice to Aldeburgh to visit his friend Edward Clodd and his wife. While referring indirectly to Emma Hardy's fondness for her company, Hardy could also confide in Clodd that it was 'a great disappointment' that 'my young friend' had been unwell and would not be able to come to Aldeburgh, on one occasion.

It is obvious that Florence Dugdale had made herself indispensable to both the Hardys, who were more than twice her age. Like a tactful daughter she brought them encouragement and a measure of practicality sorely needed from time to time in the distraught household. She remembered Mrs Hardy's birthday, 'the only living soul to do so', and she did research for Hardy when he was unable to do it himself. With her quiet, unobtrusive sympathy she deftly wove herself into their hearts, into Hardy's more securely than he knew. But this girl who brought:

> . . . *mute ministrations to one and to all*
> *Beyond a man's saying sweet . . .*[1]

was something more than a ministering angel or 'handyman'.

She had some literary ability herself, wrote verse, and had already published a number of children's stories when Hardy met her. Above all she was a critic of rare understanding, subordinating her talents and needs to those of one whom, from the first, she had recognized as a master of his art.

Amongst Hardy's lyrics we can trace several written to 'F.E.D.' There is the one dedicated to her in *Late Lyrics and Earlier* which begins with despondency—

> *I sometimes think as here I sit*
> *Of things I have done,*
> *Which seemed in doing not unfit*
> *To face the sun:*
> *Yet never a soul has paused a whit*
> *On such—not one.—*

---

[1] "After the Visit", in *Satires of Circumstance*.

and which closes with lines of deep appreciation for her devotion, not only to his daily needs, but to deeper spiritual hungers. In "After the Visit", which was published in the autumn of the year of their marriage, he speaks of her delicacy of presence. She is like a 'leaf that skims', and in the former poem the poet speaks of her as

> . . . *spiriting into my house, to, fro,*
> *Like wind on the stair.*

Her feet are as 'light on the green as thistledown ball', her walk 'so soundless' that he fancies her a phantom 'of long ago'. Another lyric not usually attributed to her inspiration is "Had you Wept",[1] in which the poet both reproaches and admires the woman with 'the large and luminous eye' for not conquering him with that best of all feminine weapons— genuine tears. The same phrase, 'large, luminous living eyes', (Florence Hardy's most striking feature, as the drawing of her by William Strang shows), is used in "After the Visit".

When Emma had died, and Hardy had passed through that period of searing reproach and intense loneliness, after knowing Florence Dugdale for more than a decade, he asked her to become his second wife. She accepted, and almost immediately after her marriage wrote that her reasons for confiding herself to Hardy were

> that I might have the right to express my devotion—and to endeavour to add to his comfort and happiness.[2]

From these intentions Florence Hardy never swerved. To the marriage she brought, in addition, a refreshing sense of humour: she smiled without bitterness at the foibles of an ageing man and rallied him with gentle gaiety. At the end of twelve months of marriage she acknowledged that it had been 'a year of great happiness', adding with emphasis, 'I am not joking'. When, in later years, Hardy's old friends praised her for her sympathetic care of the man who by now was what Arnold Bennett called 'the biggest thing in English letters, and no nonsense about

---

[1] This poem was not written to Emma Hardy as Carl Weber, p. 170, indicates. The eyes of Hardy's first wife could never have been called either 'large' or 'luminous', as her portrait shows.

[2] Letter to Sir Sydney Cockerell, p. 294.

him', whose health was decreasing, whose privacy was constantly threatened and invaded, Florence Hardy glowed with unaffected pleasure. To his old friend Edmund Gosse, whose 'faithful visitations' had cheered Hardy thirty years earlier in Arundel Terrace when he had come near bleeding to death, and who had continued to encourage and praise him when he saw his spirits drooping from lack of public and domestic appreciation, she wrote:

> I must thank you warmly for one of the kindest letters I have ever received. It gives me great happiness to know that you think I have not been a failure in taking care of my husband. Such commendation from one of his oldest and most valued friends is indeed worth having, little though I deserve it.[1]

Hardy's aversion to writing personal memoirs, and his mistrust of others handling the material for an official 'Life', were overcome by his belief in the wisdom and ability of his *Flower*, as he grew to call her in intimate moments. A month after Hardy's death she confided to their old friend, now Sir Edmund Gosse:

> With regard to the biography of my husband I have for many years been collecting material which has been somewhat roughly put into shape. T.H. allowed me to take a great many extracts from his diaries and notebooks, and supplied all the information that I required . . . T.H. left written directions about the biography—clearly stating that he wishes it to be written by me— and I am *most* thankful to find that you think I am capable of the task.[2]

She had as well the advice and aid of Sir James Barrie, Sir Sydney Cockerell and other eminent men in the literary field, both Sir Edmund and Sir Sydney being amongst Hardy's literary executors. How successfully she performed the task must be a matter of personal opinion: if one is at times baulked by her over-scrupulous reticence one has constantly to remember that, even after his death, his widow had for her husband's wishes the most conscientious respect. In that quarry, from which all other biographers must hew for their needs, one is always

---

[1] Letter dated June 10, 1922, in the Brotherton Collection.
[2] *Ibid.*, February 28 1928.

aware of her mute self-effacement before (what she rejoiced in his being) the greater literary figure. When she was once asked if she, too, did not write poetry, Florence Hardy replied with dignity that "unless a genius herself, the wife of a genius makes herself appear foolish" by proffering her work[1]—at which the shade of Emma Lavinia must have stirred uneasily.

In the year following his second marriage Hardy's favourite sister, Mary, died—she who had shared his love of painting and climbed the Bockhampton apple-trees with him as a child:

> . . . her foot near mine on the bending limb,
> Laughing, her young brown hand awave.[2]

In late years, when the sun had burst forth and the shadow of the garden gnomon had pointed at her, Hardy read into this shadow-finger a sinister warning:

> Little saw we in it,
> But this much I know,
> Of lookers on that shade,
> Her towards whom it made
> Soonest had to go.[3]

Now that she was gone, the poet who was older than either woman, wondered why he was 'not out there', just as he had done when Emma had died.

But, blossoming afresh beneath his wife's ministrations, Hardy continued to write lyric poetry. *Wessex Poems*, the *Poems of Past and Present*, *Time's Laughingstocks*, and *Satires of Circumstance* which had already appeared, were followed by *Moments of Vision*, *Late Lyrics and Earlier*, *Human Shows*, and the posthumous *Winter Words*.[4] This fertility lasted until he was eighty-seven years old, and some final revisions were made just over six weeks before his death.

The Famous Tragedy of the Queen of Cornwall appeared in 1923. With his knowledge of the work of the Anglo-Norman poet, Thomas, and Swinburne's *Tristram of Lyonesse*, and other

---

[1] Weber, p. 225.
[2] "Logs on the Hearth" in *Moments of Vision*.
[3] "In the Garden", "Looking Across" in the same volume also refer to Mary Hardy.
[4] In 1898, 1902, 1909, 1914, 1917, 1922, 1925 and 1928.

romantic handlings of this essentially Celtic romance, Hardy
set forth the tale in new guise as a one act "Play for Mummers".
The legend with its pagan, un-moral attitude, and its theme of
lovers unwittingly placed under bonds which neither could
break, through the drinking of the fatal love-potion—an action
which turned them into beings doomed to destruction, automata
of a law ill-comprehended by themselves—was one certain to
attract Hardy who had many years before discussed hypnotism,
silent influence, the negligent power of the will, and other
phenomena when dining at his London club.[1] Iseult sees the
wasting years as 'sharp entrancements': and her women see
Tristram as

> . . . *Fate-haunted, doomed to drink*
> *Charmed philtres, melting every link*
> *Of purposed faith!*

There is a curious reminder of *A Pair of Blue Eyes* in this slight
drama written fifty years after the novel. Iseult the White-
handed resembles Elfride; she has 'corn brown hair' and
'flutters' with fear. Furthermore, when Tristram casts her off
she asks the same piteous questions which Elfride had asked her
imperious lover, Knight. The Cornish girl tormentedly
questions:

> What meaning have you, Harry? You only say so, do you? . . .
> You are not in earnest, I know—I hope you are not? Surely I
> belong to you, and you are going to keep me for yours?[2]——

whereas the Breton Princess asks:

> How, Tristram mine?
> What meaning mete you out by that to me?
> You only say it, do you? You are not,
> Cannot be, in true earnest—*that I know!*
> . . . Surely I,
> *This time as always, do* belong to you,
> And you are going to keep me always yours?
> *I thought you loved my name for me myself,*
> *Not for another: . . .* [3]

---

[1] See II, p. 34.   [2] *A Pair of Blue Eyes*, p. 400.
[3] *The Queen of Cornwall*, p. 555. (Italics mine.)

The parallel is strange. *The Queen of Cornwall* was begun five years after Emma's death, and after her husband had re-visited the Cornish scene of their meeting and betrothal, near Tintagel. It is as if Hardy had gone back over the years to re-create the 'ghosts of distant days'. The surmise is confirmed in one of Hardy's letters in which he says:

> Alas, I fear your hopes of a poem on Iseult—the English, or British, Helen—will be disappointed. I visited the place 44 years ago with an Iseult of my own, *and of course she was mixed in the vision of the other*.[1]

The lyrical poetry of Thomas Hardy, who stands as the most significant poet between Tennyson and Yeats, bulks large. In the final Collected Edition, not counting the many lost and discarded poems, the published total is nearly a thousand. He is unique among English poet-novelists in having produced such a quantity of verse, and so much of it late in life when the springs of inspiration generally languish. He was aware of his own late ripening, but always insistent that poetry had been his first love, and the writing of it his first clear intention.

> I was quick to bloom: late to ripen ... I was a child till I was sixteen; a youth till I was twenty-five; a young man till I was forty or fifty.[2]

His poetry shows consistent trends throughout and, above all, a marked originality. He once told Gosse that he regarded 'the jewelled line as effeminate',[3] and it is obvious that he consciously veered away from the mellifluousness, the deep sensuousness 'loaded with ore' which had been the characteristic of English poetry in the hands of Keats, Tennyson and others. From the start Hardy appears to have been little influenced by contemporary poets, other than Swinburne and Browning, nor by his literary predecessors, with the exception of (as an adolescent) Wordsworth, who died only ten years after he was born. His poetry bears a strong resemblance to his own nature— in this respect, that beneath the quiet manner there is intensity of emotion and a great reserve of thought: secondly, the writer

---

[1] Letter dated September 20, 1916. Sir Sydney Cockerell, p. 284. (Italics mine.)

[2] II, pp. 178-9.   [3] Weber, p. 188.

enjoys the art of concealing art, just as his deceptive simplicity of bearing concealed a complex character.

Being close to the soil, closer than any contemporary poet except William Barnes, (Burns had died in 1796 and Clare in 1865), he mirrored his rural background not only in his knowledge, instinctive and acquired, but in his taste. The subjects and characters of his poems are those of the hamlet and byre: a man or woman at work pauses, with arms at rest over spade or milking-pail, to draw breath with astonishment at some reported event, and then to relish, or ponder.[1] Or, if the setting is a town one, the subject resembles some incident, either startling or tragic, in the daily life of the town-dweller reported in the newspapers. There is the immediate appreciation of the incongruity of events, or emotions, experienced by those who have lived in isolation; the dramatic is loved for its own sake, because it is grotesque, strange and inexplicable, or because there is some sharp, ironic contrast involved. Hardy is drawn by nature to the strange and violent, and his taste, revealed in the novels, is likewise apparent in the lyric poetry. But, owing to his superior intellect and education, the writer gained detachment from his native circumstances and surroundings.

The subjects first in importance in Hardy's poetry are love—generally frustrated or unhappy love—and death.[2] There are, in addition, a large number of poems which may be classed as narrative, or anecdotal: then there are the autobiographical, and finally the philosophical, wherein Hardy questions and re-questions the *why* of existence, or the problem of pain.

> There is no writer of the first rank in English literature, not even excepting the author of *Lear* and *Hamlet*, who has wrestled in spirit more arduously with [the problem of suffering] than Thomas Hardy,[3]

says one critic. The nature poems, amongst which are some of Hardy's loveliest and best known, are surprisingly small in number. A few poems are concerned with wars and war, and a few with what may be called special occasions.

[1] C. Day Lewis and Sir Maurice Bowra have pointed out these traits in *The Lyrical Poems of Thomas Hardy*, Warton Lecture, 1951, and *The Lyrical Poetry of Thomas Hardy*, Byron Foundation Lecture, 1946.
[2] See Vere Collins, *The Love Poetry of Thomas Hardy*.
[3] Rutland, p. 33.

Sometimes Hardy questions human standards in an unortho-
dox manner in his verse. Just as he had questioned the validity
of the judgments of society in *Tess* and held up chastity to a
new light, so in a lyric he holds up charity for scrutiny in
"The Blinded Bird", judging human values by Christian
standards, passionately pleading for a maimed creature.

> *Who hath charity? This bird.*
> *Who suffereth long and is kind,*
> *Is not provoked, though blind*
> *And alive ensepulchred?*
> *Who hopeth, endureth all things?*
> *Who thinketh no evil, but sings?*
> *Who is divine? This bird.*[1]

The conciseness of that stanza, the simple metre and the
Biblical phraseology, bring home praise and condemnation
more forcibly than a longer poem would do. It is an example of
Hardy's style when he is deeply moved, for there is more than
gentle pathos here (a characteristic of many of the poems), there
is rebellious emotion expressed with an effective economy of
words.

As one might expect, knowing Hardy's prose themes, many
of the poems depend on the shock of disillusion for their crisis or
ending, many are concerned with social and sexual problems.
A man drowns himself when he finds that the wife he had idolized
has been unfaithful to him; a woman pines to death when she
finds that she is not legally married to the man she loves; a girl
observes her adored in an act of common vanity and is broken-
hearted. The sorrow and poetry of existence has interpenetrated
the novels and stories, and the realism of these has invaded the
poetry, until prose and poetry complement each other.

The moods of the lyrics shade off from broad country humour,
as in the early "Bride-Night Fire" with its Barnesian flavour,
or from more delicate humour, as in "He revisits his First
School", into irony and sharp, ruthless, satirical realism. A few
poems are deeply tragic. For irony was Hardy's escape from
the unendurable which he had encountered wherever he looked,
whether in the outskirts of a great city, where mute and sorrow-

---

[1] In *Moments of Vision*.

ful lovers crossed his homeward path; or in the country, where a woman methodically goes on tidying her home before she has been able to accept the shock of her husband's death. Natures as sensitive as Hardy's must retire out of the world, escape into artistic expression of that which causes them pain or distress, or perish. This retirement is their emotional release, and creation their panacea.

If we should sum up the spirit of Hardy's poetry in two words, these would be *pity* and *irony*; *pity* for the sufferer, whether murderer or adulteress, an old horse that stumbles at its work, a bird too frail to withstand the winter blast, or a young soldier sleeping under alien stars on alien soil, ignorant of his approaching death; *irony*, which is always directed away from the suffering ones to the illogical Cause, the System which causes them to act as they do. This Promethean, this Christian, sympathy cloaks and shelters victim and villain alike. If Hardy had had more hatred in him, been more actively rebellious, he might have been a great reformer in the ecclesiastical, military or medical world, but, being an artist, he wrote out in white heat (or in a more dispassionate state many years later) that which vexed, stung, or outraged his excessive sensibility. He thrusts suffering before us with incisive strokes as Daumier does in his drawings.

Some similarities between Hardy's poetry and the early work of Donne exist. Since both men lived during an age of transition, when fresh scientific discoveries were being made and were casting religious tenets into doubt, both Donne and Hardy reveal the aching need for a faith wherewith to confirm themselves. Donne transferred his religious allegiance from one church to another and so, in part, consoled himself: Hardy was unable to do this. Yet even he, avowed agnostic, often attended services, and when walking to Stinsford churchyard declared:

> I believe in going to church. It is a moral drill, and people must have something. If there is no church in a country village there is nothing . . . I believe in reformation coming from *within* the church.[1]

The poetry of both shows that marked originality which neither

[1] Hardy to General Morgan. Blunden, p. 165.

could conceal, nor would suppress to please a sycophantic public. Both were in conscious revolt against the mellifluousness of their predecessors : each had a liking for the Gothic and strange, and a love of words for themselves, which made them import the old and invent the new. To take a single example from both, Donne introduced the word *macaron,* a coxcomb, into the language, and Hardy was fond of *fantocine* for puppet. *The Dynasts* alone exhibits many abrupt, outlandish words. An examination of the diction reveals the use of twenty-one in senses not given in the New English Dictionary, and the resuscitation of six others not in common use since the 14th, or later than the 17th, centuries.[1] Both were metrically inventive poets as well. Both were careless of poetic fame and praise, and neither was eager to rush into print. Hardy said of himself :

> *Writing* verse gives me great pleasure, but not publishing it. I never did care much about publication, as is proved by my keeping some of the verses forty years in MS.[2]

Both delight in the dramatic, and have a penetrating eye for emotional crises and the conjunction of the dissimilar, whether emotional or actual. Both are permeated with the philosophical and *scientific* thought of their day which they use allusively, and (not to draw the parallel too finely) both escaped from vulnerability into satire, or irony, as a protection against further wounding. Both had a marked awareness of sexual sin and a delicate conscience. Finally, both were morbidly obsessed with death and the horrors of the grave. In an early poem Hardy asks only of Time that in the grave he may be joined with his loved one—

> *. . . that thy worm may be my worm, Love!—*

a conceit so like Donne's that one is astonished not to be able to trace it in the earlier poet's work, whose *Flea* it resembles. There the analogy must end, for Donne was the greater poet; but Hardy's metrical debt to him has never been adequately studied.

There remains one other resemblance, between the characters of the two men : both were strongly aware of the need to regard the whole of humanity as one corporate body, and in this both were in advance of their times. Donne's "No man is an island

---

[1] See G. S. Loane, *Times Literary Supplement,* February 14, 1929.
[2] Letter to Sir Sydney Cockerell, February 28, 1922, p. 290.

entire of itself" has been too often quoted of late to call for repetition, but Hardy's insistence on this thought is little known, apart from its depiction in *The Dynasts*. A passage from two letters will suffice to give its essence:

> I would say that nothing effectual will be accomplished in the cause of *Peace* till the sentiment of *Patriotism* be freed from the narrow meaning attaching to it in the past . . . and be extended to the whole globe . . . That the sentiment of *Foreignness* . . . attach only to other planets and their inhabitants, if any.[1]

To Galsworthy he wrote six years later:

> The exchange of international thought is the only possible salvation for the world; and though I was decidedly premature when I wrote at the beginning of the S. African War that I hoped to see patriotism . . . circling the earth, I still maintain that such sentiments ought to prevail.[2]

Hardy was amongst the first to advocate a constructive policy for establishing the Jews in Palestine; and argued that if the white races had loosed such fiendishness in the world it was time to let the black and yellow have a chance. Hardy's copy of Donne's *Poems* was published in 1896 and was presented to him in 1908 by Edmund Gosse. In acknowledging the gift Hardy wrote saying that he had compunctions in accepting it since Gosse had robbed his own library in giving it to him.[3] He marked certain passages in the *Poems*, showing us that he admired "The Indifferent", "The Expiration", two lines from the second "Elegy", and the first stanza of "Song", as well as the first quatrain of the last stanza. There are also slight marks against lines in a few of the "Divine Poems", but that is all. Hardy must have known Donne long since in an earlier, lost volume, but he did not quote and re-quote him in his novels as he did other favourite poets.

His highest ambition, he confessed, was to write a lyric like Ben Jonson's "Drink to me only with thine eyes": this was 'the model he had set before him'.[4] But the joyful or serenely

---

[1] II, p. 174. Letter to Royal Society of Literature, February 8, 1917.
[2] *Ibid.*, p. 230.
[3] Letter dated July 24, 1908, Brotherton Collection.
[4] II, p. 263.

lyrical is not Hardy's most natural style. Poems such as "Weathers"—

> *This is the weather the cuckoo likes*
> *And so do I . . .—*

or the popular "When I set out for Lyonesse", are exceptional. (Hardy recognized that the latter poem had about it something of "the song-ecstasy that a lyric should have", other than an elegiac one.)[1] We remember him more for his compassion, for the harsh mockery of unrelenting irony, or even the rather humdrum recital of some minor incident. Hardy wrote poetry, not to propagate ideas, not to argue or to convert, but because poetry and the making of poetry were in the fibre of his being. Nevertheless he had an ill-founded hope that poetry might act as midwife at the birth of a new philosophy, the parents being religion and rationality, without either of which he felt that "the world must perish". "Poetry and religion" he declared, "touch each other, or rather modulate into each other; are indeed *often but different names for the same thing.*" His creed expressed in the same place, is a simple one—

> that whether the human and kindred animal races survive till the exhaustion or destruction of the globe, or whether these races perish and are succeeded by others before that conclusion comes, pain to all upon it, tongued or dumb, shall be kept down to a minimum by loving-kindness.[2]

His verse may therefore be regarded as an expression of his personal religion, by means of which he praised and blessed those things which made him joyful and cursed that which pained, saddened and oppressed him.

The majority of Hardy's notes during the last thirty years of his life, as one might expect since he was now chiefly occupied with the writing of verse, concern the art and meaning of poetry. Florence Hardy gives many of these. In 1899, after the lukewarm reception of *Wessex Poems*, the writer consoled himself by noting that:

> No man's poetry can be truly judged till its last line is written. What is the last line? The death of the poet. And hence there is this quaint consolation to any writer of verse—that it may be

[1] Letter to Sir Sydney Cockerell, January 15, 1917, p. 285.
[2] Preface to *Late Lyrics and Earlier*, 1922.

imperishable for all that anybody can tell him to the contrary;
and that if worthless he can never know it, unless he be a greater
adept at self-criticism than poets usually are.[1]

(This was a reflection of the Greek idea that no man's *life* can
be judged until it is ended.) He resents the fact that critics are
more interested in detecting a writer's alleged theological or
political beliefs than in studying his 'artistic interpretation of
life'.[2] He recognizes that appreciation of his own work is blocked
by what he calls 'the unwilling mind', a stultifying, thwarting
thing. Several days later, lamenting the labelling and stan-
dardizing of the lives and work of poets in general, he writes:

> The glory of poetry lies in its largeness, admitting among its
> creators men of infinite variety.[3]

Hardy frequently alludes to his own late blossoming and expresses his belief that old age has, for him, been of value because
it has enabled him to complete his task. This sense of having
fulfilled an intention long deferred constantly recurs. It is the
voice of the conscientious craftsman humbly reaping satisfaction from work well done. Hardy likes to think that he is not
alone in a tardy ripening:

> Homer sang as a blind old man ... Aeschylus wrote his best up
> to his death at nearly seventy ... the best of Sophocles appeared
> between his fifty-fifth and ninetieth years ... Euripides wrote up
> to seventy.
>
> Among those who accomplished late, the poetic spark must
> always have been latent; but its outspringing may have been
> frozen and delayed for half a lifetime.[4]

If *The Dynasts* had been the 'topmost cyme' of his literary
inflorescence the succeeding volumes of verse were the racemes
which clustered along the stalk.

Hardy's major concern was not for his own productions but
for English poetry at large, and one of his greatest fears was that
the war might blight it—that it might be "the first thing to go,
probably not to revive for many centuries". He urged young
writers "to stave off such a catastrophe". He feared, too, the
effect of so-called democracy on the world of letters and he saw,

---

[1] II, pp. 80-1.   [2] *Ibid.*, p. 183.
[3] *Ibid.*, p. 184.   [4] *Ibid.*

more clearly than most in his generation, the growing tendency to denigrate all but manual labour.

> Democratic government may be justice to man, but it will probably merge in proletarian, and when these people are our masters it will lead to more of this contempt and possibly be the utter ruin of art and literature.[1]

He was opposed to what he called either 'aristocratic or democratic privilege'—

> By the latter I mean *the arrogant assumption that the only labour is hand labour—a worse arrogance than that of the aristocrat*—the taxing of the worthy to help those masses of the population who will not help themselves when they might.[2]

(This was written as long ago as 1887.)

Hardy was constantly preoccupied with the thought of a growing, grieving God. Many of his notes and poems are concerned with this theme—that of a repentant Creator who should be brought to task for the suffering he has permitted, if not actually caused, who sees his error and mends his ways. Wordsworth had lain quaking on his bed at the terrible implications which the thought of a Deity who could foster evil brought him, and Hardy in *The Dynasts* (and his lesser poems) queried why, if pain might be prevented at the start, a compassionate, intelligent Deity allowed it to exist, and suffering mortals to be racked on the wheel of torture. Both of these allied thoughts may be found in the work of Greek tragedians, more especially in that of Aeschylus, who had drawn a penitent Zeus chastened by suffering and reconciled to his creatures. The tyrant and offended Master, the enemy of man, has deigned to learn from the champion of humanity who has dared to defy him. But to the question of Prometheus why he, why Io, should be tortured meaninglessly, Aeschylus gives no valid answer. Nor does the author of the Book of Job solve this heartrending problem—nor Shakespeare, Milton nor Shelley. Each poet ponders and reflects his own attitude, often at variance with the accepted beliefs of his day. But the tragedy inherent in existence remains for the percipient, the rebellious, the compassionate in each generation, to interpret in his own exceptional way.

[1] I, p. 309.   [2] *Ibid.*, p. 268.

L

After the appearance of *The Dynasts*, the apex of his literary endeavours, Hardy was granted many honours, academic and civic, and he accepted many tributes. He basked with 'characteristic quietude" in royal and international favour. No less than five Scottish and English universities conferred honorary degrees on him between the years 1905 and 1925.[1] After at first demurring he finally accepted the Presidency of the Society of Authors in 1908: the Order of Merit was conferred on him by the King in 1910, an occasion on which Hardy 'felt that he had failed in the accustomed formalities'.[2] He received an invitation to the Coronation in 1911 which, for personal reasons, he refused, and in the same year the gold medal of the Royal Society of Literature was presented to him by Yeats and Sir Henry Newbolt. He sat as a Grand Juror at the Dorchester Assizes, became a Representative Governor of the Grammar School in 1908, and later a full Governor. But the honour from Dorchester which he prized the most was the Freedom of the Borough, which he accepted in 1910 in a speech full of quiet humour:

> I may be allowed to confess that the freedom of the Borough of Dorchester did seem to me at first something that I had possessed a long while, had helped myself to (to speak plainly), for when I consider the liberties I have taken with its ancient walls, streets and precincts through the medium of the printing-press, I feel that I have treated its external features with the hand of freedom indeed.[3]

Hardy could not often be persuaded to make speeches, but on two other occasions he made felicitous ones, in 1927 when he laid the foundation stone of the new building for the Grammar School, and in 1918 when he opened a village club-room in Bockhampton. Both these occasions involved his affections, and gave him scope for personal recollections, prefaced by historical anecdotes.

Apart from his old friend and contemporary Sir Edmund

---

[1] He received an LL.D. from Aberdeen in 1905 and from St Andrew's in 1922, a Litt.D. from Cambridge in 1913, a Doctor of Letters from Oxford in 1920 and from Bristol in 1925. He was also made an Hon. Fellow of Magdalene College, Cambridge, in 1913, and of Queen's College, Oxford, in 1922.   [2] II, p. 143.   [3] *Ibid.*, pp. 143-4.

Gosse, whom someone once jocularly called 'English literature personified', there was no one of Hardy's age or stature left in the literary field. The poet was fortunate enough to receive those rare and gratifying rewards, praise and recognition before his death. That from the younger generation of writers, amongst them Sassoon, Masefield, Blunden, E. M. Forster, T. E. Lawrence, and John Cowper and Llewelyn Powys, was especially warming. The Balliol Players came thrice to Max Gate to perform the *Oresteia*, the *Hippolytus*, and *Iphigenia in Aulis* on the lawn. On the first occasion Hardy entered into their spirit of ardour, relishing the players' quick-witted way of substituting tall spikes of spirea, plucked from the garden borders, for lighted torches whose flames were invisible in the midsummer sunshine. His manner with them, and with the younger writers whom he entertained in his own home or met in those of his friends, Sir James Barrie's and others', was sincere and simple. He never patronized or talked down to them, but treated them as equals, making himself easy of approach.

In addition to the content which the act and art of writing always gave to him, the pleasure gained from recognition of his genius by the discriminating (a recognition he only half-believed in according to Charles Morgan and others), and the serenity of a sympathetic union, Hardy gained enjoyment in making visits to, and receiving them from, his old friends. He crossed from Dorset to Suffolk to be with Edward Clodd and to take part in the 150th anniversary of the birth of Crabbe, that realistic English poet whom he admitted having admired since early manhood. It was of Crabbe that he and Florence Dugdale had spoken on their first encounter and to a friend she later wrote, at her husband's direction:

> Crabbe . . . was *one* of the influences that led him towards his method—in his novels not his poetry. The report probably arose from T.H.'s saying that he owed more of his realistic style to Crabbe than to Zola.[1]

Hardy does not appear to have quoted from Crabbe, in spite of

[1] Letter to Sir Sydney Cockerell, February 6, 1919, p. 300.   Byron was also an admirer of Crabbe.

his admiration for him, and his frequent use of the work of the English poets in his novels.

He made a tour of the English cathedrals with his wife, brother and sister, between the years 1906-12, glancing at abbeys, chapels and college buildings, all of which held his interest. The gateway of Cerne Abbas was an especial favourite of his, and the great mediaeval tithe-barn there, whose roof later fell in and was replaced with cheap modern substitutes for ancient oak and thatch, had lingered in his mind as a young man to be used as the prototype for Bathsheba's barn in *Far from the Madding Crowd*.[1] Emma Hardy's nephew, who together with his sister lived at Max Gate for some years, made a drawing of the Abbey gateway, and Hardy wrote some affectionate notes on it for *The Builder*.[2] He took his wife to re-visit scenes which formerly had been dear to him and to explore fresh corners of his beloved Wessex. He even went on board English and American battleships in Portland Roads. Before old age had taken its toll of his vitality he listened to the music of Grieg and Tchaikowsky, and watched performances of plays by Ben Jonson and Shaw in London, where he talked with Gorky and Conrad, as well as numerous English writers, Bennett, Wells, Housman, Galsworthy, Kipling and others. A visit to Swinburne, the writer whom he most admired, in 1904, had been a source of great pleasure to him; with sardonic satisfaction they had compared notes on their vilification by the English press and public, being, as they thought, 'the most abused of living writers'.[3]

His novels, stories and epic poems were dramatized, and one novel was filmed. When Baron d'Erlanger staged his Italian opera based on *Tess* at Covent Garden in 1909, Hardy walked and talked with the actors on the stage on which he had appeared as a young man. In 1912 Granville Barker's adaptation of *The Dynasts* was presented at the Kingsway Theatre. There was also a drawing-room performance of *Tess* at Max Gate in 1925. Florence Hardy has given an account by one of the players, which may be supplemented by that of a personal

[1] Sir Sydney Cockerell, p. 281.
[2] February 8, 1902. Gordon Gifford was then working in Sir Arthur Blomfield's offices, into which Hardy had introduced him. Blomfield himself had died in 1899. [3] II, pp. 111-12.

friend[1] who has given me her impressions of Hardy and his home. The room, she says, was pleasant and full of budding bulbs in shallow bowls, in whose growth the poet took the keenest interest. It had been found impossible to put up all of the players at Max Gate and Hardy was concerned for those banished to hotels and lodgings. He enquired whether their rooms were warm and hoped that their beds had been properly aired. Such courteous attention to the feelings and welfare of others is borne out by another acquaintance,[2] who participated in many of the local performances of Hardy's work by the Dorchester players. His reputation was then flung wide upon the world, and actors and actresses were in nervous awe of him. Nevertheless he put one player instantly at ease by reminding her that his mother had formerly admired hers, and by apologizing for the bare stage description prefacing her name. "I hope you don't mind being called merely 'An Old Apple Woman'?" he enquired, with sincere regard for her feelings.[3]

One of the burdens of fame is the labour which accompanies it. Hardy's publishers suggested new editions and a revision of his entire work: he had likewise to be constantly on the watch against false representation and piracy in the United States. He found the extensive proof-reading exhausting both to eyes and brain. "Who cares about what one has written from hand-to-mouth forty years earlier?", was his cry. Still the work must go on, and Hardy's doggedness stood him in good stead. Another burden attending fame is the number of requests from the known and unknown to fulfil minor tasks—a friend asks for an

---

[1] Natalie Moya.   [2] Mrs Major of Dorchester.
[3] The "self-styled" Hardy Players, members of The Dorchester Debating and Dramatic Society, successfully performed adaptations of *The Trumpet Major*, *Far from the Madding Crowd*, *Under the Greenwood Tree*, *The Three Strangers* and *The Distracted Preacher*, *The Return of the Native*, *Desperate Remedies* and *Tess of the d'Urbervilles* from 1908-1924. They also gave scenes from *The Dynasts* and the *Queen of Cornwall* in 1916 and 1923. *The Dynasts* in part was also dramatized by the O.U.D.S. and performed in Oxford in 1920. In 1921 *The Mayor of Casterbridge* was filmed. It was also dramatized by Drinkwater and was played in London and Weymouth in 1926. In 1924 *The Queen of Cornwall* was put on in London: it was also set to music by Rutland Boughton and produced in Glastonbury in 1924. *Tess*, reluctantly adapted by Hardy himself and subsequently by the producer, A. E. Filmer, began at the Barnes Theatre and was transferred to the Garrick in 1925, where it ran for 100 nights.

epitaph, a regiment for a tune, a society for a motto, a stranger for a signature—those endless signatures which the writer hated making and to the giving of which he had finally to put an end. (To most of the requests, with the exception of those for his signature, Hardy replied with unfailing courtesy.) Such was the demand for Hardy's autograph that local tradespeople were besieged for cheques which the writer had given, bribing them with a larger sum than that for which the cheques were made out. American admirers came to Bockhampton during old Mrs Hardy's life-time and, like thieving magpies, tried to take, or to buy at exorbitant prices, the very straws from the thatch. People tore off branches from the trees and uprooted plants at Max Gate: some even insinuated themselves into the house by giving false names.

But fame brought gifts and tributes as well. Dorchester people danced "The Lancers" for him in the Borough Gardens, and the tune, drifting across the fields, accompanied him home. Church music was sung or played for him in the Dorchester church whose tenor bell had been the admiration of his father. Players, mummers, and carol-singers performed at Max Gate. Poets sent him a precious volume—a first edition of Keats' "Lamia," "The Eve of St Agnes" and other poems, and verses of their own. Their choice and their method of expressing their appreciation of all that Hardy had done, of all that he meant to them—the younger generation of writers—was felicitous and gratifying. They praised, his craftsmanship, his 'high endeavour, his tragic vision of life' which appealed to them, survivors of a holocaust, as so much more in keeping with truth than any other; they recognized 'the charity of that humour' which had relieved the tragedy, and the 'sympathy with human suffering and endurance' which had sweetened it.[1] To the fifty odd poets who had written Hardy verses of their own he took the trouble to reply in person, remarking with characteristic courtesy "that if they could take the trouble to write the poems he could certainly take the trouble to write the letters".[2] The gift of the Keats had been arranged by St John Ervine and the poetic tribute by Siegfried Sassoon. With his own hands, that poet with a knowledge of the sea, John Masefield, fashioned the

[1] II, p. 222.   [2] *Ibid.*, p. 192.

model of a full-rigged ship which he called *The Triumph*[1] and brought to the elder poet whom he admired.

In 1911 Hardy's friend Sydney Cockerell, Director of the Fitzwilliam Museum, had persuaded the writer to let him have many of his manuscripts for public libraries and museums, both in this country and America, and it is due to his foresight that these have been preserved and are accessible to lovers and students of Hardy's work. The poet was grimly aware that he had no descendants, and that others might 'make short shrift' with such things. In 1914 more Hardy manuscripts were sold at the Red Cross War Sales and American dealers and collectors were quick to appreciate their value. *Far from the Madding Crowd, The Melancholy Hussar, The Romantic Adventures of a Milkmaid, Human Shows, A Group of Noble Dames,* and other poems and stories are now in American public, or private, collections.

Swedish admirers of Hardy had long agitated that he should be given the Nobel Prize for Literature and there were discriminating advocates for this in his own country. In 1923 Yeats might rejoice that the honour was given less to him 'than to Irish literature and tradition'.[2] Hardy never succeeded in winning this prize but he did not greatly care. He had done all that he wanted to and when, in the same year, Sir Sydney Cockerell bought his portrait by Augustus John, Hardy remarked to his wife that "he would *far* rather have had that happen than receive the Nobel Prize—and he meant it".[3]

Unfortunately most of the portraits and descriptions of Hardy's appearance date from his later years, when painters, sculptors and writers vied with each other to interpret that wistful countenance with its seer-like eyes and expression. He was between eighty-two and eighty-three years old when the John portrait was made. Since few reactions by distinguished sitters to their likenesses are recorded, Hardy's comment—a spontaneous tribute to the painter in plain words—is of interest. He remarked:

I don't know whether that is how I look, or not, but that is how I *feel*.[4]

[1] *The Lamia* and *The Triumph* are both exhibited in the Dorchester County Museum.
[2] Cockerell, p. 272.   [3] *Ibid.*, p. 310.   [4] II, p. 253.

He also had a great fondness for a bust by Youriévitch which he preferred above all others: he sat for this when he was eighty-four and the sittings tired him.[1]

The verbal descriptions of his appearance are illuminating. When Vere Collins met Hardy he was more than eighty years of age.

> I hesitate at the word 'old', so opposed is it in its ordinary associations to the vigour of intellect and the liveliness of sentiment that marked his conversation; the quickness of his thought; the versatility of his interests; the alertness in his voice; his gestures, his walk; his keenness of sight; the clearness and steadiness of his handwriting:[2]

On looking back at that meeting many years later Mr Collins added:

> He was rather below medium height; slim; erect. His face was not strongly lined; his complexion was clear, without the dullness, sallowness, or discoloration, usually found in old, or even elderly, people. He was dressed in a brown tweed suit . . . was neat without being dapper. He spoke fluently and distinctly, with occasional emphasis to mark surprise, regret, or disapproval . . . His manner was quiet, though genial and unassuming. One cannot say he had a noticeable or impressive appearance, or manner . . . There was no expression of melancholy on his face. The photograph by Hoppé (frontispiece of the Collected Poems) gives a more faithful representation of my memory of him than the effect of tiredness in Blanche's portrait.[3]

Leonard Woolf has spoken of Hardy's 'great charm and extraordinary simplicity', and he was struck by a quality of *something which is almost the opposite of simplicity*.[4] This agrees with Charles Morgan's impressions. Hardy seemed to him 'sprightly and alert' and he uses a comparison which others made, that Hardy was 'bird-like . . . like a small bird with a great head'. He goes on to say:

> He was not simple; he had the formal subtlety peculiar to his own generation; there was something deliberately 'ordinary' in

---

[1] In the possession of Madame Youriévitch. An oil panel by William Strang (1893) in the National Portrait Gallery is the earliest of the likenesses in public collections.   [2] *Talks with Hardy at Max Gate*, p. xii.
[3] Letter to the author, February 1, 1952.
[4] Blunden, p. 172. (Italics mine.)

Thomas Hardy by Augustus John, O.M., R.A.

his demeanour which was *a concealment of extraordinary fires* ... There was in him *something timid as well as something fierce*, as if the world had hurt him and he expected it to hurt him again. But what fascinated me above all was the contrast between the plainness, *the quiet rigidity of his behaviour and the passionate boldness of his mind* ...

This contrast between the seeming-fragility of Hardy's outward form and the fierceness of the inner fire of his mind is again emphasized by John Cowper Powys.

There was much of the falcon about his aquiline nose and his hovering and 'pouncing' eye-glances, an intensity of regard that was accentuated by the slightness of his figure, by the curiously elfin tilt of his eyebrow, and by his trick of holding his head to one side, *as though the frailty of his form were constantly deprecating the terrible and august passion of his thought*.[2]

Florence Hardy describes the writer as having

... a smile of exceptional sweetness, and his eyes were a clear blue-grey. His whole aspect was almost childlike in its sincerity and simplicity, the features being strongly marked ... his nose more Roman than aquiline. The nobility of his brow was striking.[3]

In her letters she later speaks of his 'inner radiance', and the 'luminous' quality of his mind when at the height of his powers, that is when writing *The Dynasts*.[4]

But in 1927, although Sir Edmund Gosse wrote,

He is a wonder, if you like. At eighty-seven-and-a-half without a deficiency of sight, hearing, mind, or conversation. Very tiny and fragile, but full of spirit and a gaiety not quite consistent in the most pessimistic of poets,[5]

the end was drawing nigh. He went no more to watch the moon rise from a nearby barrow, nor listened eagerly for the New Year bells ringing out from St Peter's, Dorchester, or St George's Fordington.

Zest burns not so high.

.   .   .   .   .

Feet once quick are slow.

[1] II, p. 209. (Italics mine.)
[2] *The Pleasures of Literature*, pp. 612-13. Cassell & Co., 1946 (Italics mine.)
[3] I, pp. 227-8.
[4] Sir Sydney Cockerell, pp. 298 and 302.   [5] Blunden, p. 173.

L *

As the summer deepened into autumn Hardy, like one sensing his approaching end and visualizing his last resting-place, went repeatedly to Stinsford churchyard; and he reverted in mind and conversation to the earliest days of his youth. He had already made his last visit to the Bockhampton homestead. Of late these visits had saddened him since he found the house and garden 'shabby', and this made him declare he would go there no more. But on this occasion he went with the new owner of Kingston Maurward[1] and together they looked at fencing, trees and hedges, with a view to tidying and secluding his birthplace, that 'domicile of brown and green' where the birds had whistled from window ledges, or doorstep, at daybreak,[2] and the orange Crown Imperials with their tufted heads had formerly flourished in the garden—flowers which made him, even as an old man, 'give a cry of joy when he saw them'.[3] He had traced the epitaph of Robert Reason, the shoemaker,[4] on his lichened tombstone and scraped it clean: had taken Walter de la Mare to see the grave of Fanny Hurden, a girl who had been to school with Hardy, who had died at eighteen, and whom Hardy, as if foreseeing the visit of his poet friend, had lately commemorated in verses[5] more like de la Mare's than any other lines of his. The walk across the Frome meadows with their shining leats, or carriers, bright with living water, was a favourite with Hardy till the last, and the churchyard at Stinsford for him 'the most hallowed spot on earth'. In one of his most resolute poems he had resolved 'to say no more', although in the November before his death he was still writing lyrics, which he brought downstairs to share with his wife who had been in the habit of advising him about the exact, the appropriate word, or phrase, for some time past.

Then, on December 11, for the first time in his life, he sat down at his desk to write and felt unable to work—possibly at the simple country desk preserved in the Dorset Museum, which his wife tells us he had used all his life and so cared for

---

[1] Sir Cecil Hanbury.
[2] "Bird Scene at a Rural Dwelling."
[3] Sir Sydney Cockerell, p. 311.
[4] Immortalized in *Under the Greenwood Tree* as Mr Penny.
[5] "Voices from Things Growing in a Country Churchyard."

that it bore no scar or blemish. At Christmas he pondered on the Nativity and the Massacre of the Innocents. His brain was as clear, and his sense of humour as strong, as always. Outside, the snow lay in sculptured drifts and it was bitterly cold. Although he had for many years enjoyed being read to by his wife, Hardy could not now find strength for prose reading, caring only for a short poem, like de la Mare's "Listeners". One of his last thoughts and acts was for others—the signing of a cheque for the Society of Authors' Pension Fund. The night before he died he asked for "Rabbi Ben Ezra" to be read to the finish; and in the winter's dusk at the close of the following day that stanza from Omar Khayyám which closes with—

> *For all the sin wherewith the Face of Man*
> *Is blacken'd, Man's forgiveness give—and take!*

Shortly after nine o'clock on January 11, 1928, Hardy lay lifeless.

On his deathbed William Barnes had uttered a broken prayer of gratitude for life as he had known it: "I want to say—I thank God.—For all the pain—and trials—and all that I have passed through—I thank Thee."[1] That prayer and the scourging plea in Fitzgerald's lines are widely divergent in spirit. They express succinctly, and with telling emphasis, more clearly than longer comments may do, the chasm lying between the days before and after the publication of the *Origin of Species*. Yet of the sincerity of Hardy's choice, and of the fact that he found the lines of the Persian poet cleansing and consoling, there can be little doubt, knowing the man and remembering the setting and circumstances of that final reading.

Like a prophet without fame in his own country Hardy has been criticized by local people for his meanness. Despite many acts of generosity during his life he did not endow the Dorchester Grammar School, found any local scholarships, or make bequests to neighbouring churches in his Will, which provides for the reversion of moneys for the "benefit in my name of

---

[1] From an unpublished note made by Barnes' daughter, who nursed him in his last illness, in her copy of her sister, Leader Scott's, *Life* of their father. I am acquainted with it through the courtesy of Mr Giles Dugdale.

scholarships (or otherwise) of the first Wessex University that may be . . . established." Another stipulation is that his publishers shall issue an edition of his Complete Poetic Works to be on sale at a price within the means of 'poorer readers'. The most tragic fact revealed in this final will and testament, made in August 1922, when Hardy was eighty-two years of age, is that he was still hoping for an heir. In three separate clauses provision is made for "the first child of mine who shall attain to the age of twenty-one years."[1]

For those who measure success and importance in terms of possessions it is impossible to understand the artist's longing and fundamental need to simplify life, to rid it of inessentials. They despise a man who buys and keeps a single watch during the whole of his life, and disdains to purchase a carriage and pair, or a motor car. Until he was past eighty Hardy, like a good countryman, preserved the use of his legs. To him it seemed a fine thing either to walk or to cycle about the countryside, to enjoy the beauties of nature with all, not one, of his senses, buoyed up and enveloped by the air, not caged behind glass or celluloid. Clad in a 'brown holland pinafore' with a canvas satchel slung over his sloping shoulders[2] he had walked two miles and more to school, and back again, as a small boy, despite delicate health in infancy: the notion that children from outlying districts must be fetched to school in expensive taxis, the cost to be deducted from the rate-payer's pocket, would have scandalized him. Before he was eight years old he had made up his mind that he 'did not want to possess things'. Nor was Hardy interested in money or the making of money. He wished to earn sufficient to keep his wife and himself in decent comfort. His was the good craftsman's ideal, to create, as his father and Barnes had taught him, for the pleasure derived from a skilful alliance between imagination, brain and hand. At seventy-one he still scorned, when he might easily have done so, to 'write for money'.[3] He took little interest in investments and in 1915 wrote to a friend to ask his advice about the best

[1] The clause relating to the scholarship provides that the moneys are to pass to Magdalene College, Cambridge, should no such University be established.

[2] See Blunden, p. 180.

[3] Letter to Edward Clodd, Brotherton Library.

stocks and shares to buy. He thought America a sound country to invest in but the brokers had discouraged him.

> My publishers by paying up so promptly, as they always do, have put me in this dilemma of not knowing what to do with a few superfluous pounds.[1]

He had heard too many tales of the 'stressful times' of his mother's and grandmother's youth not to be anxious to safeguard the future welfare of his wife and surviving sister, and accordingly willed his fortune to them.

But the greater charge, more difficult to refute, is the constant one of Hardy's being 'a pessimist', a charge which is still being made. In a broadcast talk in 1950 he was called 'Exasperating Pessimist'.[2] The word pessimism came into the English language about 1794. No one had ever applied it to the Greek tragedians, to Shakespeare in his darker moods (in the *Sonnets*, in *Lear*, *Hamlet*, or *The Tempest*), to Gray (whom Hardy pointed out rightly deserved the apellation for his "Ode on a Distant Prospect of Eton College"),[3] to Coleridge (for his "Ode to Dejection"), or to Butler, Fitzgerald, Swinburne or Housman. Nor did anyone come to Hardy's rescue to point out that English melancholy had expressed itself since the Middle Ages in poetry, that the English spleen was a well-known 18th-century complaint, ridiculed abroad and feared at home. Against these charges the writer tried to defend himself in notes, letters, and prefaces, his bitterness and irritation at the epithet creeping out now and then in personal conversations, or in a bold note in which he declares that "if Galileo had said in *verse* that the world moved, the Inquisition might have let him alone" ...[4] He called himself in Aeschylean phrase, 'a meliorist', believing that if one looked the worst in the face, there was nothing to be feared. Hardy tried to dismiss the appellation—pessimist—from his thoughts. To Vere Collins he said, in 1920 or '22, "I suppose pessimism is an easy word to say and remember. It's only a passing fashion".[5] To Alfred Noyes he wrote in 1920 that "it was a mere nickname with no sense in it".[6] But the word and the charge rankled and the poet strove to

[1] *Ibid.*   [2] By Geoffrey Grigson.   [3] Collins, p. 63.
[4] II, p. 58.   [5] Collins, p. 63.   [6] II, p. 217.

deny it in a long argumentative preface to *Late Lyrics and Earlier*, in letters and conversations. But when all is said and done we are not impressed by these denials since something remains unexplained.

Amongst those who have striven to defend Hardy against the charge, or to mitigate its severity, are Lascelles Abercrombie, Lord David Cecil, W. H. Gardner and Edmund Blunden.[1] The first in making a comparison between the spirit of Hardy's work and that of Leopardi, says:

> Pessimism is not the denial of significance but the assertion of evil significance.[2]

In his turn Lord David Cecil writes:

> Hardy's very pessimism is of a kind only possible to one indissolubly wedded to Christian standards of value. Christian teachers have always said that there was no alternative to Christianity but pessimism, that if Christian doctrine was not true, life was a tragedy. Hardy quite agreed with them.[3]

Writing on the "hint of redemption which relieves, while it accentuates, the final agony" of Michael Henchard's death. W. H. Gardner says:

> It is the sublimity of that death scene which to my mind utterly refutes the charge of pessimism so frequently brought against Hardy. For surely, when a writer can make us feel so intensely the poignant throes of a dying soul . . . he is *ipso facto* proving to us the great value which he sets on the human soul; and only by a considerable elasticity of definition can such a valuation be called pessimistic. It is true that here, as in Shakespeare, there is no hint of survival in the paradisean or, indeed, any other sense. And Shakespeare has never been called a pessimist. Then why Hardy? Posterity will probably find it expedient to reserve the appellation for the creator of the Yahoos.[4]

After drawing attention to the less melancholy passages in Hardy's writing, which "include an element of melioration, of

[1] An anonymous reviewer of the 1927 edition of *The Dynasts* maintained that "the result is *scepticism rather than pessimism* . . . since Hardy's view is too tentative to be embodied in a system".

[2] *Thomas Hardy—A Critical Study*, p. 168. Martin Secker, 1927.

[3] *Hardy the Novelist*, p. 156. Constable, 1942.

[4] *Some Thoughts on the Mayor of Casterbridge*, English Assoc. Pamphlet 77, November 1930, p. 27. O.U.P.

submission and goodwill which is too easily forgotten in discussion of his creed ", Edmund Blunden closes his biography
with a paragraph on Hardy's darkling thoughts:

> If he was assured that our race was doomed to this disappoint-
> ment, and that the retreat from our furthest point of civilized
> intelligence and spiritual pilgrimage was imminent because the
> world was so made . . . it was not pessimism in him to admit the
> fact.[1]

One has to admire Hardy's courage and honesty in standing
by his darker convictions. He would not deflect a hair's-breadth
from what he believed in to placate his critics and attackers,
once he had thrown off the irksome yoke of early serial writing.
His integrity shines out through the gloom, and those who have
written whole books and essays on the subject have always
agreed on this.[2]

If we wish to find an explanation for this phenomenon—that
of a writer persistently charged with being something which he
himself constantly denies, we must take many factors into con-
sideration. First, casts of mind are universal: they crop up
irrespective of an age, or period. The melancholic appears and
re-appears throughout history, adding his streaks of purple and
black to the more lightly-dappled waters of his country's
literature. Secondly, a writer, even more than a painter or
musician—and Hardy was no exception to this ruling—is the
product of his age. He can not be torn from its context and
blamed for the effects of its moulding. If, as Hardy himself
maintained, "a poet should express the emotion of all ages and
the thought of his own", then we can not quarrel with him for
mirroring that thought, and for being influenced profoundly by
it.

Thirdly, attention is selective and that of the grave child, or
man, early scarred by life, will be attracted to, and stimulated
by, those very things which tear the tender fibres of his heart
and beat upon his brain. If, like Hardy, he is a country child of
a vanished age, "reared in lonely country nooks where fatalism

[1] p. 279.
[2] See R. E. Zachrisson's *Thomas Hardy's Twilight View of Life*. Stockholm,
1931; and H. C. Webster's *On a Darkling Plain*. University of Chicago Press,
1947.

is a strong sentiment", it is likely that rigid fatalism will be bound up into his being until, at the age of fifty, he will be able to paint a Joan Durbeyfield who accepts her daughter's plight with simple words of resignation, the warm-hearted dairymaids who bow before Tess' superior claims to Alec's affection with equal philosophy because 'such supplanting *is to be*', or a Napoleon who sees that the curse of life is helplessness, that he has never been his own master but always

'Ruled by the pitiless Planet of Destiny.'

Furthermore, if such a lad, who alternates between the grave and gay, is intelligent and of a questioning type of mind, interested in Greek thought, theories of religion, science, rationalism and all the complexities and contradictions of the human intellect, it is more than probable that he will be drawn, both in reading and in life itself to those aspects of tragedy which accord with his early emotional experiences connected with things seen, or merely heard. His sensitivity, one of his greatest artistic assets as well as one of his weaknesses, will cause him to be influenced by calamity and by negative trends of thought more completely, more disastrously, than someone of tougher fibre. Hardy once remarked that "it was not so much the force of the blow that counted, as the nature of the material that received the blow".[1] He was probably thinking of himself.

We have seen that, already in his late twenties, Hardy was irrevocably committed to an intellectual absence of hope, and, that his strong emotional nature suffered from this blight. He was stricken inwardly by the dual attack, first upon his emotions and then upon his intellect. He early sensed the precariousness of the balance which life called upon him to maintain. If his favourite, Aeschylus, could write—

> *Great Fortune is an hungry thing*
> *And filleth no heart anywhere—*[2]

he could mirror that fear two thousand years later in a poem called "He Fears his Good Fortune", in which the crash, long anticipated by the poet, comes in the end. If Aeschylus could

[1] II, p. 225.
[2] *The Agamemnon*, p. 60, trans. Gilbert Murray. Geo. Allen & Unwin, 1920.

cry out at the sufferings of the imagined Prometheus in the hands of a tormenting God, Hardy could carry the consciousness of pain a step further in wishing to die out of life, to remain merely a spectre, uninvolved emotionally, to sink back into the unconsciousness where he may know neither pain nor fear, as lifeless and feelingless as a stone tablet, or a picture, on a wall.[1]

Yet the devilish thing is that he can not do so while he remains actively alive, endowed more richly than most with another side to his nature which is resilient, defiant, and, in spite of all precautions, infected with that tempting, that forbidden emotion—Hope. He must attain some resolution of this conflict or perish in the struggle. Hardy did in fact attain a partial synthesis, at great cost—the subjection, the anaesthetization of his emotions in all but his writings, it would seem.

The signs of this inner struggle are evident in his verbal and written inconsistencies. He speaks confusingly with two voices—dissentient parts of himself who sit and eat at the same board yet somehow remain total strangers to each other. For example, Hardy denies, over and over again, that he writes with philosophic consistency, yet in the Preface to *The Dynasts* he likes to think that philosophers may find his work intellectually acceptable. In *Tess* he deliberately reviles the impersonal Creator whom he styles 'President of the Immortals' but he affects to believe that this is merely a figure of speech. In *Jude* he attempts to horrify and to sear the minds of his readers for cathartic purposes, and then he is wounded when they recoil. In *The Dynasts* he draws Napoleon as a puppet, or fantocine, whose every action is seemingly pre-determined, yet he wishes him to appear a free agent uninfluenced by the blind gropings of the Immanent Will.

He declares that he has only postulated an "indifferent and unconscious force, 'which neither good nor evil knows'," a narrow Necessity like that of Euripides, 'unmoral, loveless and hateless',[2] and he appears to ignore the places where he has, like Hyllus, arraigned 'the vast injustice of the Gods', either in

---

[1] "A Wish for Unconsciousness" in *Winter Words*.
[2] II, p. 217.

poetry or prose. He dismisses these denunciations as mere
'impressions of the moment . . . exclamations, in fact . . . mood-
dictated passages", wholly underrating the spirit which drove
him to express them. When Alfred Noyes corners him by
writing that he himself has never been able to conceive "a
Cause of Things which could be less in any respect than the
thing caused", Hardy retreats from the fray by replying that
the ways of Providence are indeed inscrutable, only he does not
call it Providence, a name too hackneyed and too kind, he calls
it 'The Scheme of Things'.[1]

He advocates that the Church should alter her Liturgy in
order that her teaching may be acceptable to modern minds, who
'no longer believe in the supernatural'. (Hardy was one of four
who signed a letter to the *Manchester Guardian* upon the necessity
of the reformation of the Prayer Book Services.[2]) Yet, as an old
man, he tells his wife that he will not go to church today because
he "*hates new services and new prayers*".[3]

As a child he had been, like other country children of a
bygone age, 'imaginative, dreamy, credulous of vague
mysteries', aware of the Unknown. His growing mind was
mythopoeic as well as analytical. Yet as a mature man he denied
that he was, like Jude, 'fearful, spectre-seeing always'. He told
William Archer that he wanted to see, but never had yet
beheld, a ghost. Then, as if to catch out his real, his disavowed
self, his own grandfather rewarded the believer when he was
seventy-nine.

> He saw a ghost in Stinsford churchyard on Christmas Eve . . .
> The ghost said: "A green Christmas". T.H. replied: "I like
> a green Christmas." Then the ghost went into the church, T.
> followed, to see who this strange man in 18th century dress might
> be—and found no one.[4]

The answer to the quandary, the explanation of these inconsistencies, seems to be that Hardy, who was singularly uninterested
in himself,[5] was confused: secondly, that the dichotomy between heart and head was little understood. After all his
protestations he puts the matter quite clearly in a single phrase

[1] II, pp. 216-18.   [2] See II, pp. 121-3, 225 and 246.
[3] Cockerell, p. 299.   [4] *Ibid.*, p. 305.
[5] See II, p. 108.

in a letter to another friend. His so-called 'philosophy', the amalgam of his reaction to life is, he says, nothing more than

a confused heap of impressions, like those of a bewildered child at a conjuring show.[1]

Hardy had been endowed at birth with a nature which loved all growing, all living, things. He had even tried at an early age to enter into the experience of animal life. He was gifted to a marked degree with that poetic sensibility which made him susceptible to the magic of words and imagined thought: he could share with Wordsworth that exultation which the young feel, and which the artist remembers throughout life. A passage such as—

> *The hare is running races in her mirth,*
> *And with her feet she from the plashy earth*
> *Raises a mist that glittering in the sun*
> *Runs with her all the way, wherever she doth run—*

meant something more to Hardy than it would do to an insensitive, unpoetic, child who early accepts the conundrum of life, even delights in the lethal warfare, the gladiatorial displays, between balanced antagonists.

Yet the reward for that appreciation, the senseless riddle which maddens his brain and grates his heart to the quick, is that he sees his father shoot the hare, destroy the beautiful body deprived of speed and grace, brittle it and put it in the pot, whence (further horror) it is served to him at the supper table. The exultant and wondering child, amazed at first with joy, is asked to become not only a witness to the murder of, but the cannibal who enjoys eating, his magic playmate of the fields. This is the first destruction of his belief in human kindness. Young Jude saw the rooks as

gentle friends and pensioners . . . A magic thread of fellow-feeling united his own life with theirs. Puny and sorry as those lives were they much resembled his own.[2]

The schoolmaster had told him to be kind to them: the farmer bade him starve them out. Jude perceived that "what was good

---

[1] II, p. 219.
[2] *Jude the Obscure*, p. 11.

for God's birds was bad for God's gardener". The mischief was sown.

Next, as we have seen in Hardy's life, the boy observes human beings equally savage with each other, male or female. They burn or they hang each other for transgressing man-made laws, for satisfying some urgent, natural need, such as that of filling a belly empty through no fault of its owner's. Worse still, they kill another human-being, weighting his feet with blocks ironically inscribed with the word *Mercy*[1] merely because they suspect his guilt—in order to prove their own magnanimity and rectitude. The second destruction of his belief in, his comprehension of, extolled loving-kindness has occurred. Add to this emotional strain what appears to be final conclusive proof, rational and scientific, of the senselessness of the Universe, the possible malignity of its Creator, and the final collapse of Hope is ensured.

Hope thereafter becomes indecent: to do without it is both a test and a proof of virility. Having reached this stage of hopelessness, in order to preserve one's integrity (and a belief in that of all mankind, of whom he is part) the next essential is to set about justifying one's loss of faith. A doctrine of hopelessness must be invented, if only unconsciously, for one cannot live wholly without faith in life, in human nature, in a promulgating cause. One's hatred and one's despair would be too great. First of all then, sweep out the emotions, for feeling is treacherous and betrays one. Scrutinize, classify, sterilize them, preserve them as exhibits, or disown them like troublesome, ne'er-do-well children who embarrass and inconvenience one. Declare that you "never expected much from life", or that you 'never cared for it'[2]: that you have only been looking for 'neutral tinted haps and such', while all the time it is obvious that your powers of reacting to its ferocious, its prodigal enticements are greater than those of the ordinary, the stolid, man. Refuse to be taken in by either praise or condemnation. Your aloofness will be

---

[1] These weights were tied to the feet of the lad whom Hardy's father saw hanged in 1836, four years before his birth.

[2] "For Life I had never cared greatly" in *Moments of Vision*, contains references to "conditions of doubt" and "living aloofly" in "earliest years". The other two poems referred to are "Epitaph" in *Late Lyrics*, and "He Never Expected Much" in *Winter Words*.

your armour and you will be safe, for nothing can wound you any more. Thus, towards the close of your life when an old friend sends you abundant praise, you may reply to him:

> As I have told you before, I read those things said about me by generous friends as if they were concerning some person whom I but vaguely know and whom they have mistaken for me.[1]

Or, when someone comments on another writer's definition of optimist and pessimist—the former

> appears to be one who cannot bear the world as it is, and is forced by his nature to picture it as it ought to be; and the [latter] one who cannot only bear the world as it is, but *love* it well enough to draw it faithfully—[2]

you may drily remark, "I shouldn't say 'loves'. He need not necessarily love it. It may be because he is *indifferent* enough." Hardy was not going to be drawn into an admission of love for the world at the age of eighty or more.

With her delicate sense of humour, and her devotion to her husband, Florence Hardy saw what others did not—his need to express himself dourly, and *his pleasure in doing so.*

> T.H. [she writes] ... is now, this afternoon writing a poem with great spirit: always a sign of well-being with him. Needless to say, it is an *intensely dismal poem.*[3]

The need to suffer, and to enjoy suffering, is apparent in Hardy's work. But the critics who have analysed his dark vision of life have overlooked this characteristic, and not even his wife, I think, saw how the unconscious doctrine of hopelessness was an essential synthesis of multifarious traits. At one stroke melancholy, discouragement, masochism, as well as intellectual integrity, were all appeased and satisfied by its adoption.

The circumstances attending Hardy's funeral were as superbly ironic as he himself could have wished. On the morning following his death the Dean of Westminster consented to the proposal that he should be buried in Westminster Abbey. Hardy himself would have preferred a simple country interment, and it

---

[1] Letter to Sir Edmund Gosse, June 6, 1923, Brotherton Collection.
[2] Collins, p. 62. The definition is Galsworthy's from the *Inn of Tranquillity.*
[3] Letter to S. C. Cockerell, December 26, 1920, p. 307. (Italics mine.)

had long been known by his intimates that he wished to lie with his forbears in Stinsford churchyard.[1] A swift compromise had to be made between the claims of the nation, his own wishes, and those of his widow, brother and sister. It was finally decided that his body should be cremated, that his ashes should be placed in the Poets' Corner, and that his heart should be brought back to his beloved Dorset.

On the night of January 14, therefore, Hardy's ashes rested in the dark and ancient Chapel of St Faith, beneath the august painting of the Saint (one of the few mediaeval oil-paintings on stone in the country) a fact which would doubtless have pleased the artist in him. The decision not to leave his body intact, but to practice the custom of heart-burial popular in the days of the great Crusades, might also have delighted his historical and antiquarian sense.

On the 15th, accompanied by illustrious pall-bearers including the nation's Prime-Minister, six eminent men of letters, the Master and Provost of the colleges of two great Universities, Hardy's ashes were laid to rest in Poets' Corner, with a spade-full of Dorset earth sent by a farm-labourer thrown over the casket. The Abbey was crowded, so crowded that many could not gain admission but waited patiently in the winter cold outside. There had even been a quarrel over the tickets of entry, "as if," Sir John Squire wrote, "it had been a matinée";[2] and one young girl, ignorant of the formalities and without a ticket, because she bore the family name and was dressed in seemly black, to her embarrassed astonishment found herself ushered by an unquestioning verger into the stall which sheltered the chief mourners, Florence and Katherine Hardy. At the same hour Hardy's heart was buried in the grave of his first wife in the churchyard of Stinsford, while in Dorchester a memorial service was also held in old St Peter's.

Thus, although he had never courted fame outright, Hardy's poetic genius was crowned with the ultimate national tribute. In spite of avowed agnosticism, and that running counter to the tenets of the Established Church which had enraged Bishop How and other prelates, he lay in a Christian edifice, one of the

[1] His Will stipulates that he shall be buried in the grave of his first wife in that churchyard.   [2] Blunden, p. 178.

oldest and most revered in the land. His ashes were placed next to those of that writer, Charles Dickens, whom he had not even dared to speak to as a young man, eyeing him avidly and hoping for recognition in a Hungerford Market coffee-shop.[1] But there was nothing ironic in the placing of Hardy's heart in the churchyard at Stinsford. His passionate love of his own soil and his own people would have been gratified by the thought that one day it would lie surrounded by his immediate ancestors, whilst Louisa who had shyly smiled at him in the lane, Fanny Hurden, the staunch field-women, Robert Reason, and others known and loved by him in childhood, were not far off, and in the chancel vault that romantic pair, Lady Susan O'Brien and her husband, lay side by side.

Hardy had few fears of death, although a single lyric reveals a natural shrinking from its claiming.[2] He once declared to a friend, in a peculiarly Donnian phrase, that dying seemed to him merely 'like stepping into the next room'. His attitude to an after-life was clearly and unashamedly pagan. He had early read in his copy of Aeschylus—

> . . . *For I think the slain*
> *Care little if they rise or sleep again.*[3]——

and to a friend he had written, late in life, "I shall sleep quite calmly at Stinsford, whatever happens".[4]

For Thomas Hardy had completed his task. He had enlarged the range of, and dignified, English letters. He had emphasized the importance of man. He had magnified the lowly, had been the chronicler of the lives "of those invisible ones of days gone by . . . enacted in the cottages, the mansions, the street, or on the green".[5] Through sheer fecundity and force of imagination he had created characters more real, more live, than many living beings, men and women who, clothed in the light of poetry and truth, have taken on immortality. He had extolled the Christian virtues, the worth and heroism of human love, while never flinching from acknowledging that the Church which he had

---

[1] Sir Newman Flower, p. 88.
[2] "After the Death of a Friend."
[3] *The Agamemnon*, p. 25.
[4] Letter to S. C. Cockerell, August 28, 1914, p. 278.
[5] *The Woodlanders*, p. 155.

venerated in his youth had lost her consolation for him in manhood. He had sought for God sincerely, wrestling with doubt.
He had steadfastly studied and explored those great, unceasing
problems—the existence of evil and of pain; how to reconcile
the vast world of unconsciousness (indifferent to moral values),
with the natural and human consciousness, (struggling to keep
its faith in the wisdom and benevolence of an inspiring, controlling Being, to impose value and reason on the confused
process from which it has emerged). He had unfolded the drama
of human destiny on the epic scale; had enlarged the imaginations, and stretched the taut strings, of arid minds and numbed
hearts. He had been the patient and loving observer of what, in
his beautiful Biblical phraseology, he calls

> the seasons in their moods, morning and evening, night and
> noon; winds in their different tempers; trees, waters and mists;
> shades and silences, and the voices of inanimate things.[1]

He had shown Homeric compassion for the sorely tried, and
Shakespearian pity for the birds of the brake, thicket and field.
Above all he had made a genuine criticism of life as he saw it,
bearing the ring and resonance of a great, an humble, a charitable soul.

Now the heart of him who had loved both 'planet and
star-shine' more than most, might lie in its narrow, 'yew-
arched' bed, at peace beneath

> . . . the midnight festival
> Of swarming stars, and them that lonely go,
> Bearers to man of summer and of snow,
> Great lords and shining, throned in heavenly fire.[2]

For Hardy had done 'all that he meant to do.'

[1] *Tess of the d'Urbervilles*, p. 155.
[2] *The Agamemnon*, p. 1.

INDEX

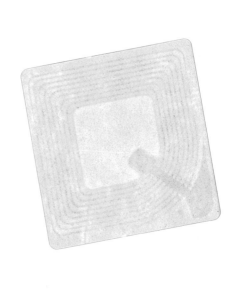